Addressing Practical Problems Through the Metaverse and Game-Inspired Mechanics

Garima Malik
Birla Institute of Management Technology, India

Dharmendra Singh
Modern College of Business and Science, Oman

Rohit Bansal
Rajiv Gandhi Institute of Petroleum Technology, India

IGI Global
Scientific Publishing
Publishing Tomorrow's Research Today

Vice President of Editorial — Melissa Wagner
Director of Acquisitions — Mikaela Felty
Director of Book Development — Jocelynn Hessler
Production Manager — Mike Brehm
Cover Design — Jose Rosado

Published in the United States of America by
IGI Global Scientific Publishing
701 East Chocolate Avenue
Hershey, PA, 17033, USA
Tel: 717-533-8845
Fax: 717-533-7115
Website: https://www.igi-global.com E-mail: cust@igi-global.com

Library of Congress Cataloging-in-Publication Data

LCCN: 2025018337 (CIP Data Pending)
ISBN13: 979-8-3693-8886-0
Isbn13Softcover: 979-8-3693-8887-7
EISBN13: 979-8-3693-8888-4

British Cataloguing in Publication Data
A Cataloguing in Publication record for this book is available from the British Library.

Table of Contents

Detailed Table of Contents

With the growing impact of mobile and internet on business and commerce, companies explored new ways to gain consumer access and attention. Research suggests that the gamification market has been consistently growing and gamification is widely used in contemporary marketing due to its ability to engage and motivate individuals. With the use of game elements, companies and marketers involved and engaged customers in an organized form of play, governed by rules and structures, that provided enjoyment and accomplishment with measurable outcomes. The avenues of enhancing customer engagement through use of gamification to improve customer relations is encouraging, particularly considering the current advancements in areas like augmented reality and virtual reality, which are expected to greatly enhance the potential for gamified experiences. In the light of above scenario, the chapter focuses on the use of gamification strategies for augmenting customer engagement and loyalty by discussing the success stories of few industry players like Duolingo, Starbucks and Snapchat.

The evolution of digital supply chains is one of the most significant transformations within modern business operations. As global markets and technological capabilities continue to evolve, businesses have been forced to adapt to new demands, operational complexities, and technological advancements. Initially, supply chains were traditionally managed through manual processes, spreadsheets, and basic Enterprise Resource Planning (ERP) systems. These systems offered limited automation, often leading to inefficiencies, delays, and a lack of visibility across the entire supply chain. However, the rise of digital technologies in the late 20th and early 21st centuries introduced a paradigm shift in how supply chains functioned. These early advancements laid the foundation for a new era in supply chain management—one driven by interconnected, real-time systems that could monitor and manage the flow of goods, services, and information with greater precision and efficiency.

This chapter discusses the aspects of applying gamification for branding within the metaverse, to address the issue of consumer interactions in the context of growing competition in the digital environment. In view of this the study uses a qualitative approach with an evaluative design that draws from various case examples of brands that have successfully incorporated gamification into their communication strategies as well as specific indicators of user engagement as well as brand loyalty. Some of the findings include; Brand engagement and attachment is enhanced through the incorporation of game elements such as; immersive experience, user generated content and reward screen. Furthermore, the research demonstrates that feedback and interaction with the unique user profile are essential for its further engagement. Lastly, this chapter established that the use of gamification in marketing within metaverse goes beyond mere product visibility since it guides in the formation of a long-term relationship with consumers through the provision of fun-related activities.

This chapter focuses on customer engagement based on the use of gamified mobile applications and virtual environments across the world while responding to the study's research question of how these technologies improve customer engagement and loyalty. Building on previous research, employing a systematic literature review and analysing case studies, the research investigates latest trends in the use of mobile applications and the impact of gamification in various sectors. Key outcomes show that individual incentives, social comparisons, and virtual environment increase engagement rates, especially with the young audience. The assessment of the given apps also emphasizes the necessity to adapt designs for different cultures and points that there is a constant need for development of new approaches to the process of

diverse gamer profiles and underscores the need for adaptive strategies in game development and marketing.

User retention is a key indicator of digital platform performance in the digital era. This study examines how gamification improves user retention by applying game-design principles to non-game contexts. The research uses psychology, user experience design, and behavioral economics to examine how rewards, points, badges, levels, and leaderboards affect user engagement and retention. Gamification increases intrinsic motivation and regular usage patterns, according to literature analysis and case analyses of platforms in education, fitness, and productivity. It admits constraints like over-reliance on extrinsic motivators and user fatigue. The findings emphasize the need for user-centered, entertaining, and meaningful gamification design. Gamification can boost user loyalty and platform sustainability done ethically and psychologically, the report suggests. This study adds to the digital behavior management debate and helps developers, marketers, and policymakers improve user experience in the competitive digital economy.

Objective of the study This study aims to understand how gamification when integrated with metaverse serves as a powerful tool for marketing and fostering brand loyalty of customers. This chapter explores how gamification in metaverse offers brand new opportunities to engage customers and win their loyalty with specific study on sports industry automobile industry, education industry and fashion industry. The ethical considerations and potential challenges are also discussed. Methodology The study is based basically on secondary data, whereby the study is done already existing data pertaining to a company or organization and sources which are internal to a company. The study also takes into account various research papers, magazines, newspapers, etc. for in-depth analysis. Conclusion The Metaverse is a real digital world where individuals may communicate, work, and play; it is no longer science fiction. It's a future where virtual and physical worlds coexist together, providing countless opportunities for companies.

This study looks at how well gamified incentive models work in India to encourage recycling, responsible plastic disposal, and a decrease in plastic use. The study investigates user motivations, preferences, and barriers to using gamified waste management systems using a mixed-methods research technique. The qualitative interviews offer detailed insights into the elements—like personal accountability, environmental concerns, and the requirement for an easily navigable platform—that motivate consumer engagement. The impact of gamified incentive models on behaviour change is further demonstrated by the quantitative survey data, which also shows how their efficacy is influenced by age, education level, and past environmental awareness. The results of this study highlights key design dimensions for creating effective gamified incentive models including balanced reward systems, user-centric design, tailored experience and smooth interaction with the trash management infrastructure. It also suggest ways to encourage long term behavioural changes and enhance consumer involvement.

The aim of the paper is to provide a thorough model that explains how Indian consumers' demographic profiles moderate the impact of various website attributes on their purchase intentions and how this helps e-retailers in the context of online shopping. We identified eight online interface features—site design, site convenience, transaction security, payment system, customer communication, delivery information, product information, and special content information—after conducting a in depth literature review. Therefore, we made an effort to ascertain the connections between

Preface

The integration of gamification and the metaverse is revolutionizing the way individuals, brands, institutions, and societies engage with digital content. This book, *Addressing Practical Problems Through the Metaverse and Game-Inspired Mechanics*, brings together researchers, educators, marketers, technologists, and policy thinkers to explore the transformative applications of gamification within virtual environments. As immersive technologies evolve, they offer new pathways to enhance engagement, build loyalty, and solve real-world problems in creative and interactive ways.

Chapter 1 introduces the foundational link between gamification and the emerging metaverse, establishing a theoretical and practical framework for understanding how game-inspired mechanics drive user engagement in immersive environments. Chapter 2 expands this vision by showcasing how brands can create loyalty through interactive storytelling, avatars, and experiential marketing within platforms like Roblox. In Chapter 3, the focus shifts to international human resource management, highlighting how virtual training and performance gamification can foster inclusion and collaboration across cultures.

The impact of gamification on brand loyalty via electronic word-of-mouth is explored in Chapter 4, while Chapter 5 builds on this by offering strategic insights into how global companies like Starbucks and Duolingo are using game elements to foster deeper customer relationships. Chapter 6 addresses the integration of gamification within digital supply chains, illustrating how immersive environments and real-time feedback loops enhance logistics and operations. Chapters 7 and 8 focus on branding and global customer engagement, revealing how interactive apps and virtual experiences amplify awareness and customer connection.

In a critical turn, Chapter 9 explores the ethical, privacy, and surveillance challenges associated with gamified systems, urging developers and policymakers to consider the darker side of digital engagement. Chapter 10 presents an in-depth analysis of India's burgeoning digital gaming sector, offering valuable insights into player behavior, preferences, and the rise of esports. In Chapter 11, the authors examine how gamification improves retention in mental health apps, a timely and relevant application given the global focus on well-being.

Chapters 12 through 14 delve into emerging and interdisciplinary applications of gamification and metaverse platforms. Chapter 12 focuses on education, exploring how immersive learning environments and gamified assessments can significantly enhance student motivation and knowledge retention. Chapter 13 investigates healthcare delivery, particularly the role of virtual reality and gamification in patient engagement, rehabilitation, and remote diagnostics. Chapter 14 takes a policy and governance perspective, analyzing how government bodies and public institutions are beginning to implement gamified citizen engagement platforms for improved public participation and service delivery.

Altogether, this volume aims to present a well-rounded, evidence-based exploration of how the fusion of gamification and metaverse technologies can address practical problems across diverse sectors. It is our hope that the insights provided here will serve as a useful reference for scholars, practitioners, developers, and policymakers who are eager to explore the future of human interaction in an increasingly immersive digital world.

We thank all contributing authors for their valuable insights and dedication to advancing this important and rapidly evolving field.

Chapter 1
Introduction Gamification in the Emerging Metaverse

Kavitha Venkatachari
https://orcid.org/0009-0001-6924-7891
Universal AI University, India

ABSTRACT

This chapter deals with the discussion of the research topic, in particular, the application of gamification in relation to the metaverse that is still in the process of formation. The study focuses on emerging issues and prospects of using the gamification approach across multiple metaverse environments. Thus, the combination of the case-study approach and surveys to capture subjective experiences of users was used. Primary conclusions point at the fact that well-implemented gamification increases user engagement and loyalty whenever a sense of community is applied in virtual environments. Nevertheless, the issues of ethical nature such as addiction and data privacy were also emerged. The evaluation suggests that while it presents a realistic opportunity for creating highly engaging and productive metavirtual environment experiences, it is crucial to weigh the consequences of using gamification. In conclusion, this chapter highlights the value proposition of gamification in the metaverse while also providing a basic guidance for game developers and business entities.

DOI: 10.4018/979-8-3693-8886-0.ch001

1. INTRODUCTION

A. Definition of the Metaverse

The term metaverse first describes virtually connected multiple shared spaces that are induced by the social presence of virtually realized physical reality as well as physically real virtual reality. It consists of AR, VR, and the Internet where its users can engage through realistic and created environments. Some of the ideas usually linked to the metaverse involve creation, social relations, and sales of virtual objects and properties by users. In the past, metaverse has been defined as enhanced virtual worlds in the 1990s, particularly "Second Life" to date more complex and integrated environments. These changes are driven by technology enhancement and growing user demands that create room for large digital universe

Over the course of several decades, the metaverse has evolved from a storybook fantasy to a complex digital world that is currently woven daily into our lives. Neal Stephenson introduced the metaverse notion first in his 1992 novel Snow Crash – an immersive and eternally vast virtual world where VR goggles enabled the individuals to This literary conception formed the basis of that enduring aspiration in technology and society: A shared, unified online sphere where there is increased interaction, creativity and trade between its dwellers. The term in recent times refers to a combination of augmented reality (AR), virtual reality (VR), and the internet so that the user can interact with immersive digital worlds in a format that incorporates seamlessly real and virtual.

Fundamentally, the metaverse revolves around the construction of long-term, co-operative contexts where users using avatars can socialize, collaborate and complete trades at the same moment. Unlike the usual digital worlds that might lack integration and functionally are limited, the metaverse seeks to build a coherent network of 3D virtual worlds. These environments are live updated, survive during user log-out and can support virtually infinite range of participants. The capacity for users to have a realistic sense of presence direct with others, digitally, is a significant feature, enabled by advances in VR /AR, haptics systems, and high-speed networking. This sense of continuity of presence with others, with others, differentiates the metaverse from the earlier online environments, with users able to make connections, collaborate, and experience things which seem real and important (Antonaci, 2019).

Significant milestones have defined the story of the metaverse since the past. Although the dream of shared virtual spaces existed in science fiction and the first computer prototypes since the 1950s, the first real practical examples came only in the 1990s. Users in Active Worlds and The Palace were empowered to roam in simulated worlds, communicate with the help of avatars, and construct their personal virtual realm. However, the several early efforts were constrained by the capability of the technology being used including slow internet connections, the rudimentary graphics capabilities and weak processing capabilities. When Second Life became available in 2003, the tipping point was reached: a lasting, community-shaped digital world including its economy, social norms, and capabilities for creation. Second Life allowed users access to the means to own, trade and manufacture virtual goods, design individual avatars and become involved in many social, education and economics programs. At its most active it had more than a million monthly users and established the foundations for a lot of functionality which later gained awareness as metaverse features.

Due to technological development, complexity and diversity of services on metaverse platforms rose to a high extent. With more availability of broadband, improved computers and graphics ability, and the explosion in popularity of mobile devices, digital immersion became a reality for a greater percentage of the population. The virtual world scenes were diversified with games such as World of Warcraft, Minecraft, Fortnite and Roblox that had mass user creativity, persistent economies and large form of social engagement. These were gaming, social networking, and creative expression amalgamated into one and allowed users to interact with digital worlds, but shaping the structure and gameplay of the virtual worlds themselves.

The metaverse is the collective imagination of the connected world-of-virtual-spaces that must be explored, in many forms, by different devices and operating systems. With AR, it is possible to view virtual features overlaid onto actual settings, thus enabling new collaborations between the physical and virtual worlds. Through digital and physical components, mixed reality (MR) technologies facilitate interaction with the metaverse through a response that flows effortlessly with the environment and movements. In spite of still active development, these technologies are rapidly approaching the point at which they will be affordable, easy to use, and widely adopted, which makes it easier for a greater number of people to interact with the metaverse.

Where possibly its greatest strength, is the metaverse's push for individual users to participate in the creation and the ongoing development of its virtual worlds. In contrast to traditional media, which depends on a small number of creators with mostly passive audiences, the metaverse enables users to become producers, as well as entrepreneurs and leaders of communities. Roblox and Minecraft have simple design capabilities that make it simple for anyone to develop games, environments, and interesting experiences, with online stores linking users to platforms where they can sell their creations at real value. The creators' empowerment has led to the development of new digital market places where digital goods ranging from virtual land to experiences can be purchased, traded and used to generate actual money value. A wide array of massive corporations are exploring the metaverse to develop marketing, retail, and customer relations, holding virtual events, introducing branded experiences, and introducing digital products that complement or supplement their traditional offerings.

Social interactions with others are a foundational aspect of what the metaverse provides. Landscape-shifting real-time connectivity over distances transforms the way people work, learn, play, and congregate in communities. The metaverse is promoting the development of virtual classroom, meetings, concerts and conferences. (Ng, 2023) These are opening up new fronts for interacting and uniting people. The pandemic accelerated the popularity of remote working and online communities demonstrating how immersed digital avenues have grown into the primary means to maintain relationships and productivity while social distancing. The metaverse is projected to play a major role in shaping realtime interactions, learning, and teamwork processes in people from different locations, backgrounds, and cultures with the continued growth (Yang, 2024)

There are additional feelings of concern for privacy, security, accessibility, and governance as the metaverse develops. When people spend more time in virtual world, share more personal data, the challenge to secure data, secure digital identity, and to improve online security become ever more pressing. Element of decentralization of metaverse platforms by which, it is difficult to implement rules and standards hence creation of innovative solutions to moderation, conflict resolution, and community governance. Industry associations, lawmakers, and bodies working with the public begin to set standards and regulations but much more needs to be done as the technology and its usage continue to evolve.

Socializing with individuals is an integral part of the possibilities metaverse provides. As in-time virtual relations across a great distance are increasingly prevalent, they change the norm of work, education, recreation, and membership within a community. By virtue of the metaverse, virtual classrooms, meetings, concerts and conferences are being held. And, with these options, interaction and community building are being rewritten. The massive proliferation of home-office setups and online community outreach as a result of the pandemic only illustrate the immense reliance now placed on digital channels for achievement of axial cohesiveness and fruitful output when people are socially distant. As more people continue growing, the metaverse may redefine how individuals in different locations, backgrounds, and cultures, learn interact and collaborate in real time.

With advancing metaverse performances, new privacy, security, accessibility, and governance issues come up. People spend more time in virtual spaces and reveal more private information, as more people need serious data protection, protected digital identities, and better online safety. The decentralized structure of metaverse platforms makes it difficult to create uniform rules and standards and lead to the necessity of finding fresh approaches to deal with moderation, conflict resolution, and community monitoring. The development of the metaverse as accessible and safe for everyone, while combating such problems as addiction, online abuse, and the inequality of internet access, is an immediate priority. Standards and regulations are already being adopted by industry organizations, governments, and public agencies, yet more regulation will be needed to support on-going development of the metaverse.

B. Organization and Narrative Flow of the Chapter

With precise structuring of the content of the chapter, the author seeks to attain systematic coherence that is on par with the review's requirements in terms of detail, empirical work and interdisciplinary nature. The introduction section emphasizes the relevance of the metaverse and gamification, determines the purpose of the chapter and places the discussion in its wider context. By providing this context at the beginning, the chapter enables readers to understand both, scope and significance of the topic against today's digital environment.

After the introductory section is done, the chapter moves on to a background aspect which introduces the basic terminology and writes about the development of both of the metaverse and gamification over time. In that regard, the authors respond to the reviewer's call to give the historical/theoretical background for understanding the metaverse and the gamification. With the help of important literature and empirical findings at this stage, the chapter prepares readers to understand the chronology of the area and the importance of current discussions.

The middle section of the chapter is formulated to cover the dominating issues investigated by the reviewer: namely, engagement of users, psychological factors, ethical aspects and technological progress. As support for recommendations, each subsection draws on systematic case studies and empirical research to point to real-world implications. For example, analysis of psychological effects borrows from the latest research on addiction and privacy issues and the section on community dynamics allows other perspectives from the users and developers. Arranged in this way, the chapter provides a shaded understanding that weighs the opportunities and the possible dangers, as well as diverse stakeholder positions.

In order to conduct a more thorough analysis of reviewer recommendations, the chapter smoothly integrates ethical guidelines and practical strategies into the primary analysis, so they become an organic part of this narrative, rather than being separated in a specific section. Including them in the essence of the analysis, the chapter provides a deeper discussion of their mutual influence and implications. The inclusion of such elements at various points in the main analysis makes the material thematically cohesive and demonstrates the way in which the technical, psychological and ethical aspects are tied together.

The second-last part of the paper describes areas for future research; it builds on previous analyses, but also pinpoints an area that needs empirical exploration. Through this standpoint, the chapter not only addresses leftover issues, but it raises further academics interests in the ever-evolving world of the metaverse.

The concluding sections recapitulate important ideas, synthesizes all the analyses, and explores both practical and theoretical impacts for the field of research, policy, and practice. The final section puts all the threads together, and the chapter's key messages as well as the relevance of ethical, empirically grounded, and stakeholder considerations for the metaverse are evident to the reader.

The chapter directs readers from the initial background information, through complete analysis with the support of empirical evidence from case studies, all the way to concluding reflections that glue the dots while maintaining the larger narrative clear and answering the need for thoroughness, balance and rigorous research.

C. Features of the Metaverse

They have realistic interfaces since the metaverse can be used to describe digital environments in which users can interact in a manner similar to fully-realized 3D space. Why These Is supported by technologies like VR and AR that have the ability to halve the real and virtual world. The most important characteristic of the spaces under discussion is interactivity defining the ability of users not only to navigate through the environment but also to engage in various activities and affect the results of such actions. Users are initiators; they have the opportunity to share their thoughts through avatars, create content, and communicate with others, feel present, and become members of this vast ecosystem.

D. Current Trends of the Metaverse

Observing the further development of the metaverse, the growth trends are overwhelming, and the application of modern technologies: blockchain, artificial intelligence, and highly efficient game engines can serve as a reference for this statement. For purposes of social interaction, business and entertainment, these technologies are fostering evolution of complex and innovative interfaces in support of the classifications (Sharma, 2024). They are increasingly being adopted across all industries ranging from the gaming, education, events, and even work from home solutions among others. Observing current trends as corporations and developers define the field, we determine that the development of the metaverse is tending towards increasing integration and immersion.

Figure 1. Metaverse ecosystem map shows all the actors and relations within this complex environment and focuses on the landscape of the metaverse along with its members as key elements for its functioning. This shared ecosystem is progressing in ever new directions and more and more contributors come up with new contestants and innovations allowing users to engage and interconnect in unprecedented ways.

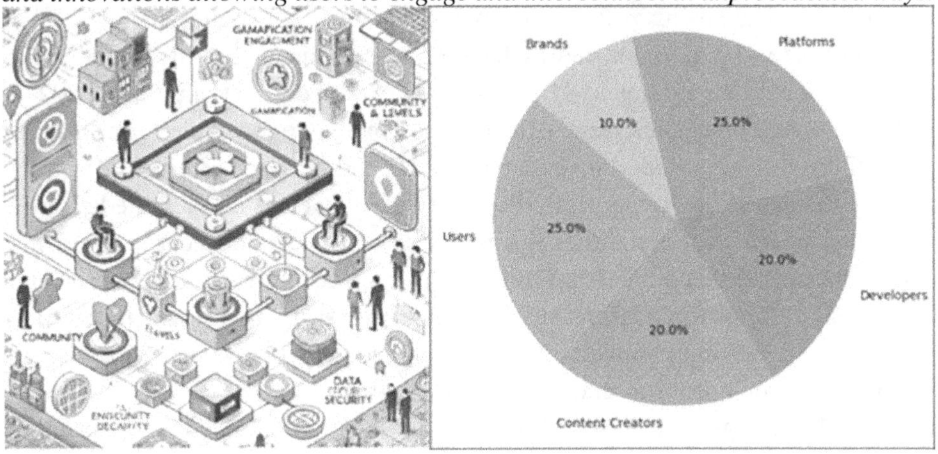

The explosive development of the metaverse is driven by such advanced technologies combined with broad cross-sector applications. As the global market is projected to skyrocket from $146.6 billion in 2024 to $1.1 trillion by 2030, the metaverse is redefining the way participants engage, work, and play in digital spaces. That growth is fuelled by the coming together of blockchain, artificial intelligence (AI), and immersive game engines that are revolutionizing digital experiences.

Blockchain At a fundamental level, blockchain provides secure decentralised digital ownership, afforded by non-fungible tokens (NFTs). With platforms like Decentraland and The Sandbox, users own virtual assets and engage with decentralised governance mechanisms. These trends signal a move away from centralised leadership towards a user-directed digital economy which is in turn enabled by DAOs and NFT marketplaces transforming the way value and participation is established within virtual spaces.

Increasingly, AI further drives this metamorphosis with intelligent avatars, personalized content, and automated moderation. AI adjusts to user preferences in real-time, leading to more inclusive and engaging virtual experiences. For business, AI enables predictive analytics and virtual assistants through which infomration and ideas can be generated, improving productivity and innovation.

In the meantime, game engines and immersive tech, like VR and AR, are starting to make the metaverse real. With VR, you see VR users in headsets and with haptic feedback devices, where AR traps digital objects in the real world. Fueled by hardware and network advances, these technologies are opening up new opportunities for entertainment, education, commerce and social interactions (Yamba-Yugsi, 2023).

The metaverse is transforming operations across sectors, including: Games: AI and blockchain give rise to player-driven economies and richer gameplay. In education, students participate in hands-on virtual learning. Retail and fashion brands, including Nike and Gucci, are using virtual storefronts to create new revenue channels. Even the metaverse is being embraced by health care and manufacturing, where tools are being used for simulation and training, and creating digital twins (Arya, 2024).

Recent developments indicate a trend toward more integrated platforms that are compatible with each other. Supercharged by 5G and next-gen internet infrastructure, the metaverse is moving from disparate virtual worlds into a united ecosystem (Flavián, 2024). It certainly helps that user's privacy and security are rising in importance and that ethical design is on the up. Decentralized governance and transparent systems are also increasingly necessary for sustainability and inclusivity.

However, challenges remain. Pinching for data privacy, standardization and digital safety would need to find their way through multi-level and big legislative and ethical framings. The digital divide is a similar threat to inclusivity, meaning it is crucial that metaverse technology is accessible for all.

2. UNDERSTANDING GAMIFICATION

Session A: Definition and Key Concepts

There is a growing concept known as the gamification, it basically entails the use of game design in a non-gaming environment with the intention of improving the experiential status of a certain activity. It harnesses Psychological States drawn from games like competition, accomplishment, team-work to promote desired behavioural patterns and patterns (Kim, 2021). The main concepts include such game design features as points, badges, and leaderboards to offer the participants concrete and visible motivation. Said in another way, gamification is not to be confused with game integrated approach which means the actual use of games in one's learning process (Gamayanto, 2024). While both seek to increase interaction and learning outcomes, gamification extends or adapts the concept of games to existing processes or systems while game based learning integrates game into the learning process (Huang, 2020).

Literature Review and Theoretical Underpinnings

Although the digital firms often incorporate gamification methods into their operations, its application has a history prior to the popular use of digital tools. The use of recognition and incentive to propagate particular action is not a new concept, early examples are manifested in awarding merit badges and the rewards programs at airlines. Between the mid 2000s, the term "gamification" gained more traction as a result of the electronic use (Smith, 2013).

The theory that has been used in supporting gamification pulls heavily from such models as Theory of Planned Behavior. According to the theory, attitudes, observed behaviors of others, and feeling of personal choice all are important in deciding if a person will use gamified platforms. All these factors combined affect the degree of success and dissemination of gamification strategies, particularly in the educational and community setups.

Empirical works read together confirm gamification greatly increases motivation, student engagement, academic results (Liu, 2024). Based on meta-analyses, the adoption of elements of game such as points, badges, and leaderboards usually brings strong motivational gains and better learning outcome, but these advantages are more pronounced if the And yet, should be mentioned, that some results suggest that the efficacy of these strategies can be sometimes questionable as some of the studies do not really reflect improvement, uncertain improvement or simply fail to show any improvement, calling for a tailored approach to implementation and design.

In a behavioral perspective, gamification proves to enhance collaboration, communication skills and digital literacy. Gaming expert many educators consider gamification to be one of the most effective ways to achieve better student learning, yet they are frequently predisposed toward adopting or rejecting gamification based on their personal views and a positive institutional environment. Further studies show how successful gamification can promote cooperation enhance interpersonal connections, and establish collective spirit, applicable for both traditional education and virtual spaces of the metaverse (Tayal, 2022).

The development of gamification, from simplest to advanced, tangible and immaterial rewards, online systems highlights its ability to change and have a crucial impact on the human behavior, education practices and the formation of the virtual community (Das, 2024). The addition of educators, developers, and user experiences heightens the discussion significantly and acts as a reminder of the opportunities and the intricacies of implementing gamification in virtual spaces such as the metaverse.

Case Studies of Gamification in the Metaverse

Roblox and Fortnite are examples of how successfully gamification can influence reality in virtual spaces. Gamification is heavily used by Roblox with badges, achievements and a thriving virtual economy as major aspects of the platform. Users, using Roblox, are free to create immersive experiences and make their works generating streams of revenue. In 2022, creators in Roblox posted a total earning of $624 million and over 3.2 billion in virtual transactions, which demonstrated its economy. The economic design of the system not only motivates contributors to engage but also gives them the chance to develop a growth mindset mindset and launch their own endeavor within the platform. Community is supported by collaborations such as NFL partnership, which brings special event challenges and virtual items, which attract different individuals and build brand interest. However, regulating the complex elements of user-generated contents, including whether or not designs are inappropriate, the coercive nature of reward structures, etc., thus presents significant oversight problems that demand that the regulation of this area be strict and that the design choices should be conscientious in nature so that the well-being and safety of all

Fortnite is an additional layer of gamification in the form of seasonal activities, common challenges for the community as well as time-limited rewards. The Fortnite team keeps on providing short duration quests, season-wise goodies, and mutual achievements to fulfill the participation needs from solo players as well as groups. Here are examples: community goal events invite participants to work towards a single effort to achieve all universal milestones, and therefore reward the group with rare items and increase social bonds. Forming the foundation of such strategies which exploit FOMO and their desire for Social bonding, these techniques increase the player retention rate as well as in-game revenue and thus facilitate player acquisition. Events like Winterfest create excitement and populate with a high number of players, thus, generating short-term interest in ultimately encouraging lag-long-term loyalty through emotional bonds.

From the evidence of these case studies, it is clear that there is a potential for carefully conceived gamification to maintain interest, promote creative expression and reinforce social networks in the metaverse (Inchamnan, 2023). They demonstrate that reward incentives when coupled with an emphasis on a user's well-being are necessary, to avoid damage to ones mental health or safety due to engagement. In demonstrations of both the advantages and the disadvantages of developing gamified virtualized spaces where autonomy in money, creativity and being with people could coexist with a dedication towards ethical development and responsible community management, Roblox and Fortnite both stand as illustrations.

B. Historical Background of the Use of Gamification

The keep going until approach has expanded on the concept of gamification since its origination and adoption by numerous sectors in the last twenty years. It is directly descended from my earliest examples – where game elements had been used for advertising or for customer engagement programs. Starting from the early 2010s, sources started pointing out the applicability of gamification to sectors ranging from educational to healthcare and employee training sectors. A timeline of gamification presents some of the key events categorized using different fields and studies that depict some of the best success stories of the attempt. For example, the site Duolingo has used the culture of achieving levels, using rewards, and using social elements for improving the language acquisition processes.

Table 1. Comparison of Gamification Elements Across Platforms gives a variety of examples of how gamification can be implemented and how similar goals can be achieved using different game elements required for the functioning of the target audience.

Platform	Points System	Badges	Leaderboards	Challenges/Quests	Social Features
Duolingo	Yes	Yes	Yes	Yes	Yes
Fitbit	Yes	Yes	Yes	Yes	Yes
Kahoot!	Yes	Yes	Yes	No	Yes
Starbucks	Yes	No	No	No	No
Minecraft	Yes	Yes	Yes	Yes	Yes

It is essential to grasp that the changes throughout its evolution are inherent in the subtleties and possibilities of utilizing gamification as an efficient intervention strategy to improve the experiences of users existent across a broad spectrum of practices. Because the analysis focuses on the manner in which various platforms incorporate gamification features, it allows to identify exemplary and novel approaches employed in enhancing engagement and satisfaction levels among end-users.

3. THE INTERSECTION OF GAMIFICATION AND THE METAVERSE

A. Why Does Gameification Matter in the Metaverse?

Due to the same reason, metaverse has adopted gamification to help in delivering the best retention and loyalty strategies to its users. In a setting where the prospects are possibly almost limitless and users producing and creating content on a large scale, the incorporation of game elements can enhance users' attention and participation. In this way platforms in the metaverse can provide positive motivators such as points, rewards and challenges in order to maintain users' engagement. This is especially relevant to virtual environments where individuals may experience many demands and issues. However, gamification enables users to become part of a community where he or she can engage himself or herself in various social related activities and goals.

B. Potential Benefits of Gamification

The potential of the gamification application in Metaverse is not only in terms of increased engagement but major motivation boost for the users and establishment of dynamic and active communities. By the introduction of game mechanics, a user becomes more active and is ready to 'play' the site since a gamer feels inspired by it due to the fact that reward features points out that they have arrived at the correct conclusion. This can increase the levels of satisfaction and enjoyment, meaning the metaverse isn't simply a place to socialize, but also a place to excel. Third, gamification promotes social features because people share common goals while engaging in activities such as completion of tasks, events and sharing of achievements.

Figure 2. The graphic benefits of gamification in the Metaverse also outlines these factors to help you explore how gamification can improve several aspects of users' experiences. Concerning motivation and involvement, community building, and many other aspects, it is incredible how the use of gamification strategies within the metaverse can be a revolution in front of established paradigms of interacting with digital scenarios. All of this benefits the user experience and at the same time, fosters the development of the metaverse as a living environment.

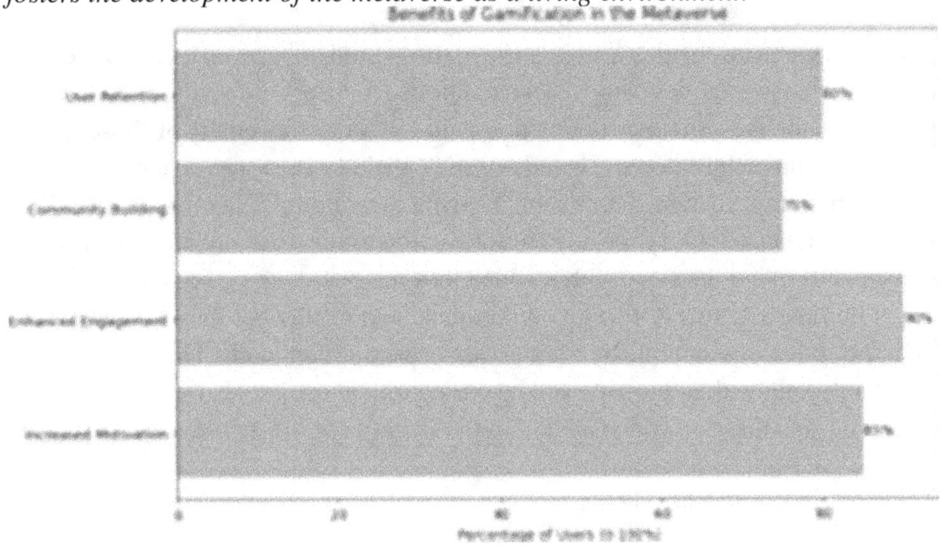

4. CORE ELEMENTS OF GAMIFICATION IN THE METAVERSE

A. Game Mechanics

Imbedded into gamification in the metaverse are vital game elements that create attractive levels and improve the overall experience. These mechanics include points, badges & a leaderboard system, and the purpose is to motivate users based on their actions. It provides feedback in terms of score which are quantifiable so as to encourage users involvement in the virtual space. Badges, however, represent the accomplishment and milestones attained and enables the users to display these symbols in their activities. This does not only increase the drive of the individual but also complements social rivalry since users can choose to have their badges situated near to that of their friends.

Forums add to this competitive tone by presenting users in the form of a leaderboard according to the number of points or achievements attained. They set an energetic social structure encouraging users to advance up the contributing ranks, making people attentive. However, in applying these elements proper balance need to be achieved; if the competition is too stiff or the rewards easily achievable, people will most likely lose interest.

Further game mechanics which can have substantial impacts on user experiences in the metaverse includes challenges and quests. As users are provided with a set of tasks, challenges imbue meaning and guide in the achievement of those goals, effectively channeling users. Threads usually include stories that help to define participation, thus making a user's involvement meaningful. This type of an aspect of storytelling can amplify the level of interaction as the users are not only dealing with a platform but the story within which they are operating is the story they help shape. For instance, users also go on missions with challenges they have to solve, tasks they have to accomplish or goals that require group work. These mechanics do not only help with motivation and intrinsic motivation, but also with team interaction and socialization which all add to the richness of the metaverse experience.

B. User Experience Design

Incorporation of gamification in the metaverse also require User experience design (UXD) for efficiency. The design of the user experience can greatly influence how users receive and utilize factors which have been incorporated into the gamification process. Two particular strategies are used, and they stem from the concept of immersion and narrative play. This kind of environment can truly be described as an illusion; users cannot simply tell the difference between real life and the digital world by using gadgets like Virtual Reality and Augmented Reality to perform their tasks. With more of the users' senses inundated—visible, audible, tangible—they are more apt to stay on task.

The narrative aspects of narrative affordances help create immersion, because they create a narrative for users to follow as they interact with their experiences. Like in any other learning context the combination of visuals and audios is crucial in boosting learners' interactions in the metaverse (Damaševičius, 2023). Good graphics and color combination and impressive animations are effective in attracting users into the experience while on the other part, sounds and music help in addition to evoking emotions that support the themes. The best of these elements applied makes the atmosphere of such a game more interesting and enjoyable. For instance, sounds can deepen the experience, while the on-screen signposts can help users have their quests pointed out to them, or inform them that their mission is complete. Visual and auditory stimulus are all that are required to turn a mundane event into a thrilling expedition.

C. Social Interaction and Community Building

Interactivity and connections are intrinsic part and parcel of gamification in the metaverse. It is noteworthy that social features play a critical role in enhancing active and engaging community within standard gamification projects. As much as possible, users like to be involved in social activities because different experiences are supplemented with social interactions that can include collaboration, competition, or communication with other people. These interactions can be assisted by gamification through offering, for instance, chat windows, collaborative tasks, and team-oriented quests.

With regards to social interaction, since game users meet friends or people with whom they are not familiar with, the act of gamification leads to togetherness. This social feature increases a platform's likelihood of attracting users because the interactions users have while using the platform make up a strong foundation of their experience. Other cooperation schemes, such as completing tasks together or performing tasks in groups, contribute to increased teamwork since users have to work together in order to achieve a shared objective. This does not only make it possible for learning to occur but also fosters desirable social interactions in context of the virtual environment.

Table 2. Understanding Game Mechanics and Their Implications on User Interaction concludes the previous chapters on game mechanics and their consequences on user engagement in metaverse context (Nicola, 2022). This table is useful in providing a reference with regard to how the various components mentioned in the definition of a good user experience fit together.

Game Mechanic	Description	Effects on Engagement
Points System	Rewards users for actions taken	Increases participation and provides immediate feedback
Badges	Visual representation of achievements	Encourages competition and motivation
Leaderboards	Ranks users based on performance	Creates competitive dynamics and drives engagement
Challenges/ Quests	Structured activities with goals	Provides purpose and enhances narrative immersion
Social Features	Allows interaction among users	Fosters community and collaboration

The core elements of gamification—game mechanics, user experience design, and social interaction—are essential for creating engaging and meaningful experiences within the metaverse. By thoughtfully integrating these components, developers can foster a dynamic environment where users are motivated to explore, collaborate, and thrive. This holistic approach not only enhances individual satisfaction but also contributes to the growth and sustainability of vibrant virtual communities.

5. CASE STUDIES AND EXAMPLES

A. Successful Gamification in Existing Metaverse Platforms

The intersection of gamification and the metaverse is exemplified by several notable platforms, including Roblox and Fortnite, which have successfully integrated game mechanics to enhance user engagement and create vibrant communities. **Roblox** is particularly noteworthy for its user-generated content model, allowing users to create and share their own games. This platform employs gamification strategies such as points, badges, and in-game currency, which incentivize players to explore, create, and participate actively in the community. Users can earn rewards for completing tasks, participating in events, or creating popular games, fostering a sense of achievement and motivation.

Fortnite, another leading platform, takes a different approach by blending gameplay with narrative elements and social interaction. The game features a seasonal model that introduces new content and challenges regularly, encouraging players to return frequently. Gamification in Fortnite includes battle passes, which offer tiers of rewards for completing specific challenges, thus enhancing user engagement through structured progression. The inclusion of social features—such as in-game events and collaborative quests—further enhances the communal experience, making it more enjoyable for players to interact with friends and other users.

Figure 3. Gamification Strategies Across Notable Platforms no longer needs any introduction, it shows how different platforms like Roblox and Fortnite have adopted different strategies and which game mechanics were important for users. This figure shows the specifics of how each of the platforms implements gamification to design engaging experience for its audience.

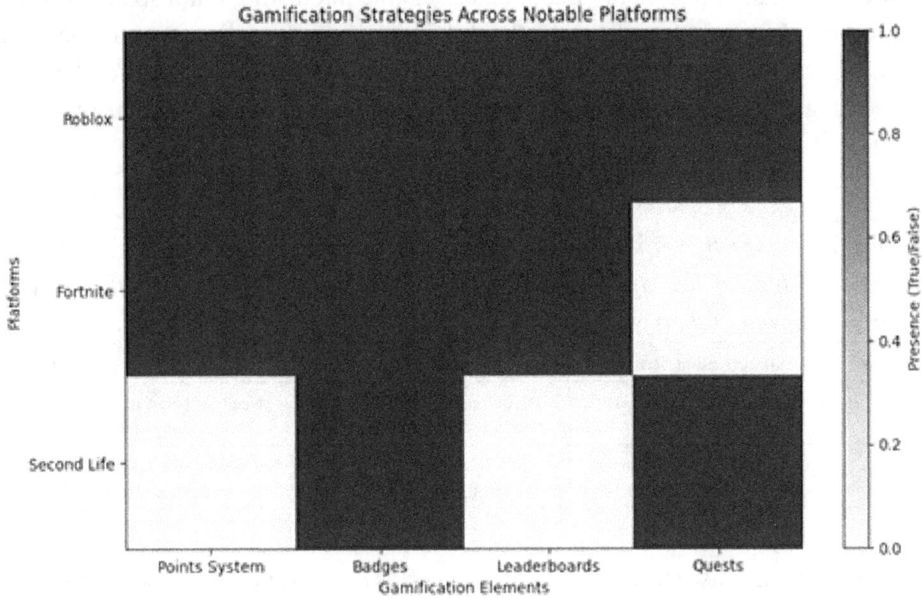

B. Lessons Learned

From here, we can draw out a number of 'success factors' for gamification on these types of networks: something that in turn allows us to outline what worked and what didn't, based on the overall level of triumph in each category. There is one distinct lesson to learn, and it is the issue of the user autonomy: The more explicit freedom people have to lead the kind of experience they have on a specific platform – whether it is through content generation, tweaking a profile, or participating in a community of some sort – the more likely they will remain loyal and satisfied. For instance, player-generated content in games like Roblox involves the players in determining how the games various aspects work like a permanent magnet to keep the players engaged. On the other hand, there are possibilities that platforms, which limit users' options or have a small amount of presented content, will not be interesting.

Another lesson is the impact of repeated update frequency and the content update especially after a period of a month or two. The same can be seen in Fortnite where the format of seasons shows how adding new tasks and ideas will help users come back to their game. It not only maintains the game interesting but also encourages learners to communicate with each other by finding friends to discuss strategies and share experience of new content. On the other hand, platforms that do not develop new strategies may find that the number of users who interact with their platform decreases with time.

Table 3. Therefore, the paper Case Study Summaries of Gamified Metaverse Experiences contains brief descriptions of the mentioned case studies, elements that played a significant role in their success and recommendations for further improvement.

Platform	Key Gamification Strategies	Success Factors	Areas for Improvement
Roblox	User-generated content, points, badges	High user engagement, creativity, community building	Need for better moderation of content
Fortnite	Battle passes, seasonal content, collaborative quests	Strong narrative, regular updates, social interaction	Balance between competitive play and casual enjoyment

To that extent, case studies of Platforms such as Roblox, Fortnite discuss the high influence of gamification within the Metaverse. Thus, game mechanics when used to improve user experiences, not only results in captivating players but also circulation of community and collaboration. Many of the elements incorporated into their projects are derived from their principles, and their accomplishments and setbacks have insights useful in future metaverse innovations. Coupled with the dynamics of these changes, this knowledge will be key to answering questions that developers of PNEs will want to address as they try to build immersive environments that are meaningful to users.

Analyzing Psychological Effects: Addiction and Privacy

A close examination of the psychological aspects of gamification reveals the potential of gamification to motivate as well as the dangers that gamification presents. The potential joy and community produced by the longing for digital accolades and accomplishments can produce feelings of fulfillment, yet it can also serve as a source of addictive behaviors, especially evident when users are bombarded with (relatively) endless repetitive tasks and rewards. The issue of user privacy is given as much importance as many gamified platforms find themselves having a huge amount of user data at their disposal, in order to facilitate personalization. Although such methods increase user attraction, they also draw attention to the need to be transparent, protect data, and take care of users' data. Successful solutions require constant tracking and the development of clear, transparent instructions on how data is processed by a user.

6. CHALLENGES AND CONSIDERATIONS

A. Ethical Concerns

Despite the fact that the use of the principle of gamification is gradually becoming more familiar in the framework of the metaverse, it is also necessary to consider several important and exciting ethical issues (Thomas, 2023). There are some drawbacks among which the development of a risk that users will become addicted and rely on the elements of gamification. In its core, gamification due to mechanics such as points, badges, and leader boards, provides the framework for generating experiences that make the users invest too much time into the virtual world. This may eliminate other daily real-life obligations and social contact, which are definitely questions about the psychological impact of long-term involvement. It is a crass imperative for developers to be sure they create a compelling experience while not implicitly encouraging addictive styles of interacting with their product.

Also, there are lots of problems connected with data security and personal information protection. When individuals play the games of the metaverse, they disclose information, choices, and behaviors that are idiosyncratic. This information can be extremely beneficial in improving user interaction and personalizing content but collects dangers in improper usage. There are cases when persons have or misuse personal information that can result in trust of the users. Recommendations for the future work include the need to ethicly approach the collection, storage, and use of data concerning the user. Such concerns must therefore be addressed through transparent policies in place to ensure cyber security, measures that provide adequate security features, and more importantly, gaining informed consent from clients on the same.

Psychological Effects of Gamification: Addiction and Mental Health

The psychological impact of gamification – some derived from components of reward mechanisms, some based on competitive dynamics, and others based on social validation – holds the ability to improve interactions among users, but this also raises questions about addiction risks, and can lead to negative consequences on long-term mental health. The users who concentrate on collecting points, badges and leaderboard spots they could become addicted to the platform use thus leading to compulsion symptoms similar to those that are present in the regular games. In order to reduce these risks, stakeholders need to produce nuanced consciousness about the intricate impact of game designs on an individual and the general digital environment.

Community moderation and user generated content are the key aspects that make a positive online climate possible within the metaverse. Strategies that focus on having a clarified sense of the norms of the community including proactive monitoring play an important role in keeping toxic interaction, harassment, and the spread of inaccurate content to a minimum. The ability of users to create content allows them to define ones online worlds and is therefore a creative urn which instills a sense of ownership, however it requires constant moderation to ensure safety and inclusivity are up to standards. Equilibrium between the promotion of creativity and instillation of oversight is paramount to developing thriving, enabling communities in the metaverse.

Metaverse platform design and operation are more influenced by new rules and ethics than ever before. To succeed, developers need to face many-sided legal and ethical challenges that include issues of privacy, the safety of the user, and the struggle against exploitative practices. Compliance with standards and an ability for an adaptation to new regulatory demands creates more robust protection for users and birthing trust and sound oversight within metaverse ecosystems. At such an analytical level, the chapter provides for a more in-depth vision of the various challenges and ethical directions that those who design and manage the gamified metaverse platforms are facing.

Stakeholder Perspectives and Ethical Engagement Guidelines

The combination of developers, users and ethicists acts to strengthen the discussion surrounding gamification in the metaverse. Developers emphasize the requirement to establish as alluring as possible and responsible systems, so that the innovation progresses hand in hand with protection of the user. It is standard for users to request the ability to track how data is handled, and what options exist to air grievances or to avoid certain functionalities. Ethics experts propose open standards based on protection of users' well-being, safeguarding privacy and equitable practices. It is possible that the adoption of such ethical principles as restrictions on ethical design and rigorous data controls, as well as on learning about digital literacy, will create safer and more accessible metaverse ecosystems (Srisawat, 2022). Such practices protect the users at the same time creating trust and ensuring the metaverse is sustainable for the future (Park, 2022).

In-Depth Analysis of User Perspectives on Ethical Challenges

The ethical perspectives of gamification in the metaverse are as much a product of technological ability as they are a product of the experience and concerns of people who call it home. The immersive, creative, and social nature of the metaverse is often tempting its users, but sometimes these very matters induce fear of addiction possibilities and threats to their private data. Typically, users report that the architecture of rewards and progress within gamified spaces motivates them to stay submerged for long stretches at a time, sometimes at the expense of their in-real-life tasks and relationships (Tsiliakos, 2024). Young consumers in particular tend to be more interested in the possibility to gain social recognition and progress in virtual activities. A sense of mastery, and ability to escape reality or receive validation from others in the metaverse are strong motivators, but such rewards can have the opposite effect on effective goal management and use as well, promoting addictive use. Results of studies emphasize that virtual embodiment, a state wherein participants feel highly involved with their avatars, is likely to enhance emotional involvement and lead to increased vulnerability to compulsive engagement, especially as technologically powered.

On the other hand, users are getting to know the privacy threats of the metaverse. Users' intimate data is constantly and heavily gathered in the metaverse, which extends further than their actions to such factors as gaze movements or facial expressions. Many of the users are uncomfortable about the lack of clear information on the methods of collecting, handling, and utilizing their data. They are scared they may have their data hacked or secretly exposed and used either by companies to their interests or used by companies to influence their actions. Such concern is exacerbated by the fact that data handling in many metaverse platforms is extremely decentralized with multiple variations in practices and poor applicability of existing privacy laws.

Real-World Examples of Ethical Gamification and Stakeholder Collaboration

Example from the leading metaverse corporations exhibit the hurdles and the progress in addressing ethical dilemmas. For instance, Roblox has introduced many parental controls, privacy settings, and community moderation tools, which are tailored to cater to younger users and establish a safe environment. Artificial intelligence and in real-time moderation by teams of people are used by the platform to monitor and respond to not appropriate behavior with the support of instructional resources that promote the exercise of respectfulness among users. Fortnite as well has introduced functions such as playtime notifications, user changeable privacy settings, and multiple reporting tools, to enable users to manage their experience and safety. In most scenarios, these strategies are developed in collaboration with external stakeholders, including, mental health professionals, child protection organizations, and experts in privacy, so as to ensure that platform guidelines reflect multiple perspectives and scholarship (Jovanović, 2022).

Throughout industries larger movements are also being created that develop common standards and best practices. For instance, the Metaverse is the platform where technology companies, standards bodies and civil society organizations meet to establish guidelines for interoperability, privacy and ethics in virtual spaces. This is a collaboration between industry, society and regulatory bodies where people are gathered to bring the metaverse on a respectful basis for technology and the welfare of its users, with inclusivity and responsibility. Diverse country-based policy makers are taking measures to resolve the issues of the metaverse through new regulations and ways of working focused on user safety, privacy, and ethical AI surrounding immersive spaces.

Data Security and Privacy Protection: Best Practices and Examples

It is especially difficult to secure data and protect the privacy in the metaverse because there is a huge quantity and high sensitivity of data collected. Leading digital platforms are deploying numerous technical and strategic methods to protect information of users. Encryption, multi-factor authentication and secure communications are the standard in practices. Regular security checkups in addition to the live continuous monitoring enables the platforms to pin down and eliminate future risks before it even manifests. Several platforms are eyeing the use of blockchain technology to add transparency and security, applying this technology's unchangeability and decentralization in a bid to provide more security for user identities and activities.

The other fundament is user autonomy in these practices. Simplified privacy dashboards enable the users to have control over the data which gets shared, with whom, and when. Users should have clear and easy-to-use consent choices and be capable of managing their operations and making informed decisions about participating in online activities. Platforms that frequently submit transparency reports have the ability to build trust by sharing information on their management of users' data, the number and content of requests received and the responses they provided on security breaches.

It is quite important to involve external experts and policymakers when responding to new risks and fulfilled legal obligations. Numerous companies are partnering with cybersecurity experts, privacy organizations, and governments in order to develop efficient compliance schemes following norms such as the GDPR.

Industry-related forums and working groups are additionally solidifying these efforts in order to encourage the sharing of knowledge, create best practices, and lead the way to improved security measures in the metaverse industry.

Ethical Gamification: Guidelines and Industry Standards

The ground for the ethical gamification in the metaverse is based upon the keystones of fairness, transparency, and upholding of autonomy of users. It is advisable to see to it that developers design their systems to protect the well-being of end users, dismiss deceptive mechanics, and encourage good interactions between end users. Clear standards for guiding the processes of dealing with rewards, progress milestones, and competition mechanisms are the essential components for promoting staying involved and avoiding the amount of dependency or exclusion that may develop amongst users.

The participation of all central stakeholders is important both in establishing and maintaining ethical guidelines. Involved in regular dialogues with users, ethicists, developers, and regulators, platforms are better equipped to identify new risks, cater to highly diverse user needs, and change their policies to reflect changing values of society. Codes of conduct, community guidelines and ethical charters are principles behind ethical conduct and continuous training and awareness building provide these across the culture of the metaverse.

New industry standards are being developed to address the unique problems presented by virtual environments. The IEEE and other organizations released ethical guidelines for XR technologies that have a significant focus of protecting the users by ensuring privacy and identity of their privacy and wellness are ensured. In addition to these standards, we see platform specific regulations and global regulatory efforts which strengthen the notions of responsible and ethical approaches to gamification in the metaverse.

With the variety of user inputs, illustrative examples, and tested ways of mitigation, this chapter enhances our understanding of the problem and the tools to counteract it. It can only move forward with active approach, open governance and engaging participation from all stakeholders. It is only possible to actualize the metaverse as a place of creativity, connection, and positive human flourishing when ethical considerations and industry best practices are central.

B. Technical Limitations

In addition to the ethic concerns, there are sundry problems encountered in the gamification based metaverse which are technical barriers to creating effective gamification in the metaverse. However, one big question is how to connect a number of technologies required to deliver an engaging experience. The integration of augmented and virtual reality and interactive aspects in the platform the project needs more funds and skills to write the platform. Making sure compatibility is achieved in the dissimilar devices and platforms poses a challenge to designers, and this results in a little user experience across the devices users may interact with. These fragments can prevent or dissuade users that are looking forward to a seamless interface experience (Daşdemir, 2022).

Other components of technical constraints include Access Issues. The metaverse is an element that needs to be user-friendly so that the individuals with one disability or another are equally welcomed. It should always be useful to note that all the elements of gamification should be developed in such a way that everybody can use them, even a disabled person. This includes adaptable interfaces, options other than using a mouse, and access for all users to be an equal part of the game. There are specific problems here that are arising for developers – in particular, while coming up with more inventive ways of using gamification, it remains important to not neglect this classical aspect as otherwise, there are less folks who can come into the metaverse in the first place.

Thus, although gamification has been implemented across the numerous metaverse benefits, it has some ethical issues and technical constraints that are needed to be solved. Computer science professionals should focus on user safety, efficient and secure data administration and usable space for diverse users. Thus, being aware of these difficulties, the metaverse can transform into an environment, which not only motivates users to generate high levels of participation but also becomes an ethical area.

7. FUTURE DIRECTIONS

A. New Directions in Explanation and Use of Games and Virtual Reality

It is envisioned that the future of gamification in the metaverse has stagewise movement for change as the integration of emerging advancements in technology for new trends through the use of artificial intelligence and augmented/virtual reality. The most interesting is the functionality of AI which is applicable in the context of adapting content and tasks according to users' behaviors and preferences (Nurtanto, 2021). This level of personalization increases the level of interaction because users is exposed to things that are in line with his/her values and therefore, meets the right motivational factors. It can also assist in real-time progression manage that would help ensure that difficulties stay at the required level of assessment and are not too difficult to frustrate the user and yet are not too easy that the user loses interest right away.

However, due to increased awareness and advancements of AR and VR features users are increasingly likely to be enthralled and engulfed with more realism and interactivity of gamified surroundings. It shows that as the components and equipment get cheaper and more widely available, more people can be introduced to these technologies. This creates new opportunities for the use of gamification, for example, games based on the mixed reality where a player moves through the real world or games that tell non-linear stories where the player could virtually experience an amazingly detailed environment. The movements over the next decade are expected to extend metaverse into an integrated system where components of the ecosystems allow people to move freely within linked virtual worlds while retaining the same identity and skills acquired in different areas.

B. Developers and Business Perspectives

As it happens, it becomes the responsibility of the developers and businesses to balance their strategies for effective utilization of the potential of gamification available in the metaverse. The suggested strategies for developers are to expand the AI &_machine learning feature to improve user experience. To be specific, through using data analytics, the developers can identify the behavior patterns of users and get a possibility to provide the users with valuable and informative experience, as well as involving them more into the project. Further, design for interfaces as well as content that is easy to understand will be hallmarks of products throughout the course, concerns for a user base to be as broad as possible for ableism.

Future development possibilities are enormous especially with metaverse in their dynamic development phase. Companies out there can work with game developers to see how they can establish synergism that will entail making games that will be in tune with the target group. For instance, it showcases opportunities for brands that can work with famous platforms to launch brands challenges or events thus using users base of these platforms to increase reach. In addition, combining gamification elements into training and education processes, which take place in the metaverse, contributes to the formation of effective learning processes that support knowledge acquisition and its application (Yamba-Yugsi, 2024).

8. CONCLUSION

A. Recap of Key Points

In this chapter, we sought to provide deep insights into the connection between gamification and the metaverse regarding its importance in boosting audience interactivity and development of active communities. We started with the definition of the metaverse and its main peculiarities – presence in the sphere of computer and virtual reality, view into immersive experience, etc. We then proceeded to define gamification and provided information on its main constituents which are points, badges, and leaderboards and information on the historical utilize of the concept in several fields. Exploring this relationship between two contexts shows that metaverse application benefits from gamification to boost engagement by utilizing game design and storytelling and thereby proactively establishing user experiences.

Furthermore, we also discussed successful examples of gamification from such platforms as Roblox or Fortnite, and learned from them useful lessons. However, it also discussed lighting the problem and evaluation with regards to the limitation and consideration of gamification; the ethical issues associated with game addition, or data privacy, and few of the implementation and access issues. Last but not the least, we focused on various future directions, including the future of AI & AR/VR and possible difficulties which developers and businesses that target to create their products in this field may face.

B. Looking into the Metaverse, Future Prospect of the Gamification

The opportunities that gamification holds for the metaverse in the future are almost endless. In turn, the ever-evolving advancements in technology appear to necessarily enhance user interactivity by providing more complex and interactive environments. Through the use of Artificial Intelligence and Augmented Reality – Virtual Reality, one can develop environment that will not only interest the user but also an environment that will respond to the user based on their behavior. Let's have a look at the continual expansion of the net and usage of interconnected virtual spaces: the ability to move between different environments while preserving the achievements and personas, in my opinion, has a future. It will probably foster users' interactive and connected experiences and may strengthen the unbroken social environment and cooperation in the metaverse (Sousa-Vieira, 2023).

C. Call to Action for Stakeholders

Based on these reflections, it is important for stakeholders such as developers, businesses, educators, and policymakers to take full participation in the future development of the gamification in the Metaverse. There is more need for the developers to keep the ethical implications where the gamification would help in improving the experience without the creation of addictive results or the treatment of the privacy of the users' information in a bad way. Companies need to look for ways of engaging the users through developing new forms of partnerships and solutions that would lead to creation of best practices in the gamification. These developments can be useful to educators where they develop a conducive environment to enhance learning with little lengths of focus or retention. Lastly, recommendations should be made that address user data privacy, as well as accessibility to equally impact the metaverse.

With cooperation and concentration on responsible innovation, various stakeholders can use gamification to create enjoyable experiences in the metaverse with potential for a positive influence on the digital society that will be favorable to all members.

REFERENCES

Antonaci, A., Klemke, R., & Specht, M. (2019, August). The effects of gamification in online learning environments: A systematic literature review. In Informatics (Vol. 6, No. 3, p. 32). MDPI. DOI: 10.3390/informatics6030032

Arya, V., Sambyal, R., Sharma, A., & Dwivedi, Y. K. (2024). Brands are calling your AVATAR in Metaverse–A study to explore XR-based gamification marketing activities & consumer-based brand equity in virtual world. *Journal of Consumer Behaviour, 23*(2), 556–585. DOI: 10.1002/cb.2214

Damaševičius, R., & Sidekersniene, T. 2023, September. Designing immersive gamified experiences in the metaverse for enhanced student learning. In *2023 International Conference on Intelligent Metaverse Technologies & Applications (iMETA)* (pp. 1-6). IEEE.

Das, T., Ganesh Kondamudi, S., Dawood Babakerkhell, M., Pal, D., Roy, R., & Funilkul, S. (2024). Intention for enhancing metaverse-based learning using gamification among university students: A study using Delphi and structural equation modelling approaches. *Cogent Business & Management, 11*(1), 2380016. DOI: 10.1080/23311975.2024.2380016

Daşdemir, Y. (2022). A brain-computer interface with gamification in the Metaverse. *Dicle Üniversitesi Mühendislik Fakültesi Mühendislik Dergisi, 13*(4), 645–652.

Flavián, C., Ibáñez-Sánchez, S., Orús, C., & Barta, S. (2024). The dark side of the metaverse: The role of gamification in event virtualization. *International Journal of Information Management, 75*, 102726. DOI: 10.1016/j.ijinfomgt.2023.102726

Gamayanto, I., Wibowo, S., & Prayitno, A. (2024). The Concept of gamification, metaverse & AI to develop hybrid learning systems inside education. [International Journal of Information System and Technology]. *IJISTECH, 7*(6), 370–378.

Huang, R., Ritzhaupt, A. D., Sommer, M., Zhu, J., Stephen, A., Valle, N., Hampton, J., & Li, J. (2020). The impact of gamification in educational settings on student learning outcomes: A meta-analysis. *Educational Technology Research and Development, 68*(4), 1875–1901. DOI: 10.1007/s11423-020-09807-z

Inchamnan, W. (2023). Gamification Pedagogy Trigger Design for Creative Experiences in Metaverse Class Room. [JASET]. *Journal of Applied Science and Emerging Technology, 22*(2), 251539. DOI: 10.14416/JASET.KMUTNB.2023.02.003

Jovanović, A., & Milosavljević, A. (2022). VoRtex Metaverse platform for gamified collaborative learning. *Electronics (Basel), 11*(3), 317. DOI: 10.3390/electronics11030317

Kim, J., & Castelli, D. M. (2021). Effects of gamification on behavioral change in education: A meta-analysis. *International Journal of Environmental Research and Public Health, 18*(7), 3550. DOI: 10.3390/ijerph18073550 PMID: 33805530

Liu, C. C., Lin, Y. Y., Lo, F. Y., Chang, C. H., & Lin, H. M. (2024). From readers to players: Exploring student engagement in a gamified metaverse and its effect on reading interest. *Education and Information Technologies*, •••, 1–27.

Ng, P. H., Chen, P. Q., Sin, Z. P., Jia, Y., Li, R. C., Baciu, G., Cao, J., & Li, Q. 2023, November. From classroom to metaverse: a study on gamified constructivist teaching in higher education. In *International conference on web-based learning* (pp. 92-106). Singapore: Springer Nature Singapore. DOI: 10.1007/978-981-99-8385-8_8

Nicola, M., (2022). gamification marketing in metaverse contexts: can the employment of immersive gamification experiences that leverage customer's creativity and sociality be a useful tool to influence customer engagement in metaverse applications?.

Nurtanto, M., Kholifah, N., Ahdhianto, E., Samsudin, A., & Isnantyo, F. D. (2021). A review of gamification impact on student behavioral and learning outcomes. iJIM, 15(21), 23.

Park, S., & Kim, S. (2022). Identifying world types to deliver gameful experiences for sustainable learning in the metaverse. *Sustainability (Basel), 14*(3), 1361. DOI: 10.3390/su14031361

Sharma, W., Lim, W. M., Kumar, S., Verma, A., & Kumra, R. (2024). Game on! A state-of-the-art overview of doing business with gamification. *Technological Forecasting and Social Change, 198*, 122988. DOI: 10.1016/j.techfore.2023.122988

Smith, E., Herbert, J., Kavanagh, L., & Reidsema, C. (2013). The effects of gamification on student learning through the use of reputation and rewards within community moderated discussion boards.

Sousa-Vieira, M. E., López-Ardao, J. C., Fernández-Veiga, M., & Rodríguez-Rubio, R. F. (2023). Study of the impact of social learning and gamification methodologies on learning results in higher education. *Computer Applications in Engineering Education, 31*(1), 131–153. DOI: 10.1002/cae.22575

Srisawat, S., & Piriyasurawong, P. (2022). Metaverse Virtual Learning Management Based on Gamification Techniques Model to Enhance Total Experience. *International Education Studies, 15*(5), 153–163. DOI: 10.5539/ies.v15n5p153

Tayal, S., Rajagopal, K., & Mahajan, V. 2022, March. Virtual reality based metaverse of gamification. In *2022 6th International Conference on Computing Methodologies and Communication (ICCMC)* (pp. 1597-1604). IEEE. DOI: 10.1109/ICCMC53470.2022.9753727

Thomas, N. J., Baral, R., Crocco, O. S., & Mohanan, S. (2023). A framework for gamification in the metaverse era: How designers envision gameful experience. *Technological Forecasting and Social Change*, *193*, 122544. DOI: 10.1016/j.techfore.2023.122544

Tsiliakos, M., & Bassing, S. 2024, April. Eduverse: Exploring Gamification and the Metaverse in Architectural Pedagogy. In *ACCELERATED DESIGN, Proceedings of the 29th International Conference of the Association for ComputerAided Architectural Design Research in Asia (CAADRIA) 2024, Volume 3, 59-68* (pp. 59-68). Association for Computer-Aided Architectural Design Research in Asia (CAADRIA).

Yamba-Yugsi, M., Contreras-Espinosa, R. S., & Eguia-Gomez, J. L. 2024. Exploring the Emerging Potential of the Metaverse in Education: Gamification, Advantages, and Limitations. In *Navigating Virtual Worlds and the Metaverse for Enhanced E-Learning* (pp. 111-133). IGI Global.

Yamba-Yugsi, M., Contreras-Espinosa, R. S., Maldonado-Mahauad, J., & Gomez, J. L. E. (2023). EXAMINING THE OPPORTUNITIES OF THE METAVERSE AND GAMIFICATION IN EDUCATION: Benefits, and constraints. *Video Journal of Social and Human Research*, *2*(2), 47–64. DOI: 10.18817/vjshr.v2i2.32

Yang, W., Fang, M., Xu, J., Zhang, X., & Pan, Y. (2024). Exploring the Mediating Role of Different Aspects of Learning Motivation between Metaverse Learning Experiences and Gamification. *Electronics (Basel)*, *13*(7), 1297. DOI: 10.3390/electronics13071297

Chapter 2
Gamified Brand Engagement in the Metaverse Strategies for Customer Loyalty

Pooja Sehgal Tabeck
https://orcid.org/0000-0001-7473-3096
Symbiosis Institute of Business Management, Noida, Symbiosis International University, Pune, India

ABSTRACT

Gamification and the metaverse are reshaping brand engagement by offering immersive, interactive experiences that go beyond traditional marketing. This chapter examines how combining game elements with virtual environments fosters emotional, cognitive, social, and transactional engagement, enhancing customer loyalty. Gamification encourages active participation through challenges and rewards, while the metaverse provides a 3D digital space for real-time interaction. Case studies such as Sunsilk City and Hyundai Mobility Adventure on Roblox show how brands use avatars, storytelling, and virtual simulations to connect with tech-savvy consumers. Sunsilk empowered young women through educational games, while Hyundai showcased future mobility in themed digital parks. Key strategies include personalization, emotional connection, continuous engagement, and seamless brand integration. These gamified metaverse experiences offer brands an innovative way to build lasting relationships with their audiences.

DOI: 10.4018/979-8-3693-8886-0.ch002

INTRODUCTION

Digitization and penetration of internet around the world has changed the business perspective and interaction with customers. Digitization has been incorporated into many facets of business domains and day to day life of individuals. The growing desire of companies to stay ahead in the competition and interact with their empowered customers has led them to adopt many new- age technologies. Among these the focus is on proactive user experience and brand engagement, a realm that has given rise to an entirely new market for gamified applications in Metaverse.

The concept of gamification been widely accepted across various industries. With advent of metaverse, it has gained renewed interest, prompting both companies and customers to delve deep into the emerging field. The Metaverse is a blend of three-dimensional virtual world that integrates Internet, Augmented Reality, and virtual reality (Arya et al.,2024). Games and digital fashion brands are at forefront of Metaverse (Lee et al.,2023). The combination of these with gamification not only generate attention about the brands rather provide a unique experience all together. The gamification characteristics affordance and perceived value and metaverse property of flow state together improves engagement for brands (Cha et al.,2024).

Virtual gaming features lead users towards the more engagement as they are easily able to interact and engage with brands through their avatars, storytelling, gif or any other gamification style created by the company (Bousba et al.,2022). This results in better experience, engagement and loyalty.

The metaverse creates an interactive and immersive environment where gamified marketing activities generate both hedonic and utilitarian values for brand which results in brand engagement. Contrary to traditional marketing activities brand engagement in gamified metaverse context is output of experience rather than only value-based assessments (Al-Adwan et al.,2025).

Initially gamification and metaverse integration has been seen in luxury brand scenario where gamification driven immersive commerce in metaverse enabled luxury brands to offer virtual store fronts, virtual try on feature. This has given unique experience to luxury customers of the brands i.e. Gucci, Zara, Ralph Lauren, Adidas and Burberry (Koohang et al.,2023). As technology trickle down the same integration has also been adopted by various brands including FMCG(Unilever) and Furniture (Ikea). Gamification plays a significant role in different domains of brand engagement and has a potential to contribute for better engagement with customers through enjoyment and pleasure in metaverse era (Thomas et al.,2023).

In view of gamified brand engagement in metaverse the present chapter will try to explore following research questions:

RQ1: What are the key differences between traditional gamification and gamification in the Metaverse?
RQ2: How does gamified brand engagement operate within the Metaverse, and what are its implications for customer loyalty?
RQ3: What is the nature of gamified brand engagement in the Metaverse?

LITERATURE REVIEW

Gamification takes its DNA from gaming where game design principals and elements integrated in non-game environment. The main objective of gamification is to transform processes, or products into a game like structure that drive behavioral changes (Hamari et al.,2023). Gamification helps companies to use game design principal in non -game context. With the help of gamification, the experience of users can be enhanced and learning process become easier. Metaverse supports the gamification with animation and make the learning process enjoyable and memorable. (Afacan,2023). In context of brands it will increase brand experience and recall rates.

Metaverse is defined as the convergence of digital and physical universe, where customers can effortlessly navigate and interacting with others. Metaverse environment helps people to enjoy hyper realistic virtual environment, interactions, experience and transactions. Metaverse is radically different from previous technologies in three parameters include functionality, interoperability and impressiveness (Buhalis et al.,2023). Functionality takes advantage of an immersive virtual world where users can interact, work and socialize by customizing their avatars, MR/VR headsets and other gadgets (Dwivedi et al.,2023). Metaverse also provides an interoperable environment where users can interact with others across different virtual worlds. Metaverse impressed its users with haptic cues and multi-sensory and multi-sensory reference points which induces their imagination and fantasy (Pero,2022).

Yadav et al., (2024) adopted the 7P framework to examine the impact of metaverse and its components on consumers and firm level outcomes. Authors discussed about products in metaverse which can take the form of digital goods such as avatars & NFTS. Pricing involves dynamic pricing whereas place refers to virtual locations. Promotions in Metaverse can utilize immersive campaigns and engage users. People is pertaining to interaction between brands and users while the processes discussed about products and brands in the metaverse must be fluid and user-friendly

Metaverse presents the distinctive opportunity for companies to enhance engagement and brand identity (Aiolfi et al.,2024). There are four types of engagement possible in the world of metaverse namely interactive, social, experiential, economic and emotional. Interactive engagement delves into user's interaction in digital environment from manipulating virtual objects to navigating into different spaces. Social engagement sheds light on social interaction. Customers can meet, communicate and collaborate in real time settings. Experiential engagement provides deep sense of involvement through adventures, challenges, games or simulations. Economic engagement focuses on economic activities of buying and selling through goods. Emotional engagement fosters strong emotional connect by offering interaction, experience, creativity and discovery (Bilgihan et al.,2024).

Brands have adopted metaverse in various contexts namely brand extension, gamified advertising, virtual storefronts and many more. Metaverse and gamification also provide the opportunities to analyze and predict consumer behavior. Virtual tracking, gesture recognition, emotional analysis and eye tracking in metaverse environment helps companies or brands to understand engagement and experience (Rane et al.,2023).

In the world of gamified metaverse customers want to create their unique identity and appearance. The motivation for self-expression in virtual environment not only enhances user engagement with the platform but also develops a strong emotional bond. The brands and the companies which have been able to utilize the gamified metaverse environment for their marketing and advertising actions develops a closer approach and relationship not only with their immediate customers but also with their potential customers (Sidorenko-Bautista,2025).

Zhang et al., (2025) provided a framework by establishing a relationship between games and metaverse in tourism domain. Their study highlighted impact of user experience on engagement and impressiveness. Authors suggested the tech savvy customers have more enjoyment and confidence which raises their engagement towards the game. Further engagement and impressiveness have impact on attitude and loyalty which turns these users into brand evangelists.

Differences in Traditional Gamification and Gamification in Metaverse

Interactivity and Engagement: In contrast to traditional marketing, which typically involves passive content consumption through channels like television ads and print media, gamification in the Metaverse promotes active user participation. Users engage through interactive elements, such as virtual challenges or quests, fostering deeper emotional connections with the brand. Gamification allows customers to engage with product or brand in a fun and non -intrusive way.

Immersive Experiences: The Metaverse leverages augmented and virtual reality to create immersive brand experiences that traditional marketing cannot replicate. This immersive nature allows consumers to experience products in a virtual environment, enhancing their understanding and appreciation of the brand.

Real-Time Feedback: Gamification mechanisms in the Metaverse allow for immediate interaction and feedback. Brands can dynamically adapt their offerings based on consumer behavior and preferences, which is more challenging in traditional marketing where campaigns often run on fixed schedules. Implementing virtual customer service through digital avatars of customer service agents will definitely provide real time feedback to customers and enhance their experience (Payal et al.,2024).

Social Connectivity: Marketing in the Metaverse promotes social interactions among users, enabling shared experiences and community-building around brands, which is less prevalent in traditional advertising. Consumers can discuss experiences, compete with friends, and share achievements, creating a community that advocates for the brand.

Data-Driven Insights: The digital nature of the Metaverse provides brands with extensive data on user interactions and behavior. This data can inform marketing strategies far more efficiently than traditional methods, where feedback loops often take longer to establish.

Cost Efficiency: Virtual products in the Metaverse can reduce manufacturing costs and environmental impact since brands can offer 'virtually wearable' products. Traditional marketing typically incurs significant costs related to product production, distribution, and physical marketing materials

Figure 1. Gamification in Metaverse

Nature of Engagement in Gamified Metaverse Environment

Agarwal et al., (2025) described about four customer engagement types which are relevant to gamified metaverse environment. These engagements are as following:

Cognitive Engagement: Customers are convinced to alike the brand if brand information is aligns to their feelings, information and experience. Customers devote more time in connecting brand information to their personal knowledge (Su et al.,2019). Gamified metaverse provide a platform to brands to work on this parameter to enhance cognitive engagement. Consumers who engage actively with a brand tend to exert greater cognitive effort in processing and comprehending brand-related information Cognitive engagement allows users to understand the features and characteristics of the brand which will lead to customer buying decisions. Drivers of cognitive engagement include knowledge sharing, involving expressing opinions, and genertaing ideas for enhancement (Algharabat et al.,2020).

Social Engagement: Kim et al., (2021) noted that user engagement can be enhanced through interaction with other customers /users in gamified Metaverse environment. The social engagement includes sharing experience with other users, participation in activities and fostering relationships. This engagement leads towards brand advocacy through positive word of mouth among users.

Emotional Engagement: The degree of excitement, pleasure and satisfaction with brand measures about emotional engagement of customer (Aljuhmani et al.,2022). Emotional engagement signifies the depth of customer's intensity and commitment is often simulated by series of brand-initiated activities or interactive communications (Dwivedi,2015). Customers who are actively engaged tend to associate positive emotions with their use of a product or brand (Cheung et al.,2021). The emotional engagement can enhance customer retention and loyalty towards the brand.

Transactional Engagement: Transactional engagement involves actions and behaviors associated with purchasing of brand. In the gamified metaverse environment consumers can establish virtual wardrobes for premium conducts and done transactions using cryptocurrency. Immersive experience can engage customers longer than physical transactions and increase the chances of buying (Spajić et al.,2022). Interactivity and ease of operation can enhance the smooth transaction experience through dynamic pricing and real time support.

Gamified Brand Engagement in Metaverse

The nontraditional consumer looks for authentic, personalized and engaging experience from marketers. Customers wants that marketers make them feel important and provide them customized product and experience. The following strategies will help brands to provide unique experience and engagement to their customers in gamified metaverse environment.

Intimacy and Commitment: The gamification marketing activities in metaverse have created the immersive experience for potential customers. The consumer involvement depends upon their internal needs, values and interests (McClure et al.,2020). The gamification activities designed as per involvement constructs help consumers to develop positive perception towards the brand which result in enhanced intimacy.

Customization: Gamified experience can be customized and designed as per individual consumer. The personalized design, interactions and challenges make them feel important and valuable for the brand. Allowing customers to create their own avatars enhances brand engagement. The customization nurtures emotional connect as customers are able to express themselves with the help of their avatars (Payal et al.,2024).

Continuous Updates & Rewards: To enhance engagement of customers with brands gamification in metaverse provide continuous updates and rewards. Continuous updates are related to level of challenges while rewards include perks and incentives. The continuous achievement on dashboards/leaderboards keep customer engage for longer duration of time.

Unified Implementation: The seamless and unified integration is required between brand and gamification. The gamification should be designed in the manner that it can reflect brand values and characteristics. A high recall value and positive word of mouth is possible with seamless and integration and unique experience with brands.

Gamification in Metaverse: A Case of Sunsilk Shampoo

Global haircare brand Sunsilk of Unilever launched a game Sunsilk city in Roblox. The game was aimed towards young women of Generation Z who are tech savvy and passionate about gaming. Sunsilk City was an immersive metaverse experience to encourage participation among young consumers. Roblox has 83 million monthly active users and 44% Roblox gamers are female. With so many women engaged in gaming and metaverse, Sunsilk had considered it as an incredible opportunity to reach generation Z and engage them with brand.

The main objective of Unilever was to change the narrative of women in games. Women are depicted as damsel-in distress or objectified as “rewards” for male characters to collect in game. With help of Sunsilk City unilever tried to break this gender stereotype.

Sunsilk City is a perfect amalgamation of metaverse and gamification in marketing scenario. The game has Mexico based bio pharmaceutical chemist and gamer Jessica Lakshmi as host, present in avatar inside the game. Lakshmi is teaching the users about the practical implication of science and technology and inspire other girls to enter in the world of science, technology, engineering and mathematics.

The game has also incorporated Sunsilk product range as a part of the narrative experience. With the vision of women empowerment, the game consists of several minigames namely Sidewalk Superstars, Blow Them away, The House of Hair and The House of Skills. Each minigame has its own unique objectives and user engagement strategy. Sidewalk Superstars has an objective of prioritize education over domestic chores while Blow Them Away empower players to fight off with toxic words and phrases used to put women down in virtual hair dryer. The House of Hair enables creativity and expression of user with their digital avatars through use of Sunsilk Haircare products. House of Skills consist of twenty online courses for users to equip them with tangible real-world skills.

The outcome was over 35 million players have played the game and it became 3rd highest rated brand experience in Roblox.

Game Based Engagement in Metaverse: A Case of Hyundai Mobility Adventure

Hyundai Mobility Adventure represents the pioneering initiative by the automobile manufacturer Hyundai, making its first foray into metaverse through the Roblox platform. Designed with the primary objective of engaging a younger, technology -oriented audience, the virtual experience seeks to transcend the boundaries of traditional interaction by offering an immersive digital environment. Within this collectively shared virtual space, gaming enthusiast can interact, share their experiences and explore Hyundai's technological innovations, product offerings and future mobility solutions.

A notable feature of Hyundai Mobility Adventure is the ability for users to create and personalize digital avatars, enabling imaginative and interactive engagement with other participants. The platform is structured about five theme-based parks, each curated to deliver unique experiential dimensions:

Festival Square serves as the central hub or base camp for users. Here, players return from their explorations to participate in festivals, vehicle exhibitions, and celebratory events, while also engaging with other players. This zone includes the opportunity to drive the IONIQ 5 and partake in three distinct mini-games.

Future Mobility City offers an ultramodern metropolitan setting where players can interact with advanced technologies, including the experience of hydrogen fuel cell systems, thereby envisioning future mobility solutions.

Eco-Forest, a recreational zone, emphasizes minimalistic living and environmental consciousness. It integrates eco-friendly technologies with elements of fantasy and slow living. This park particularly resonates with environmentally aware users and female participants due to its thematic focus.

Racing Park provides an immersive environment where users can engage with Hyundai's latest advancements in racing technologies and motorsports, delivering high-adrenaline experiences.

Smart Tech Campus simulates the professional environment of engineers and developers, allowing users to engage in sophisticated technological tasks within a virtual setting.

Through this platform, Hyundai effectively addresses both the cognitive and social dimensions of user engagement. On the cognitive front, players are encouraged to design vehicles, operate robotics, and explore urban air mobility concepts. Socially, the platform facilitates meaningful interaction among users with shared interests via personalized avatars, fostering a sense of community and collaborative learning.

Strategies for Customer Loyalty

Customer loyalty refers to a strong, enduring commitment to repurchase a product or brand consistently over time (Oliver, 1999). With a rising millennial population—many of whom have grown up immersed in video games, e-sports, and social media—the emerging metaverse is increasingly viewed as a modern-day mall: a connected space to socialize, shop, and spend time with others. Hence it is imperative for marketers to make certain strategies which helps these dynamic and tech-savvy customers to stay with them for longer duration. The engagement through innovation, psychological brand ownership and commitment on these platforms always enhances customer loyalty. Wang et al., (2024) in their study highlighted that social networking, community engagement and brand use with in the communities contribute to loyalty. Hence brands should foster their emotional relationships by engaging users on these platforms.

CONCLUSION

The convergence of gamification and the Metaverse marks a transformative evolution in the landscape of marketing and consumer engagement. Unlike traditional marketing methods, which are often linear and passive, the gamified Metaverse introduces a highly interactive, immersive, and dynamic environment that actively involves consumers in the brand experience. This transition is more than a technological advancement—it reflects a fundamental change in consumer expectations, behaviors, and the way brands build relationships with their audiences.

Gamification in the Metaverse leverages elements such as virtual reality (VR), augmented reality (AR), digital avatars, storytelling, and interactive tasks to create an experience that is not only enjoyable but also deeply engaging. These elements help stimulate emotional, cognitive, social, and transactional engagement—four dimensions that are critical for fostering lasting consumer-brand relationships. Through personalized avatars, immersive storylines, and continuous rewards, brands can create tailored experiences that resonate with users on a personal level, thereby enhancing their emotional connection and loyalty.

One of the most powerful aspects of this integration is interactivity. Consumers are no longer passive recipients of brand messages but active participants in co-creating the brand narrative. This participatory approach leads to a sense of ownership and emotional investment, key drivers of brand advocacy and repeat engagement. Furthermore, the real-time feedback and analytics capabilities of the Metaverse allow brands to respond to user behaviors and preferences almost instantaneously, ensuring that marketing efforts remain relevant, responsive, and personalized.

Another key advantage is social connectivity. The Metaverse creates a space where users can connect, compete, collaborate, and communicate with others in a shared virtual space. This fosters a sense of community and belonging—important psychological factors that contribute to brand loyalty. Through community-building and interactive storytelling, brands can amplify their reach organically, as engaged users are more likely to become brand advocates who share their experiences with others.

Cost efficiency and scalability are additional benefits. Virtual products and campaigns reduce the need for physical resources, thereby lowering environmental impact and operational costs. This is particularly beneficial for global brands looking to maintain a sustainable and flexible marketing strategy.

The case study of Sunsilk City on Roblox is a prime example of how gamified brand engagement can drive both social impact and business results. By promoting gender equality and education through interactive mini-games, Sunsilk not only reinforced its brand values but also connected meaningfully with its target audience—young, tech-savvy women. The campaign's success, with over 35 million users engaged, underscores the vast potential of such strategies when executed thoughtfully.

In conclusion, the amalgamation of gamification into the Metaverse offers brands an unparalleled prospect to craft experiences that are engaging, memorable, and emotionally resonant. It allows marketers to move beyond traditional value propositions and into the realm of experiential marketing, where user participation, storytelling, and community are the new currencies of loyalty. As the digital landscape continues to evolve, brands that can harness the full potential of gamified Metaverse environments will be better positioned to build enduring relationships with their consumers and thrive in a competitive marketplace.

REFERENCES

Afacan, N. M. (2023). Gamification in metaverse. In *Metaverse: technologies, opportunities and threats* (pp. 187–202). Springer Nature Singapore. DOI: 10.1007/978-981-99-4641-9_13

Agarwal, R., Badghish, S., Yaqub, M. Z., & Pandey, R. (2025). Customer engagement through metaverse-empowered retail channels: Role of personalization. *International Journal of Retail & Distribution Management*, *53*(6), 467–484. DOI: 10.1108/IJRDM-07-2024-0344

Aiolfi, S., & Luceri, B. (2024). See you on the Metaverse: A bibliometric expedition through the Metaverse landscape. *Technological Forecasting and Social Change*, *207*, 123605. DOI: 10.1016/j.techfore.2024.123605

Al-Adwan, A. S., Yaseen, H., Alkhwaldi, A. F., Jafar, R. M. S., Fauzi, M. A., & Abdullah, A. (2025). Treasure hunting for brands: Metaverse marketing gamification effects on purchase intention, WOM, and loyalty. *Journal of Global Marketing*, •••, 1–25. DOI: 10.1080/08911762.2025.2463897

Algharabat, R., Rana, N. P., Alalwan, A. A., Baabdullah, A., & Gupta, A. (2020). Investigating the antecedents of customer brand engagement and consumer-based brand equity in social media. *Journal of Retailing and Consumer Services*, *53*, 101767. DOI: 10.1016/j.jretconser.2019.01.016

Aljuhmani, H. Y., Elrehail, H., Bayram, P., & Samarah, T. (2022). Linking social media marketing efforts with customer brand engagement in driving brand loyalty. *Asia Pacific Journal of Marketing and Logistics*, *35*(7), 1719–1738. DOI: 10.1108/APJML-08-2021-0627

Arya, V., Sambyal, R., Sharma, A., & Dwivedi, Y. K. (2024). Brands are calling your AVATAR in Metaverse–A study to explore XR-based gamification marketing activities & consumer-based brand equity in virtual world. *Journal of Consumer Behaviour*, *23*(2), 556–585. DOI: 10.1002/cb.2214

Bilgihan, A., Leong, A. M. W., Okumus, F., & Bai, J. (2024). Proposing a metaverse engagement model for brand development. *Journal of Retailing and Consumer Services*, *78*, 103781. DOI: 10.1016/j.jretconser.2024.103781

Bousba, Y., & Arya, V. (2022). Let's connect in metaverse. Brand's new destination to increase consumers' affective brand engagement & their satisfaction and advocacy. Journal of Content. *Community & Communication*, *15*(8), 276–293.

Buhalis, D., Leung, D., & Lin, M. (2023). Metaverse as a disruptive technology revolutionising tourism management and marketing. *Tourism Management*, *97*, 104724. DOI: 10.1016/j.tourman.2023.104724

Cha, S. S., Kim, C. Y., & Tang, Y. (2024). Gamification in the Metaverse: Affordance, perceived value, flow state, and engagement. *International Journal of Tourism Research*, *26*(2), e2635. DOI: 10.1002/jtr.2635

Cheung, M. L., Pires, G. D., Rosenberger, P. J., Leung, W. K., & Sharipudin, M. N. S. (2021). The role of consumer-consumer interaction and consumer-brand interaction in driving consumer-brand engagement and behavioral intentions. *Journal of Retailing and Consumer Services*, *61*, 102574. DOI: 10.1016/j.jretconser.2021.102574

Dwivedi, A. (2015). A higher-order model of consumer brand engagement and its impact on loyalty intentions. *Journal of Retailing and Consumer Services*, *24*, 100–109. DOI: 10.1016/j.jretconser.2015.02.007

Dwivedi, Y., Hughes, L., Wang, Y., Alalwan, A. A., Ahn, S., Balakrishnan, J., ... & Wirtz, J. (2023). How metaverse will change the future of marketing: Implications for Research and Practice Psychology and Marketing.

Hamari, J., Xi, N., Legaki, Z., & Morschheuser, B. (2023). *Gamification. In Hawaii International Conference on System Sciences* (p. 1105).

Hyundai. (n.d.). *Hyundai vitalizes future mobility in Roblox Metaverse space* [Press release]. https://www.hyundai.news/eu/articles/press-releases/hyundai-vitalizes-future-mobility-in-roblox-metaverse-space.html (Retrieved March 8, 2025)

Karta. (n.d.). *Sunsilk City*. https://www.karta.game/project/sunsilkcity (Retrieved March 8, 2025)

Kim, J., & Ha, J. (2021). User experience in VR fashion product shopping: Focusing on tangible interactions. *Applied Sciences (Basel, Switzerland)*, *11*(13), 6170. DOI: 10.3390/app11136170

Koohang, A., Nord, J. H., Ooi, K. B., Tan, G. W. H., Al-Emran, M., Aw, E. C. X., Baabdullah, A. M., Buhalis, D., Cham, T.-H., Dennis, C., Dutot, V., Dwivedi, Y. K., Hughes, L., Mogaji, E., Pandey, N., Phau, I., Raman, R., Sharma, A., Sigala, M., & Wong, L. W. (2023). Shaping the metaverse into reality: A holistic multidisciplinary understanding of opportunities, challenges, and avenues for future investigation. *Journal of Computer Information Systems*, *63*(3), 735–765. DOI: 10.1080/08874417.2023.2165197

Lee, C. T., Ho, T. Y., & Xie, H. H. (2023). Building brand engagement in metaverse commerce: The role of branded non-fungible tokens (BNFTs). *Electronic Commerce Research and Applications*, *58*, 101248. DOI: 10.1016/j.elerap.2023.101248

McClure, C., & Seock, Y. K. (2020). The role of involvement: Investigating the effect of brand's social media pages on consumer purchase intention. *Journal of Retailing and Consumer Services*, *53*, 101975. DOI: 10.1016/j.jretconser.2019.101975

Nayak, A., Patnaik, A., Satpathy, I., Patnaik, B. C. M., & Baral, S. K. Metaverse: The Transformation of Customer Engagement with Brands in the Digital Age. In Green Metaverse for Greener Economies(2024) (pp. 270-284). CRC Press.

Oliver, R. L. (1999). Whence consumer loyalty? *Journal of Marketing*, *63*(4, suppl1), 33–44. DOI: 10.1177/00222429990634s105

Payal, R., Sharma, N., & Dwivedi, Y. K. (2024). Unlocking the impact of brand engagement in the metaverse on Real-World purchase intentions: Analyzing Pre-Adoption behavior in a futuristic technology platform. *Electronic Commerce Research and Applications*, *65*, 101381. DOI: 10.1016/j.elerap.2024.101381

Pero, J. (2022). *Sorry, Metaverse is the word of the year whether you like it or not.* Inverse.

Rane, N., Choudhary, S., & Rane, J. (2023). Metaverse marketing strategies: enhancing customer experience and analysing consumer behaviour through leading-edge Metaverse technologies, platforms, and models. Platforms, and Models (November 3, 2023).

Sidorenko-Bautista, P., Castillo-Abdul, B., Herranz-de-la-Casa, J. M., & Abellán-Hernández, M. (2025). Marketing, advertising, and branding in Fortnite: How do brands and companies connect today to audiences through the metaverse? *Cogent Social Sciences*, *11*(1), 2458058. DOI: 10.1080/23311886.2025.2458058

Spajić, J., Mitrović, K., Lalić, D., Milić, B., & Bošković, D. (2022, September). Personalized brand experience in metaverse. In *10th International Conference on Mass Customization and Personalization–Community of Europe (MCP-CE 2022)* (pp. 21-23).

Su, N., Mariadoss, B. J., & Reynolds, D. (2019). Emotional and cognitive involvement of consumers with hotel brands on social networking sites. *Journal of Hospitality and Tourism Insights*, *2*(4), 377–390. DOI: 10.1108/JHTI-10-2018-0064

Thomas, N. J., Baral, R., Crocco, O. S., & Mohanan, S. (2023). A framework for gamification in the metaverse era: How designers envision gameful experience. *Technological Forecasting and Social Change*, *193*, 122544. DOI: 10.1016/j.techfore.2023.122544

Wang, Z., & Yang, X. (2024). Building brand loyalty through value co-creation practices in brand communities: The role of affective commitment and psychological brand ownership. *Journal of Research in Interactive Marketing*.

Yadav, S., Pandey, S. K., & Sharma, D. (2024). Marketing beyond reality: A systematic literature review on metaverse. *Management Research Review*, *47*(7), 1029–1051. DOI: 10.1108/MRR-06-2023-0456

Zhang, J., Quoquab, F., & Mohammad, J. (2025). "Do video game players dream of metaverse traveling?" The role of gamification technology and game immersion experience. *Tourism Review*. Advance online publication. DOI: 10.1108/TR-09-2024-0821

Chapter 3
Gamified International Human Resource Management in the Metaverse

Vibhanshu
https://orcid.org/0009-0003-2739-7757
GNIOT Institute of Management Studies, India

Dhrity Gulati
DAV Institute of Management, India

ABSTRACT

This chapter covers the application of gamification in IHRM in the metaverse and the associated issues in this particular virtual environment. The study focuses on exploring the possible means of improving communication, training, and multi-country cooperation through using the game-based methods in the context of a multinational staff. This paper uses a case study analysis of academic and employing organizations and a review of the literature to establish trends in the application of gamification in the enhancement of discrete areas of human resource management particularly recruitment, training and performance management. Some of the key discoveries suggest that gamification creates motivation and cultivating culture of inclusion though embracing technologies has its drawbacks. Finally, the chapter argues that proper gamified IHRM practices can make a considerable impact on workforce shifts and stresses distant cultural sleight adjustments and continuous technological advancements to harness optimal outcomes in the metaverse.

DOI: 10.4018/979-8-3693-8886-0.ch003

1. INTRODUCTION

Technology has however brought changes in human resource management as firms seek to engage and manage a global workforce. Drawing on the notion of gameful thinking, this chapter explores the idea of gamified IHRM in the context of a metaverse or a virtual space that provides increased opportunities for communication and cooperation (Rozak et al., 2023). It is important for organizations that would like to exploit the utilization of gamification and virtual environments to enhance the employee dynamics and performances to understand the integration..

A globalized and remote-digitalized workforce has demanded a significant change in HRM practices. Automation of HRM processes has changed, especially on remote recruitment, training, motivation, and cross-border employee management. This is a significant change in the functioning and thinking of HRM about its role. From such developments as artificial intelligence, virtual reality, and the metaverse, the fundamentals in the way HR works are being changed as well as new opportunities arising in workforce management (Aydin, 2024). With the metaverse, however, there is an ever-present virtual space spilling over into the real world in an entirely new fashion, allowing employees to be granted extraordinary opportunities to network, cooperate and learn. In tandem with this continuous digital reality, organizations are adding gameful approaches and gamification to HR practices with a view to increasing engagement, motivation, and performance.

Point scoring, award of badges, and leaderboards are part of the gamification strategy. HRM adoption has been realized through the use of gamification, with possibilities of turning routine processes into more exciting ones. Whereas former motivations are bound to be oriented on a single type of motivator, gamification takes into account both intrinsic and extrinsic drivers. Research in academia confirms that using gamification in HR processes greatly increases workers' engagement levels and business results. For example, the gamification of onboarding, training and performance management allows for a more interactive environment, allows for faster skill development, provides real time feedback and promotes adaptive team work. Primarily from the psychological perspective, gamification is the most effective one as it is aimed at promoting achievements' motivation, encouraging one's competitiveness, as well as contributing to the continual growth of somebody's character. Such aspects are major driving forces in professional groups.

When metaverse is included into gamified HRM, organizations are provided with an ability to create global digital workspace in which employees are empowered to use it to connect and work together efficiently. Employees can immerse themselves into simulations as avatars, work in animated virtual team building exercises, and participate in real time simulations that recreate real world situations. Companies can create HR platforms that promote not only a physical presence but also worldwide partnership and flexibility. To demonstrate, workers can enjoy individualized metaverse training whereby they can practice realistically without the consequences of real-world errors. Also, the use of avatars and digital workspaces makes it easy for one to participate while eliminating some of the cultures that are barriers to effective teamwork across the borders.

Even with the difficulties IHRM faces regarding application of gamification and the metaverse, the possibilities of employee engagement and productivity are still high. Employers implementing these technologies have to ensure they understand how to develop and implement gamified experience specific in achievement of key strategic objectives considering the varied cultures of their work force. In the HRM space, a good practice in gamification focuses on the introduction of game design which explores fundamental concepts such as goal generation, feedback loops, and an excellent user experience, instead of purely being visually attractive. Goals have to be specifically adjusted in their setting to ensure that they are achieved. The approach/methods through which objectives are achieved must be engaging and user-friendly while active responses should be able to elicit immediate relevance-engagement. The system should not become complex to use, therefore, increasing access for a wider audience, but not lose flexibility to meet various cultural and learning needs.

In the perspective of the deployment of gamified HR systems in virtual environments, there is the need for cultural integration. Organizational strategies for motivation, HR implementation, and work regulations need to change in order to accommodate the local context such as cultural mores, morals, ideologies and communication. Think about the fact that engagement strategies that rely on competition so much might be a non-accessible option in all cultures, and elsewhere considered too demanding or even detrimental. For teams of many-facets, the use of responsive measures of inclusion and equity that fit culturally resonant language, symbols, and rewarding structures is critical. It is vital that inclusion and equity be realized for; it is less than either one of them to develop a diverse workforce. In order to improve the positive impacts of gamification on engagement and performance, optimization of organizational efficiency, and the transformation of cultural attitudes, organizations need to combine employee feedback with continuous observation of cultural trends.

In IHRM, the benefits of metaverse and gamification extend beyond enhancing business engagement as well as productivity (Prabowo,, 2023). The implementation of these tools results in establishing the culture that values learning and motivates employees to be experimental and competent in repeating critical assignments. By working in the metaverse, employees can experiment with skill experimentation, collect constructive feedback, and incrementally boost their self-confidence during safe psychological operation. Through this learning methodology, the employees obtain skills to handle the rigors and uncertainties of modern business especially those that require agility and quick recovery .

Also, human resource management is subjected to perennial challenges especially during periods of increased remote and hybrid working arrangements. It is also important for organizations to bring in HR gamification and the metaverse to enhance not only engagement, but also collaboration among the remote employees. Remote working often loses out on social bonding which perpetuates informal team bonds and collaborative unity. The metaverse can enable the construction of simulating meeting spaces that recreate vital workplace social interactions (Induji, 2024). These technologies support employee engagement and motivation by introducing gamification to the learning process, incorporating recording progress and highlighting it, providing individual feedback and publicly rewarding performance positively.

Although the promise of the metaverse for gamified IHRM exists, corporations continue to face major barriers to the use of these methods. Technology-inefficient, lacking a viable user training system, and resource constrained organizations face various ethical issues that concern data privacy. Companies face a choice over introducing strict governance in order to create trust or over successful IT system compliance which is sensitive to the need of meaningful supervision. Additionally, the perception that gamification is insincere in the company may end up destroying the attainment of corporate goals. It is possible to supply both willing and unwilling employees with incentives to engage them and include the implementation strategy's real aspects in their decision-making.

The ongoing success of the IHRM games in the metaverse depends on advancing technological capabilities and employees' altered expectations. Having AI, VR, AR, blockchain technologies will increase the effectiveness of gamified HR systems due to their ability to offer secure personalization and flexibility of applications. With AI, personalization and adjustability will be improved, while maintaining a secure operation. Gamified program successes will be measured through data analysis and a need to perpetually maintain a feedback loop. If organizations are sluggish adopting the culture into social and digital channels while also implementing efficient governance and studying technological limits, they will become left out in the benefits of these changes.

For companies working to increase global employee engagement and productivity, it is necessary to make the HR management use metaverse and gamification in its service. If organizations can use the principles of gameful thinking and virtual reality, they can bring a huge leap in terms of efficiency and responsiveness of their human resource practices.

1.1 Definition of Key Concepts

Gamification is the use of game-thinking techniques in realms beyond games for the purpose of increasing engagement, motivation and learning. Introducing points, badges and leader boards, arulgaf applies mechanics to change mundane activities into fun tasks and motivates people to accomplish the objectives. When applied to HRM, the focus on gamified is the reinforcement of recruitment processes, staff training and performance evaluations.

In HRM, gamification refers to bringing game-related aspects into workplace activities in order to increase employee motivation, engagement, and skill learning. HRM will show that the use of such things as points, badges and leader boards in work processes can really energize workers, build interest and enhance their performance. Many workers respond better and are more effective when training programs embrace gamified aspects according to studies.

The scope of IHRM is, so to speak, believed to include all efforts in respect to the international management of human resources with the objective of assisting the organizational objectives and upholding competitive greatness. As Boxall notes, IHRM deals with the perceived human resource problems that people of a multinational experience, especially in international subsidiaries and in the general set of human resource problems experienced during internationalization. IHRM involves both known HRM functions such as recruitment, selection, training, and performance, and global skills management and supervision of overseas staff.

Metaverse is defined as an integrated virtual reality world where digital experiences and physical surroundings mix so well to enable fluid interactions in permanent virtual environments. Lee and colleagues define the metaverse as a virtual world that meshes with the physical world that allows users to interact using avatars and engage in real-time immersive activities.

IHRM or sometimes referred to as cross-national human resource management occurs when the management of human resources takes places on the global stage with respect to culture, laws, and practices which differ in one country to another. IHRM comprises numerous functions such as sourcing, talent management, training, and performance evaluation; these activities must be done under different cultural standards and realities.

The metaverse is an extended reality environment comprising AR, VR, and other synchronous persistent online spaces. Activities or transactions that can take place include communication or collaboration with other users of a particular domain in real time. Such environment thus gives organizations a chance to design their human resource practices afresh providing a new way of creating new forms of relations between employees and employers.

In this research, case studies and literature reviews are used where a diverse range of academic institutions and companies conducting gamified IHRM practices in the metaverse is included. Business schools –such as INSEAD, Wharton and MIT Sloan– have adopted gamified metaverse settings for business learning; the students are able to digitally implement mergers and pursue supply chain issues. These institutions harness such platforms as Microsoft Mesh, Meta's Horizon Workrooms, VR tools to develop immersive and inclusive borderless collaboration and learning experiences.

Now this approach has been implemented in onboarding, training and performance programs not only in terms of academia but also outside across different multinational companies and HR sectors as well. The metaverse is used by these organizations as a means of providing immersive onboarding before induction and developing consistent employee participation and retention using gamified elements. This study provides a thorough review of the current situation and promising practices of gamified ICHR within the metaverse, using case studies of academia and industry.

1.2 Importance

For metaverse and gamified IHRM, understanding its importance cannot be understated, especially given trends current in the field of IHRM and technology. Main drivers for the adoption of digital tools to support and improve the HR processes in organizations are flexibilisation, qualification and efficientisation of the human resources management. Their widespread usage, increased decentralization of work and people's desire to engage more within the workspace are some of the aspects making gamification a rather worthwhile approach. In addition, the means and ways of deliberating gamified approaches characterize the metaverse further as the environment is supportive and interactive compared to the geographical limitations approach.

The introduction of gamification in IHRM processes in a metaverse is a revolutionary opportunity for organizations to foster enhanced participation and cooperation of human capital anywhere in the world.

Figure 1. An outline on implementing gamification in IHRM at the Metaverse

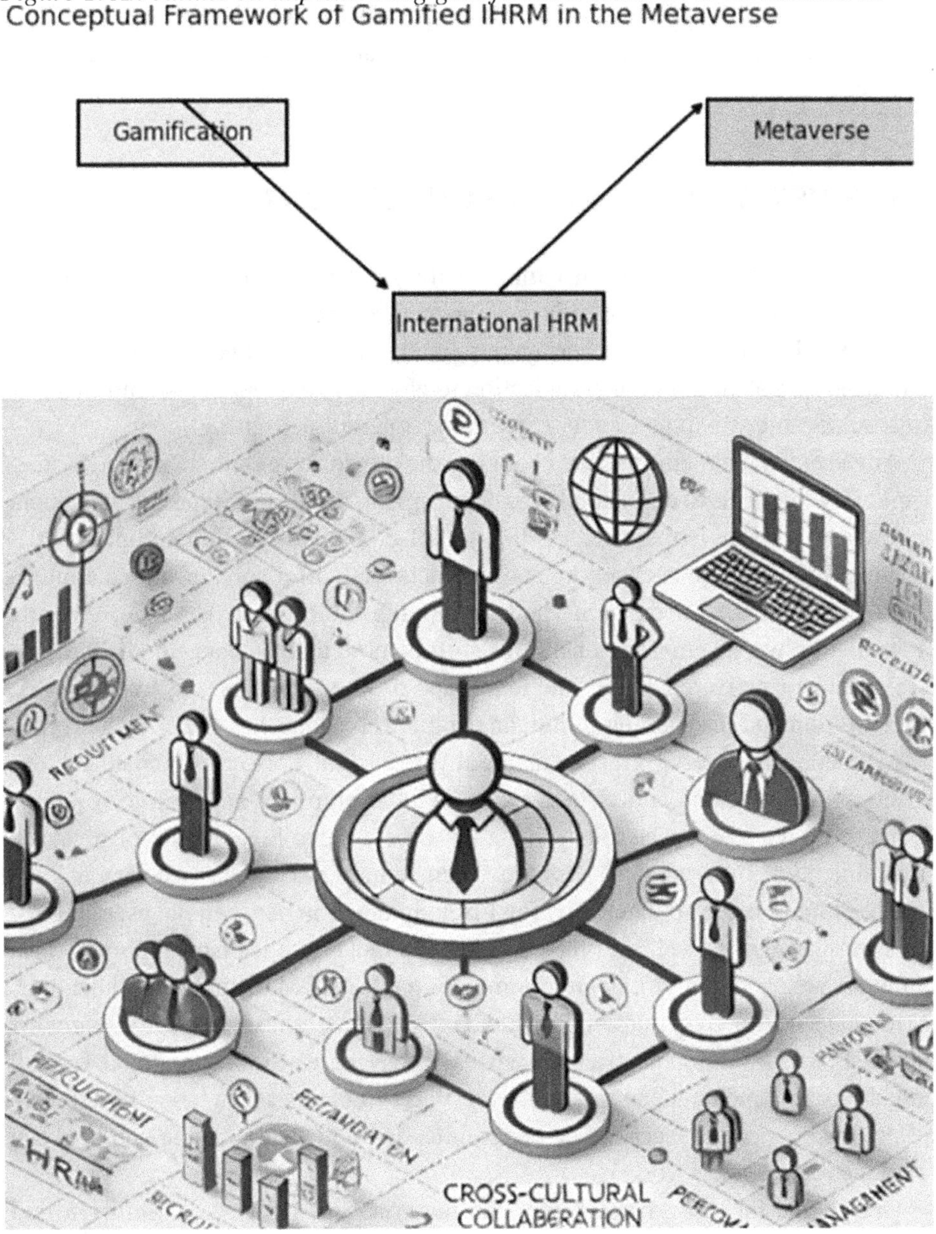

This figure indicates the use of gamification in the metaverse's IHRM systems with the collaborative roles of engagement, motivation, and cultural adaptation.

In the next sections, a detailed discussion of the interconnection and the benefits of using gamification for IHRM while operating within the metaverse will be provided Further, figure 1 presents the conceptual framework of this integration (Thomas,, 2023).

2. THE METAVERSE: A NEW FRONTIER FOR HRM

This is especially true as structures in the modern world of human resource management continue to be defined, and the metaverse comes out as a revolutionary platform to the setup. As a highly engaging, interactive and networked environment, it holds great potential for an organisation to engage and develop it's employees in ways achievable, albeit to a lesser extent in an operational setting.

Advances in the metaverse are changing the dynamics of human resource practices, allowing firms to chart employee engagement, development and management in new and innovative manners. As the tide of globalization and the digital era is growing, the HR edge is changing and the metaverse offers organizations a multi-dimensional escape for engaging and developing their employees independently of standard physical environments. This shift is more than a change in technology, it is a transformative change in the landscape of how organizations expect work, collaboration and the training of human capital to be done.

In essence, metaverse is a constant, real-time virtual world which enables interaction with augmented and virtual reality, AI and premium networking solutions (Dastane et al., 2022). The metaverse allows for a much higher level of presence and immersion than what is possible when working with the two-dimensional collaboration tools available today. Real-time interaction between the user and his/her surroundings; as well as, other users in the metaverse is also supported. This immersive exposure in virtual environments enables HRM to enable organizations to recreate social dynamics, unplanned interactions, and cooperative vigor as prevalent in conventional offices in virtual ecosystems. Staff can attend formal, brainstorming, spontaneous sessions as avatars, engaging in immerse worlds that reflect the nuances of face-to-face communication and minimize the gap between remote and on-site co-workers.

One of the biggest advantages of the metaverse to HRM is its ability to aid recruitment and talent acquisition (Sharma et al., 2023). Through metaverse technology, virtual job expos across the globe, virtual interviews and detailed 3D job demonstration is possible for organizations. Through this, organizations can be able to reach out to diverse network of potential hires anywhere in the world. Operationally, realistically simulated practices are available to job seekers where they actually do real tasks that aid recruiters to evaluate their competencies, critical-thinking abilities, and employability to the company culture.

A critical aspect in which the benefits of the metaverse are already being enjoyed in HR is talent acquisition and recruitment (Dutta et al., 2023). Organizations can organise virtual job fairs, give immersive interviews, and offer realistic job previews in the metaverse; which enables access to a global talent pool disenfranchised by geography. Virtual job scenarios give candidates the opportunity to show what they can do in simulated work environment to help recruiters assess their practical skills, analytical mindsets, and interactions with company culture, in a safe and realistic setting. The use of these techniques translates into better assessment of potential employees and greater understanding of the organization's culture and professional standards on their part leading to better hiring decisions.

The traditional way of introducing new hires in organizations through the use of paperwork and basic orientation sessions in the metaverse changes these dynamics fundamentally. Through hiring, individuals are able to move around virtual office spaces, communicate with colleagues through avatars, and interact in joint training exercises that encourage early networking and a sense of belonging in the organization. Simulating real world scenarios allows employees to rehearse their job responsibilities, receive immediate feedback, and exhibit confidence before they are placed in their actual job positions. Immersion into the metaverse during onboarding is especially meaningful in the background of remote or hybrid work where keeping cultural alignment and team unity is even more valuable (Mahajan et al., 2018).

In the field of training and development, the metaverse, a powerful and transformational technology, leaps out. Companies can design dynamic immersion learning modules, simulations and role play sessions replicating complex sever high stress situations safely and within a confined virtual environment. For instance, doctors can rehearse surgeries; engineers can troubleshoot equipment; and customer service workers can manage difficult situations all in the metaverse. By providing practical learning opportunities, the metaverse helps accelerate the learning process and promotes the fact that employees will more easily remember and use what was taught.

HRM integration into the metaverse largely transforms the way performance management is carried out. Cliché as they are with complaints about lack of objectivity and lack of frequency, standard performance reviews can benefit from real-time information collected from virtual workplace activities for performance assessment. Objective measurement can be enhanced due to virtual simulations, as well as benchmarked activities and immediate feedback which turns employees into empowered people with clear steps to improvement. Managers can observe how teams operate, monitor progress of the employees, and jump in instantly to facilitate the growth and overcome hurdles. Such a clean and constant system of performance evaluation fosters an atmosphere of responsibility, continual improvement, and prompt recognition.

The metaverse brings a new set of practices to deal with the long-standing issue of employee engagement in HRM. Being immersive and gamified, virtual spaces make a more exciting and rewarding workplace where people perform well understood, tackle them jointly, and take part in substantive team-building activities. Myth busting and relationship building between people from different departments and in different geographic locations more easily occurs at virtual networking events, social gatherings, and informal interactions. The metaverse supports inclusivity with inclusive platforms giving employees from various backgrounds, capabilities, and choice a chance to be fully involved in the organizational activities.

The ability of the metaverse to transform and create the next workforce arrangements on an international level has some merit. Breaking down physical boundaries enable companies to go beyond their local talent, providing a space where diverse perspectives meet, inspire both innovation and creative problem-solving. Remote teams are fully capable of collaboratively functioning together, using the metaverse to ideate solutions, overcome dilemmas, and think of new proposals fits in seconds. The outcome of this network promotes faster adaptation in organizations and fosters employee thinking in lieu of critical global leadership and cultural awareness for today's global markets.

In spite of immense promise the metaverse holds for HRM, its adoption is hindered with a host of problems. Adoption of strong technology, adequate bandwidth, and correct training will enable wider use to get the most out of the metaverse. There is a need to attend to security and privacy because of the virtual nature of HR in metaverse world; managing the data of employees presents substantial ethical concerns regarding consent, openness, and data confidentiality. Businesses require to have transparent policies and excellent safeguards in place so that employees' rights are both respected and trust created in regards to metaverse technologies.

Cultural barriers are also to be considered, especially when there are less accustomed, or at ease with the idea of immersive digital spaces, employees. From generational gaps to digital skill gaps and urgency to connect in person can shape how and where metaverse-based HR solutions are accepted and where they make an impact. To fill these gaps, companies are required to invest in change management, providing their employees with extensive training, and participation in designing and implementing virtual HR strategies. It can help organizations successfully step into the metaverse and maximize the possibilities involved by encouraging a wide, experimental, and learning-fuelled approach.

The changing environment with technology and workers' expectations will have a major bearing on the HRM in the metaverse (Loia, 2025). Advances in artificial intelligence, machine learning, and an earlier mentioned advanced analytics will figure to propel more customized, dynamic, and data-driven HR practices with blockchain's hope. As the line between the real and virtual continues to blur, enterprises that incorporate the metaverse for innovation, employee engagement, and growth are also advancing toward securing and sustaining top talent in a constantly transforming global environment.

2.1 Description of the Metaverse

The metaverse is distinguished by three key characteristics: These are immersiveness, interactivity and connectivity.

Realism encompasses the extent of possible interactions between users and particular environment, which make participants to have a feeling of being physically in the virtual environment. This is amplified presence makes learning and engagement much better during training sessions or any form of collaborative sessions such as team-building activities.

It enables users to chat in real time, which helps you to communicate and collaborate with people from different parts of the word. Employees in the metaverse get to engage their avatar in relations with other employees, work on projects together, and undergo a simulation of real life where it sharpens their problem-solving ability.

Connectivity augments the capacity of the metaverse to bring together people and teams of people across the world. This characteristic creates understanding within the organizations and encourages realization of talents and potentials from as many diverse perspectives as possible, in turn, it creates idea generation and problem solving diversification.

2.2 Global Implication in Workforce Management

What this means for the management of the global workforce in reference to metaverse is quite staggering. With this digital landscape, organisations could transform the conventional techniques of human resource management to fit the contingent working model. The options for virtual onboarding and training, as well as virtual performance management, in an engaging environment make the process much more pleasant for the new employee and help new hires to transition to new positions seamlessly.

In addition, the metaverse needs to be ongoing and provide ways for learning and development to continue so that users can acquire new resources and engage in effective, live and location-independent training. It is particularly timely in today's rapidly evolving business world where existing competencies alongside new ones would require constant upgrading.

This is much different from more conventional HRM approaches, which potentially are highly face-to-face and static, dependent on direct discussion with employees and worksheet-like training aids; the metaverse environment is far more interactive, with instantaneous feedback.

Table 1 provides a comparison of traditional and metaverse-based HRM as well as how metaverse based HRM can improve engagement, collaboration and flexibility of the international workforce. This table displays a side by side of traditional HRM methods and the progress made possible by metaverse technology, particularly in relation to workforce engagement, collaboration, and global flexibility.

Table 1. Comparison between traditional human resource management and the latter counterpart in the metaverse.

Aspect	Traditional HRM	Metaverse-based HRM
Interaction Mode	Primarily in-person or via email	Virtual interactions using avatars
Training	Classroom-based sessions	Immersive, interactive simulations
Accessibility	Limited by location and time	Accessible anytime, anywhere
Engagement	Passive participation	Active, gamified experiences
Feedback Mechanism	Periodic performance reviews	Real-time feedback through interaction

This table aims to show the possibility that the metaverse has in changing the dynamics of HRM practices; further, how it can be useful in the current business environment, demonstrating how it can be beneficial in promoting the workforce engagement and adaptability beyond what is currently seen in the existing literature. As the future developments of the metaverse unfold, its characteristics will become more relevant to the discussion of the potential future of HRM and promoting innovative solutions for employee-related strategies.

3. HUMAN RESOURCE MANAGEMENT: EXTRINSIC MOTIVATION THROUGH GAME DESIGN

Gamification is a powerful approach in HRM that enhances traditional practice through techniques of gamification. Through gamification's principles, organizations can only sensibly increase engagement, effectively train their workers, and harvest a greater productivity. We discuss how gamification can be used to enhance motivation and participation, and we present a variety of examples, all related to the integration of gameification in HRM.

3.1 The Role of gamification in Engagement and Learning

Organizations can easily hurdle the barriers brought about by less motivation and engagement amongst the staff by involving gamification. When the elements of points, badges, leaderboards, and challenges are introduced to traditional processes, employees find work to be enjoyable and helpful. Through utilizing these game elements, organizations create a culture where employees are motivated to achieve completion and accomplishment of milestones, in a manner that is not tiring to them.

Using playful activities and gamification, traditional learning experiences are transformed into more effective and attractive learning experiences. Playing of a gamification card, enterprises can easily plug the loopholes of the traditional passive methods of training. Learners will retain more knowledge if information is presented in an interesting manner; thus, the workforce is more focussed.

3.2 Uses of Gamification in the HRM

Gamification brings valuable versatility to HRM, including recruitment, training, and performance management, as well as others. More and more organizations are adopting gamification in their recruitment process, using game-based assessment to efficiently screen and profile candidates without the cumbersome and endless process of hiring practices. Likewise, it facilitates the company's quest to hire the best talent and gives a better view of how a candidate will fit into the company's culture.

In training specifically, gamification makes learning opportunities come to life through involvement with realistic simulations and role play scenarios. The role plays provide a forum for testing of new behaviors and instant feedback for the employees through these instruments, which facilitate new skill acquisition.

For example, game-like features bring performance management benefits like goal setting, use of objective appraisal processes. Companies can utilize a proven strategy from the game theory to develop a strong incentive framework through which continuous feedback is easily accomplished and employees are encouraged in their work to meet performance standards while directing their efforts to the organization's strategies.

Figure 2. Gamification techniques across HRM functions

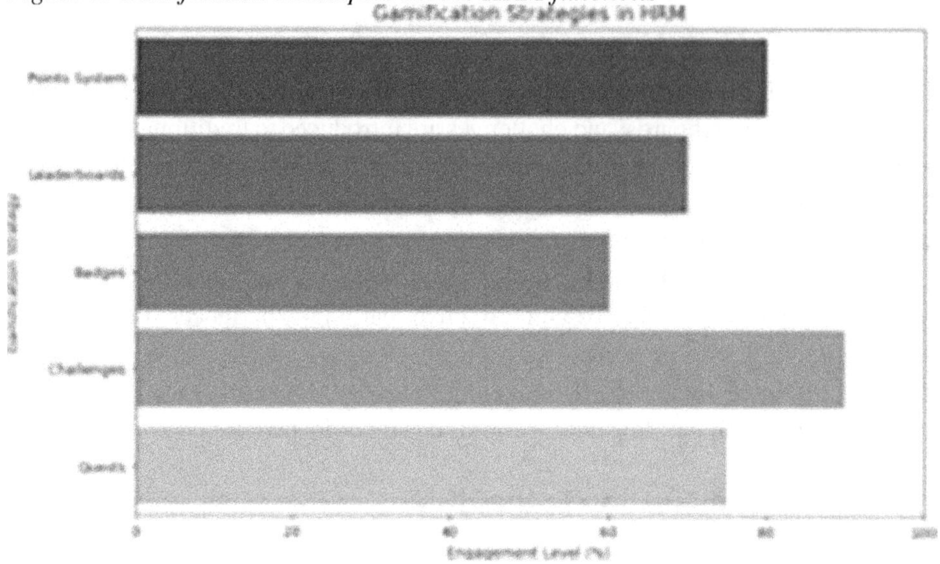

The figure shows the use of different gamification strategies for HRM AS such as recruitment, training and performance management, followed by the impact on employee engagement and organizational success.

It is also seen from figure 2 that different gamification techniques are used in different areas of HRM to improve engagement and organizational performance Generally, the following uses of gamification theories are displayed across the map:

As the concept has shown, gamification has the potential of being a revolutionary way not only in shaping better HRM experiences but in enhancing the overall organizational experiences of a set of employees. Through bringing gamification into the efficiency of hiring, training and performanceevaluation and management of employees, organizations can help create an engaging and positive company culture that not only improves employees' satisfaction, but also delivers organization's goals, objectives and outcomes.

4. THE INTEGRATION OF GAMIFICATION WITH IHRM IN THE METAVERSE

The ability to incorporate gamification into IHRM in the metaverse offers organisations the chance to revolutionize employee engagement, interaction and training. In this part of the paper, practices for designing game like experiences will be discussed as well as how culture plays a key role in strategy execution globally.

4.1 Designing Gamified Experiences

Gamified experiences should not just be fun, but also captivating, hence the need to take time and come up with or consider the following aspects. The remaining key things include setting good objectives, using attractive game mechanics and guaranteeing that an experience is convenient for the user.

But it is very possible to start with Goals and objectives that are Smart and are in line with the given organizational goals and objectives. It is important for employees to know where to direct their efforts, goals offer the means by which this is achieved and in turn gives direction and a sense of mission. By introducing attractive elements of the game, like the concept of tasks and goal, people's self-motivation as well as the social motivation can be improved. For instance, attaching a points card to the end of each training module encourages those involved to contribute and feel good about themselves once they are through.

Moreover, the aspect of the functionality for users should be taken into account as well. The last feature of the gamified platforms is the easy to use interface that should not hinder the employee use of the content in the platform. Feedback mechanisms are also important; Constant updates as to performance and progress are provided to the users.

4.2 Culture Integration in the Process of Gamification

During the process of deployment of gamified processes in IHRM, the most important issue to address for the improvement of successful engagement across intercultural teams. The cultural perspective dictates that organizations should find ways of harmonizing their gamification strategies with the multiple cultures that are at work.

These factors were identified as the cultural influences that can be a cause of game elements acceptance among employees. For example, the perceived motivator called competition, which is effective in one culture, may be regarded as pressure or as a negative factor in another culture. It is crucial for engendering tailored gamified experiences that will capture the interest of all employees.

However, it is necessary to pay attention to the language or communication patterns for the targeted audience. This is part of addressing localized content; a company should ensure that the game operations correspond to the cultural needs of the teams involved. It is recommended that organizations should seek to undertake cultural reviews to better understand how to develop effective gamification strategies that meets different companies' cultural expectations of its employees.

Table 2 describes examples of effective applied gamified IHRM initiatives that shed light on how different organizations have incorporated gamification in the IHRM system within the metaverse. These examples illustrate the idea that various forms and methods can be used together with effectively employing gamification and using it for positive results.

Table 2. The visual representation of organisations undertaking gamified HRM strategies in the Metaverse

Organization	Initiative Description	Key Outcomes
Company A	Gamified onboarding program in a virtual environment	30% faster integration of new hires
Company B	Interactive training simulations for skill development	25% increase in training retention rates
Company C	Virtual team-building games for cross-cultural teams	Enhanced collaboration and team cohesion

This table illustrates concrete examples of organisations that have been efficient in embedding gamified IHRM practices within the metaverse, and it displays the methods of implementation used and the associated outcomes.

Figure 3. A gamification framework to increase workforce participation in the Metaverse

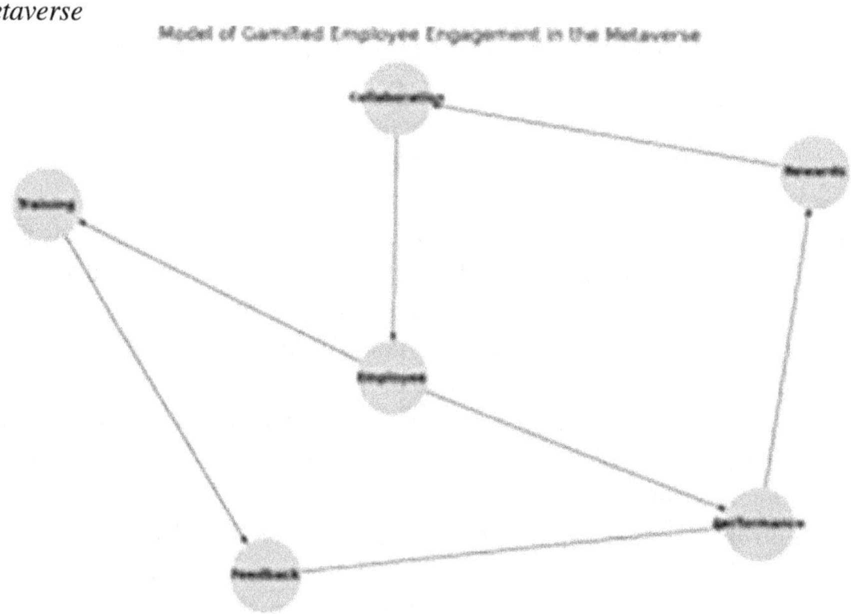

The figure above shows the proposed gamification system aimed at increasing worker dedication and cooperation in the world of the metaverse applications. Figure 3 displays an image that represents the arrangement of gamification framework elements meant to encourage employee engagement in metaverse settings (Daşdemir, 2022).

By mixing gamification strategies in IHRM in the metaverse enterprises can promote better employee engagement and reputation inspiring efficiency and performance. On the bright side, these well engineered games and associated processes guided by cultural elements and industry best practices provide great value and efficiency in involving teams in various parts of world. As going ahead, the gamification will inevitably form the corner-stone in the development of the metaverse at the expense of companies who will be seeking to unlock its full potential in various aspects such as HRM.

5. CHALLENGES AND CONSIDERATIONS

Although gamification and metaverse have potential in IHRM, it is of great essence to evaluate the challenges and the pertinent factors therein, carefully. This section covers the technology's constraints, ethical issues, and takeover and usage by employees. Although the impetuses to gamification and metaverse of IHRM have the potential for revolutionary game-changer in terms of workplace engagement, the learning outcomes, and development of organizational transformation, there is a need to be proactive in understanding the vast range of challenges related. Adoption of HRS gamification and metaverse is affected by many obstacles that include technical issues, as well as operational difficulties, ethical considerations, as well as doubts about employee engagement, and the need for buy-in. The success of results obtained from these innovations requires intense planning and strategic implementation for the enhancement of their effectiveness and minimizing their risks.

The introduction of the gamification and metaverse technologies in IHRM, however, usually meets significant impediment caused by the continuous technological barriers. Companies that happen to have financial or operational limitations struggle to acquire the infrastructure, like stable internet interfaces, state-of-the-art hardware, and easy-to-use software applications that are needed to provide vibrant virtual worlds. Technology is dynamic and fast-moving and so adds to these problems since new platforms and tools pass out of currency rapidly and with much effort being needed in upgrading and training staff. Digital infrastructural shortages especially in the less economically developed areas come to deprive the smaller firms of the financial resources and make them further the gap between the innovation-capable and limites organizations. Moreover, introducing new tools to HR infrastructure can cause incompatibility and workflow hiccups, and difficulties in data accuracy.

Building, deploying, maintaining complex systems for gamification and metaverse on HR requires specialist knowledge which organizations can fill by remodeling their employees' skills or hiring specialist consultants. Other than the technical issues, there are unique practical barriers to the adoption of gamification in IHRM. Creating effective gamified processes involves a greater complexity than simply adding points, badges, and leaderboard to traditional HR functions.

Foolish gamification campaigns can lead to undesirable effects, such as diminished motivation, little participation, even employee dissatisfaction where incentive mechanisms seem unjust or minor. There is the likelihood that the system can be manipulated such that employees seek the rewards without really getting involved with the targeted learning or also performance tasks. These methods can undermine the credibility of HR practices as well as the willingness of employees to take HR-related extravagant attitudes that do not help them to reach organization goals. The upfront cost of transitioning to gamification, including the purchase of software and hardware and the training of employees, is sometimes great. It is extremely important for organizations to examine the promised ROI and ensure that the gamification endeavors should contribute to greater strategic goals and not become just another popular but perhaps a shallow approach.

Gamification and metaverse approaches to HRM require proactive approaches to the ethics of HRM. Organizations' collection and analysis of a large amount of employee data to inspire customized offers and assess performance frequently sparks fundamental concerns on privacy, consent, and data security. It may raise concerns on the uses of their data, with the possibility of those who can view it and whether that data may be used for monitoring or enforcement outside their pact. Being open about data collection and use policies are very important to promote and achieve trust and fulfill the various relevant legal and regulatory norms. It is an ethical issue on the ability to manipulate the employees using gamification (Sharma, 2024). If you state what gamification helps achieve, highlight how its benefits are significant, and show how it shows the way to personal accomplishments and organizational success, the number of supporters and the reluctance level will increase. When employees get to engage in the design of gamified processes, they become more a part of it and the resulting outcomes are made tailored and are significant and user oriented. Gluing there is continuous support, regular training, and feedback loops for everyone to participate and apply more which will make the staff feel more prepared as they go along.

The other important aspect includes the ability to ensure the ongoing viability and sustainability of gamification and metaverse programs. The same initial excitement might be lost if the same systems become stale or if new changes creating a buzz are not implemented to stay abreast of changing needs. Continuous monitoring, assessment, and adjustment are required to preserve engagement and facilitate the gamified HR efforts to change and fit to achieve the aims of organizations. Such endeavors require continued investing in resources, active leadership engagement, as well as a willingness to take new approaches and learn the outcomes of such. Companies need to establish quantifiable objectives for their gamification pursuits, gather to understand how users engage and are effective, and use this information to improve their tactics. By recognizing accomplishment and commending accomplishment along with open dialogue concerning barriers and scope for improvement, one will maintain growth and flexibility.

Overlooking the challenges could have severe negative effects on the organizations. Poor implementation of gamification can erode organizational culture and reduce employee trust as well as cut down morale. Failure to pay due consideration to ethical issues in data privacy or fairness can lead to compliance challenges, bad image of the organization, reduced trust by employees. Technical hitches or lack or goodwill may lead to the wastage of resources and which can stop one from adopting innovation. Alternatively, those that proactively deal with these impediments by making them secure. The purpose of gamification is, therefore, to build motivation and engagement but poor implementation may trigger the underlining psychological response resulting in compulsive actions, strain of mind, or disrespectful competition among employees. There is a proven correlation between a high quantity of gamification and data overload and deterioration of sincere intrinsic motivation, as employees tend to prioritize extrinsic achievement more than intrinsic growt The integration of gamification and the metaverse into the world of HR management is met with exciting new windows of opportunities, but a vast network of challenging technological, practical, ethical and human hurdles (Lim, 2024). It is of key importance to organization that seeks to utilize these innovations for better engagement, learning and performance in today's workplace as they prioritize thoughtful and strategic attention to these challenges. If cultivated with every opportunity, a responsible approach can take organizations to gamified HR settings that are equally effective, engaging, and just, sustainable in the long term.h in the personal or professional sphere.

5.1 Technological Barriers

The primary segment of the obstacles is technologically oriented and is tightly related to the difficulties that organizations experience during the implementation of gamification and usage of the metaverse. It is quite possible that many organizations might not have the infrastructure, resources or the know-how to create and sustain advanced forms of gamification. That is, problems of incompatible systems, lack of bandwidth, or insufficient user support may act as barriers to its implementation.

Moreover, the latter type of knowledge is volatile, which may be an issue for organizations because of the fast development of technologies. It appears that as updated tools and platforms are developed, firms are required to reinvest and upgrade to keep up with the growing trends. This can be very cumbersome especially for organizations that are not well endowed and may end up paying a lot of money from their limited resources to implement projects that do not meet impact their targeted beneficiaries.

5.2 Ethical Considerations

The following are necessary principles for the adoption of gamification into IHRM: Ethical considerations are very critical in IHRM. Privacy, protection from data and fairness remain among the most costly challenges to such applications.

By adopting game-based technologies, companies are able to read valuable information regarding work force performance and factors that drive workers. It is necessary that such data is managed in accordance with regulations to maintain employee rights and only for the intended purpose. Companies must establish and execute robust protecting methods to guarantee that workforce performance and trigger data should be private.

In addition, it is imperative to ensure that the gamification practices in existence are practiced with levelness. Organizational leaders need to be especially careful preventing establishing systems that unjustly undermine some groups of consumers or individuals. Take for instance if most gamification tasks encourage competition between teams then those employees who do not find it easy to blend within such competition structures may end up becoming isolated or felt alone. The balancing and equitable application of gamification techniques will play a positive role toward establishing a proper organisational set up and fostering staff trust.

5.3 Employee Resistance and Acceptance

Another important point to highlight in connection with gamification in the workplace is the unwillingness or opposition expressed by employees on the part of these initiatives. Employees may regard gamification as misguided or empty, maliciously believing that the manager only wants to force them towards activities that they are actually not interested in. When employees are skeptical, participation levels drop and in long term gamification initiative may not be effective.

6. FUTURE TRENDS OF IHRM GAMIFIED IN THE METAVERSE

Given the ever-shifting nature of IHRM, the effective use of gamification in the metaverse is set to revolutional IHRM in the future. This section focuses on new and potential technologies that are believed to affect the gamified IHRM and gives probable expectations of future development in this innovated area. The opportunity for IHRM in the metaverse with the help of digital innovation, changing needs of the workforce, and business globalization, will lead to a very new chapter in management of HR. While companies strive to attract, groom, and keep the best talent around the world, the use of gamification in metaverse environments is gearing up to revolutionize the orientation of HR procedures and the practice through which staff interact with their careers. The synergy between innovations such as AI, VR, AR, blockchain and IoT, is setting HRM up for a new chapter that is highly participatory, analytics driven, and individualized to each employee's experience.

The increasing complexity and ease of the technologies in the technologies in the immersive form are a decisive factor in determining the direction of gamified IHRM in the metaverse. The acceleration of developments makes VR and AR common-place business tools, while not only for major technology firms, gaming industry, or private business types, but for all. Their implementation in HRM is increasing and facilitating the establishment by organizations of elaborate and persuasive virtual environments for their employees. Using these technologies, the employees can do realistic simulations, team projects and training exercises related to actual work environment scenarios, working at home or in comfortable settings. The onboarding stage may be made an interesting journey for newcomers to explore how they work in the digitally-enabled environment, interact with other avatars and achieve work-based tasks that precondition them to the requirements of organisation. Additionally, VR training simulations allow participants to manage difficult events (crisis scenarios or intercultural communications), creating a safe learning environment wherein experimentation, and error are treated as essential steps toward mastery.

There can be no doubt about the importance of AI in promoting the gamification of HRM (Singh, 2022). Organization will be able to conduct personalized training for their employees because of the development in AI; each individual is guided by his or her skill set, interests, and aspirations. With AI, employers can monitor live performance of employees, there are speedy feedback and advice to improve skills and areas that keep repeating to be trained in time through refresher programs. The high degree of personalization ensures that HR initiatives continue to be of relevance and excitement, thus promoting continuous skill learning. Blockchain technology integration is an important innovation in gamified IHRM in the metaverse. Due to decentralized and transparent nature, blockchain is a perfect choice for overseeing digital credentials, rewards, and achievements. With the help of blockchain, employees can get their validated badges, certificates or tokens after they complete their training, meet their performance criteria, or demonstrate leadership in the metaverse. With blockchain, employees can enjoy secure and mobile, but nonetheless, verifiable digital assets that allows them to carry on with their career achievements overtime for presentation. Using blockchain, it is now possible to create DAOs, allowing employees to participate in company's governance and decision-making through accessible and gamified voting mechanisms. The topic of ethics and psychology concerning gamified HRM in Metaverse will be on the agenda in the future. With organizations going deeper in data collection and analysis of employee behaviors, preferences and performance, there will be more attention paid to privacy, consent, and data security. Open policies on data and clear data protection and communications in-time will be very important in creating trust and ensuring compliance. HR specialists will also need to be acquainted with the fact that gamification can, against all intuition, promote unhealthy competition or stress, so that the mechanics of it should focus on personal development, team work, and intentional motivation, rather than unchecked productivity.

The employee wellness focus and mental health, in particular, should play a key role at developing the gamified IHRM in the next few years. Employees are likely to interact with animated wellness challenges, mindfulness apps and peer networks in the metaverse, and endeavors towards self-maintaining their physical and mental self are enhanced. In the metaverse, organizations can leverage its immersive and sociable aspects, to create venues for staff to interact, collaborate, and gained access to tools on enhancing their well-being and resilience. Conscious of the direct effect of well-being on productivity, the HR strategies now consider employee wellness to be a primary component achieving effectiveness in organizations.

Technology developments will continue to blur the lines between work and play to form more energetic, entertaining and even captivating workplaces in terms of the range and scope of activities. Employees will pursue career tasks, gain rewards on milestone accomplishment and engage in collaborative venture that relates with the organizations' objectives. Rapid and drastic positive reactions will help to create a workplace environment that emphasizes unending improvement and collaborative success. The metaverse will gamify lifelong learning through immersive experiences where employees get to explore new skills, try out different role models and keep up with what the market is evolving into all with fun and interactive feedback.

Integration of IoT and the metaverse will enhance the validity and interest of HR-virtual settings. With the help of IoT, the real-time data sources such as bodily health, workplace conditions, output measures etc. are gathered to compile in metaverse settings to manufacture personalized and environment friendly scenarios. For example, a wellness commotion in the metaverse may vary its challenges in accordance with an employee's physiological data, like heart rate or stress to encourage wellness and balance. Using this combination of real-world experiences and virtual worlds, organizations are given the opportunity to develop larger initiatives focused on their employees and improve their bond.

6.1 Emerging Technologies and Their Impact

Several cutting-edge digital technologies come to forward as exciting ways in evolving gamified IHRM in the emerging metaverse environment:

Artificial Intelligence (AI) can be a gamechanger for the field; much more personalized learning and development strategies are possible. AI can use performance insights to shape the next steps and to ensure that the gamification matches the progress needs of the employees. Furthermore, using AI-generated analytics helps organizations to tweak the elements that shape the usage of gamification continuously through monitoring current usage (Gamayanto, 2024).

Virtual Reality (VR) and Augmented Reality (AR) also play a very important role in spreading out knowledge and sharing learning through collaboration. VR provides the added benefit of enabling the conducting of training simulations in which workers can learn without endangering actual organization success. It increases the potential for interaction between the virtual and actual spaces by digitally overing digital content upon realities, which increases the engaging appeal of the activity for employees. Blockchain technology brings enhanced openness and security to gamified environments. Blockchain technology confirms the credibility of gamified incentives and rewards, as each achievement and credentials are successfully identified and stored in reliable and not-capable-to-be-altered system.

6.2 Predictions for the Future of IHRM in the Metaverse

With the flex work becoming the new norm for years to come, the metaverse will play the strategic role connecting distributed teams and strengthening bonds between individuals. Employers will ensure that arrangements that reflect in-person interactions are carried out on specific gamified environments, to foster corporate social relations.

In addition, there will be an increased dependency on data analytical tools in determining the nature of gamified IHRM. Companies will leverage analytics to determine the success of game-based initiatives and adapt changes based on big data, to strategically develop proactive and engaging programs to optimize engagement and retention. Table 3 includes guidelines of future trends in relation to HRM, which can be used by organizations to map strategic changes.

Table 3. Evolutional changes and guidelines on implementing gamified IHRM in virtual environments

Trend	Implication for HRM
Increased use of AI	Personalized learning and performance insights
Expansion of VR and AR	Enhanced immersive training and collaboration
Adoption of blockchain	Improved security and transparency in rewards
Greater focus on data analytics	Data-driven decision-making in HR practices

The table provides essential trends, advanced technologies, and practical recommendations to companies that want to implement gamified IHRM inside the metaverse. An emergent tech within the scope of metaverse strengthens these features of gamified IHRM: engagement, learning, and collaboration. To be competitive and create a focused, working team, organizations have to embrace these trends with proactive steps. Adoption of gamified IHRM is anticipated to change HR processes and the manner in which organizations develop their talent and pursue high performance in the context of rapid change.

7. CONCLUSION

Combining gamification with IHRM in the metaverse is a shift in organizational relationships with people, but mainly it is a development of a new evolution in employment. This chapter has looked at three key areas of gamification, IHRM and the metaverse to understand how these power the engagement, learning and performance of the employees. ICT introduces gamification and IHRM combination into the metaverse as a pivotal shift toward an arrangement between employers and their worldwide workforce (Shah, 2025). When looked at from beyond the technology narrative, this blend is a revolutionary rethinking of how people relate and work in their jobs. The combination of a gamification, IHRM and metaverse technology allows organizations to create work environments that are not only engaging and adaptive, but in consideration of the increased global workforce are also compatible (Getman, 2025). By adding these principles into HRM, these routine procedures become lively engagement that attracts and engages employees. However, for example, leaderboards allow employees to compete with each other and encourage a friendly rivalry process, badges and achievements contribute to the advancement process by recognizing primary achievements. Research in this area is fast emerging and shows that over 9 out of every 10 workers believe that the integration of game elements promotes their level of engagement and output, with emphasis on the critical effect in regards to workplace motivation. The incorporation of the game-based strategies to the HR processes increases the enjoyment at work and ensures individual ambitions are connected to the organization's goals bringing unity of purpose.

Meanwhile, International Human Resource Management involves management of human resources within an international context, the complex issues of disparate cultural norms, legal frameworks and business levels. Today's organization needs to figure out how HR practices can be applied across the board globally but account for and appreciate the cultural and legal differences in each of the regions while binding the whole organization together. With the help of the metaverse, a singular, long-lived virtual space powered by VR and AR, organizations have a new way to counter these challenges. Bavohane eliminates the literal borders of one's location so that remote workers from all corners of the globe and people of all walks of life can communicate, work on projects, and establish solid relationships, irrespective of the distance between them. The convergence of gamification and IHRM within the metaverse triggers a vibrant exchange that highly enhances the response of personnel, learning, and outcomes. As employees take an active part in their development, spurred on by clear objectives, instant feedback, and relevant prizes then engagement increases. The metaverse provides gamified experiences, such as virtual scavenger hunts, interactive simulations and team challenges, which build a shared sense of success and promote better communication and collaboration, across departments and geographies (Mukherjee, 2024).

This new situation represents a big change for learning. It is possible that in-person/ passive learning strategies may fail to capture the staff's attention or provide meaningful, practical experience for geographically diverse groups. On the other hand, the metaverse emerges as a platform that offers employees the engaging, interactive learning space where they can practice skills, solve problems and receive instant feedback in simulated environments. For instance, virtual reality simulations allow employees to practise difficult discussions, solve the technical issues, or to deal with complicated business issues in a secure and controlled setting. Experiential learning has been shown to address retention and skill acquisition much better than learning from lectures or reading material. In addition personalized training modules can cater to various employees' individual requirements and methods and ensure that all the employees receive adequate and effective learning experiences.

Despite these obstructions, the convergence of gamification and IHRM in the metaverse is ready to open new possibilities for organizational change. In the process, organizations can create thriving work cultures that actively engage employees, and help them elevate, rather than merely manage employees, to promote genuine empowerment. Current developments in technology hold the promise of improving the likelihood of personalized, adaptive and meaningful HR approaches of the future. By adopting these innovations, organizations can become pioneers of innovation that will allow them to gain the war against talent in a quickly increasingly complex and tentative market.

7.1 Summary of Key Points

Figures covered in this chapter include defining aspects of gamification as well as why it matters in increasing motivation and engagement of the workforce. In this paper, we looked at examples of using gamification in recruitment, training, and other areas of HRM, focusing on the prospects of using such solutions in the virtual environment. In addition, we discussed issues that organisations may encounter, with technology issues, ethical issues, and issues with employee engagement being highlighted as major problems; the cultural context of gamification was also discussed as a necessity due to diverse cultures around the world. New technologies including AI, VR, AR and blockchain were seen to be the enablers of future trends of gamified IHRM the direction for more individualised and data-enabled HRM practices.

7.2 Recommendations for Practitioners

In order to assist HR practitioners who want to introduce gamification into their companies, below are fundamental suggestions. First and foremost obtaining the required technologies solutions is of utmost importance. Gamification will require organizations to use high-end tools such as AI, VR, and AR in order to be practical. Second, thoughtful design is crucial. The enhancement of performance and participation is markedly enhanced when specific, meaningful goals are established, engaging game features are included, and an easy-to-use interface is available. Third, cultural sensitivity should be of primary concern. Creating gamification strategies, aligned and respecting the diversity of the workforce, minimises feelings that people are left behind, and increases the level of participation. Fourth, forward looking strategies for gamification should be informed by a commitment to ethical and privacy conscious practices. Transparency, fairness, and the protection of employee data should be at the top of the list for organizations in the pursuit of earning trust through gamified sort of methods. Finally, employee engagement is vital. By involving staff in decision making, responding to their concerns in a timely manner and sharing rationale behind gamification use, as well as positive results of this type of implementation, it may increase interest and participation of employees. Such adherence by HR experts is supportive of the effective integration and the engagement merits of gamification

7.3 Bottom Line on Evolution of HRM in the Metaverse

This means that the existence of HRM in the metaverse is a radical change in how organisational workforce is managed and fostered. Looking into the future, the opportunities for improvement of the employee experience, encouraging employees for collaborative work and boosting their performance through use of successful elements of gamification in HR practices will be on the rise. By becoming receptive to this change and by preparing for the new trends and tools, companies can restore themselves as leaders in effective HR management strategies that can reach vibrant and happy talent. Looking ahead the issue will be to seize these opportunities as well as to solve the ethical and pragmatic issues associated with the current trend. Exploring the metaverse represents an opportunity for a better and improved thought and working process of human resource management.

REFERENCES

Aydin, O., Karaarslan, E., & Narin, N. G. (2024). Artificial intelligence, vr, ar and metaverse technologies for human resources management. *arXiv preprint arXiv:2406.15383.*

Daşdemir, Y. (2022). A brain-computer interface with gamification in the Metaverse. *Dicle Üniversitesi Mühendislik Fakültesi Mühendislik Dergisi, 13*(4), 645–652.

Dastane, O., Rafiq, M., & Turner, J. J. (2024). Implications of metaverse, virtual reality, and extended reality for development and learning in organizations. *Development and Learning in Organizations, 38*(5), 27–32. DOI: 10.1108/DLO-09-2023-0196

Dutta, D., Srivastava, Y., & Singh, E. (2023). Metaverse in the tourism sector for talent management: A technology in practice lens. *Information Technology & Tourism, 25*(3), 331–365. DOI: 10.1007/s40558-023-00258-9

Gamayanto, I., Wibowo, S., & Prayitno, A. (2024). The Concept of gamification, metaverse & AI to develop hybrid learning systems inside education. [International Journal of Information System and Technology]. *IJISTECH, 7*(6), 370–378.

Getman, A. P., Yaroshenko, O. M., Demenko, O. I., Lutsenko, O. Y., & Prokopiev, R. Y. (2024). Gamification for staff motivation: Impact on work efficiency and corporate culture at the international level. *Journal of Economics and Management, 46*, 274–299. DOI: 10.22367/jem.2024.46.11

Induji, R. T., & Somasundari, K. M. VinothKumar, K.R., Swapna, S., Brindha, S. and Kumar, S.K. (2024). Entry of the Metaverse in Human Resource Management: A Paradigm Shift in Workplace Dynamics. In *Anticipating Future Business Trends: Navigating Artificial Intelligence Innovations: Volume 1* (pp. 73-80). Cham: Springer Nature Switzerland.

Lim, D. H., Lee, J. Y., & Park, S. (2024). The metaverse in the workplace: Possibilities and implications for human resource development. *Human Resource Development Review, 23*(2), 164–198. DOI: 10.1177/15344843231217174

Loia, F., Capolupo, N., & Adinolfi, P. (2025). Training me softly. Metaverse-based immersive and gamified learning through a knowledge management perspective. *Journal of Knowledge Management, 29*(5), 1465–1489. DOI: 10.1108/JKM-08-2024-0929

Mahajan, S., Pandey, P. K., Behera, J., Pandey, P. K., & Beg, R. A. (2018). *Hybrid Work Models, Metaverse Integration, and Talent Management Strategies: Navigating Post-Pandemic Realities*. Green Metaverse for Greener Economies.

Mukherjee, S., & Gupta, G. (2024). Re-Imaging Human Resource Strategic Approaches: Adoption of Metaverse. In *The Role of HR in the Transforming Workplace* (pp. 95-103). Productivity Press.

Prabowo, S. H. W., Murdiono, A., Martha, J. A., Zutiasari, I., & Murad, S. M. A. (2023). May. Gamification of Ubiquitous-Based Learning Media as an Initiative of Open-World Metaverse Conversion for Problem Based Learning (PBL) in Business and Management Courses. In *BISTIC Business Innovation Sustainability and Technology International Conference (BISTIC 2022)* (pp. 86-97). Atlantis Press. DOI: 10.2991/978-94-6463-178-4_10

Rozak, H. A., & Fachrunnisa, O., Sugiharti, Taswan, & Fitriati, I. R. (2023, August). Metaverse and Modification Needs of Human Resources Management Practices and Policies: An Overview. In *International Conference on Intelligent Networking and Collaborative Systems* (pp. 285-294). Cham: Springer Nature Switzerland. DOI: 10.1007/978-3-031-40971-4_27

Saeed, A., Ali, A., & Ashfaq, S. (2024). Employees' training experience in a metaverse environment? Feedback analysis using structural topic modeling. *Technological Forecasting and Social Change, 208*, 123636. DOI: 10.1016/j.techfore.2024.123636

Shah, R., Shah, S., & Pathak, P. (2025). Metaverse work culture: The emergence of virtual-first companies and HR's role. *Strategic HR Review*. Advance online publication. DOI: 10.1108/SHR-03-2025-0029

Sharma, W., Lim, W. M., Kumar, S., Verma, A., & Kumra, R. (2024). Game on! A state-of-the-art overview of doing business with gamification. *Technological Forecasting and Social Change, 198*, 122988. DOI: 10.1016/j.techfore.2023.122988

Singh, A., Lakhera, G., Ojha, M., Mishra, A. K., & Kumari, J. (2022). Exploring the Use of Gamification in HR Processes for Staff Engagement in Hotels and Restaurants. In *AI, Blockchain, and Metaverse in Hospitality and Tourism Industry 4.0* (pp. 253-262). Chapman and Hall/CRC.

Thomas, N. J., Baral, R., Crocco, O. S., & Mohanan, S. (2023). A framework for gamification in the metaverse era: How designers envision gameful experience. *Technological Forecasting and Social Change, 193*, 122544. DOI: 10.1016/j.techfore.2023.122544

Chapter 4
Impact of Gamification on Brand Loyalty:
Exploring the Mediating Role of e-WOM

Rukshar Rukshar
https://orcid.org/0009-0007-0442-4213
Jamia Millia Islamia, India

Anam Khanam
https://orcid.org/0000-0001-5655-8618
Jamia Milia Islamia, India

M. D. Sajjad
https://orcid.org/0009-0001-8545-5391
Jamia Milia Islamia, India

Sarita Nagvanshi
https://orcid.org/0009-0007-0442-4213
New Delhi Institute of Management, India

ABSTRACT

This research seeks to examine the impact of gamification on brand loyalty through mediating the role of e-WOM. Data was collected from 287 individuals who frequently use online e-commerce platforms and are acquainted with mini-games like quizzes, spin-wheels, and task completion. through both online and offline questionnaires. The collected data were then analysed using Partial Least Squares Structural Equation Modeling (PLS-SEM), utilizing the Smarts PLS 4 software. The findings of this study reveal a significant positive relationship among gamification and brand loyalty and e-WOM. Additionally, the results support the mediating role of e-WOM in

DOI: 10.4018/979-8-3693-8886-0.ch004

the relationship between gamification and brand loyalty. The study employed cross sectional data which limits generalization. Primary data was collected with the help of a questionnaire which could lead to inaccurate results. Moreover, the study investigated the impact of gamification as a whole variable instead of examining their individual impact such as points, badges, and leaderboards.

INTRODUCTION

Social media and internet usage have altered how businesses operate as well as how consumers behave (Dwivedi et al., 2021). Marketers are adjusting to the constant changes in the corporate environment by employing cutting edge marketing techniques to increase product awareness, engage consumers and also help them make better decision about what to buy. A growing number of companies are competing for market dominance by attracting in active customers. As a relatively new paradigm for engaging consumers, gamification is applied as a strategy to influence and motivate people to participate in education, marketing, training, networking, and health-related activities (Bunchball, 2010). The term "gamification" describes the use of aspects of game design elements outside of games (Deterding et al., 2011). This modern method engages the target population and encourages behavioural change in a variety of contexts. In the fields of education, health, media, and crowdsourcing-based online communities, it has grown in popularity as a tool for maintaining consumer engagement (Hassan & Hamari, 2020) (Smiderle et al., 2020). According to Doğan-Südaş et al., (2023), gamified apps are assumed to motivate users to visit the app more frequently, which could lead to habit formation or behaviour change. T-Mobile Tuesdays, for instance, provides a range of incentives to encourage customers to visit their app frequently, like every Tuesday. Additionally, gamified apps encourage users to share their experiences through word-of-mouth communication on various online social media platforms by offering a variety of incentives that can be earned and redeemed through engagement, such as badges, points, visual tokens or symbols, leaderboards, or cash prizes. Hamari, (2013), have describe the use of gamification in various context such as promotion of greener energy consumption, fostering TV channer loyalty, encouraging people to take care of their health and even gamifying the tracking of life goals. By using game-like elements such as scoreboards, points, and personalized fast feedback, gamification aims to create a game-like experience, motivate and guide users' behaviour, and increase users' engagement with the "play" tasks (Sigala, 2015) (Lee & Hammer,

2011). These elements give users a sense of ownership, flow, and purpose when they are completing the "play" tasks (Pavlus, 2010).

Recent researches provide evidence that gamification has a positive relationship with a important brand-related outcomes, including brand engagement (Xi & Hamari, 2020), brand attitude (Yang et al., 2017), brand loyalty (Hwang & Choi, 2020), and brand love (Hsu & Chen, 2018). The effectiveness of gamification in strengthening customer-brand interactions is confirmed by these researches. However, gamification's use in marketing contexts is still relatively new as pointed out by Koivisto & Hamari, (2019), suggesting that further research is necessary to fully understand its wider behavioural consequences.

In particular, the relationship between gamification and electronic word-of-mouth (e-WOM) has remain underexplored in the literature, which has mostly concentrated on the impact of gamification on user engagement. Bitrián et al., (2021), discovered that gamification increases user engagement in mobile applications, and that this increased engagement has a favourable impact on the willingness of users to recommend apps to others. In the same way, Meenakshy et al., (2020) looked at the travel industry and emphasized how intrinsic motivation—particularly enjoyment—drives e-WOM behaviour through gamified experiences.

Despite these efforts, previous research has mostly focused on the relationship between gamification and engagement without thoroughly examining the ways in which gamification may have a direct impact on electronic word-of-mouth (e-WOM), especially in digitally branded environments like mobile applications or virtual platforms like the metaverse. Given the increasing significance of digital ecosystems in influencing consumer behaviour, this poses a serious research vacuum.

Furthermore, it has been acknowledged that e-WOM plays a significant role in influencing consumer choices. A Nielsen survey from 2015 found that consumers place a very high value on e-WOM trust, ranking it second only to traditional word-of-mouth communication. Given its scale and persuasive strength, it is crucial and timely to comprehend the mechanisms underlying e-WOM, such as gamification. Thus, this study aims to address this gap by investigating the impact of gamification directly and indirectly through e-WOM and also mediation effects of e-WOM. The study aims to respond to some research issues.

RQ1. How does gamification influence electronic word-of-mouth (e-WOM) and consumers' brand loyalty?
RQ2. How does electronic word-of-mouth (e-WOM) influence consumers' brand loyalty?
RQ3. Does electronic word-of-mouth (e-WOM) mediate the relationship between gamification and consumers' brand loyalty?

LITERATURE REVIEW

Gamification, a modern marketing and promotional tool, is known to elicit good emotions. Nonetheless, previous research has rarely addressed how gamification influences brand loyalty; this study identified how gamification affects consumer loyalty (Al-Zyoud, 2021). Gamification's new trend has led to a growth in the popularity and rise of games in marketing activities, making them desirable to marketers. Gamification is becoming increasingly popular among marketing executives. Gamification can be considered as a novel approach to increasing brand awareness and loyalty, innovation, and online user engagement. According to Aksoy et al. (2015), consumer loyalty is generated by the interactions and relationships that customers form and develop with a company, product, service, or brand. Firms that communicate through social media, in particular, are more likely to have a positive brand image and higher perceived service quality, which can increase consumer loyalty (Al-Zyoud, 2021).

Evidence suggested that firms use gamification primarily to improve consumer loyalty, positive word-of-mouth, and engagement (Leclercq et al., 2017). Playful consuming experiences were revealed to be major predictors of consumers' cognitive, affective, and behavioural involvement (Zaib et al., 2019). Gamification dynamics, electronic word of mouth, and enjoyment exert a positive and significant effect on urge to impulsive buying. Among gamification dynamics, reward, status, self-expression, and altruistic behaviours have an effect on creating enjoyment, but competition and achievement have no positive and significant effect (Aghdaie et al., 2022). The role played by gamification in the interplay of influencer traits, continuous usage intentions of platforms, and electronic word-of-mouth (e-WOM) within online platforms. The primary emphasis of this investigation lies in examining the various facets of gamification this finding revealed a significant impact of network exposure arising from gamification on users' intentions for continuous platform usage.

Furthermore, the assessment of gamification, taking into account both utilitarian and hedonic factors, shows a significant impact on e-WOM. This shows that social media users who participate in gamified events are more likely to promote them to their friends and family. Furthermore, attitudes have demonstrated to be an important element, influencing both users' long-term usage intentions and e-WOM (Pandey et al., 2024). WOM contributors write reviews about products/services provided by business venues and WOM consumers read reviews and use them to form attitudes and make purchase decisions. Gamification elements such as points and badges, awarded to WOM contributors for various reasons, and displayed to WOM consumers, have a dual role in WOM context. First, points awarded for user contributions help motivate WOM contributors to increase their participation. Second, badges awarded to users for visiting business venues signal prior experience or competence, and they help determine how WOM consumers perceive WOM contributors and form their judgments based on the reviews (Wang et al., 2018).

Hajarian and Hemmati (2020) used gamification to encourage consumers to suggest products to one another via Word of Mouth. The proposed recommendation system has been deployed on an e-commerce website. Experimental results suggest that the proposed strategy is effective in increasing consumer sales and unique visits. Using the suggested WOM recommendation system, the average number of female customer visits increased by 116% while the average number of male customer visits climbed by 100%. Furthermore, the ratio of unique clients to purchases has fallen by 7%. This means that the number of purchases by customers has increased. According to Butt and Ahmad (2024), perceived utility, amusement, and enjoyment have a favourable impact on consumer word-of-mouth and loyalty. Furthermore, gamification components such as fun and playfulness improve the perceived usefulness of mobile payments. It indicates how happy and excited users are with WeChat Hongbao. Furthermore, the positive moderating effect of intimacy on the hypothesised links indicates that all three generations are likely to adopt gamified money features. Wang et al. (2017) investigated the effect of gamification on WOM. This study contributes to and enriches the WOM literature by introducing a new feature - reviewers' activity history.

Gamification is one method for increasing mobile app users' brand loyalty. We hypothesize that the regularity with which people employ immersion, achievement, and social elements is related to brand loyalty. It was discovered that customers must frequently engage immersion and achievement-related features in order to experience significant brand loyalty. On the contrary, we discovered that users who rarely use at least two gamification elements had low brand loyalty (Mattke & Maier 2021). Chien and Wu (2015) studied the relationship between mobile gamification design elements, brand experience, and brand loyalty, while Al-Zyoud (2021) investigated how gamification affects consumer loyalty and its impact on purchase and e-WOM sharing behaviour. Gamification techniques can improve customer loyalty outcomes by examining some real-world examples where marketers have had mixed success implementing gamification in their loyalty programs (Lem et al., 2022).

In today's marketing environment, gamification has become a potent force. It had a significant indirect impact on customer engagement, which influences brand loyalty and ultimately influences customer buying intentions. According to Punwatkar and Verghese (2025), this study highlights the importance of gamification in changing consumer behavior and the value of encouraging user engagement and brand loyalty to influence purchase decisions. Theoretically, it contributes to the brand marketing literature by recognizing gamification as a new predictor of brand attachment. It also contributes to the gamification literature by proving that achievement-related gamification features increase brand attachment through intrinsic reasons rather than extrinsic motives in the setting of an online brand community (Yang et al.,2022).

Gamification had a substantial and positive impact on customer experience; it also has a positive and major effect on user customer brand engagement, which in turn has a positive and significant impact on customer experience. It also indicated that customer brand engagement serves as a bridge between gamification and customer experience (Jami Pour et al., 2021). This research seeks to examine the impact of gamification on brand loyalty through mediating the role of electronic-words-of-mouth.

CONCEPTUAL FRAMEWORK OF THE STUDY

A gamification conceptual framework is a structured model that helps in the design, implementation, and evaluation of gamified systems. Gamification is the use of game design elements in non-game contexts, and its impact can be observed in increased user engagement, motivation, and behavioural outcomes across various domains such as education, business, and health (Deterding et al., 2011).

Figure 1. Conceptual framework model

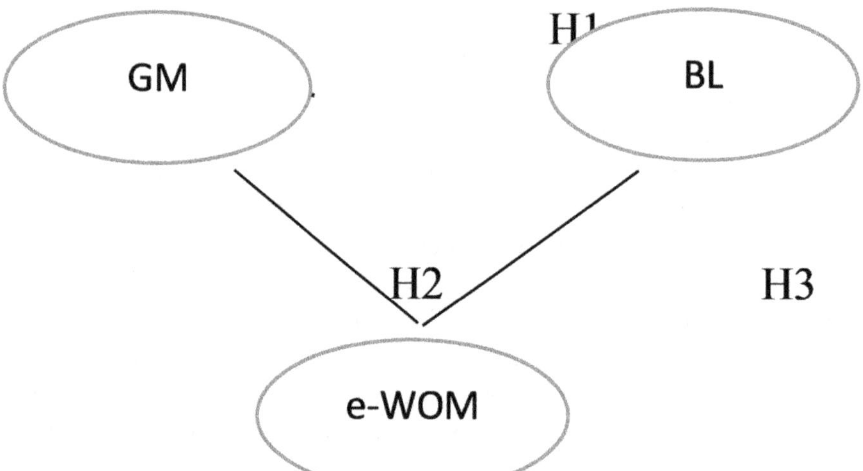

HYPOTHESES DEVELOPMENT

Gamification and Brand Loyalty

Gamification significantly enhances brand loyalty by increasing customer engagement, fostering emotional connections with the brand, and encouraging repeat interactions (Nobre et al.,2021) and the application of gamification in marketing strategies leads to increased brand engagement and loyalty by enhancing perceived enjoyment and brand value (Hofacker et al.,2016).

H1: Gamification has a significant impact on brand loyalty.

Gamification and e-WOM

Gamification symbols signaling experience that accompany WOM lead to perceptions of positive WOM contributors as more competent. This leads to important changes in behavioral outcomes such as willingness to visit buy and willingness to recommend the reviewed outlets (Wang et al., 2020).

H2: Gamification has a significant impact on e-WOM.

e-WOM and Brand Loyalty

e-WOM acts as a mediating variable between customer satisfaction, trust, and loyalty, enhancing consumer-based brand equity (CBBE). This indicates that positive e-WOM can strengthen brand loyalty by building trust and satisfaction among consumers Saleem (M. & Ellahi 2018). The impact of e-WOM on brand loyalty among Generation Z users of the OVO digital payment platform found that e-WOM significantly contributes to brand loyalty. The research highlighted that quality and quantity of e-WOM, sender expertise, and consumer satisfaction are critical factors influencing brand loyalty (Yolanda & Purwitasari 2020).

H3: e-WOM has a significant impact on brand loyalty.
H4: e-WOM significantly mediates the relationship between gamification and brand loyalty.

RESEARCH METHODOLOGY

Instrument Development

The tool used in this study was created by modifying a 5-point Likert scale, ranging from "strongly disagree" to "strongly agree," based on previous research. The scale for assessing gamification was derived from the work of (Hsu & Chen, 2018). Consumer loyalty was measured using the framework from (Chaudhuri & Holbrook, 2001) and the electronic word of mouth component was adopted from the research conducted by Goyette et al. (Goyette et al., 2010)

Sampling and Data Collection

Data was gathered through both digital and face-to-face methods. Links to online surveys were shared across multiple social media channels, such as WhatsApp, Instagram, email, and Facebook. Participants had the choice to fill out the survey either electronically or on paper during field visits. The study utilized convenience sampling and a cross-sectional research design. The target group included individuals who frequently use online e-commerce platforms and are acquainted with mini-games like quizzes, spin-wheels, and task completion. The questionnaire was divided into two parts: Part A gathered demographic details (Table 1), while Part B focused on the study's proposed hypothesis. Out of the 400 questionnaires distributed, 299 were returned, and 287 were found suitable for analysis after screening. The survey achieved a response rate of 71.75%.

DATA ANALYSIS

Respondent's Demographic Profile

The demographic characteristics of the respondents are presented in Table 1. The sample comprised 52.26% male and 47.74% female participants. Regarding marital status, 35.19% were married, 64.11% were single, and 0.70% were divorced. In terms of educational qualifications, 56.10% held undergraduate degrees, 33.80% held postgraduate degrees, and 10.10% completed other courses.

Table 1. Demographic profile of respondents

Particular	Categories	Frequency	Proportion
Sex	Male Female	150 137	52.26 47.74
Marital	Married Single Divorced Widow	101 184 2 0	35.19 64.11 0.70 000
Education	Graduate Master PHD Other	161 97 000 29	56.10 33.80 000 10.10
Are you familiar with gamified shopping apps (e.g. loyalty points, badges, rewards)?	No 12 Yes 287 Grand Total 299		

Data Analysis Procedure

The research utilized SmartPLS4 to test the proposed hypotheses. The selection of PLS SEM for data analysis was primarily due to its appropriateness for managing small sample sizes (Chin et al., 2003) The analysis adhered to a two-stage approach, assessing both the measurement and structural models.

Measurement Model Evaluation

To assess the measurement model, the study examined internal consistency, convergent validity, and discriminant validity. Table 2 displays the means, standard deviations, and loadings for all constructs involved in the research. Convergent validity refers to "the extent to which different measures reflect the same conceptual construct" (Dinev & Hart, 2004) As shown in Table 2, all three constructs met the required criteria, with loadings above 0.7, composite reliability exceeding 0.7, and average variance extracted (AVE) greater than 0.5 (Hair et al., 2017) Additionally, Cronbach's Alpha values, which measure internal consistency, were above 0.7(Fornell & Larcker, 1981) thereby confirming the constructs' convergent validity. Discriminant validity was evaluated using the Fornell-Larcker criterion, cross-loading, and the Heterotrait-Monotrait ratio. Discriminant validity is defined as "the extent to which a measure is adequately distinguishable from related constructs within the nomological net" (Dinev & Hart, 2004). According to Table 4, the Fornell-Larcker criterion demonstrated that the square roots of the AVE for the constructs—BL (0.730), GM (0.779), and e-WOM (0.641)—were higher than the correlation values between each construct and others, thus confirming discriminant validity as per the Fornell-Larcker criterion.

Table 2. Mean, SD and loadings of constructs

Construct	Item Code	Mean	SD	Loading
Gamification	GM1	3.797	0.913	0.888
	GM2	3.881	0.904	0.91
	GM3	3.801	0.953	0.833
	GM4	3.85	0.891	0.896
E-WOM	e-WOM1	4.129	0.877	0.784
	e-WOM2	3.619	1.054	0.766
	e-WOM3	3.801	0.931	0.82
	e-WOM4	3.951	1.009	0.823
	e-WOM5	3.668	0.938	0.808
Brand loyalty	BL1	3.451	0.94	0.721
	BL2	3.605	0.921	0.877
	BL3	3.853	0.935	0.881
	BL4	3.731	0.954	0.887
	BL5	3.741	0.970	0.892

Table 3. Cronbach's Alpha, composite reliability and average variance

Construct	Cronbach's Alpha	composite reliability	average variance extracted
Gamification	0.905	0.934	0.779
E-WOM	0.862	0.899	0.641
Brand loyalty	0.905	0.934	0.730

Table 4. Discriminant validity–Fornell-Larcker criterion

	BL	GM	e-WOM
BL	**0.712**		
GM	0.558	**0.736**	
e-WOM	-0.031	-0.251	**0.869**

Table 5 displays the cross-loading criterion, showing that the loadings for each construct surpassed their respective cross-loadings with other constructs in the columns. This result verifies the establishment of discriminant validity according to the cross-loading criterion. Table 6 shows the Heterotrait-Monotrait (HTMT) ratio for the constructs, and since all constructs had an HTMT value below 0.85 (Henseler et al., 2015), the discriminant validity of the measurement model was confirmed.

Table 5. Discriminant validity–loading and cross-loading criterion

	BL	GM	e-WOM
BL1	**0.721**	0.557	0.585
BL2	**0.877**	0.699	0.554
BL3	**0.881**	0.694	0.600
BL4	**0.887**	0.710	0.545
BL5	**0.892**	0.709	0.550
GM1	0.694	**0.888**	0.554
GM2	0.730	**0.910**	0.549
GM3	0.676	**0.833**	0.468
GM4	0.692	**0.896**	0.545
e-WOM1	0.507	0.508	**0.784**
e-WOM2	0.326	0.301	**0.766**
e-WOM3	0.460	0.425	**0.820**
e-WOM4	0.602	0.504	**0.823**
e-WOM5	0.647	0.575	**0.808**

Table 6. Discriminant validity–Heterotrait-Monotrait criterion (HTMT)

	BL	GM	e-WOM
BL	0.854		
GM	0.792	0.882	
e-WOM	0.662	0.600	0.801

Structural Model Evaluation

Before assessing the structural model, it is crucial to examine multicollinearity to ensure the validity of the results. The Variance Inflation Factor (VIF) values ranged from 1.651 to 3.952, all below the threshold of 5, indicating no multicollinearity issues within the model (Hair et al., 2014). Subsequently, the structural model was evaluated using the coefficient of determination (R2) and predictive relevance (Q2). Table 7 reports the R2 value for e-WOM as 0.361, suggesting that gamification accounts for 36.1% of the variance in e-WOM. Similarly, the R2 value for brand loyalty is 0.681, indicating that e-WOM explains 68.1% of its variance. Thus, the coefficient of determination is considered acceptable for this study. According to Chin (1998), R2 values should exceed 0 or 0.1 to be deemed acceptable. Additionally, the model's predictive validity (Q2) was assessed using the blindfolding method. Since the Q2 values were above zero, Hair et al. (2017) concluded that the model is a good predictor. As shown in Table 8, the PLS-SEM data indicates that gamification significantly positively influences brand loyalty (β= 0.792, t= 29.614, p= 0.000), supporting H1. Furthermore, gamification has a significant positive effect on e-WOM (β= 0.600, t= 13.482, p= 0.000), supporting H2. Moreover, e-WOM positively and significantly impacts brand loyalty (β= 0.292, t= 6.964, p= 0.000), thus supporting H3.

Table 7. Structural model assessment

Construct	R^2	Adj. R2	Q2
BL	0.681	0.679	0.624
e-WOM	0.361	0.358	0.355

Table 8. Results of Hypothesis Testing

	Original sample	Standard deviation	T statistics	P Value	Decision
GM -> BL	0.792	0.027	29.614	0.000	Supported
GM -> e-WOM	0.600	0.045	13.482	0.000	Supported
e-WOM -> BL	0.292	0.042	6.964	0.000	Supported
GM -> e-WOM -> BL	0.175	0.027	6.403	0.000	Supported

Mediating Analysis

The proposed conceptual model posited individual mediating relationships, which were evaluated using a bootstrapping method applied to 5,000 sub-samples. As presented in Table 8, the mediation hypothesis (H4) was assessed among Gamification, electronic word-of-mouth (e-WOM), and brand loyalty. Upon the introduction of the mediator, the specific indirect effect was found to be significant (β= 0.175, t=6.403, p=0.000), indicating partial mediation (Hair et al., 2017). The statistical analysis corroborated that the mediation effect of e-WOM between Gamification and Brand loyalty, as hypothesized in H4, was statistically significant.

CONCLUSION

The purpose of this study was to investigate how gamification affects brand loyalty and electronic word-of-mouth (e-WOM), as well as how e-WOM mediates the relationship between gamification and brand loyalty. Knowing how interactive and game-like aspects affect consumer behaviour has become essential in the increasingly digital marketing landscape. This study adds to the expanding body of knowledge by empirically confirming that gamification not only improves user engagement but also acts as a tactical tool to generate e-WOM and cultivate enduring brand loyalty.

Firstly, the results confirm that brand loyalty is positively impacted by gamification (H1). This supports the idea that gamified experiences increase brand connection and user involvement, which leads to long term loyalty (Hwang & Choi, 2020). Sigala, (2015) revealed that TripAdvisor's fun ware system greatly increased customer involvement during trip planning, which had a good impact on satisfaction and repeat business. Similarly, Abou-Shouk & Soliman (2021), showed that the intention to apply gamification in the tourism industry increases customer engagement and brand loyalty. Additionally, the value components of gamification—such as achievement, social connection, and entertainment—promote brand love, which in turn fosters brand loyalty (Torres et al., 2022).

Secondly, gamification has a considerable impact on e-WOM, as the research confirms (H2). This implies that gamified experiences motivate consumers to post about their satisfying brand experiences on the internet. According to previous research, gamification can increase user satisfaction and engagement, which encourages users to participate in e-WOM activities (Hamari, 2013). Leaderboards, point systems, and virtual incentives, frequently generate a feeling of accomplishment that users wish to share on social media or in reviews, so naturally increasing e-WOM. Bitrián et al., (2021), discovered that gamified elements in mobile apps greatly increase user engagement and motivate users to share their experiences online. Similarly, Meenakshy et al., (2020), highlighted how intrinsic motivators, especially enjoyment, encourage users to create electronic word-of-mouth in the tourism industry. According to their research, gamification, particularly when it is intended to provide a fun and fulfilling experience, motivates users to interact with digital platforms more thoroughly and refer them to others.

Thirdly, this study confirms that e-WOM significantly influences brand loyalty (H3), aligning with previous research across industries. Valmohammadi et al., (2024) found that e-WOM positively impacts e-brand loyalty, especially when moderated by brand love. In the cosmetics sector, (Fatmawati & Amanati, 2023) reported that e-WOM, driven by positive brand experiences, directly enhances customer loyalty. Similarly, (Ghosh et al., 2023.) showed that e-WOM fosters trust and engagement, which are key to building loyalty in luxury branding. In online retail, Ilhamalimy &

Ali, (2021) demonstrated that e-WOM builds trust, which then influences purchase intent an antecedent to loyalty. These findings reinforce the role of e-WOM as a key mechanism in cultivating lasting brand relationships.

Further, the study demonstrates that the relationship between gamification and brand loyalty is mediated by e-WOM. This was corroborated by Hutter et al., (2013), who discovered that user interactions on MINI's Facebook page increased brand awareness and purchase intention through electronic word-of-mouth (e-WOM), demonstrating how social engagement converts into loyalty. This demonstrates that e-WOM is a crucial mechanism that connects gamified experiences to sustained brand loyalty.

This study offers empirical proof that gamification is an effective strategic tool for boosting brand loyalty and electronic word-of-mouth (e-WOM). The findings demonstrate that gamification has a direct impact on both brand loyalty and e-WOM, but that e-WOM also acts as a mediator, enhancing the relationship between gamified experiences and enduring customer loyalty. Previous research from a variety of industries supports these findings, highlighting the significance of creating gamified experiences that are rewarding, socially connected, and engaging. Using gamification can increase consumer engagement, encourage peer-driven advocacy, and ultimately leads to more loyal customers as firms compete in more digital and interactive marketplaces

Limitations

The findings of the study provide valuable insights but there are few limitations that should be acknowledged. Firstly, the study employed a cross-sectional design which limits the ability to establish causality. So, in future longitudinal studies can be carried out to study changes in consumers' behaviour overtime. Secondly, questionnaires were used for data collection which can provide inaccurate answers due to social desirability. To address this, future research could incorporate alternative methods such as experiments or in-depth interviews to gain richer and more reliable data. Thirdly, the study focussed on the effect of gamification as a whole without examining their individual contributions i.e. points, badges, leaderboards. So, incorporating these elements can provide more insights in future research.

REFERENCES

Abou-Shouk, M., & Soliman, M. (2021). The impact of gamification adoption intention on brand awareness and loyalty in tourism: The mediating effect of customer engagement. *Journal of Destination Marketing & Management, 20*, 100559. DOI: 10.1016/j.jdmm.2021.100559

Aghdaie, S. F. A., Ansari, A., & Telgerdi, J. (2022). Analysing the impact of gamification dynamics and e-WOM on impulsive buying. *International Journal of Procurement Management, 15*(1), 40–61. DOI: 10.1504/IJPM.2022.119840

Aksoy, L., Keiningham, T. L., Buoye, A., Lariviere, B., Williams, L., & Wilson, I. (2015). Does loyalty span domains? Examining the relationship between consumer loyalty, other loyalties and happiness. *Journal of Business Research, 68*(12), 2464–2476. DOI: 10.1016/j.jbusres.2015.06.033

Al-Zyoud, M. F. (2021). The impact of gamification on consumer loyalty, electronic word-of mouth sharing and purchase behavior. *Journal of Public Affairs, 21*(3), e2263. DOI: 10.1002/pa.2263

Al-Zyoud, M. F. (2021). The impact of gamification on consumer loyalty, electronic word-of mouth sharing and purchase behavior. *Journal of Public Affairs, 21*(3), e2263. DOI: 10.1002/pa.2263

Al-Zyoud, M. F. (2021). The impact of gamification on consumer loyalty, electronic word-of mouth sharing and purchase behavior. *Journal of Public Affairs, 21*(3), e2263. DOI: 10.1002/pa.2263

Bitrián, P., Buil, I., & Catalán, S. (2021). Enhancing user engagement: The role of gamification in mobile apps. *Journal of Business Research, 132*, 170–185. DOI: 10.1016/j.jbusres.2021.04.028

Bitrián, P., Buil, I., & Catalán, S. (2021). Enhancing user engagement: The role of gamification in mobile apps. *Journal of Business Research, 132*, 170–185. DOI: 10.1016/j.jbusres.2021.04.028

Bunchball, I. (2010). Gamification 101: An introduction to the use of game dynamics to influence behavior. *White paper, 9*, 1-18.

Chaudhuri, A., & Holbrook, M. B. (2001). The Role of Brand Loyalty / 81 The Chain of Effects from Brand Trust and Brand Affect to Brand Performance: The Role of Brand Loyalty. In *Journal of Marketing* (Vol. 65).

Chien, W. J., & Wu, Y. L. (2015). The Effect of Mobile Gamification on Brand Loyalty.

Chin, W. W., Marcolin, B. L., & Newsted, P. R. (2003). A Partial Least Squares Latent Variable Modeling Approach for Measuring Interaction Effects: Results from a Monte Carlo Simulation Study and an Electronic-Mail Emotion/Adoption Study. *Information Systems Research*, *14*(2), 189–217. Advance online publication. DOI: 10.1287/isre.14.2.189.16018

Deterding, S., Dixon, D., Khaled, R., & Nacke, L. (2011, September). From game design elements to gamefulness: defining" gamification". In *Proceedings of the 15th international academic MindTrek conference: Envisioning future media environments* (pp. 9-15). DOI: 10.1145/2181037.2181040

Deterding, S., Sicart, M., Nacke, L., O'hara, K., & Dixon, D. (2011). Gamification. using game-design elements in non-gaming contexts. In *CHI'11 extended abstracts on human factors in computing systems* (pp. 2425-2428).

Dinev, T., & Hart, P. (2004). Internet privacy concerns and their antecedents - measurement validity and a regression model. *Behaviour & Information Technology*, *23*(6), 413–422. Advance online publication. DOI: 10.1080/01449290410001715723

Doğan-Südaş, H., Kara, A., & Karaca, E. (2023). Effects of gamified mobile apps on purchase intentions and word-of-mouth engagement: Implications for sustainability behavior. *Sustainability (Basel)*, *15*(13), 10506. DOI: 10.3390/su151310506

Dwivedi, Y. K., Hughes, L., Ismagilova, E., Aarts, G., Coombs, C., Crick, T., Duan, Y., Dwivedi, R., Edwards, J., Eirug, A., Galanos, V., Ilavarasan, P. V., Janssen, M., Jones, P., Kar, A. K., Kizgin, H., Kronemann, B., Lal, B., Lucini, B., & Williams, M. D. (2021). Artificial Intelligence (AI): Multidisciplinary perspectives on emerging challenges, opportunities, and agenda for research, practice and policy. *International Journal of Information Management*, *57*, 101994. DOI: 10.1016/j.ijinfomgt.2019.08.002

Fatmawati, I., & Amanati, A. K. (2023). How does consumer experience with cosmetics products create EWOM, satisfaction, and loyalty? *Jurnal Manajemen Bisnis*, *14*(1), 53–71. DOI: 10.18196/mb.v14i1.14525

Fornell, C., & Larcker, D. F. (1981). Evaluating Structural Equation Models with Unobservable Variables and Measurement Error. *JMR, Journal of Marketing Research*, *18*(1), 39–50. Advance online publication. DOI: 10.1177/002224378101800104

Goyette, I., Ricard, L., Bergeron, J., & Marticotte, F. (2010). E-WOM scale: Word-of-mouth measurement scale for e-services context. *Canadian Journal of Administrative Sciences*, *27*(1), 5–23. DOI: 10.1002/cjas.129

Hair, J. F., Hult, G. T. M., Ringle, C. M., Sarstedt, M., & Thiele, K. O. (2017). Mirror, mirror on the wall: A comparative evaluation of composite-based structural equation modeling methods. *Journal of the Academy of Marketing Science*, *45*(5), 616–632. Advance online publication. DOI: 10.1007/s11747-017-0517-x

Hajarian, M., & Hemmati, S. (2020, September). A gamified word of mouth recommendation system for increasing customer purchase. In *2020 4th International Conference on Smart City, Internet of Things and Applications (SCIOT)* (pp. 7-11). IEEE. DOI: 10.1109/SCIOT50840.2020.9250209

Hamari, J. (2013). Transforming homo economicus into homo ludens: A field experiment on gamification in a utilitarian peer-to-peer trading service. *Electronic Commerce Research and Applications*, *12*(4), 236–245. DOI: 10.1016/j.elerap.2013.01.004

Hamari, J., & Koivisto, J. (2013, June). Social Motivations To Use Gamification: An Empirical Study Of Gamifying Exercise. In *ECIS* (Vol. 105, No. 5, pp. 18-19).

Hassan, L., & Hamari, J. (2020). Gameful civic engagement: A review of the literature on gamification of e-participation. *Government Information Quarterly*, *37*(3), 101461. DOI: 10.1016/j.giq.2020.101461

Hassan Butt, A., Ahmad, H., Muzaffar, A., Irshad, W., Usman Mumtaz, M., & Zubair Ahmad Khan, T. (2024). WeChat Gamification: Mobile Payment Impact on word of mouth and customer loyalty. *Spanish Journal of Marketing - ESIC*.

Henseler, J., Ringle, C. M., & Sarstedt, M. (2015). A new criterion for assessing discriminant validity in variance-based structural equation modeling. *Journal of the Academy of Marketing Science*, *43*(1), 115–135. Advance online publication. DOI: 10.1007/s11747-014-0403-8

Hofacker, C. F., De Ruyter, K., Lurie, N. H., Manchanda, P., & Donaldson, J. (2016). Gamification and mobile marketing effectiveness. *Journal of Interactive Marketing*, *34*(1), 25–36. DOI: 10.1016/j.intmar.2016.03.001

Hsu, C. L., & Chen, M. C. (2018). How gamification marketing activities motivate desirable consumer behaviors: Focusing on the role of brand love. *Computers in Human Behavior*, *88*, 121–133. DOI: 10.1016/j.chb.2018.06.037

Hsu, C. L., & Chen, M. C. (2018). How gamification marketing activities motivate desirable consumer behaviors: Focusing on the role of brand love. *Computers in Human Behavior*, *88*, 121–133. DOI: 10.1016/j.chb.2018.06.037

Hutter, K., Hautz, J., Dennhardt, S., & Füller, J. (2013). The impact of user interactions in social media on brand awareness and purchase intention: The case of MINI on Facebook. *Journal of Product and Brand Management, 22*(5/6), 342–351. DOI: 10.1108/JPBM-05-2013-0299

Hwang, J., & Choi, L. (2020). Having fun while receiving rewards?: Exploration of gamification in loyalty programs for consumer loyalty. *Journal of Business Research, 106*, 365–376. DOI: 10.1016/j.jbusres.2019.01.031
Hwang, J., & Choi, L. (2020). Having fun while receiving rewards?: Exploration of gamification in loyalty programs for consumer loyalty. *Journal of Business Research, 106*, 365–376. DOI: 10.1016/j.jbusres.2019.01.031
Ilhamalimy, R. R., & Ali, H. (2021). Model perceived risk and trust: e-WOM and purchase intention (the role OF trust mediating IN online shopping IN shopee Indonesia). *Dinasti International Journal of Digital Business Management, 2*(2), 204–221. DOI: 10.31933/dijdbm.v2i2.651

Jami Pour, M., Rafiei, K., Khani, M., & Sabrirazm, A. (2021). Gamification and customer experience: The mediating role of brand engagement in online grocery retailing. *Nankai Business Review International, 12*(3), 340–357. DOI: 10.1108/NBRI-07-2020-0041

Koivisto, J., & Hamari, J. (2019). The rise of motivational information systems: A review of gamification research. *International Journal of Information Management, 45*, 191–210. DOI: 10.1016/j.ijinfomgt.2018.10.013

Leclercq, T., Poncin, I., & Hammedi, W. (2017). The engagement process during value co-creation: Gamification in new product-development platforms. *International Journal of Electronic Commerce, 21*(4), 454–488. DOI: 10.1080/10864415.2016.1355638

Lee, E., Hammer, B., Kim, J. K., Page, Z., Emrick, T., & Hayward, R. C. (2011). Hierarchical Helical Assembly of Conjugated Poly (3-hexylthiophene)-block-poly (3-triethylene glycol thiophene) Diblock Copolymers. *Journal of the American Chemical Society, 133*(27), 10390–10393. DOI: 10.1021/ja2038547 PMID: 21627317

Lem, A. J., Liddicoat, C., Bissett, A., Cando-Dumancela, C., Gardner, M. G., Peddle, S. D., Watson, C. D., & Breed, M. F. (2022). Does revegetation cause soil microbiota recovery? Evidence from revisiting a revegetation chronosequence 6 years after initial sampling. *Restoration Ecology, 30*(8), e13635. DOI: 10.1111/rec.13635

Mattke, J., & Maier, C. (2021). Gamification: Explaining brand loyalty in mobile applications. *AIS Transactions on Human-Computer Interaction, 13*(1), 62–81. DOI: 10.17705/1thci.00142

Meenakshy, M., Saxena, R., & Srivastava, M. (2020). Gamification: Increasing electronic word of mouth in tourism. *SCMS Journal of Indian Management*, *17*(4), 51–62.

Nieto-Escamez, F. A., & Roldán-Tapia, M. D. (2021). Gamification as online teaching strategy during COVID-19: A mini-review. *Frontiers in Psychology*, *12*, 648552. DOI: 10.3389/fpsyg.2021.648552 PMID: 34093334

Pandey, S., Kumar, A., & Sharma, A. (2024). Sustainable solar drying: Recent advances in materials, innovative designs, mathematical modeling, and energy storage solutions. *Energy*, *308*, 132725. DOI: 10.1016/j.energy.2024.132725

Pavlus, J. (2010). The game of life.(Cover story). *Scientific American*, *303*(6), 43–44. DOI: 10.1038/scientificamerican1210-43

Punwatkar, S., & Verghese, M. (2025). Investigating the impact of gamification on customer engagement, brand loyalty and purchase intent in marketing. *Journal of Applied Research and Technology*, *23*(1), 94–102. DOI: 10.22201/icat.24486736e.2025.23.1.2592

Sigala, M. (2015). Gamification for crowdsourcing marketing practices: Applications and benefits in tourism. *Advances in crowdsourcing*, 129-145.

Sigala, M. (2015). The application and impact of gamification funware on trip planning and experiences: The case of TripAdvisor's funware. *Electronic Markets*, *25*(3), 189–209. DOI: 10.1007/s12525-014-0179-1

Smiderle, R., Rigo, S. J., Marques, L. B., Peçanha de Miranda Coelho, J. A., & Jaques, P. A. (2020). The impact of gamification on students' learning, engagement and behavior based on their personality traits. *Smart Learning Environments*, *7*(1), 3. DOI: 10.1186/s40561-019-0098-x

Torres, P., Augusto, M., & Neves, C. (2022). Value dimensions of gamification and their influence on brand loyalty and word-of-mouth: Relationships and combinations with satisfaction and brand love. *Psychology and Marketing*, *39*(1), 59–75.

Valmohammadi, C., Asayesh, F., Mehdikhani, R., & Taraz, R. (2025). Influencer marketing, ewom, e-brand experience, and retail e-brand loyalty: Moderating influence of e-brand love. *Journal of Relationship Marketing*, *24*(1), 66–92. DOI: 10.1080/15332667.2024.2405292

Wang, L., Gunasti, K., Shankar, R., Pancras, J., & Gopal, R. (2018). (Forthcoming). Impact of gamification on perceptions of word-of-mouth contributors and actions of word-of-mouth consumers. *Wang, L., Gunasti K., Shankar, R., Pancras, J. Gopal, R., Impact of Gamification on Perceptions of Word-of-Mouth Contributors and Actions of Word-of-Mouth Consumers, MISQ. Management Information Systems Quarterly.*

Wang, L., Gunasti, K., Shankar, R., Pancras, J., & Gopal, R. (2018). (Forthcoming). Impact of gamification on perceptions of word-of-mouth contributors and actions of word-of-mouth consumers. *Wang, L., Gunasti K., Shankar, R., Pancras, J. Gopal, R., Impact of Gamification on Perceptions of Word-of-Mouth Contributors and Actions of Word-of-Mouth Consumers, MISQ. Management Information Systems Quarterly.*

Wang, T., Fan, L., Zheng, X., Wang, W., Liang, J., An, K., Ju, M., & Lei, J. (2021). The impact of gamification-induced users' feelings on the continued use of mHealth apps: A structural equation model with the self-determination theory approach. *Journal of Medical Internet Research, 23*(8), e24546. DOI: 10.2196/24546 PMID: 34387550

Xi, N., & Hamari, J. (2020). Does gamification affect brand engagement and equity? A study in online brand communities. *Journal of Business Research, 109*, 449–460. DOI: 10.1016/j.jbusres.2019.11.058

Yang, C., Yang, P., & Feng, Y. (2022). Effect of achievement-related gamification on brand attachment. *Industrial Management & Data Systems, 122*(1), 251–271. DOI: 10.1108/IMDS-02-2021-0088

Yang, Y., Asaad, Y., & Dwivedi, Y. (2017). Examining the impact of gamification on intention of engagement and brand attitude in the marketing context. *Computers in Human Behavior, 73*, 459–469. DOI: 10.1016/j.chb.2017.03.066

Yolanda, F. (2020). Pengaruh Electronic Word Of Mouth Di Media Sosial Instagram Terhadap Brand Loyalty OVO (Survei Terhadap Pengguna OVO Pada Generasi Z) (Doctoral dissertation, Universitas Mercu Buana Jakarta).

Zaib Abbasi, A., Hussain, K., Kaleem, T., Rasoolimanesh, S. M., Rasul, T., Ting, D. H., & Rather, R. A. (2023). Tourism promotion through vlog advertising and customer engagement behaviours of generation Z. *Current Issues in Tourism, 26*(22), 3651–3670. DOI: 10.1080/13683500.2022.2144156

Chapter 5
Gamification Strategies for Enhancing Customer Engagement and Loyalty

Ruchi Khandelwal
https://orcid.org/0000-0002-5826-4573
Amity School of Business, Amity University, India

Deepa Kapoor
https://orcid.org/0000-0002-7755-1631
Amity School of Business, Amity University, India

ABSTRACT

With the growing impact of mobile and internet on business and commerce, companies explored new ways to gain consumer access and attention. Research suggests that the gamification market has been consistently growing and gamification is widely used in contemporary marketing due to its ability to engage and motivate individuals. With the use of game elements, companies and marketers involved and engaged customers in an organized form of play, governed by rules and structures, that provided enjoyment and accomplishment with measurable outcomes. The avenues of enhancing customer engagement through use of gamification to improve customer relations is encouraging, particularly considering the current advancements in areas like augmented reality and virtual reality, which are expected to greatly enhance the potential for gamified experiences. In the light of above scenario, the chapter focuses on the use of gamification strategies for augmenting customer engagement and loyalty by discussing the success stories of few industry players like Duolingo, Starbucks and Snapchat.

DOI: 10.4018/979-8-3693-8886-0.ch005

INTRODUCTION

Technological advancements have had a lasting impact on how companies do business and attract customers. As businesses turn to online platforms, there is an increased need to attract, engage and retain customers. With the advent of smartphones, companies gained easy access to stay connected with their customers and involve them in the value co-creation processes (Kennedy & Guzmán, 2016). As brands continue to explore novel methods to connect with customers, from offline to online to omnichannel presence, there is a noteworthy improvement in customer engagement and customer experiences. (Eigenraam et al., 2018; Kumar et al., 2019). Research suggests that since the beginning of this century, the gamification market has been consistently growing and is poised to reach USD 38.42 million by 2026 (Mordor Intelligence, 2020). Gamification is a key strategy in contemporary marketing due to its ability to engage and motivate individuals. Gamification strategies are used by companies and marketers to involve and engage customers in an organized form of play, governed by rules and structures, that not only provide enjoyment but also a sense of accomplishment with measurable outcomes. (Seaborn & Fels, 2015). This customer engagement is beneficial to companies in more than one ways. First, gamification adds value by motivating customers to adopt behaviours linked to gamified applications, and their interactions generate data that companies can leverage to gain better insights into their customers (Eisingerich et al., 2019). Additionally, when customers share their game outcomes with friends, it amplifies the impact of social network influence also (Kumar & Pansari, 2016). The chapter discusses the elements of gamification and its importance in influencing customers through enhanced engagement and brand loyalty to drive purchase intentions. Through case analysis of strategies employed by marketers such as Starbucks, Duolingo, and Snapchat, the potential of gamification as a potent tool that can impact the entire customer journey in today's marketing landscape is highlighted.

BENEFITS OF GAMIFICATION

The strategy of gamification has emerged as one of the most effective tools for influencing individuals' behaviour. These techniques offer a multitude of advantages. Below are some of the primary benefits and justifications for why businesses may consider incorporating gamification into their marketing efforts:

- **Build Brand Awareness**

Games serve as an effective marketing instrument due to their enjoyable nature and the fact that they are frequently viewed as non-intrusive methods of promotion. They help in establishing a favourable image of your company and have the potential to influence consumers' future purchasing decisions. Implementing gamification in marketing also enhances social shareability. Marketing through gamification provides entertainment to customers while simultaneously informing them about company products or services. Certain marketing games, such as quizzes or puzzles, serve educational purposes as well (Topuzova, 2025).

Brands are constantly seeking ways to engage their existing audience, reach new audiences, or re-engage with past audiences. In a crowded digital landscape, standing out and creating a memorable brand is essential. Incorporating gamification in marketing enables the creation of interactive experiences that leave a lasting impression on consumers. Through memorable games and challenges, the brand's identity becomes intertwined with positive emotions and enjoyable moments.

- **Increase Customer Engagement**

Interactive campaigns are transforming marketing by engaging customers through immersive experiences rather than traditional one-way communication. At the core of this approach is the development of an interactive narrative or activity that encourages customer participation. Gamification in campaigns often involve storytelling, puzzles, quizzes, or virtual simulations, inviting customers to take an active role (Segmentify, 2024).

This participatory model shifts the customer from a passive recipient of information to an active participant in the brand's story. Interactive experiences fulfill consumers' desire for stimulation and challenge, aspects that traditional marketing often lacks. Gamification makes brand interactions more dynamic and enjoyable, encouraging consumers to spend more time engaging with content.

- **Better Conversion Rates**

The duration of a visitor's stay on a website holds significant importance in digital marketing, as it is closely linked to the likelihood of conversion. When users dedicate more time to a website, they generally engage more thoroughly with the content, leading to a deeper understanding and appreciation of the brand's offerings. Longer visits increase the chances of users encountering persuasive calls-to-action, such as special offers or newsletter sign-ups, which can further motivate them towards a conversion. The primary advantage of gamification is the boost in user participation, leading to improved conversion rates in digital marketing as a result of integrating gamified elements.

Brands that incorporate gamified elements into their strategies often observe a 7X higher conversion rate, directly attributed to the added entertainment and reward value (Baldwin & Baldwin, 2024). For example, offering a 'spin-to-win' feature where users can earn discounts or prizes can significantly boost participation and create a sense of immediate gratification.

- **Non-Intrusive Data Collection**

In the realm of digital marketing, gamification emerges as an essential instrument for gathering zero-party data, which refers to the information that consumers voluntarily share in return for an enjoyable experience. This enables brands to customize their upcoming marketing strategies while building trust by considering user privacy. Over the past few years, marketing has shifted from being product-centric to a more consumer-centric approach. Games within marketing are based on permission, as customers willingly opt-in and share their contact details to participate or claim prizes.

The utilization of gamification in marketing also facilitates the collection of valuable customer data, allowing marketers to gain insights into consumer behaviour through the monitoring of analytics. The data can then be utilized to track user behaviour, motivations, and demographics. While data is undeniably a highly asset for businesses, concerns regarding data privacy have led to a shift towards more transparent and consensual data collection methods. (Simms, 2019). The incorporation of gamification in marketing presents a subtle and respectful approach to gathering valuable insights through zero-party data collection. Players willingly provide information as they engage with games, surveys, or interactive quizzes, thereby fostering trust and enabling brands to effectively personalize their marketing efforts while honouring user preferences and privacy.

- **Enhances Brand Loyalty**

Transforming leads into customers is always beneficial; however, to achieve optimal results, fostering their loyalty is essential. Strategies in marketing aim to enhance brand loyalty, with gamification serving as a powerful method for achieving this goal.

Effective gamification requires the incorporation of captivating gaming components across different domains, including education and business, to boost engagement and motivation, ultimately leading to greater brand loyalty. Gamified content serves to increase motivation and maintain customer engagement, which in turn fosters increased brand loyalty, while also portraying your company as one that values and appreciates customer loyalty. There are numerous ways to utilize gamification to enhance brand loyalty, such as implementing loyalty programs which often involve earning points or making a specific number of purchases in exchange for rewards, discounts, or other perks (Bullock, 2024). Badges and leaderboards also prove to be useful in this context. When customers feel their loyalty is valued, they are more likely to continue patronizing your company or participating in activities you organize. Gamified experiences provide a memorable means for consumers to interact and connect with the brand

GAMIFICATION AND ITS ELEMENTS

Gamification is understood as a system that applies game design elements to contexts beyond gaming to effect behavioural change among individuals (Hofacker et al., 2016). Gamification is the practice of creating systems, services, and activities to evoke experiences and motivations like those found in games, with the additional objective of influencing user behaviour (Huotari & Hamari, 2017). This approach often draws inspiration from game design by integrating game mechanics or similar elements into the intended environment. In general terms, gamification is characterized as the integration of game design elements into non-game activities to foster engagement among individuals (Deterding et al., 2011).

Over recent years, gamification has found applications in a variety of fields, including information systems, eLearning, marketing, and social sciences. It encompasses various design principles and systems aimed at influencing, engaging, and motivating individuals, groups, and communities to promote specific behaviours or achieve desired outcomes (Glover, 2013). Gamification involves incorporating the essence of games - fun, play, transparency, design, and challenge - into real-world objectives, rather than solely for entertainment purposes (Palmer et al., 2012). In an era where mobile devices, screens, and gaming consoles increasingly shape our daily experiences, it is evident that games serve not only as sources of entertainment but also as powerful tools for engagement.

The use of gamification is often aimed at enhancing customer satisfaction through the effective engagement and excitement of individuals, as well as the improvement of playfulness, mastery, and immersion experiences (Ryan et al., 2006). By incorporating gamified features into non-game contexts, gamification emphasizes the notions of games, fun interaction, and gaming design (Seaborn & Fels, 2015). Within business contexts, gamification refers to the design of products and services that facilitate game-like experiences, thereby creating value and eliciting more favourable responses from customers (Huotari & Hamari, 2017).

Gamification marketing is a strategic approach where businesses utilize game-based elements to enhance engagement on their marketing communication channels. It is characterized by the utilization of game design elements to augment the value of non-game products and services while simultaneously encouraging behaviours that create additional value for customers. Gamification involves integrating playful and competitive elements into marketing strategies, transforming customers into active participants in the narrative of a brand, and turning ordinary interactions into unforgettable experiences. Figure 1 presents the three key dimensions of the Gamification feature, as provided by researchers (Bitrián et al. (2020), Luarn et al. (2023), and Qian et al. (2022), Xi & Hamari (2019). The following are the features of Gamification:

1. **Immersion-related features** are primarily designed to engage the player in self-directed exploration, incorporating game mechanics such as avatars, narrative storytelling, personalisation, and role-playing elements.
2. **Achievement-related features** strive to enhance the players' feelings of success, utilizing mechanics such as badges, challenges, goals, leaderboards, and progression indicators.
3. **Social interaction-related features** are primarily designed to facilitate users' social engagement, incorporating game mechanics such as teams, groups, and competitions.

Figure 1. Gamification features

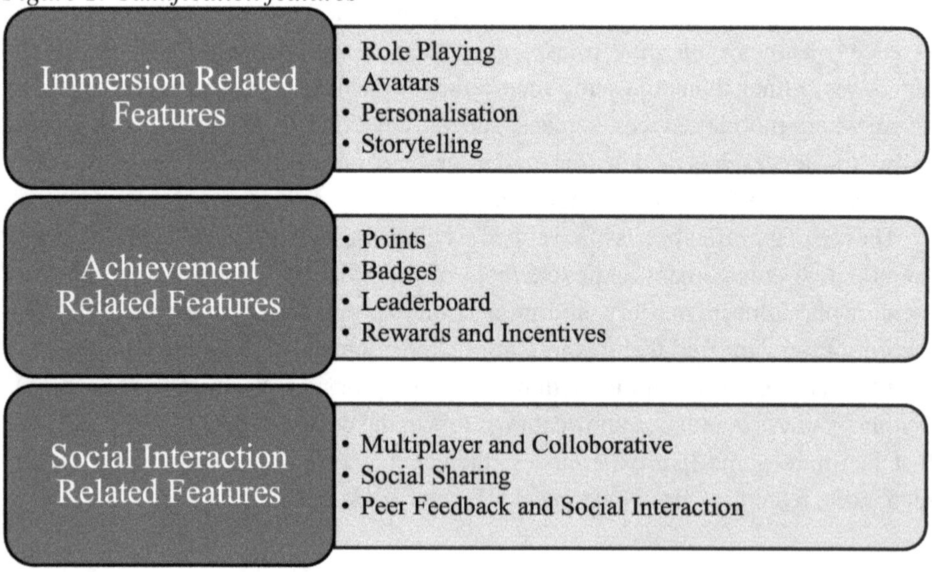

Immersion-Related Features

In the context of gamification, immersion signifies the integration of components such as avatars, role-playing dynamics, storytelling, and personalization to captivate players in self-guided explorative tasks (Xi & Hamari, 2019). These attributes promote a deeper cognitive engagement in self-directed thought. Avatars and personalization provide players with an enhanced sense of independence and a greater willingness to engage in the game.

Gamification employs narrative elements to establish an emotional bond with users. Through stories, characters, and settings, it provides a way to relate to and empathize with the learning journey. Immersive-related elements in gamification can be of the following forms:

- **Role-playing**. The integration of a storyline or narrative enhances the significance of tasks. The challenges and quests linked to role-playing foster a connection between the user and their character or narrative, introducing an emotional aspect to the gaming experience.
- **Avatars**. These allow users to craft a visual representation of themselves within the gamified environment. An avatar on a gamified platform grants users the opportunity to design a virtual version of themselves that others will recognize and associate with – it becomes their digital identity.
- **Personalisation** Users can customize their avatars, reflecting their personalities and preferences, which leads to a more tailored and engaging experience.. They facilitate personal expression and enrich the immersive experience, thereby boosting engagement, ownership, and investment in the activity.
- **Storytelling:** Avatars can be woven into narratives, allowing users to embody characters within a story, deepening immersion and engagement.

Achievement-Related Features

Achievement elements allow users to experience a sense of success and receive rewards while engaging in various tasks within games (Shen et al., 2020). When users can earn rewards or trophies through their involvement, they are likely to view their interactions with the gamified system as both valuable and significant (Högberg, Shams, & Wästlund, 2019). Features related to achievement are typically associated with a more cognitive approach, emphasizing goal-oriented engagement and behavior., Landers et al., 2017, Baek et al., 2015). The most widely recognized elements of achievement-related features in gamification are:

- **Points:** Points function as a feedback tool, offering users concrete metrics of their efforts. Users accumulate points by completing designated actions or reaching specific milestones. As noted by Lee & Hammer (2011), points effectively encourage desired behaviours by providing rewards for task completion.
- **Badges:** Badges function as digital representations of achievement. Deterding et al. (2011) suggest that badges provide users with a feeling of accomplishment and acknowledgment for attaining particular milestones. Although badges can boost intrinsic motivation, their effectiveness is heightened when users view them as indicators of personal development or mastery, rather than merely as incentives for task completion (Hamari et al., 2014). Badges are given for accomplishments or expertise in specific areas and these visual markers of progress motivate users to remain engaged with the system.
- **Leaderboards:** Leaderboards present the rankings of participants according to their performance and achievements. They foster a competitive atmosphere, motivating users to strive for a higher rank. Leaderboards provide a social comparison between users, creating competition and potentially encouraging performance improvement. However, they may also demotivate individuals who perceive themselves as low-ranking, potentially causing disengagement (Burke, 2014). Balancing competition with collaboration is important for maximizing engagement (Deci et al., 1999).
- **Rewards and incentives** -These serve as external motivators to promote desired behaviors, encompassing both virtual and real-world rewards, such as discounts, access to exclusive content, and prizes. By providing such incentives, gamification encourages users to engage actively, complete tasks, and enhance their overall level of participation.

Social Interaction Features

Social interaction-related features primarily facilitate user engagement (Jang et al., 2018) and encompass game mechanics such as teams, groups, and competitions (Hamari & Tuunanen, 2014; Koivisto & Hamari, 2019; Peng et al., 2012; Snodgrass et al., 2013; Yee et al., 2012). A fundamental aspect of gamification is its capacity to harness social engagement, motivating users to interact not only with the platform itself but also with fellow users. This interaction fosters connections, collaboration, and friendly competition among participants. The main elements of Social Interaction features are:

- **Multiplayer and Cooperative Elements:** The integration of multiplayer and cooperative features encourages collaboration, teamwork, and social connections. Cooperation within gamified environments boosts engagement by enabling users to unite in pursuit of shared objectives, thus fostering a sense of community (Koivisto & Hamari, 2019). Collaborative tasks enhance user satisfaction, as individuals feel a bond with others through common challenges, which can promote sustained engagement over time (Deterding et al., 2011).

- **Social Sharing:** Social sharing permits users to showcase their accomplishments, milestones, or brand-related content on platforms like Facebook, Instagram, or Twitter. This integration not only boosts engagement but also enhances brand visibility and social credibility. Research by Hamari et al. (2014) demonstrated that social sharing markedly boosts user engagement in gamified environments, particularly when individuals can showcase their progress to friends or peers. Users are more inclined to remain active in gamified systems when they can share their advancements with their social circles, resulting in heightened interaction and social affirmation. Nonetheless, studies also indicate that an overemphasis on social sharing may lead to superficial engagement or the pressure to uphold a specific social persona (Zichermann & Cunningham, 2011).
- **Peer Feedback:** Peer Feedback provides users with the opportunity to offer insights, commendations, or constructive criticism regarding the achievements of others. Harrington et al. (2015) observed that systems incorporating peer feedback and social recognition enhance user satisfaction, as individuals feel acknowledged and valued within the community.

GAMIFICATION AND CUSTOMER ENGAGEMENT

There is an increased use of gamification by companies all over the world including marketing giants like Samsung, Coca-Cola and Nike who are actively engaging customers and cultivating strong associations leading to better marketing outcomes (Burnett, 2019). Gamification binds together the fundamentals of drive (motive), competitive spirit and compensation inducing user engagement on one hand and fostering brand loyalty on another which impacts purchase intention (Punwatkar and Verghese, 2025).

Customer Engagement is described as encompassing several key factors: Customer Lifetime Value (which measures the total revenue a business expects from a customer throughout their relationship), Customer Referral Value (the financial benefit a business gains from customers acquired through referrals), Customer Influence Value (the potential a customer has to influence others' purchasing decisions and perceptions of the brand), and Customer Knowledge Value (the insights a company collects about its customers to better understand their needs, preferences, and behaviours, leading to improved products, services, and customer experiences) (Kumar et al., 2010). Research results indicate that Gamification has a positive influence on all aspects of customer engagement (Hermawan and Tjhin, 2023). Previous studies have explored the impact of gamification on customer engagement across a variety of focus areas, including sports activities (Hamari and Koivisto, 2015), social networks (Harwood and Garry, 2015), brands (Berger et al., 2017), healthcare services (Hammedi et al., 2017), and online communities (Leclercq et al., 2017).

The power of gamification lies in its ability to engage essential human desires such as achievement, progress, and social connection. Offering users clear objectives, feedback, and tangible rewards, shifts them from being passive observers to active participants, fostering greater engagement and investment in the brand (Punwatkar and Verghese, 2025). For instance, a fitness app may incorporate gamified elements like progress tracking, virtual challenges, and social sharing to encourage users to exercise consistently and meet their fitness goals. In this case, the sense of accomplishment from completing challenges or earning achievements acts as a strong motivator, helping maintain user engagement over the long term. Gamification seeks to create an immersive, game-like experience, aiming to motivate and guide user behaviour while increasing engagement with play-based tasks, through game-inspired techniques such as scoreboards, points, and instant personalized feedback. These elements help users feel a greater sense of ownership, flow, and purpose when interacting with these tasks. In consumer-focused websites and mobile apps, businesses leverage gamification to encourage the use of eCommerce platforms, ultimately boosting customer loyalty, brand awareness, and effective marketing engagement. In addition, gamification utilizes principles of behavioural psychology to shape consumer behaviour and decision-making. Rewards, both tangible (e.g., discounts, freebies) and intangible (e.g., badges, status), trigger dopamine release in the brain, reinforcing desired behaviours and creating positive connections with the brand. Moreover, the competitive aspect introduced through leaderboards or peer comparisons can tap into users' competitive nature, motivating them to surpass others and gain recognition within the community.

Consumer engagement can be harnessed through motivation, intrinsic or extrinsic that directs consumers to invest their resources towards the company or the brand. People naturally tend to participate in activities they find enjoyable and fun, regardless of rewards. Intrinsic motivations have a lasting impact on behaviour, while extrinsic motivations are driven by the desire for external rewards. Behaviours influenced by extrinsic motivations tend to be short-term and intense but rely on the ongoing availability of incentives (Hammedi et al., 2019). A recent study by Hassan (2017) identifies four key intrinsic motivations that drive customer engagement: purpose, mastery, autonomy, and relatedness. Purpose-driven motivations stem from the need to feel that one has a mission to fulfil. Mastery reflects the desire to acquire new skills and reach a level of excellence. Autonomy involves the sense of freedom to act according to personal preferences. Lastly, relatedness is the feeling of belonging to a community. Fulfilling these four motivations fosters greater engagement over time. Even in cases where extrinsic motivation (rewards) is being used, they must engage one of the intrinsic motivations to create long-term behavioural change, as is the case with customer engagement.

Another important aspect leading to customer engagement is the experience that the gamified elements provide. A well-curated game experience can result in high levels of engagement of customers wherein customers can experience immense enjoyment, time distortion (not registering the passage of time), complete immersion (ignoring other things that may demand attention), and curiosity. The essential enjoyment and cognitive benefits of gamification work together to influence customer emotions and satisfaction. This results in a type of experiential engagement described by Pansari and Kumar (2017) as "true love" representing the highest level of engagement. It reflects the experiences of customers who are deeply invested in the relationships they build and sustain with key objects.

The incorporation of gaming elements into marketing strategies has become a growing trend across various industries, with companies using gamification to enhance user experiences, boost engagement, and influence consumer behaviour (Yadav & Dangi, 2023). This move towards gamified interactions represents a strategic effort to improve customer engagement and satisfaction, ultimately transforming the dynamics of consumer-brand relationships.

GAMIFICATION AND CUSTOMER LOYALTY

Oliver (1999) defines consumer loyalty as "a strong commitment to repeatedly purchase or patronize a preferred product or service in the future, leading to consistent same-brand or same-brand-set purchases, even in the face of situational factors and marketing strategies that could encourage switching behaviour." Aksoy et al. (2015) argue that consumer loyalty is influenced by the interactions and relationships consumers build with a business, product, service, or brand. Liu et al. (2019) define customer loyalty towards a brand as a strong emotional and behavioural commitment to repeatedly buy a product or service, while Martínez-López et al. (2020) highlight its resilience against external influences and marketing tactics. For example, consumers remain loyal to brands like Apple or Samsung despite alternative options. Gamification, which incorporates game-like elements into marketing (such as points or leaderboards), enhances customer engagement and promotes brand loyalty (Wahyu Karyadi et al., 2023). Flipkart, for instance, uses its mobile app to reward customers with points on every purchase which can be redeemed for future purchases, encouraging repeat visits. The relationship between gamification, customer engagement, and brand loyalty is interconnected, with increased engagement leading to stronger brand attachment and higher loyalty, which in turn boosts consumer purchasing decisions. Therefore, integrating gamification into marketing strategies is shown to positively influence brand loyalty and consumer buying intentions.

Al-Zyoud (2020) concluded that gamification not only contributes positively to building customer loyalty but also through motivational and emotional involvement, increases consumer's intention to engage further driving a positive attitude toward the company, product, or brand. This influences their purchase intention as well as motivates them to share positive word-of-mouth about the firm.

SUCCESSFUL GAMIFICATION STRATEGIES OF COMPANIES

By incorporating game-like features into routine transactions, Starbucks not only enhances the customer experience but also establishes a standard for retail innovation. The gamification strategy of Starbucks significantly elevates engagement and loyalty, demonstrating how traditional businesses can prosper by embracing modern digital strategies. The main gamification strategies adopted by Starbucks are as follows:

1. Starbucks

Personalisation

Starbucks provides an experience that is highly personalized as they customize promotions and rewards for each member by utilizing information derived from their purchasing patterns. If a customer frequently purchases a specific kind of beverage, they may be presented with exclusive promotions associated with that product. Starbucks enhances your account by saving details about your preferred beverages, while also sending push notifications and facilitating seamless communication, which contributes to greater user engagement and retention.

Rewards

The core of the Starbucks Rewards Program revolves around the accumulation of Stars, which act as the primary means for customers to earn points towards various rewards. Participants can earn Stars by making purchases at Starbucks using either a registered Starbucks Card or the Starbucks mobile application. By accumulating a designated number of Stars, customers become eligible for a range of rewards, including complimentary food and beverages as well as discounts on merchandise.

Customers earn Stars with each transaction, and the app incorporates gamification strategies to motivate users to collect Stars and reach higher reward levels. Features such as achievements, tiers, and visuals promote repeat purchases. Customers are surprised with a special birthday reward from Starbucks on their birthdays, enhancing the delight of their app experience.

Challenges and Progress Tracking

Starbucks frequently launches time-sensitive challenges and games in the app. These initiatives not only help retain the interest of current customers but also draw in potential new ones by utilizing seasonal themes and unique offerings.

Examples of these are Seasonal Challenges for earning extra rewards; Time-limited promotions fostering a feeling of urgency that stimulates consumer purchases; Customized Rewards include opportunities to earn tailored rewards, such as exclusive merchandise or special discounts

2. Duolingo

Online learning frequently struggled with learner retention, resulting in many individuals who enrolled in courses failing to achieve their educational objectives. Nevertheless, most EdTech companies viewed these issues as inherent limitations of online education. Duolingo aimed to tackle these issues by rethinking the approach to online language instruction. To improve the existing online language learning landscape, Duolingo shifted its emphasis from merely delivering educational services to creating an engaging, interactive, and even addictive learning experience. Duolingo adopts various gamification features to engage users and improve high retention rates:

Personalisation

App allows Profile picture customization which fosters a deeper sense of connection for the user with the product in use. Users are free to insert any image they prefer enabling users to experience a greater sense of ownership or pride in their online identity.

Storytelling

Duolingo use storytelling and real-life scenarios within its lessons. Rather than focusing solely on abstract vocabulary and grammar drills, Duolingo presents language in context. Users interact with characters and situations that reflect real-life experiences, making language acquisition more practical and relatable (Studio Zizo, 2023).

Badges

Users can earn achievement tokens on Duolingo that reflect their language skills, which are displayed on their profiles. Badges serve as an excellent mechanism to encourage users to engage more deeply with their studies, fulfilling a fundamental need for self-esteem, a powerful intrinsic motivator. Users can monitor their progress by reviewing their earned badges or sharing their achievements with friends.

Duolingo provides various mini-challenges and badges for completing specific objectives or milestones, such as mastering a skill or achieving a certain level.

Streaks

The continuous usage of the application was vital for the sustainability of Duolingo's business model. To achieve this, Duolingo implemented streaks to motivate users to practice daily, offering rewards for consecutive days of learning. Users receive rewards for consecutive days of learning, and the potential loss of a streak acts as a deterrent against skipping a day. . The excitement increases with the length of your streak, along with the pressure to maintain it, streak feature significantly influences user engagement.

Experience Points and Leaderboards

Duolingo utilizes experience points, commonly referred to as XP, which are earned as users engage in learning new languages. This concept is prevalent in many online games and serves as a straightforward yet effective way to reward participants. Beyond providing a feeling of progress and achievement, experience points also foster a sense of ownership over one's digital accomplishments. On Duolingo, learners can set a daily target for points, which can be integrated with various gamification elements. Users accumulate points by completing each course, allowing them to appear on a leaderboard. This feature enhances the motivation to excel and cultivates a competitive spirit among learners.

Social Interaction

Duolingo, although it is not designed as a social media application, takes advantage of the beneficial elements of social influence. The application motivates you to bring in friends, which is a common feature in many apps today. You can follow others, review the achievements of your friends, and see your ranking on the league leaderboards.

These elements facilitate a way to compare oneself with other users on the app, which can motivate the individual to keep using Duolingo or engage more to advance with their friends. Moreover, the app frequently indicates the locations of your friends or notifies you when they have accomplished something. This not only allows you to celebrate the achievements of friends, but it also inspires you to maintain your pace with your colleagues!

3. Snapchat

In the dynamic environment of the digital era, where social media platforms compete for users' limited attention, one strategy stands out in maintaining user engagement: gamification. Snapchat employs gamification through the following features, all designed to enhance user engagement, drive sales, and improve retention.

Personalisation

Filters and lenses by Snapchat exemplify the significant impact of personalized gamification in engaging users effectively. Snapchat filters transform selfies into artistic creations or humorous snapshots. Users have the option to transform into charming puppies, glimmering mermaids, or even swap faces with their friends

The attraction of filters and lenses lies fundamentally in their ability to cater to individual psychological preferences. Users enjoy the opportunity to customize their content based on their emotions, relevant happenings, or merely to amuse their friends. Having a sense of ownership regarding their content cultivates a stronger bond with the platform.

Lenses utilize augmented reality (AR) to deliver an even more engaging experience. The ability to share these experiences with friends, and sometimes in real-time video chats, fosters a sense of collective enjoyment and connection.

Streaks

Snapchat introduced Streaks to motivate users to log in daily, A Snap Streak indicates the number of consecutive days two users have been sharing snaps with each other. To maintain a streak between two users, at least one snap (typically a photo or video) must be sent from either party within a 24-hour timeframe.

A flame emoji ( ) along with a numeral, which signifies the duration in days that the streak has been active, appears next to the usernames to indicate the streak. The more frequently you send snaps each day, the greater your streak becomes, leading to an increased sense of commitment and involvement.

Snap Scores

The Snap Score is a feature on Snapchat that increases by one point each time a user sends or receives a Snap. In addition to individual Snaps, the score is influenced by factors such as app usage frequency, number of friends, and interactions with specific friends' Snaps. A Snap Score serves as a numerical indicator of a user's activity and engagement on Snapchat. In essence, the more actively a user engages with the platform, the higher their Snap Score will be. This score is displayed on the user's profile icon and can be located in the top left corner of the screen.

Snapchat Stories enable users to share photos and videos with friends for a 24-hour period. Interacting with friends' Stories by viewing, reacting, and responding to them can contribute to increasing one's Snap Score.

Snapchat's Snap Score, which quantifies user activity, can serve as a motivator for engagement by providing a sense of achievement and social standing, thereby encouraging users to utilize the app more frequently and interact with others.

Social Interaction

Snap Map is a feature within Snapchat that enables users to share their real-time locations with friends on an interactive map, explore various locations, and view Snaps submitted by the community from different parts of the globe.

By sharing your location with friends, you engage in a virtual treasure hunt, where the excitement lies not only in knowing your friends' whereabouts but also in the joy of exploration. Equipped with Bitmoji avatars, Snap Map allows users to embark on virtual journeys, appealing to the explorer in everyone. Additionally, it introduces a competitive aspect, encouraging users to collect more Bitmoji characters, akin to a real-world video game. Streaks and Snap Map enhance social connections by motivating users to share their experiences, explore friends in their vicinity, and remain active on the platform.

Users of Snapchat, motivated by these game-inspired interactions, demonstrate increased engagement both with the platform and one another, thereby enhancing the overall experience for users.

CHALLENGES OF GAMIFICATION

The use of gamification has become an effective method for enhancing engagement, encouraging changes in consumer behaviour, and supporting learning and development. Despite the significant advantages of gamification, there are considerable challenges associated with its implementation that must be addressed to achieve successful outcomes:

1. Over Gamification

While gamification can significantly boost user engagement, it is important to exercise moderation. Overuse of gamified features may lead to an experience that feels overwhelming or even frustrating for users. It is vital to thoughtfully choose gamification elements that are in harmony with your app's objectives and to integrate them smoothly (Flores & Flores, 2025). When game mechanics are applied excessively or inappropriately, they can detract from the authenticity of the experience. For example, if an educational platform places excessive emphasis on rewards and badges, it may diminish the intrinsic value of the educational content itself. Users may become more preoccupied with accumulating points rather than genuinely mastering the subject matter. Therefore, it is crucial to strike an appropriate balance between gamified elements and core content to preserve the integrity and effectiveness of the overall experience.

2. Designing and Implementing Effective Gamification

Designing effective gamification involves careful planning and alignment with user motivations and objectives. The game mechanics should be relevant and meaningful to the users' goals to ensure success. Poorly designed gamification can result in disengagement or frustration, especially if challenges are overly difficult or rewards do not meet user expectations. Users need to have a solid understanding of their goals and how their actions contribute to their overall progress (Baikins, 2025)

Companies should dedicate time to understanding their audience and refining the design to ensure that gamification elements enhance the overall experience rather than detract from it.

3. Regular updating Gamification Elements

Gamification requires regular content updates to ensure continued user engagement. It is crucial to evaluate user feedback, engagement statistics, and behavioral trends to find opportunities for enhancement. Consistently changing gamification features in response to user preferences and evolving trends can help maintain long-term user engagement (Smith, 2025). A lack of innovation or inadequate maintenance can result in user disengagement.

4. Effective Measurement

While methods exist to quantify the number of individuals who have engaged with a gamified experience, there currently remains a lack of tools for marketers or organizations utilizing gamification within their marketing strategies to ascertain whether their games are effectively contributing to the achievement of the objectives set forth at the outset of the development process, such as enhancing customer loyalty (Nagarajah, 2022). Organizations must define specific success metrics and monitor the effectiveness of their gamification initiatives. This process involves evaluating user engagement, satisfaction levels, and the attainment of targeted outcomes.

CONCLUSION

Gamification is more than a trendy term; it represents a tactic that is changing the way companies engage with their clients. Given that the average adult's attention span measures only eight seconds, it can be challenging to capture and maintain customer interest. Nevertheless, enhancing customer retention and fostering brand loyalty offers numerous advantages.

Gamification is not limited to gaming firms or large technology companies; it is also gaining traction in a multitude of sectors. Whether in healthcare, education, retail, or finance, gamification has the potential to change how companies engage with customers. The outlook for utilizing engagement in customer relations appears to be quite promising, particularly considering the current advancements in areas like augmented reality and virtual reality, which are expected to greatly enhance the potential for gamified experiences.

As the popularity of gamification continues to rise, it is increasingly vital to implement it in an ethical and responsible manner. While gamification can effectively enhance user engagement and foster loyalty, it is essential to evaluate the impact of these strategies on users and ensure they adhere to ethical principles. The goal of gamification should be to enrich the user experience rather than to exploit their time or attention.

Various brands employ distinct gamification strategies to enhance customer engagement and loyalty. However, for successful execution, the key point is to determine the appropriate gamification approach that aligns with your brand.

REFERENCES

Aksoy, L., Keiningham, T. L., Buoye, A., Larivière, B., Williams, L., & Wilson, I. (2015). Does loyalty span domains? Examining the relationship between consumer loyalty, other loyalties and happiness. *Journal of Business Research, 68*(12), 2464–2476. DOI: 10.1016/j.jbusres.2015.06.033

Al-Zyoud, M. F. (2021). The impact of gamification on consumer loyalty, electronic word-of mouth sharing and purchase behavior. *Journal of Public Affairs, 21*(3), e2263. DOI: 10.1002/pa.2263

Baek, T. H., Yoon, S., & Kim, S. (2015). When environmental messages should be assertive: Examining the moderating role of effort investment. *International Journal of Advertising, 34*(1), 135–157. DOI: 10.1080/02650487.2014.993513

Baikins, P. (2025, March 27). *The State of Marketing Gamification: Challenges and opportunities*. GAMIFICATION+. https://gamificationplus.uk/the-state-of-marketing-gamification-challenges-and-opportunities/

Baldwin, C., & Baldwin, C. (2024, December 27). *Gamification in marketing*. Insider. https://useinsider.com/gamification-in-marketing/

Berger, A., Schlager, T., Sprott, D. E., & Herrmann, A. (2017). Gamified interactions: Whether, when, and how games facilitate self–brand connections. *Journal of the Academy of Marketing Science, 46*(4), 652–673. DOI: 10.1007/s11747-017-0530-0

Bitrián, P., Buil, I., & Catalán, S. (2020). Gamification in sport apps: The determinants of users' motivation. *European Journal of Management and Business Economics, 29*(3), 365–381. DOI: 10.1108/EJMBE-09-2019-0163

Bullock, M. (2024, November 21). *Why Gamification is Important & Its Benefits*. Spinify. https://spinify.com/blog/why-gamification-is-important/

Burke, Brian. "Gamify: How Gamification motivates people to do extraordinary things. Bibliomotion." *Inc., Apr* (2014).

Burnett, S. (2019),"Is it time to add gamification to your loyalty strategy? Forbes", available at: https://www.forbes.com/councils/forbesagencycouncil/2019/01/22/is-it-time-to-add-gamification-to-your-loyalty-strategy/ (accessed 28 March 2025).

Deci, E. L., & Ryan, R. M. (2000). The" what" and" why" of goal pursuits: Human needs and the self-determination of behavior. *Psychological Inquiry, 11*(4), 227–268. DOI: 10.1207/S15327965PLI1104_01

Deterding, S., Dixon, D., Khaled, R., & Nacke, L. (2011, September). From game design elements to gamefulness: defining" gamification". In *Proceedings of the 15th international academic MindTrek conference: Envisioning future media environments* (pp. 9-15). DOI: 10.1145/2181037.2181040

Eigenraam, A. W., Eelen, J., Van Lin, A., & Verlegh, P. W. (2018). A consumer-based taxonomy of digital customer engagement practices. *Journal of Interactive Marketing*, *44*(1), 102–121. DOI: 10.1016/j.intmar.2018.07.002

Eisingerich, A. B., Marchand, A., Fritze, M. P., & Dong, L. (2019). Hook vs. hope: How to enhance customer engagement through gamification. *International Journal of Research in Marketing*, *36*(2), 200–215. DOI: 10.1016/j.ijresmar.2019.02.003

Flores, B., & Flores, B. (2025, March 7). How gamification engages your audience—benefits, challenges, case studies and future trends - Agility PR Solutions. *Agility PR Solutions - Media Relations. . .Streamlined.* https://www.agilitypr.com/pr-news/public-relations/how-gamification-engages-your-audience-benefits-challenges-case-studies-and-future-trends/

Glover, I. (2013). Play as you learn: Gamification as a technique for motivating learners. In *Proceedings of world conference on educational multimedia, hypermedia and telecommunications 2013* (pp. 1999e2008). Chesapeake, VA: Association for the Advancement of Computing in Education.

Hamari, J., & Koivisto, J. (2015b). Working out for likes: An empirical study on social influence in exercise gamification. *Computers in Human Behavior*, *50*, 333–347. DOI: 10.1016/j.chb.2015.04.018

Hamari, J., Koivisto, J., & Sarsa, H. (2014, January). Does gamification work?--a literature review of empirical studies on gamification. In *2014 47th Hawaii international conference on system sciences* (pp. 3025-3034). Ieee.

Hammedi, W., Leclercq, T., & Poncin, I. (2019). Customer engagement: The role of gamification. In *Handbook of research on customer engagement* (pp. 164–185). Edward Elgar Publishing. DOI: 10.4337/9781788114899.00014

Hammedi, W., Leclercq, T., & van Riel, A. (2017). The use of gamification mechanics to increase employee and user engagement in participative healthcare services: A study of two cases. *Journal of Service Management*, *28*(4), 640–661. DOI: 10.1108/JOSM-04-2016-0116

Harwood, T., & Garry, T. (2015). An investigation into gamification as a customer engagement experience environment. *Journal of Services Marketing*, *29*(6/7), 533–546. DOI: 10.1108/JSM-01-2015-0045

Hassan, L. (2017). Governments should play games: Towards a framework for the gamification of civic engagement platforms. *Simulation & Gaming*, *48*(2), 249–267. DOI: 10.1177/1046878116683581

Hermawan, J. H., & Tjhin, V. U. (2023). The effect of gamification on customer engagement in e-commerce. *Journal of Theoretical and Applied Information Technology*, *101*(19), 5952–5954.

Hofacker, C. F., Ruyter, K. D., Lurie, N. H., Manchanda, P., & Donaldson, J. (2016). Gamification and mobile marketing effectiveness. *Journal of Interactive Marketing*, *34*(1), 25–36. DOI: 10.1016/j.intmar.2016.03.001

Huotari, K., & Hamari, J. (2017). A definition for gamification: Anchoring gamification in the service marketing literature. *Electronic Markets*, *27*(1), 21–31. DOI: 10.1007/s12525-015-0212-z

Intelligence, M. (2020), Gamification market– growth, trends, COVID-19 impact, and Forecasts (2021-2026), Report, available at https://www.mordorintelligence.com/industry-reports/gamification-market (accessed 29 March 2025).

Jang, S., Kitchen, P. J., & Kim, J. (2018). The effects of gamified customer benefits and characteristics on behavioral engagement and purchase: Evidence from mobile exercise application uses. *Journal of Business Research*, *92*, 250–259. DOI: 10.1016/j.jbusres.2018.07.056

Kennedy, E., & Guzmán, F. (2016). Co-creation of brand identities: Consumer and industry influence and motivations. *Journal of Consumer Marketing*, *33*(5), 313–323. DOI: 10.1108/JCM-07-2015-1500

Koivisto, J., & Hamari, J. (2019). The rise of motivational information systems: A review of gamification research. *International Journal of Information Management*, *45*, 191–210. DOI: 10.1016/j.ijinfomgt.2018.10.013

Kumar, V., Aksoy, L., Donkers, B., Venkatesan, R., Wiesel, T., & Tillmanns, S. (2010). Undervalued or overvalued customers: Capturing total customer engagement value. *Journal of Service Research*, *13*(3), 297–310. DOI: 10.1177/1094670510375602

Kumar, V., & Pansari, A. (2016). Competitive advantage through engagement. *JMR, Journal of Marketing Research*, *53*(4), 497–514. DOI: 10.1509/jmr.15.0044

Kuo, M. S., & Chuang, T. Y. (2016). How gamification motivates visits and engagement for online academic dissemination—An empirical study. *Computers in Human Behavior*, 55(A), 16–27.

Landers, R. N., Bauer, K. N., & Callan, R. C. (2017). Gamification of task performance with leaderboards: A goal setting experiment. *Computers in Human Behavior, 71*, 508–515. DOI: 10.1016/j.chb.2015.08.008

Leclercq, T., Hammedi, W., & Poncin, I. (2018). The boundaries of gamification for engaging customers: Effects of losing a contest in online co-creation communities. *Journal of Interactive Marketing, 44*(1), 82–101. DOI: 10.1016/j.intmar.2018.04.004

Lee, J. J., & Hammer, J. (2011). Gamification in education: What, how, why bother? *Academic Exchange Quarterly, 15*(2), 146.

Liu, R., Liu, L., Lee, M., & Chen, J. (2019). When will consumers be ready? A psychological perspective on consumer engagement in social media brand communities. *Internet Research, 29*(4), 704–724. DOI: 10.1108/IntR-05-2017-0177

Luarn, P., Chen, C.-C., & Chiu, Y.-P. (2023). Enhancing intrinsic learning motivation through gamification: A self-determination theory perspective. *The International Journal of Information and Learning Technology, 40*(5), 413–424. DOI: 10.1108/IJILT-07-2022-0145

Martínez-López, F. J., Anaya-Sánchez, R., & Gázquez-Abad, J. C. (2020). Consumer engagement and loyalty in social media environments: The role of content and interaction. *Journal of Retailing and Consumer Services, 54*, 102027.

Nagarajah, A. (2022, December 20). *How gamification in marketing affects consumer behavior?* eVULX. https://evulx.com/how-gamification-in-marketing-affects-consumer-behavior/

Nicholson, S. (2012). A user-centered theoretical framework for meaningful gamification. *Gamesþ Learningþ Society, 8*, 1.

Oliver, R. L. (1999). Whence consumer loyalty? *Journal of Marketing, 63*(4_suppl1), 33–44. DOI: 10.1177/00222429990634s105

Palmer, D., Lunceford, S., & Patton, A. J. (2012). The engagement economy: How gamification is reshaping businesses. *Deloitte Review, 11*, 52–69.

Pansari, A., & Kumar, V. (2017). Customer engagement: The construct, antecedents, and consequences. *Journal of the Academy of Marketing Science, 45*(3), 294–311. DOI: 10.1007/s11747-016-0485-6

Peng, W., Lin, J. H., Pfeiffer, K. A., & Winn, B. (2012). Need satisfaction supportive game features as motivational determinants: An experimental study of a self-determination theory guided exergame. *Media Psychology, 15*(2), 175–196. DOI: 10.1080/15213269.2012.673850

Punwatkar, S., & Verghese, M. (2025). Investigating the impact of gamification on customer engagement, brand loyalty and purchase intent in marketing. *Journal of Applied Research and Technology*, *23*(1), 94–102. DOI: 10.22201/icat.24486736e.2025.23.1.2592

Qian, T. Y., Matz, R., Luo, L., & Xu, C. (2022). Gamification for value creation and viewer engagement in gamified livestreaming services: The moderating role of gender in esports. *Journal of Business Research*, *145*, 482–494. DOI: 10.1016/j.jbusres.2022.02.082

Ryan, R. M., Rigby, C. S., & Przybylski, A. (2006). The motivational pull of video games: A self-determination theory approach. *Motivation and Emotion*, *30*(4), 344–360. DOI: 10.1007/s11031-006-9051-8

Seaborn, K., & Fels, D. I. (2015). Gamification in theory and action: A survey. *International Journal of Human-Computer Studies*, *74*, 14–31. DOI: 10.1016/j.ijhcs.2014.09.006

Segmentify. (2024, July 4). *The Ultimate guide to gamification in Marketing*. Segmentify. https://segmentify.com/blog/gamification-marketing-guide/

Shen, Y. S., Choi, H. C., Joppe, M., & Yi, S. (2020). What motivates visitors to participate in a gamified trip? A player typology using Q methodology. *Tourism Management*, *78*, 104074. DOI: 10.1016/j.tourman.2019.104074

Simms, B. (2019, May 13). *5 Benefits of Using Gamification in your Digital Marketing Strategy*. #DMWF World Series. https://www.digitalmarketing-conference.com/5-benefits-of-using-gamification-in-your-digital-marketing-strategy/

Smith, B. (2025, March 17). *Gamification in Marketing: Trends for 2025*. https://www.rhapsodymedia.com/blog/gamification-in-marketing-trends-for-2025

Topuzova, I. (2025, March 13). *What is gamification in marketing?* Dot.vu Blog. https://blog.dot.vu/gamification-in-marketing/

Xi, N., & Hamari, J. (2019). Does gamification satisfy needs? A study on the relationship between gamification features and intrinsic need satisfaction. *International Journal of Information Management*, *46*, 210–221. DOI: 10.1016/j.ijinfomgt.2018.12.002

Yadav, M., & Dangi, A. (2023). The Impact of Gamification on Cognitive Brand Engagement in E?Commerce Context, *Pacific Business Review International*, 15(8).

Yee, N., Ducheneaut, N., & Nelson, L. (2012). Online gaming motivations scale: Development and validation. In *Proceedings of the SIGCHI Conference on Human Factors in Computing Systems*, Austin, Texas, USA. DOI: 10.1145/2207676.2208681

Zichermann, G., & Cunningham, C. (2011). *Gamification by design: Implementing game mechanics in web and mobile apps*. O'Reilly Media, Inc.

Zizo, S. (2023, December 3). *A gamified language learning experience: a case of duolingo*. https://www.linkedin.com/pulse/gamified-language-learning-experience-case-duolingo-studio-zizo-feb4f

Chapter 6
Transforming Digital Supply Chains With Gamification and Metaverse Integration

E. Nirupama
https://orcid.org/0009-0003-2915-0678
Saveetha School of Management, Saveetha Institute of Medical and Technical Sciences, India

S. Seenivasan
https://orcid.org/0000-0002-2155-9781
Rathinam Technical Campus, India

Kamini.S. Bhardwaj
Chandigarh School of Business, Chandigarh Group of Colleges, India

Naresh Babu Karunakaran
https://orcid.org/0009-0005-3113-4225
Sree Abirami College of Occupational Therapy, India

Guru Basava Aradhya S.
https://orcid.org/0000-0002-3335-2681
Chandigarh School of Business, Chandigarh Group of Colleges, India

P. Selvakumar
https://orcid.org/0000-0002-3650-4548
Department of Science and Humanities, Nehru Institute of Technology, Coimbatore, India

T. C. Manjunath
https://orcid.org/0000-0003-2545-9160
Rajarajeswari College of Engineering, India

ABSTRACT

The evolution of digital supply chains is one of the most significant transformations within modern business operations. As global markets and technological capabilities continue to evolve, businesses have been forced to adapt to new demands, operational complexities, and technological advancements. Initially, supply chains were

DOI: 10.4018/979-8-3693-8886-0.ch006

traditionally managed through manual processes, spreadsheets, and basic Enterprise Resource Planning (ERP) systems. These systems offered limited automation, often leading to inefficiencies, delays, and a lack of visibility across the entire supply chain. However, the rise of digital technologies in the late 20th and early 21st centuries introduced a paradigm shift in how supply chains functioned. These early advancements laid the foundation for a new era in supply chain management—one driven by interconnected, real-time systems that could monitor and manage the flow of goods, services, and information with greater precision and efficiency.

INTRODUCTION

The evolution of digital supply chains is one of the most significant transformations within modern business operations. As global markets and technological capabilities continue to evolve, businesses have been forced to adapt to new demands, operational complexities, and technological advancements. Initially, supply chains were traditionally managed through manual processes, spreadsheets, and basic Enterprise Resource Planning (ERP) systems. These systems offered limited automation, often leading to inefficiencies, delays, and a lack of visibility across the entire supply chain. However, the rise of digital technologies in the late 20th and early 21st centuries introduced a paradigm shift in how supply chains functioned. These early advancements laid the foundation for a new era in supply chain management—one driven by interconnected, real-time systems that could monitor and manage the flow of goods, services, and information with greater precision and efficiency. In the early stages of digital transformation, businesses turned to technologies such as radio frequency identification (RFID), barcode scanning, and advanced data analytics to streamline processes(Afacan, 2023). These innovations enabled improved tracking, inventory management, and logistics optimization. Virtual environments can be used to model complex supply chain networks, enabling participants to experience the flow of goods and services stages, but the potential is clear. The convergence of these technologies offers businesses a dynamic way to enhance efficiency, boost engagement, and create innovative experiences for customers, employees, and other stakeholders. While traditional digital supply chain technologies continue to play a vital role in optimizing logistics, inventory, and data management, gamification and the metaverse bring a layer of interactivity and immersion that promises to redefine the future of supply chain management(Agenda, 2015). As these technologies mature, we can expect to see an increasingly interconnected and immersive supply chain ecosystem, one that not only improves operational efficiency but also fosters deeper connections between people, technology, and businesses around the world.

THE CHALLENGES OF TRADITIONAL SUPPLY CHAINS: INEFFICIENCIES AND OPPORTUNITIES FOR IMPROVEMENT

Traditional supply chains, while foundational to global commerce for centuries, face a myriad of challenges that hinder their ability to efficiently and effectively meet the demands of the modern market. As supply chain management practices evolved, the growing complexity of global trade, technological advancements, and shifting consumer expectations have highlighted the inherent inefficiencies within traditional supply chain models.(Bartle, 2004; Bell, 2008) These inefficiencies, often stemming from outdated processes, lack of integration, and limited visibility, present significant obstacles for businesses striving to maintain competitive advantage in an increasingly fast-paced and interconnected world. While traditional supply chains have provided a framework for operational success, the need for innovation and adaptation has never been more critical. This discussion aims to explore these inefficiencies and identify the various opportunities for improvement in the traditional supply chain framework, focusing on technological advances, process optimization, and strategic shifts that can enable organizations to overcome traditional challenges. Traditional supply chains are often designed with a focus on cost minimization and efficiency, without adequately considering the need for agility. When unexpected events occur, such as supplier disruptions or shifts in consumer demand, traditional supply chains are ill-equipped to quickly pivot or respond. (Berggren & Iselid, 2023). By embracing technologies such as 3D printing, companies can reduce their reliance on centralized manufacturing facilities, allowing for localized production and faster response times. In addition, implementing just-in-time (JIT) strategies or adopting a hybrid supply chain model that blends traditional methods with new, more adaptive approaches can help businesses respond more effectively to sudden shifts in demand or unexpected disruptions. Sustainability also presents a significant opportunity for improvement. By embracing circular economy principles and focusing on sustainable sourcing, energy-efficient transportation, and waste reduction, companies can improve their environmental performance while meeting growing consumer and regulatory demands for sustainability. Adopting green technologies, such as electric delivery vehicles or renewable energy sources, can help reduce the carbon footprint of traditional supply chains and create a more environmentally friendly operation. In conclusion, traditional supply chains are beset by a variety of inefficiencies, including poor communication, fragmented systems, lack of visibility, limited flexibility, and environmental impact(Cali et al., 2022a). However, these challenges also present numerous opportunities for improvement. By embracing technological innovation, optimizing processes, and incorporating sustainability into their operations, businesses can create more efficient, adaptable, and resilient supply chains.

THE POTENTIAL OF GAMIFICATION AND METAVERSE INTEGRATION: ENHANCING SUPPLY CHAIN PERFORMANCE

The rapid advancements in digital technology have ushered in a new era of supply chain management, where companies are increasingly exploring innovative strategies to boost performance, increase engagement, and create a more immersive experience for stakeholders. Among the most promising innovations are gamification and the integration of the metaverse, both of which offer groundbreaking potential to enhance supply chain performance. By leveraging gamification principles and metaverse technologies, companies can transform traditional supply chain operations, improving efficiency, visibility, collaboration, and overall engagement across all stages of the supply chain. As global competition intensifies and consumer expectations continue to evolve, businesses must leverage these technologies not only to streamline processes but to foster a more connected, transparent, and dynamic supply chain ecosystem.(Cali et al., 2022b) This analysis explores how gamification and the metaverse are poised to revolutionize supply chain performance, offering new opportunities for optimization, employee engagement, decision-making, and collaboration. The integration of gamification into supply chain management represents a natural progression, offering companies the ability to enhance motivation, incentivize behaviors, and drive performance through interactive and engaging strategies(Castronova, 2008). In traditional supply chains, employees, stakeholders, and partners often interact with systems that are operationally driven, with limited opportunities for engagement beyond basic tasks. By utilizing virtual spaces to showcase the journey of products, from raw material sourcing to delivery, companies can create a fully transparent and engaging experience for consumers. Virtual tours of production facilities, warehouses, and distribution centers can allow customers to track the movement of goods and learn about the environmental and ethical practices behind their purchases. (De Giovanni, 2023)This transparency builds consumer trust and loyalty while promoting greater corporate social responsibility. In addition, the metaverse allows brands to interact with customers in innovative ways, such as hosting virtual events, offering gamified experiences, or creating immersive brand storytelling that strengthens the connection between the business and its audience.

GAMIFICATION IN SUPPLY CHAINS: A NEW APPROACH TO ENGAGEMENT AND MOTIVATION

One of the most promising and transformative strategies that have gained traction in recent years is gamification—applying game mechanics, principles, and elements to non-game environments to boost engagement, motivation, and performance. While gamification has been widely used in marketing,(Delgado, 2022) education, and customer engagement, its integration into supply chain management is still emerging as a powerful tool that holds the potential to revolutionize how companies operate and manage their operations. By embedding gamified elements into supply chain processes, businesses can motivate employees, improve efficiency, encourage healthy competition, and promote a culture of continuous improvement. create a competitive atmosphere that motivates (Delmerico et al., 2022) employees to strive for excellence and improve their performance. This not only leads to improved efficiency but also boosts morale, creating a positive feedback loop where high performance is continuously rewarded. Furthermore, gamification enables companies to create an ongoing feedback loop where employees can continually assess and improve their performance. As employees work toward achieving specific objectives, they are provided with feedback in real-time, allowing them to make immediate adjustments and improve outcomes.(Fajar et al., 2022) This ongoing feedback mechanism creates a sense of continuous improvement, which is essential in supply chain management, where responsiveness and agility are critical for success.

Types of Gamification: From Points and Badges to Leaderboards and Challenges

This analysis explores the different types of gamification, focusing on their application, potential benefits, and the ways in which these elements can be leveraged for maximum impact. Points are one of the most ubiquitous and fundamental components of gamification. At its core, the point system is a way to quantify effort, achievement, and performance in a structured and measurable way. Points are awarded to individuals when they complete a task, reach a milestone, or exhibit a desired behavior. In many gamified systems, points serve as the basic currency for tracking progress, incentivizing actions, and providing feedback to participants. A supply chain project can collectively earn points based on their collaboration and achievement of shared goals, such as reducing lead times or minimizing stockouts. This approach fosters teamwork and collective responsibility, encouraging employees to work together toward common objectives while still providing individual recognition for performance. Additionally, points provide a low-cost, easily implementable tool for driving engagement and tracking progress in real-time. Badges are another popular form of gamification, offering a visual representation of achievements, skills, or milestones. Badges serve as symbols of accomplishment and recognition that acknowledge an individual's effort, proficiency, or progression within a gamified system. Unlike points, which accumulate over time, badges are typically awarded for specific achievements or accomplishments. For example, (Hadavi & Alizadehsalehi, 2024)an employee who consistently meets performance targets in a warehouse might earn a "Top Picker" badge, while a supply chain manager who successfully reduces supply chain costs could receive a "Cost Optimizer" badge. When used strategically, badges can foster a sense of accomplishment and pride, motivating individuals to strive for higher levels of performance. Warehouse workers, logistics personnel, and supply chain managers can all be ranked based on their performance in these areas. For example, a warehouse worker who consistently meets picking accuracy targets or a logistics tea(Harapan et al., 2020)m that reduces transportation costs might appear at the top of the leaderboard, gaining public recognition and a sense of accomplishment. The competitive aspect of leaderboards encourages individuals to continuously improve, as they strive to outperform their peers. The real-time nature of leaderboards creates a dynamic and engaging environment where employees are constantly aware of their standing, leading to increased focus and determination. Leaderboards can also promote collaboration among teams, as employees work together to achieve collective goals and improve their rankings. For instance, a team of supply chain professionals might work to reduce lead times, and their collective success could be reflected in their rank on the leaderboard. by adding elements of surprise or novelty. (Jiang et al., 2021)For example, a "flash challenge" might involve a sudden task that appears on the system for a limited time, encouraging participants to act quickly in order to complete the task and earn rewards. The use of time limits, random challenges, or "boss-level" challenges that require higher levels of performance can keep the gamified system dynamic and fresh, preventing it from becoming repetitive or boring and challenges are the most common elements used in gamified systems, each offering unique benefits and serving specific purposes. Points provide a simple and measurable way to track progress, while badges offer visual recognition of achievements.

Gamification Use Cases in Supply Chains: From Inventory Management to Logistics and Transportation

Gamification is particularly effective in areas like inventory management, logistics, and transportation, where efficiency, accuracy, and timeliness are crucial to the smooth functioning of supply chains(Kadry, 2022). This section explores key use cases of gamification within these core areas, highlighting how it can address specific challenges, boost performance, and foster a more engaged workforce employee who consistently maintains an error-free inventory record could earn the "Inventory Accuracy Expert" badge, motivating them to continue performing at a high level. This feedback helps employees track their accuracy, speed, and productivity in real-time, allowing them to adjust their approach as needed. Visual progress trackers and leaderboards also foster a sense of competition and collaboration, further motivating employees to achieve their best performance. Logistics and warehouse operations are integral to the functioning of supply chains, and they often involve complex processes such as order picking, packing, sorting, and shipping. In many traditional environments, workers may become disengaged or experience burnout due to the repetitive nature of these tasks. Gamification offers a powerful way to improve performance, increase motivation, and foster a more collaborative and engaging work environment.(Kaede et al., 2023): Gamification can also be applied to improve fuel efficiency and route optimization, both of which are crucial for reducing operational costs. For example, drivers can participate in challenges that encourage them to reduce fuel consumption by using more efficient driving practices, such as maintaining steady speeds, reducing idle times, or optimizing routes. The driver who achieves the lowest fuel consumption within a given period could be rewarded with points, badges, or other incentives. Similarly, challenges can be designed to optimize delivery routes, with drivers being rewarded for reducing the total time or distance traveled while still meeting delivery deadlines. Gamified Training for Drivers: Gamified training programs for drivers can help them develop safer and more efficient driving practices. (Kafilaleh & Asadi, 2022)For example, a training simulation might include different road conditions, traffic scenarios, and vehicle performance challenges.

THE METAVERSE: A NEW FRONTIER FOR SUPPLY CHAIN INNOVATION

As global supply chains become increasingly complex, businesses are seeking innovative ways to solve long-standing challenges such as inefficiencies, delays, disruptions, and lack of real-time visibility. The metaverse offers a promising solution, providing a space where companies can simulate, monitor, and optimize supply chain processes in real-time. By embracing immersive virtual environments(Lee et al., 2015), businesses can transform their supply chain models from reactive to proactive, gaining the ability to predict potential problems, visualize data, and collaborate more effectively with stakeholders, all within a shared virtual ecosystem. This new frontier holds immense potential, offering everything from virtual warehouses and logistics hubs to digital twins and augmented reality interfaces that could dramatically enhance operational visibility, decision-making, and collaboration across the supply chain(Lee, 2022). Moreover, with the use of blockchain technology, the metaverse allows for secure, transparent transactions, ensuring that every interaction within the ecosystem can be traced and verified in real time. Additionally, digital twins for a variety of scenarios without the risk of costly mistakes or disruptions. Collaboration is at the heart of modern supply chains, where companies rely on numerous external partners, suppliers, and stakeholders to ensure the smooth flow of goods and services(Madakam et al., 2015). By leveraging virtual tours, 3D models, and real-time video streams, businesses can assess the status of their supply chain partners in a more efficient and effective way, cutting down on travel time and expenses. While the full integration of the metaverse into supply chain operations may still be a few years away, early adopters are already seeing the benefits of leveraging virtual spaces for tasks such as product design, testing, logistics optimization, and supplier collaboration.(Madgule et al., 2023) As the metaverse becomes more accessible and mainstream, it will continue to reshape the way companies think about supply chain innovation, offering a wealth of new opportunities to improve efficiency, reduce risks, and create more resilient, agile supply chains.

Metaverse-Enabled Supply Chains: Enhancing Collaboration and Visibility

While initially popularized in the world of entertainment and gaming, the potential of the metaverse has extended far beyond its original applications, finding growing relevance in sectors such as healthcare, education, and, importantly, supply chain management.(Nwakanma et al., 2022) The integration of the metaverse into supply chains offers an innovative approach to addressing longstanding challenges, particularly in the areas of collaboration and visibility, two factors that are critical to the success of any modern supply chain. In this intricate ecosystem, visibility and collaboration are key to maintaining operational efficiency, reducing risk, and ensuring customer satisfaction. For example, AR-enabled smart glasses can display real-time data overlays, such as inventory counts or shipping status, overlaid onto the physical environment. This empowers warehouse workers, logistics personnel, or maintenance teams to access critical information on the spot, without needing to consult multiple systems or reports. Blockchain technology, which is often integrated with metaverse platforms, can also play a key role in enhancing transparency and ensuring the security and traceability of supply chain transactions. With blockchain, every transaction or movement of goods is recorded in a decentralized, immutable ledger, allowing supply chain participants to verify the origin, status, and movement of products at any stage of the process. This creates a transparent and auditable record, making it easier to trace products from source to destination and providing stakeholders with confidence that the information they are receiving is accurate and trustworthy. In addition to improving real-time collaboration and visibility, the metaverse also offers supply chain managers the ability to conduct simulations and scenario planning in a fully immersive, virtual environment (OMIgroup, 2022).

Metaverse Use Cases in Supply Chains: From Virtual Warehouses to Digital Twins

Notably, the development of virtual warehouses and digital twins—two of the most promising metaverse use cases—has already begun to reshape how companies manage, optimize, and innovate their supply chain operations(Park, 2021). These innovations have the potential to improve real-time tracking, enhance collaboration, optimize warehouse management, and streamline logistics, all of which are crucial to achieving more efficient and resilient supply chains. Warehouses are central hubs in the supply chain, serving as critical points where goods are stored, managed, and prepared for distribution. However, traditional warehouses face several challenges, such as inefficient layouts, lack of real-time visibility into inventory, poor management of labor resources, and difficulty responding to sudden shifts in demand. In a conventional setting, warehouse managers rely on software and spreadsheets to track inventory, which can lead to inaccuracies or delays in updating stock levels, leading to stockouts, overstocking, or operational inefficiencies. This includes tracking the movement of materials through manufacturing plants, monitoring inventory levels, and assessing the status of shipments and deliveries. With the integration of IoT sensors and other data sources, the digital twin continuously updates its virtual model in real time, ensuring that supply chain managers always have access to accurate, up-to-date information. If a delay or issue arises—such as a transportation disruption or inventory shortage—managers can see the immediate impact on the supply chain and use the digital twin to evaluate different solutions, such as rerouting shipments or adjusting production schedules. For example, digital twins can simulate the effects of a factory closure or labor strike, allowing supply chain managers to explore alternative sourcing or production strategies that can minimize the disruption's impact on the broader network(Pooyandeh et al., 2022).

Figure 1. Digital twin metaverse

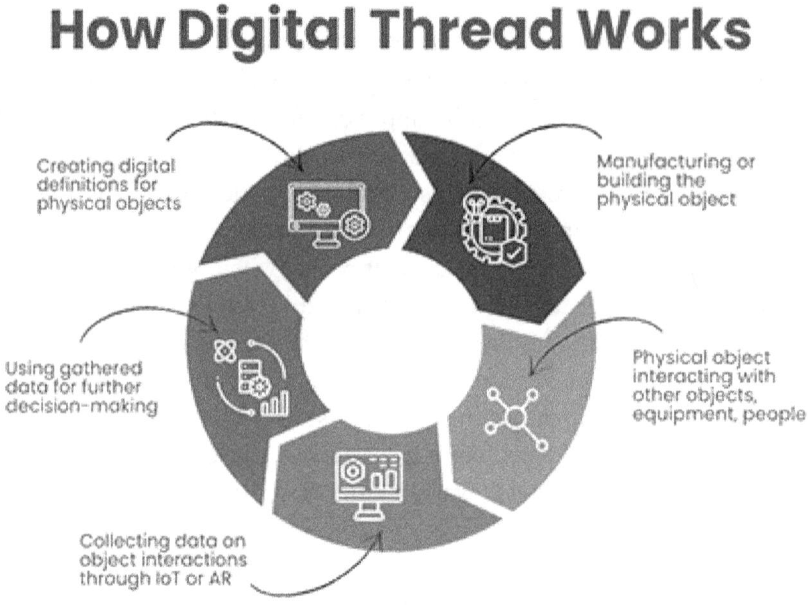

Improved Risk Management: Digital twins allow businesses to simulate potential disruptions or challenges and develop contingency plans to mitigate risks before they materialize. Predictive Analytics: By analyzing historical data and simulating future scenarios, digital twins help businesses predict and prepare for future events, reducing the likelihood of unanticipated disruptions. Enhanced Decision-Making: Businesses can test different strategies, forecast outcomes, and optimize processes in the virtual space before making costly decisions in the physical world. Cost Savings: Digital twins help reduce operational costs by enabling proactive maintenance, improving supply chain efficiency, and preventing the need for expensive emergency repairs or last-minute fixes.. Virtual Logistics Hubs: Optimizing Transportation and Distribution Logistics is a cornerstone of supply chain operations, and virtual logistics hubs within the metaverse offer significant potential to optimize transportation and distribution processes. In these digital spaces, businesses can simulate and monitor the movement of goods throughout the supply chain, from factories to warehouses and ultimately to end customers. Virtual logistics hubs allow supply chain managers to visualize transportation routes, assess traffic patterns, and simulate various logistical challenges to identify the most efficient and cost-effective solutions. For example, virtual logistics hubs can model shipping routes to determine the fastest and most economical paths for transporting goods. By integrating real-time data, such as weather conditions, traffic patterns, and port congestion, the metaverse can offer logistics managers valuable insights into the optimal delivery routes(Prabadevi et al., 2023). Additionally, digital twins of transportation assets like trucks, ships, and planes can be created to track the status of shipments in real time, monitor vehicle performance, and predict maintenance needs. The virtual environment also offers an opportunity for collaborative problem-solving. Logistics teams, suppliers, and customers can meet in a shared virtual space to discuss issues, analyze data, and make decisions in real time. (Zhang, 2023)This collaborative approach is especially valuable in complex supply chains where multiple stakeholders are involved and quick, coordinated action is required to address disruptions or delays.enefits of Virtual Logistics Hubs in the Metaverse: optimized Routes and Transportation: Virtual simulations allow companies to evaluate the best routes for transporting goods, taking into account factors such as weather, traffic, and road conditions improved Real-Time Visibility: The digital representation of transportation assets offers continuous monitoring of shipments, allowing for better tracking and faster resolution of issues.

Benefits of Gamification and Metaverse Integration in Supply Chains: Increased Efficiency and Productivity

The integration of gamification and the metaverse into supply chains represents a groundbreaking shift in how businesses can optimize operations, boost employee engagement, and foster collaboration across complex networks. Supply chains are often the backbone of any business, with efficiency and productivity directly influencing a company's bottom line. However, traditional supply chain systems are often hampered by inefficiencies, lack of real-time data, communication barriers, and siloed workflows. By incorporating gamification techniques and metaverse technologies into supply chain management, companies can unlock new levels of efficiency, improve decision-making, enhance collaboration, and drive productivity. Gamification—the use of game-like elements such as points, badges, leaderboards, and challenges—has become a highly effective tool for driving employee engagement and motivation across various industries. In the context of supply chains, gamification can address some of the most persistent challenges, such as low employee morale, lack of motivation, and difficulty in managing repetitive or manual tasks. By incorporating game mechanics into everyday processes, companies can create an environment where workers are incentivized to perform better, improve their skills, and contribute to the overall success of the supply chain. One of the primary benefits of gamification in supply chains is its ability to increase engagement and motivation. When employees are given clear goals, instant feedback, and rewards for their performance, they are more likely to take ownership of their tasks and work more efficiently. (Zhang et al., 2023)For example, warehouse workers might earn points or badges for quickly and accurately picking and packing orders, leading to faster processing times and fewer errors. These rewards can be tracked via digital platforms, creating a competitive yet collaborative environment where workers strive to improve their performance. Over time, this can result in faster order fulfillment, higher accuracy, and fewer operational disruptions. Gamification also fosters healthy competition and teamwork among employees. In large, dispersed supply chains with many participants,(Yang, 2023) it is critical to maintain alignment and coordination among different teams.

Leaderboards and team-based challenges allow employees to compete while still working toward the same organizational goals. This collaborative element ensures that supply chain participants remain engaged and focused on meeting targets, thus boosting productivity across the entire network. Moreover, gamification offers an effective tool for training and skill development. Employees can undergo training modules designed as games or simulations, where they earn rewards for mastering new skills or completing tasks correctly. This form of interactive learning is more engaging than traditional training methods, and it allows employees to immediately apply their knowledge in real-world scenarios. Over time, this helps employees build expertise and gain confidence in their roles, leading to a more skilled workforce and a more efficient supply chain. Key Benefits of Gamification in Supply Chains: Enhanced Motivation and Engagement: Gamification fosters a more motivated workforce by providing clear goals, rewards, and feedback, driving better performance across supply chain tasks. Improved Efficiency: By incentivizing employees to complete tasks more quickly and accurately, gamification helps reduce delays and errors, resulting in faster, more efficient operations While gamification improves the efficiency of individual tasks within the supply chain, the metaverse takes the concept of collaboration to a whole new level. The metaverse, a shared, virtual environment that integrates the physical and digital worlds, offers unprecedented opportunities for improving supply chain operations through enhanced collaboration, real-time data access, and immersive visualization.(Vijayakumar et al., 2024) By creating virtual spaces for supply chain stakeholders to interact, share information, and make decisions in real time, the metaverse can bridge communication gaps, improve transparency, and streamline workflows. This real-time collaboration is crucial when responding to disruptions, such as stock shortages or shipping delays, as it allows for quick decision-making and faster resolution.(Sugumaran et al., 2024) Additionally, by having a shared virtual space, team members from different locations can access and interact with the same data simultaneously, fostering better communication and reducing misunderstandings that can lead to inefficiencies.The metaverse also improves productivity by making data more accessible and actionable.

The combination of gamification and the metaverse can also enhance training and skill development(Sreenivasulu et al., 2022). In a virtual training program, workers could be taught best practices for warehouse management, logistics planning, or inventory control in an interactive, game-based environment. As they progress, they could receive immediate feedback, rewards, and performance rankings based on their actions, driving continuous improvement in skills and knowledge. within a set period, with each team member contributing their expertise. These challenges foster a sense of community, increase motivation, and encourage the sharing of knowledge across teams.

Challenges of Implementing Gamification and Metaverse Integration in Supply Chains

The integration of gamification and the metaverse into supply chain management offers vast potential for enhancing efficiency, collaboration, and productivity. However, as with any transformative technology, the implementation of these innovations comes with a unique set of challenges—both technical and organizational—that companies must navigate. While the promise of gamification and metaverse-enabled supply chains is compelling, overcoming these challenges is essential to realizing their full potential. These challenges can broadly be categorized into technical hurdles, organizational barriers, and cultural obstacles, each requiring careful planning, strategy, and investment to overcome.The technical challenges associated with implementing gamification and the metaverse in supply chains primarily revolve around the infrastructure required to support these innovations, the integration with existing systems, and the scalability of the solutions across diverse supply chain environments.Both gamification and metaverse technologies are data-intensive and require robust technological infrastructure to function effectively. For gamification, the platform on which it is implemented needs to be able to handle the tracking of employee performance, achievement milestones, and the distribution of rewards. e, the metaverse's reliance on virtual reality (VR) and augmented reality (AR) requires that employees have access to headsets and other devices, which may not be financially feasible for all businesses. The lack of this infrastructure could create a significant barrier to adoption, particularly in industries or regions where digital infrastructure is underdeveloped. Poor integration can lead to data silos, inaccurate reporting, and inefficiencies, negating the benefits of gamification and metaverse integration. Moreover, integrating gamification features into day-to-day supply chain operations requires careful consideration of how performance data will be captured, analyzed, and reported without creating additional work or complexity for employees.(Sreenivasulu et al., 2022) The lack of effective integration between systems could also lead to operational disruptions during the transition phase.As supply chains evolve and expand, scalability becomes an important consideration when implementing gamification and metaverse technologies. For instance, a gamification platform may work well in a small warehouse environment but may struggle to scale across a global supply chain with multiple locations, vendors, and distribution centers. Similarly, metaverse simulations and virtual spaces must be adaptable to the varying complexities of supply chains(Truong et al., 2023).

The costs associated with training employees, maintaining the necessary hardware, and ensuring that all stakeholders are onboard with the new technologies can be substantial. Supply chains that span multiple countries may also face challenges in aligning different regulatory standards, language barriers, and regional technolog. Clear communication, leadership buy-in, and employee involvement in the implementation process are essential for gaining the support of all stakeholders. Another significant challenge is the need to upskill employees to effectively use gamification and metaverse technologies. For many supply chain professionals, these new tools represent a significant departure from the traditional systems they are used to. While gamification itself may seem straightforward, understanding how to engage with and make the most of a gamified system requires new skills, including familiarity with performance metrics, progress tracking, and virtual collaboration tools. Similarly, working in the metaverse often requires new capabilities, such as navigating virtual environments, interacting with digital twins, and understanding how data is presented in immersive spaces.The gap in skills can be particularly pronounced among employees with limited exposure to digital technologies. For example, workers in traditional industries, such as warehousing or transportation, may lack the technical know-how required to use augmented or virtual reality systems effectively. Similarly, employees who are not familiar with game mechanics may struggle to engage with gamified systems designed to incentivize and motivate their performance.To overcome this challenge, companies must invest in comprehensive training programs that equip employees with the skills they need to use these new technologies. These programs should be tailored to the specific needs of different departments and roles within the supply chain and should emphasize hands-on experience with the tools. Moreover, businesses should consider offering ongoing support and refresher courses to ensure that employees remain confident and competent as they adapt to these new systems.

Overcoming Barriers to Adoption: Strategies for Successful Implementation of Gamification and Metaverse Integration in Supply Chains

The integration of gamification and metaverse technologies into supply chains promises to revolutionize operations, enhance collaboration, and drive performance across all sectors of the supply chain, from inventory management to logistics. However, while the potential benefits are clear, organizations often face significant barriers when adopting these advanced technologies. From technical challenges to organizational resistance, the hurdles that businesses must overcome can be daunting. To successfully implement gamification and metaverse systems, organizations must develop comprehensive strategies that address the multifaceted barriers to adoption and ensure smooth transitions that are sustainable in the long run. This discussion will explore effective strategies for overcoming these barriers and enabling the successful integration of these transformative technologies into supply chain operations.The technical challenges of implementing gamification and metaverse systems in supply chains are often the first obstacles organizations must address. These challenges can range from infrastructure limitations to difficulties integrating new technologies with existing systems. For companies to successfully implement these technologies, it is essential to invest in upgrading their IT infrastructure.To overcome this barrier, businesses can begin by conducting an audit of their existing infrastructure and identifying areas that need upgrading(Wang et al., 2022) .

This might involve investing in cloud-based systems that can scale as the supply chain grows, ensuring high bandwidth for real-time data transmission, or procuring enable businesses to add new features or expand existing functionalities without significant disruption. Pilot projects are another effective way to test the scalability of these systems, allowing businesses to assess their performance and capacity before full-scale implementationagers, and other stakeholders may resist change, particularly when the new systems alter long-standing processes or require them to learn new skills. Organizational resistance can take many forms, from skepticism about the benefits of these technologies to a lack of confidence in their ability to use them effectively. To overcome these barriers, businesses must implement strong change management strategies that emphasize communication, training, and leadership involvement.averse integration to all stakeholders.(Ramakrishnan et al., 2022) This includes not only the employees who will be directly interacting with these technologies but also executives, managers, and other decision-makers who play a key role in the adoption process. Providing clear explanations about how these technologies will improve operational efficiency, increase engagement, and enhance decision-making can help alleviate concernst is also important to dispel myths or misconceptions about gamification and the metaverse. For example, some employees may fear that gamification will be used to punish poor performance, while others may worry that the metaverse will replace traditional methods of collaboration. By offering workshops, webinars, or informational sessions, businesses can provide an open forum for employees to ask questions, voice concerns, and better understand the potential advantages of these technologies.. Instead of rolling out the systems across the entire organization at once, businesses can start with smaller, more manageable pilot programs in specific departments or regions. This allows employees to familiarize themselves with the new technologies, experience the benefits firsthand, and provide valuable feedback that can be used to refine the systems before a broader rollout.

CASE STUDY: GAMIFICATION IN SUPPLY CHAIN MANAGEMENT: A REAL-WORLD EXAMPLE

Gamification has become an increasingly prominent tool in supply chain management, offering solutions that enhance employee engagement, improve operational efficiency, and drive productivity. By applying game-design elements like points, badges, leaderboards, and challenges to supply chain operations, companies have found innovative ways to motivate employees, streamline processes, and improve overall performance. This case study explores a real-world example of gamification applied in supply chain management, illustrating how it can be successfully integrated into a complex business environment to achieve tangible results. In particular, this case focuses on a large multinational retailer, Walmart, and how it has used gamification in its warehouse and logistics operations to optimize performance and increase (Rather, 2023)worker satisfaction.Walmart's approach to gamification in its warehouses involved several key steps to integrate game mechanics into the day-to-day operations of its distribution centers.The first step in Walmart's gamification strategy was to identify the key performance indicators (KPIs) that could be tracked and incentivized through gamification. These KPIs included metrics like the number of items picked, the accuracy of order fulfillment, .Walmart's next step was to design a gamified experience that would appeal to warehouse employees and provide them with incentives to perform better. The company developed a gamification platform that included elements commonly found in video games, such as points, badges, and levels. Employees could earn points for completing tasks like picking products accurately, meeting daily quotas, and maintaining high levels of efficiency. The more tasks completed, the higher the score, and the more opportunities employees had to unlock achievements and rewards.In addition to individual rewards, Walmart incorporated a competitive element into the system by introducing leaderboards.

These leaderboards displayed the top performers in different categories, creating a sense of friendly competition among employees. Those who ranked at the top were often recognized in company-wide communications or received tangible rewards like gift cards, paid time off, or even monetary bonuses. (Singh, 2023)The social aspect of gamification—seeing their names on leaderboards or receiving peer recognition—helped to motivate employees and foster a sense of pride in their work.Another key aspect of Walmart's gamification strategy was the incorporation of team-based challenges. These challenges allowed warehouse teams to compete against one another to achieve shared goals, such as completing a certain number of orders within a set timeframe. By promoting teamwork, Walmart encouraged employees to collaborate, share best practices, and work toward common objectives, which ultimately enhanced overall performance.Teams that succeeded in meeting their targets could earn collective rewards, such as team outings, group lunches, or additional paid time off. These team-based rewards helped foster a sense of camaraderie and boosted morale. In contrast to individual-focused rewards, team-based incentives also encouraged employees to help each other improve, thereby creating a more collaborative and supportive work environment.. Leveraging Technology for Real-Time Feedback Walmart made use of technology to ensure that feedback and rewards were delivered in real-time. Each warehouse employee had access to a personalized dashboard where they could see their progress, compare their performance with others, and track their achievements. ested in their work, knowing that their contributions were being recognized and rewarded. Walmart reported a reduction in turnover rates in warehouses that had implemented gamification, as employees felt more motivated to stay and improve their performance.. Enhanced Collaboration and TeamworkWhile gamification often focuses on individual performance, Walmart's inclusion of team-based challenges played a crucial role in fostering collaboration and improving teamwork. Warehouse employees began working together more effectively, sharing tips and strategies to improve performance.(Tlili et al., 2023).

CASE STUDY: METAVERSE-ENABLED SUPPLY CHAINS: A REAL-WORLD EXAMPLE

The metaverse—an interconnected, immersive virtual world where digital and physical experiences converge—has emerged as a transformative technology with the potential to revolutionize supply chains. By integrating metaverse technologies such as augmented reality (AR), virtual reality (VR), and digital twins, organizations can gain unprecedented insights, enhance collaboration, improve visibility, and optimize operations across the entire supply chain. This case study explores a real-world example of how a leading global logistics and e-commerce company, DHL, has adopted metaverse technologies to enhance its supply chain operations, improve decision-making, and increase operational efficiency. Specifically, the case focuses on DHL's exploration and implementation of metaverse-driven supply chain initiatives, including the use of digital twins for warehouse management and AR for real-time operational visibility.Background: DHL and the Need for Innovation in Logistics DHL, a division of the German logistics company Deutsche Post, operates one of the world's largest logistics and supply chain networks, offering services that range from express delivery to warehousing, freight transportation, and supply chain optimization. With a vast and intricate network that spans across more than 220 countries and territories, DHL faces numerous challenges related to optimizing supply chain processes, maintaining operational visibility, and meeting customer expectations for speed, accuracy, and efficiency.As the global logistics industry became more complex due to the rise of e-commerce, fluctuating demand, and the increasing importance of real-time data, DHL recognized the need to innovate its operations to remain competitive.(Xu et al., 2022). In addition, DHL partnered with Siemens to develop digital twin technology for its warehouses, providing a robust platform for real-time monitoring and simulation. Collaborations with these industry leaders helped DHL accelerate the implementation process and ensure that the technologies met the company's needs and standards.DHL understood that successful adoption of metaverse technologies would require extensive training and employee buy-in. (Widiyanti et al., 2022)As part of the implementation process, the company conducted employee workshops and training programs to familiarize workers with the new technologies.

Employees were trained on how to use AR devices, navigate VR training modules, and interact with digital twin interfaces.The company also involved employees early in the pilot projects, gathering feedback and making adjustments to the technologies based on user experience. This collaborative approach helped ensure that the systems were user-friendly and that employees felt comfortable using the new tools in their day-to-day operations.The adoption of metaverse technologies had a significant positive impact on DHL's supply chain operations. Some of the key benefits that the company realized include:One of the most significant advantages of implementing metaverse technologies was the enhanced visibility DHL gained across its supply chain operations. With the digital twin technology in place, DHL was able to monitor warehouse operations in real-time, allowing management to identify inefficiencies and bottlenecks quickly. The ability to simulate different scenarios and optimize processes based on real-time data helped DHL make more informed decisions, reducing delays and improving resource allocation.Additionally, integrating these technologies into existing systems and processes required careful planning and coordination, especially as some locations had legacy systems that were difficult to update.DHL also faced the challenge of ensuring that its digital twins remained accurate and up-to-date, as real-world data from warehouses had to be continuously fed into the digital models. Maintaining this data flow required a robust IT infrastructure and ongoing monitoring.The key lesson from DHL's metaverse integration is the importance of conducting pilot projects before full-scale implementation. By starting small and gathering feedback from employees, DHL was able to refine the technology and make necessary adjustments before rolling it out across its entire network.

Best Practices in Gamification and Metaverse Integration: Lessons from Industry Leaders

The integration of gamification and metaverse technologies into supply chains represents a significant leap forward in how organizations approach operational efficiency, employee engagement, collaboration, and innovation. By leveraging these technologies, companies can create dynamic, immersive, and interactive environments that offer not only improvements in productivity but also transformative shifts in how organizations manage their processes, foster employee engagement, and deliver value to their customers. This comprehensive approach, however, requires careful planning, strategic implementation, and consistent optimization. In this discussion, we examine best practices in the integration of gamification and the metaverse in supply chains, drawing from lessons learned by industry leaders who have successfully adopted these innovations.One of the fundamental lessons from industry leaders is the importance of starting with a clear understanding of the business objectives behind adopting gamification and metaverse technologies. Before jumping into the deployment of these technologies, organizations need to ensure that they are aligned with their broader goals, whether these are related to improving operational efficiency, enhancing employee engagement, optimizing customer experience, or driving innovation.For instance, DHL, one of the leading logistics companies, started its journey into the metaverse by identifying specific pain points The lesson here is that businesses must not simply adopt gamification and metaverse technologies because they are trendy but because they have a direct impact on the key drivers of business success.For example, Walmart undertook extensive collaboration with employees when piloting gamification techniques in its warehouse operations. Workers were trained on how to use gamified systems that tracked performance metrics such as order fulfillment speed and accuracy.

Crucially, feedback from these warehouse employees was incorporated into the refinement of the system, allowing the company to adapt and tailor the system to fit the actual needs of its workforce. This created a sense of ownership among the employees and significantly improved engagement with the new technology.Similarly, when(Qin, 2022) Maersk, a global leader in container shipping and logistics, experimented with virtual reality to train its teams, they ensured that employees from various departments—including logistics, This constant iteration allowed L'Oreal to maintain the relevance of the technology and ensure that the training was effective and up to date.Additionally, Siemens, a global technology company, developed a metaverse-driven industrial training program, where employees could practice operating complex machinery in a safe, virtual environment. Siemens has also embraced gamification to encourage knowledge-sharing and innovation within its workforce. The company's efforts to foster a culture of experimentation and ongoing learning in the use of digital tools highlight the value of nurturing an adaptable and forward-thinking mindset. By encouraging employees to experiment with new gamified systems and virtual environments, Siemens effectively used the metaverse to drive continuous improvement in training and operational performance. This seamless integration ensured that employees had an immersive, real-time view of product movements is vital to establish clear, measurable goals before implementing these technologies, as well as to continue gathering feedback to make iterative improvements.For example, FedEx measures the success of its gamified logistics system based on key metrics like order accuracy, delivery speed, and employee productivity.(Yan, 2022) The company then uses this data to optimize the game mechanics, ensuring that employees stay motivated while still achieving organizational goals. Similarly, L'Oréal's use of VR training programs includes specific KPIs to track employee progress and engagement, allowing the company to adjust training modules and gamified elements accordingly.

Future Directions for Research and Practice: Exploring the Integration of Gamification and Metaverse in Supply Chains

The integration of gamification and the metaverse in supply chain management is still in its early stages, yet it holds transformative potential for the future of operations, collaboration, and customer engagement. As the digitalization of supply chains accelerates, the opportunities to harness these technologies to optimize processes, increase engagement, and enhance performance will continue to expand. However, to fully realize the potential of gamification and metaverse integration, ongoing research and practice will be crucial to address existing challenges, explore new applications, and advance the capabilities of these technologies in supply chains. The future directions for research and practice in this area will require interdisciplinary collaboration, technological innovation, and an exploration of both theoretical and practical frameworks to ensure that the integration of gamification and the metaverse delivers substantial value for businesses, employees, and customers alike.Does it lead to sustainable performance improvements, or does it risk creating dependency on rewards, leading to a decline in intrinsic motivation once the rewards are removed?Moreover, research could explore the effects of different gamification mechanics on different types o A balanced approach to gamification that aligns with an organization's culture and values could prove key to achieving positive outcomes in supply chain settings. Exploring the Intersection of Gamification and Metaverse Technologies in Supply Chains As the metaverse continues to develop, its potential for integration with gamification is an exciting area for future research. While both gamification and the metaverse are promising individually, their intersection could unlock new dimensions of supply chain innovation. For instance, research could focus on how gamified experiences can be integrated within metaverse environments to enhance training, collaboration, and decision-making in supply chains.One promising avenue is the use of virtual warehouses and digital twins in the metaverse, where supply chain teams can interact in real-time with a virtual representation of their physical operations. Within these virtual environments, gamification can be introduced to encourage performance metrics, optimize workflow, and increase engagement among supply chain employees.

Research could investigate the best practices for integrating gamified elements into these immersive metaverse settings to foster competition, collaboration, and knowledge-sharing among supply chain stakeholders.Additionally, the use of the metaverse in virtual testing and simulation environments offers opportunities to explore how gamified scenarios could help supply chain teams solve complex problems. For example, companies could use virtual simulations in the metaverse to test different operational strategies or manage crises like supply chain disruptions, and gamification could incentivize teams to find the most optimal solution. Future research could investigate how the combination of gamification and metaverse simulations can lead to improved decision-making and faster problem-solving capabilities in high-stakes situationsAnother area of exploration lies in the use of the metaverse for cross-organizational collaboration in supply chains. The metaverse could facilitate a shared virtual space where supply chain partners, including manufacturers, suppliers, and logistics providers, can collaborate and problem-solve in real-time. Research could focus on how gamified interactions within these virtual spaces can improve communication, enhance transparency, and foster trust between supply chain stakeholders, leading to more effective joint decision-making.One of the major challenges faced by organizations looking to implement gamification and metaverse technologies in their supply chains is the issue of integration with existing systems and ensuring interoperability. As many businesses still rely on legacy systems, the ability to integrate new technologies into these infrastructures is critical. Future research should focus on developing frameworks, tools, and protocols that enable seamless integration of gamified and metaverse-based applications into existing supply chain platforms, such as enterprise resource planning (ERP) systems, warehouse management systems (WMS), and customer relationship management (CRM) software.Moreover, interoperability between different virtual platforms and technologies will be essential for ensuring that supply chains can leverage the full potential of the metaverse and gamification.

CONCLUSION

The convergence of gamification and the metaverse offers a unique opportunity for businesses to leverage these technologies in tandem, transforming how supply chain operations are managed, optimized, and experienced by both employees and customers alike.At the heart of the digital supply chain revolution is the ability to drive efficiency, enhance collaboration, and foster innovation. Gamification, when integrated into supply chain operations, offers the potential to incentivize behaviors, streamline workflows, and create an environment where employees are motivated to meet and exceed performance benchmarks. By embedding game-like elements such as rewards, challenges, leaderboards, and progress tracking into daily tasks, businesses can encourage greater engagement and performance from workers at all levels of the supply chain. This shift not only helps increase productivity but also cultivates a culture of continuous improvement, as employees become more invested in their work and motivated by achievable goals. In the context of the metaverse, its ability to offer immersive, 3D virtual environments opens new doors for supply chain management. The metaverse allows organizations to create digital twins of physical supply chain processes, enabling real-time simulations, monitoring, and decision-making in ways that were previously unimaginable. For instance, digital twins can represent everything from individual warehouses and transportation networks to entire supply chains, providing instant insights into operational performance, inventory levels, and equipment conditions. Additionally, advances, the synergy between these technologies will likely serve as a cornerstone for the next phase of supply chain transformation. Enhanced Employee Engagement and Motivation significant aspect of the future of digital supply chains involves creating environments that engage and motivate employees. Traditional supply chain models often suffer from high turnover rates, low morale, and a lack of incentive for employees to perform at their best. Gamification, when applied strategically, addresses these challenges by offering an interactive, rewarding experience for workers, fostering both individual and team-based engagement. The use of points, badges, challenges, and leaderboards makes work more enjoyable, turning mundane tasks into stimulating activities and aligning employee goals with company objectives. Moreover, the metaverse offers an opportunity to take employee engagement to the next level by offering virtual, gamified environments where workers can interact with digital avatars, attend immersive training sessions, and collaborate in real-time with colleagues across the globe. In the warehouse setting, for instance, gamification can be integrated with AR/VR tools, where employees receive visual feedback on their performance and are given real-time, virtual training that feels just as effective as hands-on, in-person learning. By making the workplace more engaging, dynamic, and educational, businesses can improve worker satisfaction, reduce attrition, and foster a deeper sense of purpose and loyalty within their teams. Furthermore, gamification and metaverse-driven supply chain innovations can provide employees with a sense of achievement and recognition. Performance-driven gamification elements, combined with the ability to visualize progress in virtual worlds, will create a more immersive and rewarding employee experience, where workers are encouraged to learn, grow, and continuously enhance their skills. The next frontier in supply chain management is the enhanced ability for real-time collaboration and end-to-end visibility. Historically, traditional supply chains have struggled with fragmented systems, disparate data sources, and a lack of real-time access to critical information, which can result in delayed decision-making and inefficient operations. The integration of gamification and the metaverse into supply chains will bridge these gaps by offering both the data-driven insights of digital twins and the immersive, interactive capabilities of virtual environments. The metaverse, for instance, enables the creation of virtual supply chain ecosystems, where stakeholders—whether internal teams, suppliers, or customers—can access and interact with a shared, dynamic digital representation of the supply chain. This collaborative virtual space allows for seamless communication, decision-making, and problem-solving across borders and time zones. Supply chain managers can, for example, use the metaverse to simulate the effects of disruptions, test alternative strategies, and coordinate responses with key partners in real-time, all while gaining deeper insights into how changes in one part of the supply chain might affect the entire network. The gamification aspect further enhances collaboration by encouraging competition and cooperation among supply chain stakeholders. Using challenges and incentives, businesses can incentivize teams to improve their performance metrics, such as reducing lead times, improving inventory management, or increasing on-time deliveries. Collaborative games, like team-based challenges or "quests" to optimize specific supply chain processes, create a shared sense of purpose among employees, suppliers, and partners, helping to align goals and improve overall supply chain performance. The future of digital supply chains will be driven by sophisticated analytics and artificial intelligence (AI) that can turn this data into actionable insights. Integrating gamification into the supply chain provides a platform to harness data effectively and make informed decisions. Gamified systems collect real-time data on worker performance, inventory levels, shipping times, and customer satisfaction, creating a rich data ecosystem that can be analyzed for trends, patterns, and opportunities for improvement. The metaverse, with its ability to generate real-time digital twins, also plays a crucial role in predictive analytics. By simulating various supply chain scenarios, businesses can use the metaverse to test and predict the outcomes of different strategies under varying conditions.

REFERENCES

Afacan, N. M. (2023). "Gamification in Metaverse," in Metaverse: technologies, opportunities and threats. Springer, 187–202. DOI: 10.1007/978-981-99-4641-9_13

Agenda, I. (2015). *"Industrial internet of things: unleashing the potential of connected products and services," 34*. Collaboration with Accenture.

Bartle, R. A. (2004). Designing virtual worlds. New riders, bell, M. W. (2008). Toward a definition of. *Journal of Virtual Worlds Research, 1*(1).

Berggren, N., and Iselid, F. (2023). Unlocking the fashion Metaverse: exploring the impact of external factors on innovation diffusion in the Metaverse fashion industry.

Cali, U., Ferdous, M. S., Karaarslan, E., Gourisetti, S. N. G., & Mylrea, M. (2022a). "SSI meets Metaverse for industry 4.0 and beyond," in Paper presented at the 2022 IEEE 1st global emerging technology blockchain Forum: blockchain and beyond (iGETblockchain). 1–6. DOI: 10.1109/iGETblockchain56591.2022.10087134

Cali, U., Kuzlu, M., Karaarslan, E., & Jovanovic, V. (2022b). "Opportunities and challenges in Metaverse for industry 4.0 and beyond applications," in Paper presented at the 2022 IEEE 1st global emerging technology blockchain Forum: blockchain and beyond (iGETblockchain), 1–6. DOI: 10.1109/iGETblockchain56591.2022.10087104

Castronova, E. (2008). *Synthetic worlds: the business and culture of online games*. University of Chicago press.

De Giovanni, P. (2023). Sustainability of the Metaverse: A transition to industry 5.0. *Sustainability (Basel), 15*(7), 6079. DOI: 10.3390/su15076079

Delgado, C. B. (2022). User experience (UX) in Metaverse: Realities and challenges. *Metaverse Basic Appl. Res., 1*, 9. DOI: 10.56294/mr20229

Delmerico, J., Poranne, R., Bogo, F., Oleynikova, H., Vollenweider, E., Coros, S., Nieto, J., & Pollefeys, M. (2022). Spatial computing and intuitive interaction: Bringing mixed reality and robotics together. *IEEE Robotics & Automation Magazine, 29*(1), 45–57. DOI: 10.1109/MRA.2021.3138384

Fajar, M., David, D., Sihombing, P., Kekal, H., Aditya, I., Ilham, R., & Keswara, Y. S. (2022). The Metaverse to enhance safety campaign toward shipping industry (case study: The development and implementation of Metaverse in government-owned corporation). *International Journal of Emerging Technology and Advanced Engineering, 12*(08), 1–11. DOI: 10.46338/ijetae0822_01

Girvan, C. (2018). What is a virtual world? Definition and classification. *Educational Technology Research and Development*, *66*(5), 1087–1100. DOI: 10.1007/s11423-018-9577-y

Gursoy, D., Malodia, S., & Dhir, A. (2022). The Metaverse in the hospitality and tourism industry: An overview of current trends and future research directions. *Journal of Hospitality Marketing & Management*, *31*(5), 527–534. DOI: 10.1080/19368623.2022.2072504

Hadavi, A., & Alizadehsalehi, S. (2024). From BIM to Metaverse for AEC industry. *Automation in Construction*, *160*, 105248. DOI: 10.1016/j.autcon.2023.105248

Harapan, H., Itoh, N., Yufika, A., Winardi, W., Keam, S., Te, H., Megawati, D., Hayati, Z., Wagner, A. L., & Mudatsir, M. (2020). Coronavirus disease 2019 (COVID-19): A literature review. *Journal of Infection and Public Health*, *13*(5), 667–673. DOI: 10.1016/j.jiph.2020.03.019 PMID: 32340833

He, T. (2022). From single-player games to Metaverse: A futuristic analysis of challenging legal issues in the video game industry in China. *GRUR Int.*, *71*(10), 952–966. DOI: 10.1093/grurint/ikac039

Jagatheesaperumal, S. K., & Rahouti, M. (2022). Building digital twins of cyber physical systems with Metaverse for industry 5.0 and beyond. *IT Professional*, *24*(6), 34–40. DOI: 10.1109/MITP.2022.3225064

Jiang, W., Han, B., Habibi, M. A., & Schotten, H. D. (2021). The road towards 6G: A comprehensive survey. *IEEE Open Journal of the Communications Society*, *2*, 334–366. DOI: 10.1109/OJCOMS.2021.3057679

Kadry, A. (2022). The Metaverse revolution and its impact on the future of advertising industry. *J. Des. Sci. Appl. Arts*, *3*(2), 347–358. DOI: 10.21608/jdsaa.2022.129876.1171

Kaede, S., Hiroki, S., & Shuichi, N. (2023). The Metaverse in the tourism industry: A new horizon after the COVID-19 pandemic. *Wakayama Tour. Rev.*, *4*, 32–35. DOI: 10.19002/24363839.4.32

Kafilaleh, Y., & Asadi, H. (2022). Identifying and prioritizing key branding factors in the pharmaceutical industry in Metaverse: An integrated DEMATEL-ANP approach. [TRS]. *Tobacco Regulatory Science*, •••, 3026–3034.

Lee, C. W. (2022). Application of Metaverse service to healthcare industry: A strategic perspective. *International Journal of Environmental Research and Public Health*, *19*(20), 13038. DOI: 10.3390/ijerph192013038 PMID: 36293609

Lee, H., Yoo, S., & Kim, Y. (2015). "Design and implementation of an energy trading model for smart factories," in Paper presented at the 2015 IEEE 20th conference on emerging technologies and factory automation (ETFA), 1–4. DOI: 10.1109/ETFA.2015.7301568

Madakam, S., Lake, V., Lake, V., & Lake, V. (2015). Internet of things (IoT): A literature review. *J. Comput. Commun.*, *3*(05), 164–173. DOI: 10.4236/jcc.2015.35021

Mahadev Madgule, N. (2023). Vinayaka, Yeshwant M. Sonkhaskar, Dhiren Ramanbhai Patel, R. Karthikeyan, P. Selvakumar,(2023). Mechanical properties and microstructure of activated TIG welded similar joints of Inconel alloys by desirability approaches. *Materials Today: Proceedings*, *77*, 528–533. DOI: 10.1016/j.matpr.2022.12.250

Nwakanma, C., Njoku, J., Okafor, C., & Kim, D. (2022). "Prospect and industry issues of Metaverse and digital twin adoption in nigerian maritime," in Paper presented at the Proceedings of the 1sth international Conference on maritime IT convergence. South Korea: Jeju Island, 1–4.

OMIgroup. (2022). Open Metaverse interoperability group. Omigroup. Available at: https://omigroup.org/

Özdemir Uçgun, G., & Şahin, S. Z. (2023). How does Metaverse affect the tourism industry? Current practices and future forecasts. *Current Issues in Tourism*, *27*(17), 2742–2756. DOI: 10.1080/13683500.2023.2238111

Park, J. H. (2021). The direction and implications of the content industry in the Metaverse era. *SSRN*, (21), 6–5. DOI: 10.2139/ssrn.4194255

Pooyandeh, M., Han, K., & Sohn, I. (2022). Cybersecurity in the AI-based Metaverse: A survey. *Applied Sciences (Basel, Switzerland)*, *12*(24), 12993. DOI: 10.3390/app122412993

Prabadevi, B., Deepa, N., Victor, N., Gadekallu, T. R., Maddikunta, P. K. R., & Yenduri, G.. (2023). Metaverse and the fashion industry: A systematic literature review. *J. Glob. Fash. Mark.*, *15*(1), 131–154. DOI: 10.1080/20932685.2023.2270587

Qin, Y. (2022). Investment potential analysis on Chinese stock market in Metaverse-take VR industry as a sample. Paper presented at the 2022 7th international conference on financial innovation and economic development (ICFIED 2022), 1001–1007. DOI: 10.2991/aebmr.k.220307.165

Ramakrishnan, T., Mohan Gift, M. D., Chitradevi, S., Jegan, R., Hency Jose, P. S., Nagaraja, H. N., & Hailegiorgis, S. M. (2022). Study of numerous resins used in polymer matrix composite materials. *Advances in Materials Science and Engineering, 2022*(1), 1088926.

Rather, R. A. (2023). Metaverse marketing and consumer research: Theoretical framework and future research agenda in tourism and hospitality industry. *Tourism Recreation Research*, •••, 1–9. DOI: 10.1080/02508281.2023.2216525

Singh, K. (2023). Evaluation planning for artificial intelligence-based industry 6.0 Metaverse integration. Intelligent Hum. Syst. Integration (IHSI 2023). *Integrating People Intelligent Syst., 69*(69). Advance online publication. DOI: 10.54941/ahfe1002892

Sreenivasulu, A., & Manimozhi, T. Satheesh kumar P., Selvakumar P. and Singh P.,(2022). "The Model of Smart Sensing Device For Sensitive Nanoclusters Modification in Sensing Properties," 2022 2nd International Conference on Advance Computing and Innovative Technologies in Engineering (ICACITE), Greater Noida, India, 2022, pp. 1043-1047, DOI: 10.1109/ICACITE53722.2022.9823846

Sugumaran, K. M. D., Pandiyarajan V., Y. B S, Selvakumar P. and M. S, (2024). "Analysis of Electromyography Signals for Control of Mechanical Prosthesis using Machine Learning Techniques," 2024 2nd International Conference on Intelligent Data Communication Technologies and Internet of Things (IDCIoT), Bengaluru, India, 2024, pp. 1059-1067, DOI: 10.1109/IDCIoT59759.2024.10467707

Tlili, A., Huang, R., & Kinshuk, X. (2023). Metaverse for climbing the ladder toward 'industry 5.0'and 'society 5.0. *Service Industries Journal, 43*(3-4), 260–287. DOI: 10.1080/02642069.2023.2178644

Truong, V. T., Le, L. B., & Niyato, D. (2023). Blockchain meets Metaverse and digital asset management: A comprehensive survey. *IEEE Access : Practical Innovations, Open Solutions, 11*, 26258–26288. DOI: 10.1109/ACCESS.2023.3257029

Vijayakumar, G., Rajkumar, M., Rajiv Chandar, N., Selvakumar, P., & Duraisamy, R. (2024). Muniyandi Rajkumar, Rajiv Chandar N, Selvakumar P and Ramesh Duraisamy, (2024). Environmentally friendly TDS removal from waste water by electrochemical ion exchange batch-type recirculation (EIR) technique. *Environmental Science. Water Research & Technology, 10*(4), 826–835. DOI: 10.1039/D3EW00793F

Wang, X., Shi, T., Bai, W., Peng, K., Li, J., & Shi, Y. (2022). "The research of Metaverse application in intelligent railway passenger station," in Paper presented at the international conference on Metaverse, 111–117. DOI: 10.1007/978-3-031-23518-4_10

Widiyanti, D. E., Kim, E. B., & Shin, S. Y. (2022). "Enhancing the use of Metaverse in industry: advertisement management system," in *Proceedings of the korea communications society conference*, 753–754.

Xu, M., Ng, W. C., Lim, W. Y. B., Kang, J., Xiong, Z., Niyato, D., Yang, Q., Shen, X., & Miao, C. (2022). A full dive into realizing the edge-enabled Metaverse: Visions, enabling technologies, and challenges. *IEEE Communications Surveys and Tutorials*, *25*(1), 656–700. DOI: 10.1109/COMST.2022.3221119

Yan, R. (2022). "A sustainable fashion industry business model revolution based on the Metaverse: practices and reciprocal processes,", 4. Econ. Manag., 363–369. DOI: 10.54097/hbem.v4i.3526

Yang, L. (2023). Recommendations for Metaverse governance based on technical standards. *Humanities & Social Sciences Communications*, *10*(1), 1–10. DOI: 10.1057/s41599-023-01750-7

Zhang, R., Wen, K., Cai, R., & Liu, H. (2023). The application of Metaverse in the construction industry: Exploring the future architectural trends of virtual and real integration. *J. Civ. Eng. Urban Plan.*, *5*(3), 65–72. DOI: 10.23977/jceup.2023.050309

Zhang, S. (2023). "Metaverse technology enabled figure skating industry upgrade," in Paper presented at the 3rd international conference on internet, education and information technology (IEIT 2023), 383–394. DOI: 10.2991/978-94-6463-230-9_45

Chapter 7
Fostering Brand Awareness and Customer Loyalty With Gamification in the Metaverse

Sarika Koluguri
https://orcid.org/0009-0003-1542-3102
KG Reddy College of Engineering and Technology, Moinabad, India

Keshav Sudam
https://orcid.org/0009-0006-5000-8264
Indis Vivacity Kondapur, Hyderabad, India

ABSTRACT

This chapter discusses the aspects of applying gamification for branding within the metaverse, to address the issue of consumer interactions in the context of growing competition in the digital environment. In view of this the study uses a qualitative approach with an evaluative design that draws from various case examples of brands that have successfully incorporated gamification into their communication strategies as well as specific indicators of user engagement as well as brand loyalty. Some of the findings include; Brand engagement and attachment is enhanced through the incorporation of game elements such as; immersive experience, user generated content and reward screen. Furthermore, the research demonstrates that feedback and interaction with the unique user profile are essential for its further engagement. Lastly, this chapter established that the use of gamification in marketing within metaverse goes beyond mere product visibility since it guides in the formation of a long-term relationship with consumers through the provision of fun-related activities.

DOI: 10.4018/979-8-3693-8886-0.ch007

1. INTRODUCTION

1.1 Overview of the Metaverse

Augmented reality, virtual reality, the internet and more combined in one area that gives the opportunity to interact with users in metaverse. As a concept it describes a digital world that mirrors the physical and it comprises of social networks, games, a commerce marketplace among others. Some of these features include user created content that lasts beyond a single session, multiuser that occurs concurrently and in real-time. In contemporary marketing, the metaverse is its exciting area where brands are trying to tap consumers in a new and unique way. CCR is a pioneer in the application of metaverse technologies in marketing that allows its clients to create environments for direct customer interactions and experiences otherwise impossible in conventional marketing niches.

1.2 Gamification Explained

Web gamification is the use of game design techniques in different environments other than games in order to improve user experience. This approach uses features including points, badges, leader boards, and challenges in order to ensure that participation as well as achievements are enhanced. The principles of gamification are based on the concepts of intrinsic and extrinsic motivation systems which motivate inherent contentment and fun to user and extrinsic approach that motivates user's behavior (Kumari, 2023). Taking the case of brand engagement, gamification is perfect as it alters the buying process into rewarding processes. Having closed the way Looker's audience perceives brands, it's says that through the use of game mechanics, it'll be easier to present emotionate brand stories that influence the consumer (Sharma, 2024).

1.3 Purpose of the Chapter

This study aims to assess facts and identify role of gamification when it comes to the metaverse as well as the general brand association and commitment. When marketing in virtual environments, it becomes important to know when and how to successfully approach and utilize the user. Specifically, this chapter will desire to know how brands can use the concept of gamification to engage consumers in a way that leads to improved connection. More specifically, this chapter aims to discuss the role of gamification in the context of the metaverse and present the most important recommendations and strategies, opportunities and risks for marketers interested in successfully engaging with virtual audiences through various games and applications in the nearest future.

2. THEORETICAL FRAMEWORK

2.1 Understanding the Psychological Perspectives of Games

Analyzing the background of psychological uses of gamification also plays an important role of applying it in the marketplace. Core to this is a dichotomy of motives; intrinsic and extrinsic motivation. Intrinsic motivation means doing the activity for the sake of doing it, for the sake of having the fun of the activity, the fun the game give. Thus, while intrinsic motivation is based on the desire to respond to the content within the activity, extrinsic motivation is predicated on the offer of points, badges, or other prizes that are outside the context of the activity. This way, gamification is capable of inspiring powerful experiences across the entire user range by tapping into both extrinsic and intrinsic motivators.

Engagement mechanics is the conceptual approach used to describe the specific tactics used to interest and retain a user. Such mechanics embrace setting goals, feedback, and social sharing in addition to improving the user experience leads to satisfaction and accomplishment related to other users. If well incorporated within brand initiatives, these engagement mechanics result in increased user retention and more profound brand affection.

2.2 Brand Awareness and Loyalty

Brand recognition and brand identity are two major concepts in marketing and both are measured differently. Brand familiarity relate to the extent a brand is known by the consumers, and this is classified in terms of the recall rates and brand recognition studies. On the other hand, brand loyalty is defined as long-term consumer's tendency to repurchase or support a particular brand, where metrics that may be used include repeat purchase rate and customer life time value.

One most notable connection is the one between gamification and brand loyalty. It helps create richer engagement environments in that it turns static brand engagements into dynamic ones. Now, when consumer engaged into the gamified activities, he/she will probably have a positive perception towards the brand and therefore brand loyalty will have occurred. Compared to traditional promotional strategies, the use of gamification offers real potential for brands to foster emotional bonds with consumers in a manner that will only deepen the relationship (Rane, 2023).

Table 1. Comparison of gamification techniques and their psychological impact

Technique	Psychological Impact	Example Application
Points System	Encourages competition	Leaderboards
Badges	Provides a sense of achievement	Milestone rewards
Challenges	Promotes engagement through tasks	Quests and missions
Social Sharing	Fosters community interaction	Shareable achievements
Progress Tracking	Visualizes user journey	Progress bars and levels

The table above shows how several types of gamification build on psychological concepts to motivate users, which is a basis for analysing their value in consolidating brand equity within the metaverse.

3. GAMIFICATION STRATEGIES IN THE METAVERSE

3.1 Designing Engaging Experiences

Laying down memorable experiences is crucial when companies are aiming at interacting with clients through the metaverse. These interactions occur in virtual worlds and other similar environments in which users can interact and participate in ways which fit well. It is thus possible for brands to capitalize on the specificities of these themed environments in a given digital application of space by proposing experiences that are appropriately stimulating of exploration and aesthetic expression and that bring the user closer to the brand.

Thus, information generated by users can be seen as critical to the development of engagement of the metaverse. Brands must ask themselves whether that community is engaging and empowering users to build their environment or to create their own content be it virtual avatars, levels for games or new storylines, etc. It also increases the level of user engagement with the brand and helps to achieve group interaction among users, leading to even greater strengthening and protraction of the brand. If the users are involved in the brand story and are essentially given the role of co-authors, it is easy to motivate them emotionally and have them promote the brands (Wanick, 2023).

3.2 Interactive Campaigns

Having communicational campaigns within the metaverse is a massive opportunity for brands to market to buyers effectively in the metaverse. What is especially important, virtual environments allow offering consumers series of amazing experiences that can be engaging at the same time. Positive examples show that combining elements of games into the marketing mix is unobtrusive; it keeps consumers more engaged and loyal.

For example, in virtual scavenger hunts, the brands offer amusement to users in a form of a game; at the same time, they also help consumers know more about the offered products or the organization's values and missions. They generally involve admittance to an activity wherein one has to complete puzzles or missions in order to find facts about a brand or have access to rewards. Such experience not only attract consumers' attention to the product but also make them search for the product, and more importantly, the probability of consumers' recalling the brand is high in the blue ocean of digital world.

Another best practice that brands have used in the metaverse is interactive storytelling. This application enables the users interact with narratives that are based on choices, which can make brands develop interpersonal relations with consumers. For example, a fashion brand might create a storyline of trying on some outfits for a character in a game and then purchasing what has been tried on (Zaki, 2024). An engagement of this sort not only improves the interaction level which defines a user's involvement with a particular brand but also evokes emotions of brand commitment (Öztürk, 2023).

Such campaigns might employ several elements including but not limited to: The challenge, the reward and the share buttons which helps to engage the users. There are different types of challenges, starting from specific tasks that can be solved to creative contests through which customers will be immersed in a brand. When these challenges are presented to consumers in a format of points, badges, or even exclusive content for accomplishing them brands can help create positive reinforcement by encouraging consumers to complete these challenges over and over again.

In addition, it should not be mentioned that the social component of these campaigns is also significant. With this, others as a means of sharing one's experience on the social media platforms or within the metaverse, brands get a wider coverage. If the users showcase their achievement or join group, they become promoters of the brand across the social media platforms without having to directly advertise; new users are attracted to the brand due to sponsored content.

Combining interactivity and gamification of different categories of campaigns within the metaverse, brands can create active and engaging consumer experiences. Hence, developing innovative approaches and appeals that incorporate promotional messages in the content shared with the target audience, firms can foster a passionate team of brand messengers (Bilgihan, 20234). The possibility for growth in this area is huge, and it is expected that the brands that actively use these technologies would achieve great results in terms of users' attention and their loyalty to a particular brand.

There are several ways brands can determine the effectiveness of these interactive campaigning, including: engagement rates, completion rates on the tasks set in games, and the amount of user generated content. Also, monitoring social communication and feedback will also help estimate the perception of the brand resulting from the campaign. Through the evaluation of these metrics, brands are able to improve future campaign objectives, and overall performance, leading to long term users' loyalty.

Figure 1. Key gamification elements in the metaverse

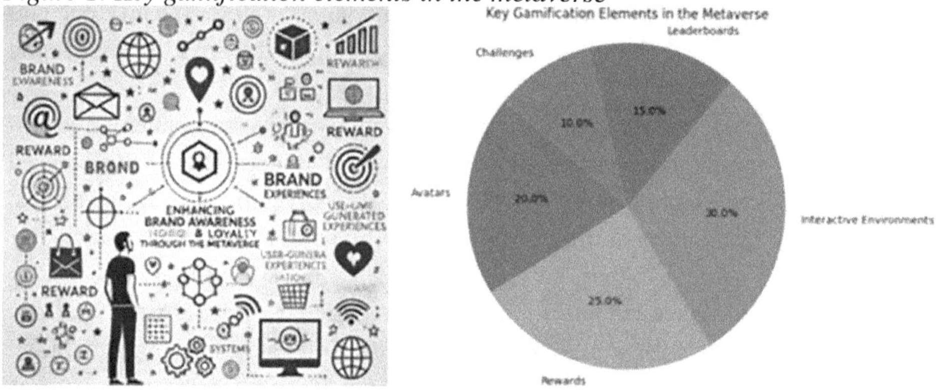

This figure visually represents the essential gamification elements that drive engagement within the metaverse, including avatars, rewards, challenges, and social interactions. These components work together to create a holistic user experience, reinforcing the brand's presence and encouraging long-term loyalty (Oluwaseyi, 2024).

Figure 2. User engagement cycle in gamified experiences

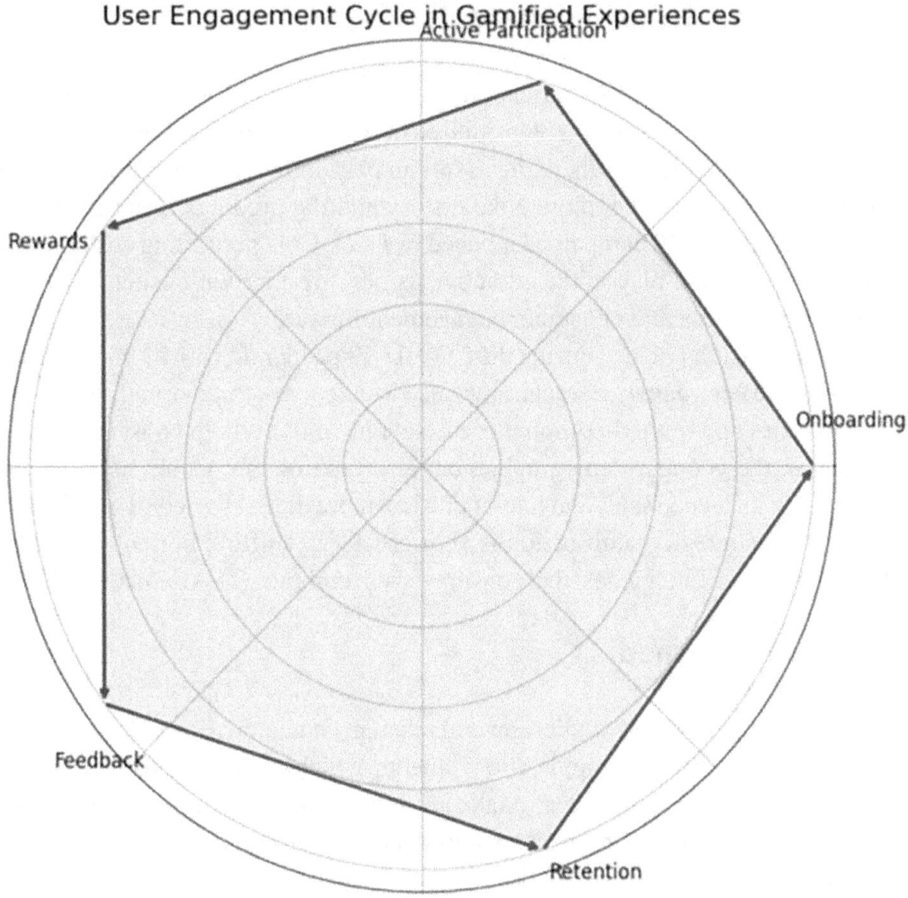

This figure illustrates the cyclical nature of user engagement in gamified experiences, highlighting key stages such as onboarding, active participation, rewards, feedback, and retention. Each stage represents an opportunity for brands to deepen their connection with users, demonstrating how effective gamification can lead to sustained engagement and loyalty in the metaverse.

4. CASE STUDIES

4.1 Successful Brands in the Metaverse

Many brands have used gamification features in the metaverse to reach users: their unique advertising concepts help build customer trust. Some of the most famous ones are Nike's "Nikeland" where the users can play games, chat and receive some incentives as long as they explore Nike history and the products. Another typical example is the Covid-19 campaign launched by Coca-Cola permitting customers to create their avatar and play in the attractive games, together with using it to move their brand awareness and consumer engagement forward.

Also, Gucci has advanced during the COVID-19 pandemic with its online Gucci Garden in the Roblox game; users can navigate virtual rooms, wear virtual clothes and buy accessories and limited-edition pieces. Not only did this help boost the brand's awareness in the younger demographic, but also proving that games as a concept can positively influence sales and interaction in a more digital society. These brands represent how strategic gamification is very crucial in shifting normal marketing methods into active fun 'games' that consumers will embrace (Dos Remedios, 2023).

4.2 Lessons Learned

By evaluating these case studies, several inherent characteristics and trends identified in various gamification applications emerge, which will be discussed in greater detail below. The first major idea to take away from the consolidated information presented in this paper is the necessity to connect game-related activities to the brand and its principles (Arya, 2024). New studies have also shown that messages associated with core branding tend to perform better when incorporated in gamification initiatives. Moreover, it is the aspect of promoting community participation; permitting users to discuss their experiences and to challenge each other provide better user experience and create user identity.

The second is the application of data analytics for tracking user's activity and preferences are important. Consequently, theoretical knowledge of what captures the attention of the users will prompt a consistent improvement of strategies that brands deploy to appeal to the consumers. Last but not the least it becomes crucial to balance game with brand; sometimes brand and game both becomes confusing rather then adding value to it.

Table 2. Case study analysis of brand engagement in the metaverse

Brand	Gamification Strategy	Key Outcomes
Nike	Nikeland virtual experience	Increased user engagement and brand loyalty
Coca-Cola	Personalized avatar experience in games	Enhanced brand visibility and interaction
Gucci	Gucci Garden on Roblox	Elevated presence in younger markets and sales growth
Adidas	Virtual sneaker drops and challenges	Boosted online sales and community building
Fortnite (Epic Games)	Collaborations with major brands	Significant brand reach and cross-promotion opportunities

This table shows the potential used in brands across the metaverse and outcomes achieved by strategies through the use of gamification. Such information may be useful to other brands in formulating their proper models of gamification.

5. MEASURING SUCCESS

5.1 Key Performance Indicators (KPIs)

For the evaluation of implemented gamification concepts in the metaverse, brands need to define objective measurable goals that incorporate brand recognition and loyalty as their principal metric. Some of the typical measures that are used when calculating brand awareness are brand recall rates, coverage rates marketing communications and the click through rates, likes, shares, comments, and other engagement parameters received across social media sites (Bousba, 2022). For brand loyalty, such measurements as customer retention coefficient, the frequency of repurchase, or customer lifetime value, all give information about how well the brand retains the audience.

Some of these KPIs require tools that support data collection in the monitoring process. Other tools include Google Analytics, social media insights, and customers relationship management software which gives you full information about the users' engagement and subsequent activities (Сизикова, 2024). Moreover, the tools, which are employed to measure customers' activity when they interact with a brand's game, including game analytics, may facilitate the assessment of customers' engagement (Nicola, 2022).

5.2 Analyzing User Feedback

Usually, thanks to the analysis of the comments given by the users, it is possible to fine-tune the goals of the gamification process as well as improve the overall user experience. Consumer participation brings about understanding ofconsumer expectations, their attitude and likely opportunities for enhancing the product. This one can involve acting with the user, surveys, polls and focus groups which can provide the qualitative data as well as quantitative results.

It is possible to track conversations people have on social platforms, incorporate feedback forms into the gamified experience, as well as analyze the content that the users created. It also assists brands in understanding user satisfaction and in the process, create the feel of community since consumers feel appreciated. Including user feedback into designing and development activities help brands to refine the idea of gamification as organically as possible.

Figure 3. KPI framework for measuring brand loyalty in the metaverse

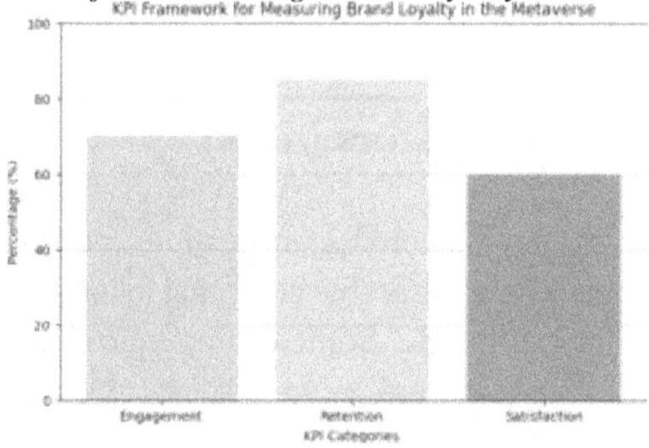

This figure describes a preliminary taxonomy of KPIs reflecting brand loyalty in the context of the metaverse as well as suggestions for how these KPIs can be quantified. More significantly, it emphasises process areas of engagement, retention and customer satisfaction that lay down a framework for brands and thus helps to guide the industry in evaluating how effective an attempt at gamification (Mittal, 2023).

Table 3. KPIs for evaluating gamified marketing campaigns

KPI	Description	Measurement Method
Engagement Rate	Frequency of user interaction	Analytics tools, user logs
Retention Rate	Percentage of returning users	Cohort analysis
Customer Satisfaction	User feedback and ratings	Surveys and reviews
Completion Rate	Rate of users completing gamified tasks	In-game tracking
Social Sharing	Volume of user-shared content	Social media analytics

The given table provides an outline of basic KPIs which can be applied to the assessment of the gamified marketing campaigns' effectiveness. Through the tracking of these KPIs, brands are also able to consider their applicability as well as aim to further optimise methods of reaching and retaining users.

6. CHALLENGES AND CONSIDERATIONS

6.1 Potential Pitfalls of Gamification

Although the use of gamification can improve the overall spect of the user engagement and, thereforeBrand loyalty, it 'comes with some specific difficulties'. First, by the fact that there may be too many options and the users get tired of changing from one platform to another. While the number of brands using gamification increases, the audience might experience the problem of the overload of gamified offerings. From this saturation, audiences get used to such tricks and thus lose interest and instead of being useful to their daily lives, they end up coming across fake innovate ideas. It indicates that brands should not depend upon gamification as the single powerful tool instead they should aim at generating suitable and valuable experiences that can be shared with target customer groups.

As mentioned previously, ethical factors are central to gamification, where it is essential to assess how feasible they are to incorporate into practice. This is especially important to brands as they seek to advance their engagement goal; brands have to make sure that with gamification, they do not capitalize on user susceptibilities or create negative user habits like sinful use of mobile screens or unhealthy chasing after the rewards. Confidentiality in the process of obtaining information from the user is also crucial to correct relationships (Safitri, 2024). From this paper, it is evident that brands should be careful about designing the gamification aspects that could otherwise influence users in negative ways and instead follow the guidelines that will help to create a positive experience among users.

6.2 Future Trends

Several considerations are in a preparedness to define the direction of development in the metaverse in the coming future. Here is one specific forecast: The development of new technologies as AI, machine learning, and others to integrate more intelligent gamified environment (Rane, 2023). In real time analysis of user behavior brands help to properly adjust their gamification to individual users, which leads to satisfaction of the users.

Furthermore, it can be supposed that decentralised approaches and the exploit of the blockchain technology can also affect gameification strategies. These technologies can enable people to own objects into virtual worlds, that is, invest on their experiences such as NFTs. Additionally, we will continue to observe how the increasing metaverse adoption could be overshadowed by a focus on the gamification of social connections. Brands that help build a real community for the consumers will probably be more effective (Mazzù, 2024).

However, there are challenges with gamification, and brands have to ensure that they counter those challenges as they strive to adopt the different strategies through the evolving metaverse.

7. CONCLUSION

7.1 Recap of Key Insights

Drawing from the previous chapter of this paper, this chapter has focused on how gamification could revolutionize brand endorsement and affinity in the metaverse. Essential findings indicate that there are certain peculiarities of the gamified experience that may dramatically enhance users' engagement: the given context, such as the environment, user contents, and campaign, and interactive ones. Intrinsically linked motivational factors, as well as extrinsic motivational factors aligned with a brand allow for the development of meaningful consumer-brand relationships rather than simple marketing strategies. These case-studies contextualize Nike and Coca-Cola to show how major brands use gamification techniques to induce community engagement and increase the overall engagement of their users for their particular brands.

In addition, the presentation focused on how success can be best measured in terms of clearly defined KPIs and how the role of user feedback underlines the requirement of brands to fine-tune the approach effectively. But there is a need to be careful of some of the drawbacks that may be experienced by brands and consumers as follows; That is user fatigue and the ethical issue that may accompany game based activities.

7.2 Final Thoughts

Thus, we outline the further prospects of using brands and engaging consumers through gamification features in the metaverse. With advancement in technology, brands will be able to get better and efficient techniques of developing game like experiences using game gamification strategies. The application of AI, machine learning, and distreading block chains will allow users to engage at much more profound levels and levels of engagement hence, brand loyalty (Lamba, 2024).

Lastly, it is apparent that brands which incorporate innovation as a primary priority alongside ethical relevancy and community engagement will be best seated for success within the metaverse. This suggests that brands can sue meaningful consumer engagements and relevant and exciting experiences to make sense of this bourgeoning and changing digital environment so as to usher in a new dispensation in marketing that will be based on pro-consumer experiences and brand loyalty.

REFERENCES

Сизикова, А. (2024). Tools of Brand Promotion Metaverse. *Коммуникации. Медиа. Дизайн*, *9*(3), 135–158.

Arya, V., Sambyal, R., Sharma, A., & Dwivedi, Y. K. (2024). Brands are calling your AVATAR in Metaverse–A study to explore XR-based gamification marketing activities & consumer-based brand equity in virtual world. *Journal of Consumer Behaviour*, *23*(2), 556–585. DOI: 10.1002/cb.2214

Bilgihan, A., Leong, A. M. W., Okumus, F., & Bai, J. (2024). Proposing a metaverse engagement model for brand development. *Journal of Retailing and Consumer Services*, *78*, 103781. DOI: 10.1016/j.jretconser.2024.103781

Bousba, Y., & Arya, V. (2022). Let's connect in metaverse. Brand's new destination to increase consumers' affective brand engagement & their satisfaction and advocacy. *Journal of Content. Community & Communication*, *15*(8), 276–293.

Dos Remedios, L., 2023. The influence of the Metaverse on Brand Management: A study. *communities, 2*(2), p.5.

Kumari, H., & Gujral, H. K. (2023). A STUDY ON GAMIFICATION & ITS EFFECTS ON CONSUMER BEHAVIOUR. *International Journal of Advanced Research in Computer Science*, *14*(4).

Lamba, S. S., & Malik, R. (2024). Retention in the Metaverse: Customer Engagement Using Big Data. In *Augmenting Customer Retention Through Big Data Analytics* (pp. 291-309). Apple Academic Press.

Mazzù, M. F., Pozharliev, R. I., & Della Sala, I. (2024). How Metaverse Creates Value for Luxury Brands. In *Sinergie-SIMA Conference 2024 «Management of sustainability and well-being for individuals and society*.

Mittal, G., & Bansal, R. (2023). Driving force behind consumer brand engagement: the metaverse. In *Cultural marketing and metaverse for consumer engagement* (pp. 164–181). IGI Global. DOI: 10.4018/978-1-6684-8312-1.ch012

Nicola, M. (2022). Gamification marketing in metaverse contexts: can the employment of immersive gamification experiences that leverage customer's creativity and sociality be a useful tool to influence customer engagement in metaverse applications?.

Oluwaseyi, J. and Stilinski, D., (2024). The Strategic Implications of the Metaverse for Brand Building and Customer Experience.

Öztürk, B. and Hersono, R., (2023). Playing to Win: How Gamification Can Boost Customer Engagement and Turn Non-Fans into Brand Advocates.

Rane, N. (2023). Metaverse marketing strategies: enhancing customer experience and analysing consumer behaviour through leading-edge Metaverse technologies, platforms, and models. *Available atSSRN*. DOI: 10.2139/ssrn.4624199

Rane, N., Choudhary, S. and Rane, J., (2023). Metaverse for Enhancing Customer Loyalty: Effective Strategies to Improve Customer Relationship, Service, Engagement, Satisfaction, and Experience. *Service, Engagement, Satisfaction, and Experience (November 1, 2023).*

Safitri, A., Husin, N., Arifah, I. D. C., Dewi, R. S., Kharisma, F., & Kautsar, A. (2024, January). Metaverse User Experience, Customer Engagement, and Brand Awareness Relation as SMEs Marketing Strategies in Virtual Worlds. In *2024 ASU International Conference in Emerging Technologies for Sustainability and Intelligent Systems (ICETSIS)* (pp. 1092-1096). IEEE. DOI: 10.1109/ICETSIS61505.2024.10459506

Sharma, W., Lim, W. M., Kumar, S., Verma, A., & Kumra, R. (2024). Game on! A state-of-the-art overview of doing business with gamification. *Technological Forecasting and Social Change*, *198*, 122988. DOI: 10.1016/j.techfore.2023.122988

Wanick, V., & Stallwood, J. (2023). Brand storytelling, gamification and social media marketing in the "metaverse": A case study of the Ralph Lauren winter escape. In *Reinventing fashion retailing: Digitalising, gamifying, entrepreneuring* (pp. 35–54). Springer International Publishing. DOI: 10.1007/978-3-031-11185-3_3

Zaki, Y., Wu, M. S., Hamdan, A., & Alsharabi, H. (2024). A Conceptual Framework for Metaverse Marketing Strategies in the Fashion Industry: Exploring the Role of Brand Experience and Brand Equity. In *Opportunities and Risks in AI for Business Development* (Vol. 1, pp. 311–321). Springer Nature Switzerland. DOI: 10.1007/978-3-031-65203-5_28

Chapter 8
Global Customer Engagement Through Gamified Mobile Apps and Virtual Experiences

Kajal Chauhan
https://orcid.org/0009-0006-5000-8264
Lloyd Business School, Greater Noida, India

Krity Gulati
Lloyd Business School, Greater Noida, India

ABSTRACT

This chapter focuses on customer engagement based on the use of gamified mobile applications and virtual environments across the world while responding to the study's research question of how these technologies improve customer engagement and loyalty. Building on previous research, employing a systematic literature review and analysing case studies, the research investigates latest trends in the use of mobile applications and the impact of gamification in various sectors. Key outcomes show that individual incentives, social comparisons, and virtual environment increase engagement rates, especially with the young audience. The assessment of the given apps also emphasizes the necessity to adapt designs for different cultures and points that there is a constant need for development of new approaches to the process of gamification. Finally, the chapter posits that gamification when incorporated with strategic purpose can enhance the fellowship between customer and business, consequently delivering better results thus, providing a guide for businesses that aim to utilize these tools.

DOI: 10.4018/979-8-3693-8886-0.ch008

1. INTRODUCTION

International customer communication on the other hand is defined as the manner and approach used by these firms to establish and maintain relationships with customers in different parts of the world. It includes all the contacts that brand create with its customers intending to foster loyalty, satisfy the consumers and consequently make sales. This paper recognizes that with the globalization of markets, managing customer relations globally is a significant test to success in today's cut throat markets.

As a recent phenomenon, the use of gamification has been an effective technique in improving customers engagements by incorporating game mechanics in non-video game environments. Including the features like points, rewards, challenges, social sharing businesses can design experiences that are exciting to customer. In addition to influencing people into participating in the process, the approach also leads to a sense of accomplishment to the users and hence, higher likelihood of brand commitment. Therefore, gamification is being used as a critical element in the strategies to create effective marketing and customer services.

Today, smart applications for mobile devices and virtual/mixed reality are critical to engaging customers worldwide. The advance in information communication technology such as smartphone and the internet is therefore presents business with the opportunity to access customers at anytime and at any place. Mobile application helps to communicate directly and establish a loyal audience through offering and buying simple processes, while virtual scenarios, including AR and VR, design an engaging space for customer familiarization. Altogether, these technologies do not only enhance the customers' experience, but also let the brands, the gathering of the crucial information which can be used for enhancing the further engagement.

Figure 1. Customer journey map

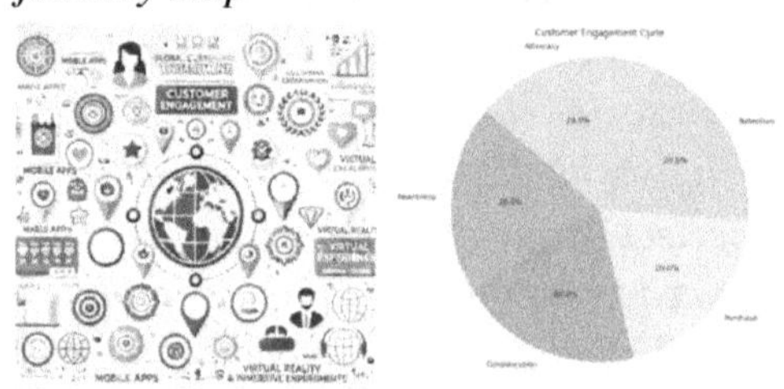

In this paper, thus, the Customer Engagement Cycle, illustrated in Figure 1, has been used to depict forces in play over the lifecycle of customer engagement. This figure represents a Customer Journey Map that enlightens clients on the process they undergo in considering a particular product, buying it and using it, and even recommending it to other potential buyers. It will also help businesses better manage how they engage customers on an international level, using knowledge of this cycle to target those clients where they are most receptive to certain kinds of outreach.

Over the past few years, there has been a rise in research examining gamification as a way to keep customers interested in mobile applications. Based on their investigation, De Canio, Fuentes-Blasco and Martinelli (2021) suggest that what leads shoppers to make purchases via mobile apps is mainly having fun, focusing on the app and sharing the experience with others. Chinese consumers involved in their research proved that gamification helps in engaging them with shopping and also indirectly leads to a higher intention to purchase. It is suggested that the most useful gamified apps encourage achievement and also give people a chance to interact with others.

According to Harwood and Garry (2015), if a gamified system is to motivate customers, it must ensure both intrinsic and extrinsic forms of motivation are present. It is highlighted that most people lose interest in gamification if it only offers basic or easily exhausted rewards. A strategy is successful when it combines important challenges, offers freedom to the user and provides useful feedback, boosting users' motivation and encouraging them to stay loyal for a long time. The authors from this year's study by Hammedi, Leclercq and Poncin (2019) also argue that gamification works best when users' values are part of it and when there is a mix of rewards that are given as well as those the user earns themselves.

Several research studies have examined how using gamification enhances the engagement of customers. According to Hollebeek, Das and Shukla (2021), gamified loyalty programs work better than traditional ones in increasing customer loyalty, their desire to take part and download the company's app. What they learned is that having fun and enjoying the program greatly impact the link between gamification and customer loyalty and self-gains play a big role too. It indicates that the use of gamification in managing customers motivates individuals both to participate and to support the business. Authors Bitrián, Buil and Catalán (2021) reveal that gamification in mobile apps motivates users because it rewards them and allows them to achieve success. They have concluded that providing a combination of challenges and benefits, as well as fresh updates, help keep users interested.

The studies consider the general digital environment where gamification is found. Rasool, Shah and Islam (2020) identify that customer involvement today is affected by excellent digital services, content made for each individual and interesting interactivity. They believe that concentrating on how users interact with a website helps companies gain more attention and gamification provides the best ways to make a website both enjoyable and relevant as technology advances. The author investigates the connection among gamification, brand love, customer involvement and how likely people are to repurchase, using Nike Run Club as an example. Results suggest that gamification improves people's relationship with the brand and acts to enhance engagement with the brand. Gamification, according to the study, both boosts the satisfaction with a brand and encourages people to shop again, sharing useful tips with brand managers wanting to solve the same problem.

Other studies in this field focus on how engaging with a brand impacts the effect of gamification on customers. The authors found that in online grocery retailing, adding fun challenges and interactive games boosts customers' satisfaction and helps keep them loyal to a brand. Based on the research, when gamification is combined with other aspects of building a brand and includes personalization and interactivity, its effectiveness increases significantly. This coincides with Yadav et al.'s study (2022), revealing how gamification leads to customers spending more time on the app and being more loyal.

Studies done in different industries show that gamification is flexible. The authors reveal how playing games in managing finances and following set targets results in better understanding of finance as well as increased loyalty to the brand. Högberg and colleagues discuss the use of augmented reality in shopping, where customers enjoy interacting with the product and are encouraged to buy. According to Jang, Kitchen and Kim (2018), including personalized achievements and streaks in mobile exercise apps boosts people's interest in using the app and also increases their likelihood of buying similar ones. All of these studies suggest that gamification succeeds in many industries and can increase people's interest in the short and long terms.

It is very important for global mobile app-based games to be adaptable to different cultures. In 2020, Kamboj, Rana and Drave observed that in some cultures, workers are led by the idea of working with a group, while in others they value challenging rivals. According to De Canio et al. (2021), it is important to adapt the main features of a game to suit the local audience. Falco (2020) studied gamification in China's luxury market and discovered that people who care about their status react well to using augmented reality (AR) and enjoying exclusive online rewards. Thus, the best way to use gamification is to make it flexible and adapted to local cultures, so that a wide range of people can take part in games adapted to their markets.

People who write on gamification point out a number of problems and ethical concerns linked to it. These scholars (Harwood and Garry) say that, if people receive too much external motivation, they can lose their internal desire to keep doing their work. In Rasool et al. (2020), it is mentioned that user trust in personalized gamification needs to be protected by following regulations, since there are some data privacy issues. Hammedi et al. (2019) argue against malicious design and encourage using good practices in gamification to allow users to make their own choices and build trust in a brand. Therefore, it is important for gamified systems to support users, be unbiased and be designed considering what is best for them.

In the upcoming years, the literature suggests that several new patterns are shaping the future of using gamification to engage customers. AI and machine learning are helping apps provide different challenges and rewards depending on what a user does. The grouping of augmented and virtual reality is making experiences more enjoyable and using blockchain technology makes rewarding users more secure and transparent. According to scholars, its success in the coming years relies on providing memorable, ethical and culturally relevant games that inspire people to stand behind the brand.

The evidence shows that proper implementation and design of gamification push customers to become more involved in using mobile apps and other virtual platforms. It applies mental triggers to initiatives, ensures enjoyable experiences for users and provides clear results everywhere for any business. Yet, its success lies in maintaining a balance between encouraging rewards, ethics and new ideas, as people in this age need more from their work.

2. THE CONCEPT OF GAMIFICATION

The use of game design features and mechanics in a field that is not a game is defined as gamification. This approach makes daily tasks less of a chore while integrating aspects like; points, badges, leaderboards and challenges. The general objective of gamification is to provide various incentives: intrinsic and extrinsic, so that interactions with the application shall become more engaging and beneficial for a user. Applying aspects of game design, firms can deliver a desired experience, which will elicit achievement and competition from customers.

The psychological basis of gamification is derived from many theories of motivation and behavior. The major theory includes Self-Determination Theory (SDT) which holists the issues of intrinsic motivation. Therefore, gamification can contribute to the increase of intrinsic motivation based on the needs for mastery, autonomy and relatedness. Also, the extrinsic rewards that are employed by other applications and services, such as accumulating points and earning gifts, can also encourage people's interest to a certain product or service. Such psychological factors make it possible for the businesses to apply the right techniques that will make people play games while at the same time fulfilling their needs.

As you can see in Table 1, some game mechanics can encourage users to do different things. Because these aspects rely on behavioral psychology and motivational theory, they play a big role in encouraging users and making them happy. When businesses rely on these elements, ordinary tasks can be made more exciting and playful. It leads to more people using the app, results in loyal customers and boosts their interest in the products and services.

Points play a crucial role in the design of games. Points indicate how much you have achieved and how far you have advanced. There are points available for playing a game, taking part in a task, answering a quiz or logging in every day. Players feel accomplished because the results of what they do appear quickly. People like that achievements in work can be easily measured. A point system is motivational because it helps people work toward their goals or earn rewards for their actions.

Point systems often go together with badges which are given as a reward for reaching different achievements. Unlike points, badges exist to highlight what you can do and how well you do it. Badges are usually given whenever someone successfully completes a tough or unusual activity. For a lot of users, these achievements in the form of game tokens inspire pride, make them feel good about themselves and are useful in starting and continuing conversations. The badge system helps satisfy humans' need for knowing they are competent and appreciated by others. When people are acknowledged by others for their hard work, they usually keep up and face more challenges.

Using leaderboards in a game helps players compete with one another. When users are ranked by their number of points or completed tasks, leaderboards cause a lively competition between them. For such people, viewing their stats encourages them to excel and be better than their competition. When updated frequently or set up by category, time or type of users, leaderboards commonly engage the audience strongly. But if leaderboards aren't used with respect to players, some may feel discouraged when they fall behind the primary players. For this reason, successful games with levels often switch their leaderboards, providing chances for all users to advance.

Usually, point systems, badges and leaderboards are the main parts of many systems based on games. As long as all these elements are present, they encourage various types of users: personal progress for some, achievement recognition for others and competing for others. Combining all these parts can develop an experience that is interesting for people of many types.

On top of the main three, other engagement tools can be just as important. With a progress bar, you can see your advancement to a particular objective. Although they seem straightforward, they are helpful: the motion of a bar filling lures a person into finishing the task. Since people recall unfinished things better due to the Zeigarnik effect, they are drawn to complete their unfinished chores.

In most gamified areas, challenges and quests are also frequently used. They provide users with particular goals and explain what should be achieved by a given time. Challenges motivate people to get involved and try to achieve specific goals. Many times, they include earning points, badges or getting access to new things within one planned game activity. Many quests use storytelling, making players care more about the quests. If a story is well-written, it gives each task a purpose and makes learning more enjoyable.

The learner's progress is considered and the amount of difficulty increases steadily without getting too tough. Moving up in experience can give you access to extra things which can truly excite the player. If a game is easy to advance in, players are motivated to come back frequently.

Taking part in social interaction is also highly effective in gamification. Whenever people participate in a community together, learn together or play games, they usually engage more. Since people are social, gaming with social options lets them meet the essential need for social bonding. These features make ordinary games an opportunity for players to work or compete with each other.

Special rewards such as money, can strongly impact someone's behavior. Although joy, craving new knowledge and mastering a skill are best for lasting enthusiasm, lower-cost and free offers, as well as using a points system, are a good way to encourage more people to try out the app. The benefits offered should be distributed in balance. Dependence on outer or external rewards often reduces our motivation from inside. Such gaming systems encourage users to engage more by using rewards as one way among many, unlike most rewards systems today.

The purpose of all these elements is to make the process more delightful, interesting and helpful for accomplishing business goals. If users enjoy using an app, platform or service, they will tend to come back again. As a result, users recall the company more often, enjoy using their products and become more devoted to the brand. People who love using an app may turn into reliable customers and those loyal customers may spread the good news about the platform to their social circle.

Integrating these different ways effectively can lead to results that support a company's strategy. One way to encourage learning is for an e-learning system to award points, use progress measurements, offer badges and set up leaderboards for students to compete against each other. Alternatively, a fitness app could have challenges, different levels and features to help users share their progress online. Both situations make it possible for people to find doing ordinary or tough work to be enjoyable and inspirational.

In addition, you cannot expect effective gamification to be the same for every situation. Your offer should be made just for each individual. New types of systems analyze data and apply machine learning to customize their games for each player. If a business understands its players' actions, likes and habits, it can update the game with challenges of varying difficulty, timed rewards and different types of feedback. Therefore, each person gets an experience that is tailored to their characteristics and the way they prefer to learn.

Besides encouraging users to use a product, gamification gives businesses access to useful information. Gamified features allow companies to observe what signals their target audience, where they are losing interest and how to improve. As a result, changes can be made to products continuously based on what users require. For example, if the majority of users quit the application before meeting the challenge goal, the business can consider if the task is challenging, takes too much time or lacks rewards and adjust the issue by making the challenge better suited for users.

Gamification is useful in applications that businesses use too. Some companies apply game-based approaches to better engage workers and help them learn. Gamification can include rewarding workers when they reach new learning goals and using dashboards that promote competitiveness between groups.

Key gamification elements and their effects are shown in the Table 1 where one can see that various game mechanics may affect users' activity. Constituents including point systems motivate users in terms of garnering points for certain tasks accomplishing while badges are symbols of accomplishment. Leaderboards add a degree of competition whilst giving users a target to strive for unlike with the previous tip. All these elements help to make the experience more appealing that way making your customers happier and more loyal. So when those elements are properly combined these business create the right gamified experiences that target an increased interaction with their products and services.

Table 1. Key gamification elements and their effects. This table outlines various gamification elements, their definitions, and their potential effects on user engagement and motivation.

Gamification Element	Definition	Effects on User Engagement
Points System	A scoring mechanism that rewards users for completing tasks or activities.	Increases motivation and encourages participation; users strive to accumulate points.
Badges	Visual symbols of achievement awarded for reaching specific milestones.	Provides recognition and a sense of accomplishment; fosters a feeling of progression.
Leaderboards	Rankings that display users' performance relative to others.	Introduces competition, motivating users to improve their performance to climb the ranks.
Challenges/Quests	Tasks or missions that users can complete for rewards.	Engages users through goal-setting; encourages exploration and repeated interaction.
Levels/Progression	A system where users advance through stages based on their achievements.	Creates a sense of advancement and growth; keeps users engaged over time as they aim for higher levels.

continued on following page

Table 1. Continued

Gamification Element	Definition	Effects on User Engagement
Social Sharing	Options for users to share achievements and progress on social platforms.	Builds community and enhances user engagement; encourages social interaction and competition.
Feedback Mechanisms	Immediate responses to user actions, such as notifications or progress updates.	Keeps users informed and motivated; reinforces behaviors and encourages continued participation.

This table serves as a concise reference to illustrate how different gamification elements can influence user behavior and enhance engagement in various contexts

3. MOBILE APPS AS ENGAGEMENT TOOLS

Smartphone applications have become almost indispensable tools in people's ability to interact with brands and services. Overall, there has been an increase in the use of mobile applications across the world due to enhanced smart phone usage and ease. Using the latest figures available, mobile applications are said to capture more than 90% of the total mobile time consumers spend, making them a vital aspect in the current world. People are turning more to applications that allow smooth interaction, quick access to services, and relevant material. In response to this trend, designing attention-grabbing and easy to use applications remains as important for business organizations as it has ever been.

Some of the characteristics that can boost engagement in mobile applications are incentives, and the rank list. Re-points or discount depending on the tasks or content, which users accomplish or download, makes use of rewards systems. It will not only encourage users to open the app more they would want but also be loyal to the brand. On the other hand, leaderboards add competition to the picture to make users want to play the game with the aim of outdoing his/her counterparts. Showing the positions depending on active usage or other performance, people would be motivated in an attempt to move up the ranks.

Figure 2. Mobile app usage and engagement rates

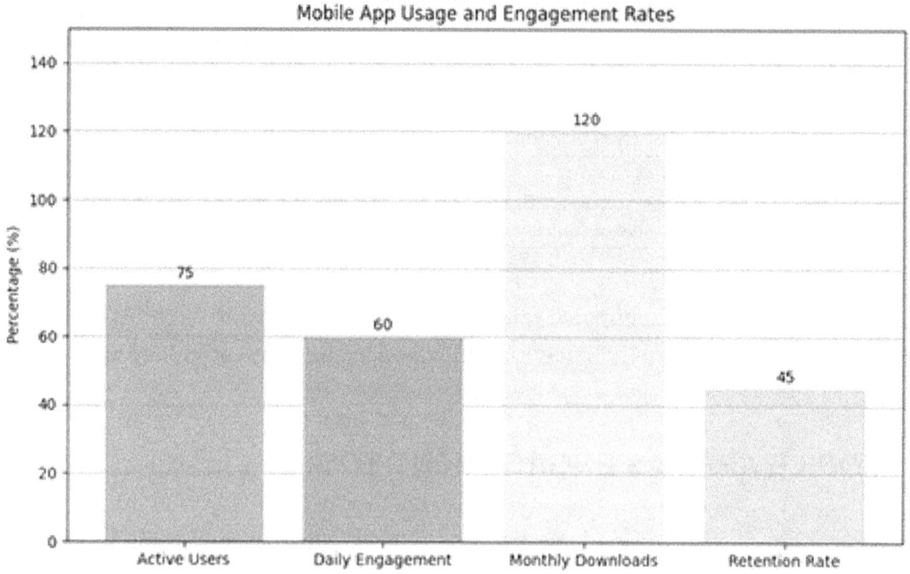

Mobile application usage and engagement rate is presented on the figure 2 and it shows that the above said features are useful for the desired attention grabbing in the user. Here are some of the trends; average time spent per app, the level of engagement in the areas that apply gamification, and the download rates year on year. By using the above-mentioned knowledge, businesses can enhance understanding of user behavior in order to improve the methods that encourage users' active usage of their mobile applications not just one time, but after it as well.

4. VIRTUAL EXPERIENCES: AN EMERGING FRONTIER

Virtual experiences are defined here as digital environments, virtual spaces in which people can interact with content, objects and environments to some extent. Such experiences may involve augmented reality, where digital objects are added on objects around us in real life and virtual reality where users are provided with totally computer generated environments. Some of virtual experiences include; virtual spatial augmented reality apps where customers get to see products in their environment; virtual reality models that afford customers a virtual tour of properties or even tourist attractions. With advancement of technology these currently are essential tools that would help brands to engage their audiences and come up with memorable touch points.

The value of the AR and VR in contrast with a more conventional approach is rooted in the novelty and interactivity that the technologies bring to the marketing table. These technologies promote improved interaction as users are able to engage with product and services of interest on a more human level. For example, customers can try some new clothes on via AR or see how some furniture will look in their homes via AR; people can be teleported to exotic locations through VR or get real-life-like training. Through employment of these technologies, customer satisfaction and engagement is achieved through improvement of memorable experiences.

Several cases demonstrate the effectiveness of virtual interactions in different fields. For instance, IKEA's augmented reality app- IKEA Place allow customers to see how furniture would look in real life before purchasing, thus increasing buyers' satisfaction and a low number of returns. Likewise, Nike has used VR for product exposure to encourage users to interact with products in an environment that is virtual, ultimately raising awareness around new products. In these examples we can see how virtual experiences help to increase client interest and attract customers in a particular brand.

Table 2 presents a simple analysis of AR and VR in relation to their uses, users' experience, and engagement level. Making this comparison makes it easier to discover the most suitable way of using these technologies to actively engage the customers. With the help of these considerations brands are able to make informed decision about using AR or VR based on the audience the brand is targeting or what level of brands interaction is required.

Table 2. Comparison of AR vs. VR in customer engagement

Aspect	Augmented Reality (AR)	Virtual Reality (VR)
Definition	Enhances the real world with digital overlays.	Immerses users in a fully digital environment.
User Experience	Interaction with both physical and digital elements.	Complete immersion with no physical world.
Accessibility	Often accessible via smartphones and tablets.	Requires specialized hardware (VR headsets).
Applications	Retail (virtual try-ons), navigation, education.	Gaming, training simulations, virtual tours.
User Engagement	Encourages immediate interaction with surroundings.	Provides deep, immersive experiences.
Cost	Generally lower development and implementation costs.	Higher costs due to hardware and software needs.
Target Audience	Broad audience, suitable for casual users.	Typically targeted at enthusiasts and professionals.

Simply put, gamification relies on the attraction of playing, receiving rewards and achieving to build stronger feelings between businesses and their customers and makes them faithful over the long run. Gamification works well as a motivation tactic because it is based on theories, including the Self-Determination Theory which puts weight on what motivates people to feel intrinsic motivation. If mobile apps use points, badges, leaderboards and challenges, it can appeal to people's requirements and motivate them to keep using, actively interact and stand by the brand. Apps such as Nike Run Club and Strava, use achievement badges, tracking results and sharing with others to keep users motivated to set and obtain their personal goals, while also enjoying the spotlight within a large group. Having two main goals encourages users to interact more with the app and feel both connected to others and part of the community. Gamification has allowed both Starbucks and Sephora to increase customer loyalty by providing rewards for repeated visits, inspiring their customers to take part in fun events each season and encouraging them to tell others about the brands. Such programs keep evolving over time in reaction to users' preference and opinions. Entertaining people is made easier and more fun now because virtual experiences using AR and VR allow users to interact with things virtually and interactively. Using apps such as IKEA Place, customers are able to imagine furniture at home and reduce their doubts, while with VR from Marriott Hotels or Audi, they experience virtual trips and have more exciting links. Such technologies draw the attention of young people interested in innovation, individual choices and interaction and help brands obtain specific information about what their customers prefer and tend to do which can guide future decisions.

Instead of focusing on one sector or area, applying gamification to mobile apps follows a common pattern found across the globe. Revolut and Monzo as well as other apps in the financial category now include features such as games and charts that help many people better control their finances. Financial management apps help users change their ways by introducing attainable goals and encouraging them with small bonuses, making users more loyal at the same time. With Duolingo and Kahoot!, learning a language and getting involved in school has become much more exciting, fun and addictive by adding points, different levels and quizzes. Its ability to help users ranges from motivating competition and achievements to supporting teamwork and online communities. Rewards, competition, levels and storylines as different game mechanics should be chosen to support the purposes of the app as well as engage its expected users. Thus, people from societies that celebrate succeeding individually are likely to enjoy competing, while those from collectivist societies are more likely to enjoy working together. For a brand to tap into global markets, it must show cultural friendliness, since the things that encourage people and their behaviors are not the same everywhere. Cultural relevance of the game is achieved through localizing not just its words but also elements such as gameplay, rewards and even the looks of the game.

Because of AI, machine learning, AR and VR, mobile apps can now be personalized for each user at the moment they play. AI can help by proposing new features or products for each person, depending on their actions and provide personalized reminders if a user appears close to leaving. Thanks to biometric features in gaming, challenges and Bonuses can be modified based on a user's feelings or actions, increasing their loyalty to the game. Even with these new innovations supporting gamified strategies, we must continue to consider ethical matters involving people's data, agreements and how algorithms function. Since apps are gathering more and more information about consumers, brands have to be transparent and safe while respecting the latest rules such as the GDPR. The good reputation gamification strategies gain from being ethical will win the hearts of customers and support their companies for a long time.

A number of studies and examples prove that mobile apps and virtual experiences using games help to keep customers engaged. If gamification is put in place strategically, numerous studies show it can increase user interest, make individuals more satisfied, keep them coming back and result in them spending more time in apps, completing multiple tasks and becoming loyal. You achieve success by designing and continuously improving the mechanics in games, relying on data and the comments from users. For a brand, it is important to determine its purposes, identify what encourages their audience to play and choose which game elements can best help reach the goals set. Despite login system can include things that show progress, alert users and instantly update their accomplishments to help motivate them. When challenges and rewards are updated, people remain interested in playing and can share their successes or compete with their peers. The top gamified apps make sure that users can easily play games within the app without getting distracted from what it's supposed to do.

Global customer service is being transformed by new technologies and is being guided by psychology and culture. The use of AI, AR and VR with data analytics will help brands improve experiences for everyone and learn even more about their customers' preferences. Similarly, both brands and developers should stay attentive, innovate and show strong ethics while dealing with user engagement, ensuring their data is secure and meeting the needs of people from various cultures. Most companies nowadays gain a valuable tool in gamification and virtual reality to attract global customers, connect with them on a deeper level and build loyalty despite the tough competition online. Those who manage to balance pleasure, rewards, consideration of users' privacy and freedom will connect with customers over a long period and do well in this field.

5. INTEGRATING GAMIFIED ELEMENTS IN MOBILE APPS

For maintaining the distinction between the entertainment and productivity domains, design of gamified mobile applications has to follow four principles. Some of the possible techniques for managing the implementation of gamification includes defining the type of goals for gamification, understanding the target audience, and choosing correct game elements which will affect the users positively. For example, if the goal is to retain the users, adding a little badge to the user's profile when they have been active in the app may be very useful. For the same reason, creating missions or a competition of some sort may help the users find more about the application, thus improving the experience.

It should be noted that long-arm solutions for the creation of attractive user experiences through gamification are best simplistic. The actual user interface for the target product should be quite clear so that the user will know how he or she is going engage in gamified actions. Other feedback includes things like progress bars, and alerts on how well the user is doing or how successful he or she is, it motivates them. It also updates challenge and reward regularly that makes contents fresh and provide continuous engagement. Furthermore, the mechanisms like sharing achievements, or competition with friends are of great value and can improve the overall user experience by engaging the community more actively.

In evaluating effectiveness and relevance of gamified elements, therefore there must be set goals that can be quantified in light of the general goal of the apps. Some key metrics expected for determining engagement success are the rates of user retention, average time spent on engaging content, success rate in completing the tasks embodied in the theme of engagement, and users' feedback scores. The following Table 3 shows these metrics, for the convenience of app developers and marketers, presenting a range of factors that reflect the success rate of applied gamification techniques. Thus, it is possible to incrementally adjust gamification strategies based on the given metrics reflecting user behaviour in businesses.

Table 3. Common metrics for evaluating engagement success

Metric	Description	Importance
User Retention Rate	Percentage of users who return to the app over time.	Indicates the effectiveness of engagement strategies.
Average Session Duration	Average time users spend in the app per session.	Reflects user engagement and interest in content.
Completion Rate of Tasks	Percentage of users who complete gamified challenges.	Shows the effectiveness of gamification in driving actions.

continued on following page

Table 3. Continued

Metric	Description	Importance
User Feedback Scores	Ratings or reviews provided by users regarding their experience.	Provides qualitative insights into user satisfaction.
Churn Rate	Percentage of users who stop using the app over a period.	Helps identify retention issues and the need for improvement.
Social Sharing Metrics	Frequency of users sharing achievements on social media.	Indicates community engagement and brand visibility.
In-app Purchases	Revenue generated from in-app transactions.	Measures monetization success and user investment in the app.

These tables provide a concise overview of the comparison between AR and VR in customer engagement and the metrics used to evaluate engagement success.

Figure 3. Conceptual model for mobile gamification app

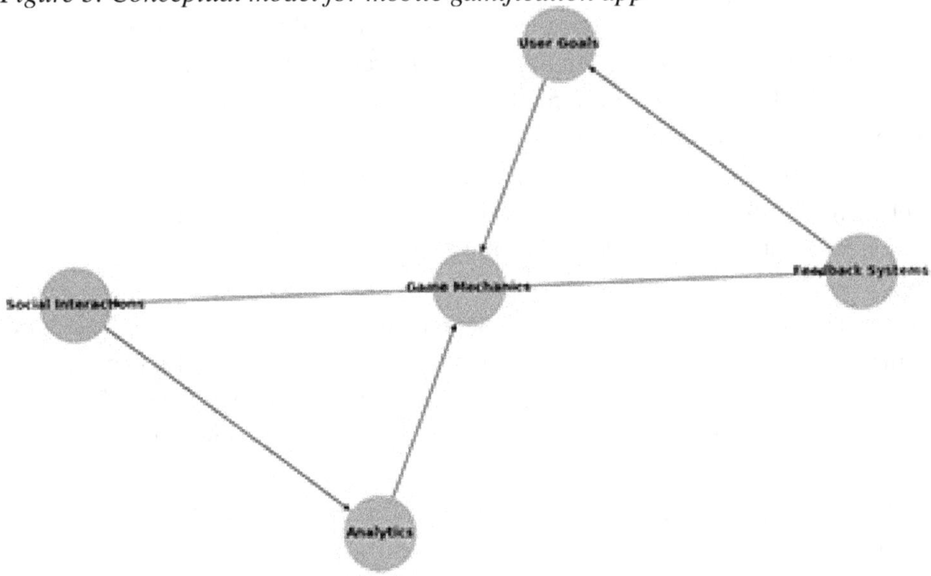

In the next section, Figure 3 outlines a conceptual model for mobile gamification app development with key factors for a good gamified application. With this model showing the duality between user goals, mechanics, feedback and analytics aspect, this work has demonstrated the need to consider different area so as to design entertaining mobile apps. When using this framework, developers will be able to create not only engaging gamified elements but also elements that users will stay satisfied.

6. GLOBAL PERSPECTIVES ON ENGAGEMENT

While designing the gamification strategies and the mobile apps, there are particular cultural differences which are likely to affect the use. Culture affects how people view incentives, rivalry, and cooperation, and the reasons that make them use an app. For instance, there is the idea that group outcomes are preferable to personal ones may mean that more group-focused problems and shared motivators may be more compelling. Variance in these cultures causes business organizations to appropriate the form of gamification to address the expectation of various groups, thereby improving user commitment.

Examples of different areas also give useful information on how cultural issues influence the effectiveness of gamification. For example, in Japan the elements of story and social communication are perpetual thus mobile games in this culture may include both. A notable example is the mobile game "Line: Disney Tsum Tsum," which perfectly implemented characters people love and the substance of cooperation that is popular in Japan into the game. On the other hand within the United States, merit and competition are the leading values, thereby apps that support manifestation of individual goals for example fitness tracking apps containing comp[etitive characteristics perform well in the society.

To fit business strategies into various markets, it is important to assess cultural probes in business by conducting relevant market analysis. Some of the tactics that should be adopted for better flexibility and adaptability include the following adaptability flexibilities that must be charged to reflect expectations within a given region should reflect the following: For example, making the offer relevant to the culture of the country it is operating in or changing the competitiveness of an application increases the usage it receives. Moreover, communicate with the local influencers or partners may help learn about the right message and marketing strategies for the target audience.

Through approaching the issues of gamification and app designing taking into account cultural peculiarities, commercial organizations can develop applications that will be appealing to audiences globally. Not only does this make the customer relationship stronger, but it also builds the brand's clientele, making businesses ready for the interconnected world of e-commerce.

To implement game elements in mobile apps, one should possess both technical knowledge and an understanding of people's minds, as well as adapt the approach over time with advice from real users and their needs. Brands that have achieved significantly in mobile games usually begin with clearly set business objectives, then make sure these objectives are fulfilled by matching them with mechanics their players are likely to enjoy. Starbucks added goals, time-based deals and status levels to its rewards program, so users had an incentive to buy other items and visit the stores more often. Shoppers enjoyed going to the coffee shop because they were constantly encountering special features, challenges and gifts as they advanced through the ranking system. Similarly, the language learning app from Duolingo reminds users to use the app regularly and hardly leaves them feeling bored. This shows that gamification should be done in a way that engages users, so they do not become bored once the interesting new rewards are gone. Leading companies usually use points, badges, rewards and other external stimuli, in addition to helping their members feel valued, enjoy freedom and bond socially. As a result, apps like Strava and Peloton encourage users to join virtual events, set their own goals and tell others online about what they've done.

Evaluating the success of gamified engagement can lead to better results now and in the future. Brands have to measure their performance by looking at user retention, average time in the app, the number of app uses, finishing tasks in the game and scores on customer satisfaction surveys. They help understand users' experiences with gamified aspects and show the areas that need improvements. Should daily active users fall after the release of a new challenge, it could mean that the task is too hard or doesn't provide users with enough rewards, so a reconstruction may be required. In addition to numbers, feedback and discussions from users, surveys and web analysis may highlight the reasons behind their choices, what makes them upset and what they still need. Finally, this process allows businesses to continue shaping their gamification approach, introducing extra missions, prizes and ways for people to interact. Especially, highly successful gamified systems can easily change as new trends, user habits, technology and competitors appear. During COVID-19, fitness and wellness apps quickly provided remote events, at-home challenges and support options to maintain their customers' motivation since fitness events couldn't happen in person.

Though gamification attracts and leads customers for many brands, companies should make sure they are doing it right by protecting their customers and being responsible. It's challenging to avoid focusing on fast results that may hamper the company's future loyalty with its customers. depend on external rewards. Consequently, brands should create enjoyable games that have meaning for users and fit within their personal interests and values. Users could be given flashcards, work with others in groups or be encouraged to do art and literature projects. Another problem is "dark patterns," where companies use certain styles to encourage people to make choices that are not helpful for them. If a gamification system is ethical, users must understand it, agree and feel it helps them rather than controls them. People tend to trust brands that care about ethics and those that manage their reputation in fraudulent ways may not last long and could easily get in trouble with authorities.

Now, technologies such as artificial intelligence and machine learning, businesses can offer personalized gamification to their users. Recognizing trends in users' behavior, AI can propose new activities and courses for them, while machine learning can detect signs of a user getting bored and intervene to entice them back. A mobile banking app can utilize AI to encourage users to save or test their financial knowledge and then reward them as they achieve their personal financial aims. Furthermore, machine learning can be used in a retail app to organize users depending on their usual purchases and offer unique incentives, loyalty programs or games that are suitable for each user. However, these advancements could make people's data less secure and reduce their control over their own privacy. Firms should make it clear to users how and why they collect their data, as well as what users can do with the data. Government regulations such as the GDPR must be followed to ensure users feel safe on website.

First, those implementing gamified engagement strategies should study the target audience, define clear objectives, find the best game themes and test and improve the experience after each use of the app or experience. For gamification to work smoothly and support the business, representatives from product management, design, development, marketing and data science groups should collaborate. Brands must understand that gamification requires consistent effort and adapting to new ideas, discoveries and what users now expect from them. A user-focused and ethical use of data allows gamification to design mobile apps and online games that attract people and sustain their loyalty and value.

7. CHALLENGES AND CONSIDERATIONS

However, applying gamification for customer engagement has many advantages and downsides that companies have to be alert to. One typical problem is over-justification, according to which users may be eager to be rewarded with points and badges rather than being motivated from within. This can have the effect of a real lowing down of the interested clientele in the product or service that is being marketed. This is because the users will only open the app with the Aim of getting the points and not necessarily building a relationship with the various brands. Hence, K path remains acceptable for companies to deal with the dilemma of providing extrinsic and intrinsic motivation at the same time through the meaningful and enjoyable rewarding experiences.

Another crucial aspect to consider, is data protection and anonymity while applying gamification is also of top priority. Since most apps require access to private user data for purposes such as use customisation and monitoring of use data, app owners must ensure that the data is secure. It appears that users are smarter today and ready to claim their right to privacy; they can be reluctant to open an application that will not explain how their data will be used or when their information will be secured. Businesses need to follow rules like GDPR and must be straightforward along with outcomes that they produce from data. This fosters trust especially among the users so that they can interact with the remaining gamified features, fear of misuse being a thing of the past.

The other important factor is the ability to balance engagement with user experience. Still, gamified elements can boost user engagement but these features may get in the way the primary functions of the application. In fact, an interface that is filled with lot of gamification elements can be counterproductive and customers end up getting frustrated with the interface. In this case, usability should remain the design priority and games features that are integrated should not complicate the use of a product. Recurrent evaluation and gathering of feedback from the users can aid developers in making improvement on their designs away from angering users, acknowledging that gamification can improve overall satisfaction.

To overcome these challenges and considerations, different techniques must be followed for increasing the customer engagement by applying the concepts of gamification in business organizations. This will help to avoid occurrences of pitfalls on the ways to ensure the brands' long and successful cooperation with the users in overly competitive world.

A lot of studies and case examples now confirm that gamification greatly improves global engagement, changes our behavior as users and leads to a rise in loyalty across numerous areas and countries. Its main advantage is that it activates achievement, competition and social bonding which all people experience. As evidence, studies suggest that gamification increases user involvement by almost 50 percent and improves a business's profits by up to 30 percent. To maintain their success, Nike Training Club, Peloton and Duolingo award badges, place users on leaderboards and provide instant rewards, helping to encourage healthy habits in users. Because of these, dopamine is released, encouraging people to feel both successful and motivated in their daily work. Both Nike Training Club and Peloton in fitness ensure users can monitor their progress with milestones and may compete with others through the leaderboard. When users test themselves, they compete with friends and build friendships, both of which help maintain their interest for a long period. Much like SuperBetter, the Duolingo language learning app uses instant feedback and streaks to help learners become more involved and practice every day. The strength of these strategies also increases when users can share what they do, play against their friends and engage in shared events. Because of this, people using the app enjoy the experience even more and spread positive news about it, resulting in additional new users.

There is much more to gamification than just engaging people and helping them remember. With competition and support, apps encourage people to form tight-knit communities where users share a sense of belonging. Users of Fitbit can select their goals, join team games, play against others in step races and get virtual badges for reaching set milestones while viewing their stats and graphs. As a result, game players remain motivated and choose to share the fun with others, enhancing the app for the community. When someone gets rewards, it makes the app more exciting and prone to continued use and when achievements are posted on social media, the app attracts even more attention. Waze encourages people to send real-time traffic updates by rewarding them with points and bars on their profiles upon sharing. Thanks to the leaderboard and emotions system in the app, users find it fun to engage with each other and the fact that all its data is provided by the community means it is always accurate. HumanForest, a company that produces e-bikes, allows people to earn TreeCoins during their bike rides which symbolize trees that are not used when riding a bike. As a result, bike riders get enthused and tend to recommend the app as well as support its commitment to sustainability in the community.

Now that gamification is more advanced, making apps more relevant and tougher is playing a major role in shaping their future. With improvements in data and AI, apps can provide unique challenges, bonuses and events to each person which helps them stay satisfied and attached to the app. As an example, health apps use AI to check someone's fitness habits and recommend tasks that are suitable for them and education apps help each student by making exercises personalized to their needs. Nowadays, it is very important for developers to use social networks to let users communicate, compare their results and participate in group activities. As a result, using AR and VR, gamification takes user engagement to another level. Pokémon GO achieved this by displaying Pokémon on phone screens as players stepped outside and explored their area with friends. VR is being tested in retail and training apps to develop virtual worlds in which users practice, use different items or attend virtual events.

Because gamification is popular globally, the industry is expected to increase its market value from $9.1 billion in 2020 to over $30 billion by 2025. In Africa, Latin America, the Middle East and Asia Pacific, the use of these services is spreading rapidly due to new innovative ideas from these regions and the increase in e-learning, mobile banking and online shopping. Local providers and an emphasis on gamification in learning and trade are causing the African gamification market to increase by more than 60 percent. In this region, China and India are taking the lead, working on improving how users feel and using gamification to increase their attention in both finance and healthcare. Both L'Oréal and Domino's Pizza have achieved positive outcomes by using games to train their employees and boost sales, among other things. The cases above show that gamification engages customers and employees and can help achieve important business results worldwide.

Gamification comes with both pros and cons and there are issues to consider when applying it. If brands only use extrinsic rewards, users may get bored once they no longer feel the excitement of earning new ones. If users believe external incentives are not worthwhile, they might become bored with the platform. To prevent this issue, successful apps pay close attention to what's important to users. Application developers need to be mindful of ethics, as much more of our information is now handled and processed. To gain and maintain the trust of users, companies in such areas must ensure transparency, user agreement and strong data security. Showing creativity won't mean much in gamification if brands ignore users' needs and the ethical rules involved.

To sum up, the next stage of gamification will be guided by new technologies like blockchain, making it possible for players to own and trade things from various games outside their app. Thanks to this, app users might see opportunities to earn real money and interact more with the app. As virtual and augmented reality become more advanced, AI and machine learning will help customize the game and adapt the difficulties accordingly. With more competition appearing online, those who adopt these ideas and continuously advance their use of gamification will succeed in grabbing and maintaining global attention. To succeed in gamification, mobile apps and other virtual environments must ensure their experiences remain fun and rewarding while also being valuable, ethical and meet the needs of users from around the world.

8. FUTURE TRENDS

Cutting edge changes in customer engagement are taking place primarily because of technology expansion along with customer expectations. Hence, even as consumers mature and grow to expect features such as personalization and interactivity from Websites, firms have to keep reinventing themselves. Customers believe that the level of interaction of customer engagement management with customers in future will further stimulate the integration across different touch points, integrating online and offline experience. A few brands are successful in integrating all these touchpoints, and such brands are expected to create a better bond with consumers.

Forecast regarding future gamified applications and virtual environment focus on becoming even more engaging and individualized. It is quite possible that with more advancing of AR and VR solutions, such application will provide extremely captivating interactive interfaces. They will allow the brands to come up with enhanced storytelling and more engaging people's attention to interact with solutions.

Also, undertaking routine activities like shopping, learning and health will continue to be placed in the 'game context' as users look forward toSetActive and engaging experiences.

There is no doubt that the application of AI and machine learning helps in amplifying engagement. These technologies will allow brand- marketers to mine enormously huge data to address user preferences and engagement relating to personalized experiences. Using AI, its is possible to forecast the user's needs and then adjust the gamification aspects for the user based on his or her usage. Furthermore, the use of machine learning allows for the dynamic changes in processes inherent in the gamification, so that the features remain fresh and exciting to customers in the long run. Such innovation dynamic will be crucial in keeping the users engaged and building a long term patronage base.

9. CONCLUSION

Finally, the chapter focuses on the benefits of gamified M-Commerce and Virtual Experience Applications as a means to enhance global customer relations. Developing the ideas of Global customer engagement definition, the principle of gamification, and the use of the immersive technologies, we have also denoted their role for making the interaction between the brand and the customer more profound. The evaluation of the explored tendencies on the utilization of the mobile applications alongside cultural sensitivity makes it explicably clear that it essential for the existing business entities to align their operations to suit the new market. Furthermore, the assessment of risks and opportunities associated with the proposed system shows that the key issue – the focus on extrinsic motivators as well as data privacy issues – should be addressed in the same manner, using an evidenced-based approach to highlight the value of more natural, endogenous motivators for extended use of an application.

Because customer engagement has and will continue to rapidly change, future sustained innovation will be vital. This means that organizations and firms have to constantly adapt because gamification and engagement are constantly evolving due to consumers' high expectations and new technologies. [The areas of opportunity are new tools such as AI and machine learning that will improve personalization and responsiveness and, in turn, lead to deeper user engagement. Thus, focusing on such aspects provides continuous and even greater growth of brands in the constantly growing competition among companies and customers' constant focus on brands.

Since the world is entering a new phase of customer engagement, making use of gamified apps and virtual settings has proven to be fundamental for forming lasting relationships between brands and their customers. Now, thanks to improved technologies, engagement is measured by the stronger and more reliable interactions between consumers and businesses. These brands believe that engaging customers means handling their entire journey from getting interested in a brand to joining their group of supporters. In similar circumstances, true innovation occurs when organizations include gamification as part of how they deal with customers and unite it with different digital supports and company plans. As a result, the customer journey should be planned by considering what is valuable to each user and using insights from data to improve and personalize the whole experience. The best gamified systems adjust and respond to users, new technologies and any changes in society. Adapting in this way is particularly crucial in today's world market which brings together people from many cultures, features various regulations and involves a lot of competition. Achieving the best results in gamification requires spending on skilled analysts, flexible approaches to software development and working together across all departments, ensuring the programs are indeed engaging, moral, accessible and sustainable.

In this new era, more consumers value sustainability and they hope the companies they shop from also value social responsibility. Many people can take actions for good, join groups to help others and learn about protecting the environment, health and money through gamification and virtual apps. In other words, when apps encourage people to act sustainably, join charities or support local enterprises, everyone profits from their actions. It is effective for gamified systems to tug at the heartstrings by rewarding achievements with actions that benefit the world, as doing so often encourages users to take real actions. Prevalence of social impact in gamification tactics helps a brand capture and retain eco-minded customers, stand out in a competitive environment and build valued brand equity over time. In virtual spaces, attention is placed on using less energy, enabling everyone to access the environment and managing data appropriately. Now that AR, VR and AI are being adopted more swiftly, businesses should ensure that their online efforts are open to all, respect the environment and maintain ethical use of new technologies.

Since types of gamers come from various backgrounds, companies are making sure their games are enjoyable for everyone. People of all ages and technology levels are interested in games today. Nowadays, games have become connected with people from all ages, genders, backgrounds and cultures. The rise in gaming's popularity has persuaded brands to design their games to include a larger variety of people.

A good way to make gaming inclusive is to design apps and virtual worlds that can be modified to suit many users' needs. Various difficulty levels help new players by making the game easy, while excitement level is high for players who try the highest modes. Moreover, having the option to play in other languages makes the game easier for people who don't speak the same language. Because of these features, many more individuals can join in, enjoy and remain dedicated over the years. The ability to change difficulty, language and design can make digital games and apps successful for a bigger audience.

As well as technical updates, adding numerous stories, characters and backgrounds helps many users relate to the platform. A game should both run smoothly and evoke special experiences for the ones who use it. When characters in a product represent a user's identity, experiences and heritage, users usually relate to it better. Stories in games from other cultures and backgrounds help players discover ways of life and moral values, all the while engaging them in a fun setting.

The effort to welcome everyone is not only good for society; it is also a benefit for business. If users feel part of a brand, they become more trusting of it. They are usually devoted, encourage people to try the business and actively join in with the company. As a result, including different people helps brands expand and create thriving, strong-bonded communities. It also reflects how a company values social responsibility and plays a good role in today's online world.

Today, people from all over the world can join digital communities. Online gaming communities are made up of people from all parts of the world. Because the world is so connected now, including everyone is more vital and urgent than ever. When creating an experience for a shared virtual world, attention should be given to culture, language and experience differences. If a brand does not take global users into account, it can make people unhappy with its services and lose significance. Meanwhile, when inclusive design is placed first, the community of users worldwide becomes engaged with the product and its future improvements.

Playing games with others from different countries can shape the world in many valuable ways. Games provide opportunities for people from different cultures to collaborate and gain knowledge. Cooperating players can gain knowledge of how others around them think and approach different experiences. This way, people respect one another and learn to reduce their cultural biases. In a time when people can disagree on many issues, games can bring people together to accomplish challenges and achieve similar goals.

New technology is causing the difference between the real and digital worlds to fade. Brands are interacting differently with customers because of recent game features, advancements in technology and AI. In the future, customer service will involve combining both online and offline experiences for each individual in real time. Brands will be able to interact with people instantly through wearables, smart homes and devices made for the Internet of Things.

An app for health can take data from your smartwatch to guide you in exercises that suit your current state of fitness and mind. Upon finishing the challenge, the user could add points to their score or discover new functions in the app. Personal interaction helps the brand become more appealing and underlines that it values each person's needs. Likewise, these types of apps can encourage users to do certain things by showing them what's nearby.

Blockchain and decentralized systems ensure that users can handle their personal information, assets and online identities by themselves. Previously, people allowed companies to handle their information which led to privacy and security concerns. Having a decentralized system ensures more openness and more control for each person using it. If people can look after their private data and possessions safely on a platform, they are more inclined to rely on it. The significance of trust is important in place where users can spend their time, cash and feelings.

AI is playing a significant part in today's new trends. When mental intelligence improves, experimenting and tailoring games for each user will become easier. AI is able to monitor a user's actions, tastes and improvements to understand what will most appeal to them. The game adjusts itself during the experience, keeping the story interesting from start to finish. When a player starts to feel bored, the system could surprise them with a tournament or another type of game challenge. If a player needs help, the AI can provide hints, useful tips or an easier task.

But with all these developments, people have greater tasks to handle. Firms should pay close attention to any problems involving data privacy, bias in AI algorithms and ethics in AI. AI systems may become biased if the data they use is also biased. A case in point, if one playstyle gets most of the in-game rewards, it will likely hurt the experiences of particular individuals within the community. Without accessibility features, many games could leave behind people with disabilities. For a brand to ensure inclusivity, it should pay close attention to these issues even before they start affecting the user experience.

As a result, we should keep constantly learning and exploring different approaches. Teams at these companies will have a chance to improve their gamified experiences, include everyone and make a difference. In addition, this way of learning encourages brands to develop new ideas and meet users' needs quickly. These experts need collaboration, communicating and sharing information to improve the user experience.

Furthermore, teams working on gaming and virtual environments have to ensure their teams are inclusive as well. Having a variety of people on a team leads to paying attention to a variety of needs and designing something more inclusive. When companies have diversity in their teams, what they design often reflects the differences found in real life.

All things considered, internet-based gaming apps and virtual events have greatly changed the way businesses connect with customers globally. Through play, storytelling and technology, companies are able to offer impactful, meaningful and engaging experiences that help their customers stay loyal and get involved. Sustainable, inclusive and ethical engagement needs to be considered regularly and requires changes and updates to suit users' expectations. Down the road, the companies who succeed will cater to their customers, open themselves to new ideas and possibilities and make changes that matter to society. Later on, we will find that customer engagement is full of opportunities for interaction, deep involvement and excitement—and the reason for this is people who are bold enough to come up with new ideas now.

REFERENCES

Bitrián, P., Buil, I., & Catalán, S. (2021). Enhancing user engagement: The role of gamification in mobile apps. *Journal of Business Research, 132*, 170–185. DOI: 10.1016/j.jbusres.2021.04.028

De Canio, F., Fuentes-Blasco, M., & Martinelli, E. (2021). Engaging shoppers through mobile apps: The role of gamification. *International Journal of Retail & Distribution Management, 49*(7), 919–940. DOI: 10.1108/IJRDM-09-2020-0360

Falco, G. (2020). *Customer engagement through gamification marketing in China: A focus on the luxury market* [Unpublished manuscript or thesis if not published].

Hammedi, W., Leclercq, T., & Poncin, I. (2019). Customer engagement: The role of gamification. In *Handbook of research on customer engagement* (pp. 164–185). Edward Elgar Publishing., DOI: 10.4337/9781788114899.00014

Harwood, T., & Garry, T. (2015). An investigation into gamification as a customer engagement experience environment. *Journal of Services Marketing, 29*(6/7), 533–546. DOI: 10.1108/JSM-01-2015-0045

Högberg, J., Ramberg, M. O., Gustafsson, A., & Wästlund, E. (2019). Creating brand engagement through in-store gamified customer experiences. *Journal of Retailing and Consumer Services, 50*, 122–130. DOI: 10.1016/j.jretconser.2019.05.006

Hollebeek, L. D., Das, K., & Shukla, Y. (2021). Game on! How gamified loyalty programs boost customer engagement value. *International Journal of Information Management, 61*, 102308. DOI: 10.1016/j.ijinfomgt.2021.102308

Hsu, C. L. (2023). Enhancing brand love, customer engagement, brand experience, and repurchase intention: Focusing on the role of gamification in mobile apps. *Decision Support Systems, 174*, 114020. DOI: 10.1016/j.dss.2023.114020

Jami Pour, M., Rafiei, K., Khani, M., & Sabrirazm, A. (2021). Gamification and customer experience: The mediating role of brand engagement in online grocery retailing. *Nankai Business Review International, 12*(3), 340–357. DOI: 10.1108/NBRI-07-2020-0041

Jang, S., Kitchen, P. J., & Kim, J. (2018). The effects of gamified customer benefits and characteristics on behavioral engagement and purchase: Evidence from mobile exercise application uses. *Journal of Business Research, 92*, 250–259. DOI: 10.1016/j.jbusres.2018.07.056

Kamboj, S., Rana, S., & Drave, V. A. (2020). Factors driving consumer engagement and intentions with gamification of mobile apps. [JECO]. *Journal of Electronic Commerce in Organizations*, *18*(2), 17–35. DOI: 10.4018/JECO.2020040102

Rasool, A., Shah, F. A., & Islam, J. U. (2020). Customer engagement in the digital age: A review and research agenda. *Current Opinion in Psychology*, *36*, 96–100. DOI: 10.1016/j.copsyc.2020.05.003 PMID: 32599394

Raza, A., Rehmat, S., Ishaq, M. I., Haj-Salem, N., & Talpur, Q. U. A. (2024). Gamification in financial service apps to enhance customer experience and engagement. *Journal of Consumer Behaviour*, *23*(4), 1653–1670. DOI: 10.1002/cb.2294

Yadav, K., Arora, A., Yadav, R., & Saini, C. P. (2022). Gamified apps and customer engagement: Modeling in online shopping environment. *Transnational Marketing Journal*, *10*(3), 593–605. DOI: 10.33182/tmj.v10i3.2062

Chapter 9
The Dark Side of Gamification:
Ethics, Privacy, Surveillance, and Monitoring in Virtual and Gamified Environments

Uchit Kapoor
https://orcid.org/0009-0001-4845-8200
Arthkalp, India

ABSTRACT

This chapter analyses the opposite perspective on the use of game elements, the so-called gamification, and is devoted to its Ethical Issues, Privacy Aspects, and Surveillance Aspects. The study analyses how gamification can influence one's behavior and cause addiction as well as privacy invasions. Again, when using a qualitative research methodology among the case studies and relevant literature, the chapter identifies emerging patterns in data gathering activities and user surveillance. Significant findings revealed that while applying gamification increases the level of interest, it involves important ethical concerns concerning the openness and permission, which compromise user agency. The analysis concludes that stakeholders, including developers and policymakers, must prioritize ethical frameworks to balance user engagement with privacy and ethical considerations, ensuring responsible gamification practices. Ultimately, fostering awareness of these issues is essential for developing more ethical and user-centered gamified systems.

DOI: 10.4018/979-8-3693-8886-0.ch009

INTRODUCTION

Gamification is the process of using game design techniques for purposes other than playing a game and is today used as a powerful way of engaging people (Fitria, 2022). It has uses in education, marketing, healthcare systems, as well as employee training, with concepts such as points, badges, and leaderboards being implemented right into the learning process ensuring that individuals act in a way that is desired. Specifically, gamification intends to engage users by appealing to their psychological needs or rather the desire to achieve goals as they complete tasks. However, as this approach becomes increasingly accepted and used, it has essential ethical implications that need to be addressed (Rowicka, 2023).

There is a concept as the 'dark side' of gamification which means that apart from the positive outcomes of the process, it has negative consequences and ethical issues. On the positive side, gamification has the potential of creating healthier engagement and, on the negative side, manipulation, addictions, and the abuse of personal data. These issues are compounded by the fact that data capture and user monitoring are common features of gamified systems. Therefore, one will have to turn his attention to the ethical perspective of gamification, namely privacy concerns and surveillance as well as consent.

This way, it will be possible to identify which specific concerns have to be addressed to make gamified experiences more responsible. With the emergence of digital spaces that permanently monitor users' activity, it is critical to create a set of measures that need to be ethical and protect users' rights. The goal of this chapter is to discuss the factors that make the use of gamification conceptually elusive and practically challenging with a focus on the ethical dimension.

There is widespread belief that gamification can improve engagement, but researchers have recently started to mention its less obvious and significant negative side too. People who support this theory note that the influences responsible for motivation and involvement can also be twisted to manipulate, exploit and even cause harm to people. For example, Self-Determination Theory explains how trying to obtain points, badges and leaderboards in games can end up reducing a person's motivation. People may enjoy what they are doing less and become bored when the prizes or rewards are gone. Because of this phenomenon, called the overjustification effect, it is crucial that game elements in programs do not interfere with people's freedom and good health.

The field of gaming studies brings up issues of possible ethical challenges due to manipulation and changing a person's behavior (Sheetal, 2023). Systems that feature gamification are created to help users adopt certain habits that usually fit the needs of the organization or are beneficial for a business. They may use psychological techniques to develop habits in users, as users may not be aware of the difference between a habit and a decision. Sometimes, users are not fully aware that gamification is changing their behavior, thereby causing them to lose some control. Since platforms based on games are not always clear about how they operate, it's hard for users to understand all the effects their activities may have.

Many studies also point out the danger of addiction and people playing games non-stop (Packin, 2025). Often, this type of environment offers various bonuses, allows players to see how they compare on leaderboards and provides feedback at all times. These features may lift our spirits, yet they can also become addictive like present-day gamblers and social apps. Some users might start using a platform more than they planned and this can end up being harmful for them. Because people feel they have to be involved in many activities, this can cause stress and even exhaustion, mainly if there are incentives for staying active.

Some studies also focus on privacy and surveillance when discussing how gamification can be harmful. Thanks to data-driven personalization in games, more data is now being collected than ever before. In many cases, these systems track a user's actions, likes and even moods, without informing them or asking them to agree. Since the operators know and control so much about users, users often do not have equal power. This situation is concerning as it may compromise people's privacy, self-determination and the security of their personal information. Risks are most significant among youth and children, since the whole situation becomes more ethically demanding.

Many people studying this field have developed different ethical ways and standards to encourage responsible and acknowledging users while implementing gamification. Many in the field agree that transparent practices, user understanding and control are among the main principles for ethical design. As a result, users should receive understandable explanations about gathering and using their data, be able to manage what information is transmitted and contribute to the development and improvement of these systems. Even though guidelines such as data protection laws are in place, studies recommend that following the law is not enough. Members of the tech industry, along with end users and government officials, should regularly discuss new issues and methods to improve with the changing landscape of technology and demands of users.

It also examines how gamification influences society and various organizations. Badly designed games within a company can cause unfair competition, damage trust among workers and increase the power differences among members. As a result, including different backgrounds and considering various stakeholders when developing and evaluating gamified systems is necessary. If we consider all the possible pros and cons, stakeholders can build games that inspire enthusiasm, are honest, include all groups and respect everyone involved.

Dark gamification covers many aspects such as moral, mental and social considerations. Experts in psychology and ethics believe they know the mechanisms behind the unexpected problems caused by gamification. Studies that focus on evidence from real-life situations show that there can be addiction, manipulation, violations of privacy and arguments among people. It is important to use ethical principles, obey regulations and promote approaches where people are in charge, can easily observe what happens and feel beneficial. The chapter aims to add to the current knowledge about gamification by drawing from the studies mentioned above.

Table 1. Key definitions and concepts

Term	Definition
Gamification	Use of game elements in non-game contexts
Surveillance	Monitoring user behavior in digital spaces
Privacy	Protection of personal information and data
Ethics	Moral principles guiding behavior in gamified contexts

1. ETHICAL CONSIDERATIONS IN GAMIFICATION

Researchers have paid a lot of attention to the ethics of gamification. According to Kim and Werbach (2016), major concerns are exploitation and manipulation of people through gamification. What the researchers discovered is that when user participation relies on points and badges, organizations benefit at the expense of players' interests. As shown by Arora and Razavian (2021) in studies about health-tracking, using gamification techniques may cause people to become obsessed with the app, resulting in damage to their health. Many researchers mention that gamification can make people feel coerced into acting a certain way, since these techniques are often engineered to trigger the mind, but these tricks are rarely described clearly in the game's design.

Dark side problems, according to Ruggiu et al., are fueled by privacy violations that conflict with respecting choosing how an individual's data should be used. The researchers see that thanks to workplace gamification, companies have unprecedented access to employees' work habits and may use this information for purposes unknown to the staff. In addition, Benjamin (2019) indicates that gamification in society makes data harvesting seem like a fun game for people to enjoy. Similarly, according to Srivastava and colleagues (2023), incorporating certain gaming aspects directly leads to an increase in data dangers, mostly due to people wanting to do well on leaderboards.

It is clear that gamification affects our mental health and also leads to changes in engagement. These researchers (Algashami et al., 2019) found that competition in enterprise gamification systems is often set improperly, leading to stress and seclusion among staff and thus lowering the social advantages of using these systems. It demonstrates that achievement-oriented workplaces favor those who are outgoing and ignore individuals who tend to think thoroughly before acting. McCall and Baillie (2017) also see that gamification in schools can dull a learner's interest in new things by stressing measures of success too much. Kim and Werbach's earlier recommendations are supported by their latest research that, in the main, warns against the 'quantified self' trend influencing a person's self-image because of continual scoring of behavior. Arora and Razavian found that 23% of those they surveyed used fitness apps to exercise dangerously in an attempt to achieve virtual goals. The team explains in their studies how gaming can stimulate dopamine which directly influences decision-making in teens and bypasses reasoning.

In their study, Hyrynsalmi et al. (2017) analyze the link between surveillance capitalism and gamification and suggest that such systems mainly consist of Datenherrschaft, meaning that they largely exploit users' behavioral data. In their research, they prove how simple elements in games contribute to gathering psychographic information which is later used for online advertising with no mention to the game's users. Based on Benjamin's arguments (2019), it appears that public participation platforms designed using gamification, reward those who interact a lot with data rather than those who take an active part in democratic actions.

It is clear from Raftopoulos' (2014) review that the rules regarding disclosure are not yet standardized in different countries. David Vincent et al. have pointed out, in their report from last year, that games used at work rarely protect privacy as much as GDPR and COPPA standards require. In their research, Jami Pour and Binaei discovered that inadequate rules in Iran allow certain online games to target people looking for fast, immediate financial earnings.

Many new ways of addressing ethical issues have been invented thanks to these challenges. It is argued by Selinger et al. (2015) that gamification should build good character through a system of fair rewards. It works against the common practice of boosting metrics for the present by promoting growth for gamification users in the future. They achieve this by offering their privacy-by-design methodology, placing cryptography and specific controls of privacy within the underlying protocol of each game. Algashami et al. (2019) have proven that participatory design workshops can detect and handle problems that may affect society during deployment.

Gupta argues, based on his analysis, that the introduction of hyper-personalized games through generative AI will lead to even more ethical dilemmas. Based on their studies, the authors believe that adaptive difficulty and responsive emotions in games could both increase the risks of coercion and introduce additional symptoms of psychology dependency. This matches Acquisti et al.'s (2015) point that frequently using personalized gamification encourages people to exchange important data for little in return.

The researchers point out that when it comes to work, gamification can create problems with productivity. The PLS-SEM approach demonstrates that introducing factors like gamification can help online businesses gain fast results, while the ANN results suggest that an abundance of similar efforts could result in frustrated users leaving the community after six months. According to the findings, using gamification alone cannot be solution for every issue, so it's necessary to fit it within the contexts involved. In healthcare, McCall and Baillie (2017) believe serious games can bring attention to fulfilling rules rather than focusing on what matters to patients.

These systems also pose sociotechnical challenges because it is difficult for different devices to share information. According to Adams (2017), the data gathered from fitness, learning and workplace systems is used to assemble profiles of people's behaviors and support new practices for social scoring. In his (2019) work, Benjamin explained that the trend of gamification confuses employees by making them believe that monitoring their performance is just a game.

All in all, these studies highlight three areas that need further attention in AI, gamification and security: 1) How gamification impacts the mind over time, 2) Whether and how frequently cultures face the same issues with dark patterns, 3) How rules can be consistently applied when using AI in both simple and complex gamification systems. Based on what has been found, it is crucial for gamification ethics to rely on concepts from computer science, behavioral psychology, legal studies and philosophy.

Putting together views from various fields, the literature review provides a solid support for looking into ethics in gamification. Drawing together studies from health, education, work and civic groups indicates that putting attention on engagement often results in focusing less on people's true value. By doing this, game researchers and developers must emphasize ethics from the start of the design, instead of attaching them at the end.

1.1 Manipulation and Behavioral Control

The other ethical issue that such techniques raise is that of conscious manipulation of user behavior. Because the experiences designed in a gamified system appeal to human psychological buttons, which include incentives and rivalry, the system can make the users do particular activities, though thereby unknowingly. This manipulation challenges the subject's ability to make decisions to perform activities that they want or those that have been deemed appropriate by the designers. The insights obtained from the range of referenced examples of educational apps or fitness trackers demystify how gamification works and also why it engenders ethical concerns over user control and decision-making.

1.2 Addiction and Engagement

Another problem is that games sometimes can become addictive, which can be also relevant to gamified environment. Features like constant incentives and rivalry can produce a fascinating environment within which clients have an opportunity to get involved and may in turn result in an addictive pattern. It indicates that those elements that are applied to support gamification of processes can increase motivation and lead to compulsive behavior (Ibrahim, 2021)

Figure 1. Gamification strategies' impact on engagement levels, highlighting both the positive and negative outcomes of such design choices.

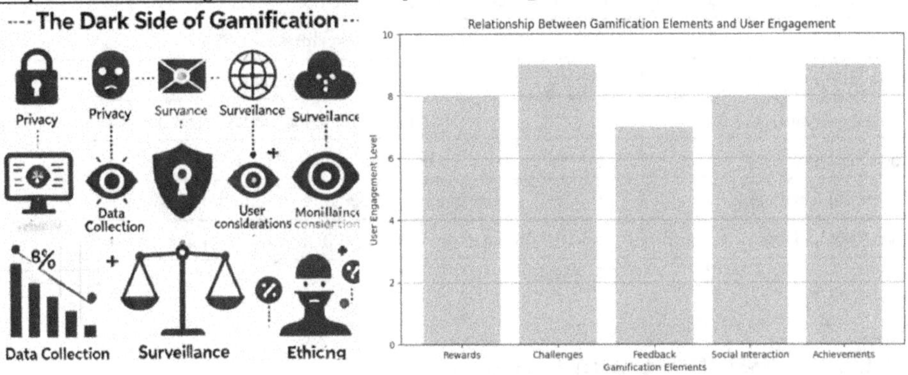

1.3 Transparency and Consent

Ethical issues of gamification require transparency to consumers and an opportunity to assume risk through informed consent (Al-Msallam, 2023). In return for points and advertising content, users give out vast amounts of personal information but are often unaware of how their information will be used. Some of the challenges include: With regards to data practices, there is often much uncertainty, which may create a considerable divide between users and the platforms that use gamification. Consequently, providing the users with enought information about data collection and usage remains as the most crucial aspect. To unpack, solving these transparency problems is crucial in developing an enshrinement of ethical uses of platforms that respect users' rights and decision (Spanellis, 2023).

2. PRIVACY ISSUES IN GAMIFIED SYSTEMS

2.1 Data Collection Practices

In gamified contexts, first- and second-order data are gathered in order to improve the general pleasure derived from interaction (Zhang, 2023). Such data can be, for instance, name and email address of the user or the data about their behavior, including the interactions they have made, the rates of completion of certain activities, and the time spent on it. Using values and metrics, developers will ensure that all users are retained through providing them with changed and tailored experience. But this raises significant privacy issues getting and sharing such vast amount of data leaves users unaware of how much data is being collected from them (Rivadeneira, 2023).

Table 2. Common data types collected in gamification

Data Type	Description
Personal Information	Name, email, age, gender
Behavioral Data	User actions, task completion, engagement metrics
Location Data	GPS coordinates, IP addresses
Device Information	Type of device, operating system, browser type
Social Media Data	Interactions with social platforms, sharing behavior

2.2 User Awareness and Control

One of the main issues that can be observed concerning the data privacy of users is encountered in gamified systems. It wherein many may not be well aware of which data is being gathered or for what purpose or how such data collected shall be utilized, which results in ignorance and lack of control of personalized data. In addition, the increased length and legalise of the privacy policies, terms of service add an extra layer of confusion to the rights of the users. To deal with these problem it is necessary to utilize measures which increase information owner control. It is, therefore, likely that this could entail reducing privacy options, offering understandable information about data utilization, and offering options to prevent or block particular data utilization. In this way, empowering users is much capable of enhancing the trust of users and promoting more ethical perspective of gamification (Rivadeneira, 2023).

Ensuring that personal information is not abused during the development of online games necessitates proper data handling. This system works by adhering to the principle that just the required data should be processed and used. Collecting less data keeps users' information more private and increases their trust. If a goal of the system is to support better health, it may not require sensitive and specific information, but only basic details about how active the user is. Moreover, it means less risk and correct handling of data to follow expected standards.

Privacy should be considered from the very start of creating a technology system. Privacy should be considered during the platform's development instead of being added as an additional step later. Before releasing any new features, you should conduct an assessment, note the routes of data across your system and agree on what data is gathered, processed and accessed by different individuals. If privacy boundaries are put in place at the beginning, all later design steps will be reviewed for privacy risks.

The use of gamification also relies heavily on being transparent. People should understand which data is being collected, for which reasons, how much time it will be saved for and what they can do with their information. Notice and policy language should be simple and easy to understand and descriptions of key events usually appear whenever a user is about to reveal private details or achievements. By providing this information, users are able to understand the details and make decisions comfortably.

Consent concepts should be strong and significant. Gamified systems ought to present users with the ability to choose if they want certain data from their use of the application to be shared or not. So, users may decide to stay anonymous in leaderboards by using pseudonyms and they can also avoid providing third parties with certain details about their performance. Making users' data accessible to them enables platforms to comply with laws and value their customers' choices.

Using advanced privacy technologies helps safeguard people's data. Applying anonymization or pseudonymization methods removes any elements that might link a person to the data. You can use differential privacy to add noise to the combined data so that the identity of individual people is protected. Homomorphic encryption and federated learning are rising technologies that allow people to analyze or process their information without moving it to external servers or unencrypted devices. They play a significant role when it comes to data related to health, finances or education.

The importance of policies in an organization matches that of advanced security systems. Strong policies for storing and deleting data prevent anyone else from obtaining personal information. Audits and reviews done often ensure that companies meet updated laws and quality guidelines.

It is important to involve and educate users when including privacy during gamification. A lot of users could be unaware of the consequences of sharing their information in games that feature online communities. Tutorials that explain what information is being gathered, easily-understandable privacy options and quick privacy tips can teach people how to control their privacy. If developers engage users in the development process, they learn the details their customers find most compelling and are more likely to produce the kinds of systems that users recognize and trust.

Connecting capturing participation, performance and engagement with protecting users' privacy is sometimes quite difficult. It is important for designers to explore the drawbacks and present users with settings that let them remain private or limit their others from seeing what they accomplish. Never should game-like elements force users to disclose more information than they plan; they should value and recognize people who participate carefully and respect their privacy as much as those who do well during games.

To design privacy-focused gamification, one should follow guidance given by laws and regulations such as the GDPR and the COPPA. Governments have implemented these regulations so that personal data is only collected if needed, that people know what they can do with their personal information and that companies protect it. If these requirements are considered in designing, it also shows users that their privacy is valued.

Designing games for education should always consider ethical issues. Those involved in developing and supporting new technology should constantly try to strike a balance between user participation and user privacy. Exchange between people who make, use and oversee games can lead to discovering new issues and deciding on best ways to handle them. When privacy is at the forefront, gamified platforms fulfill their roles in education, health, business or entertainment, all while ensuring users' trust, privacy and dignity are protected.

2.3 Case Studies

Some of the most huge privacy leaks in gamified systems suggest the significance of the threats contained in the data collection practices. For instance, a popular jogging app was found leaking users' geolocation information to third parties thus exposing movement patterns of the user (Mink, 2023). This breach brought concern into the use of personal data in gamification application and highlighted the necessity of strong protection of data. Another example was an online education service that was unable to protect participants' personal information disclosure and exposure. The evaluation of these case studies draws out the weak points existing in the gamified systems and also emphasizes the necessity for the fortification of privacy options in order to better protect the users and remain ethical in the gamification domain.

3. SURVEILLANCE AND MONITORING

3.1 Surveillance Mechanisms

Surveillance mechanisms in gamified contexts employ different technologies in order to track users' activity and their interactions. These can range from monitoring applications, analytical instruments, and an assortment of metrics accumulation tools used to Follow user vibrations across multiple mediums. For instance, health and fitness apps could use the app user's location data during the fitness challenge, while learning apps could track a student's activities through a learning management system. Such flow of data makes it easier for developers to improve on the user experience and apply learning or engagement approaches.

Figure 2. Flowchart of data surveillance processes in gamified environments

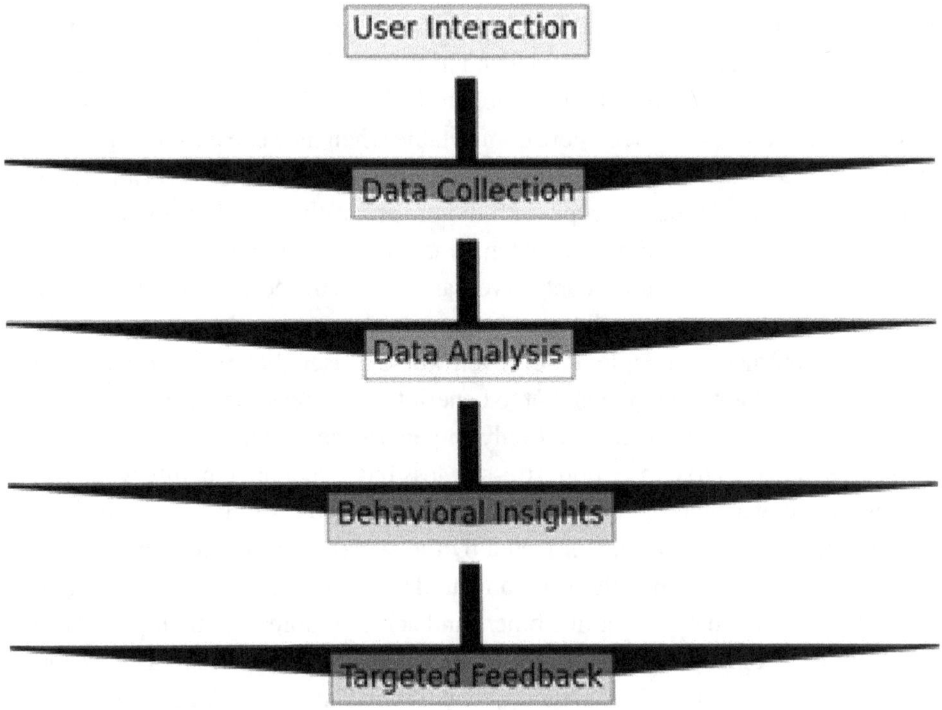

3.2 Impact on User Behavior

The kinds of surveillance that are associated with various gamified systems directly weigh on users' interactions and processes. On the hand, monitoring can foster motivation because user is being given feedback and corresponding experiences in real time. However, the proposal has implications for ethical considerations such as; privacy and autonomy respective to the client. These behaviors may constrain user to abide to certain expected behaviors that in turn, may have a potentially negative effect on there self motivation. These consequences are so complex since consumers can be exposed to privacy invasion and the pressure to participate all the time, potentially causing negative on their well-being, and experience.

Surveillance in a gamified environment feels different for each user because their perceptions are influenced by a mix of mental, social and other factors. The main argument for surveillance in gamified systems is that it helps keep people more engaged, gives them unique advice and rewards them with actual items. Still, the way people feel while using apps is often not simple. When monitoring is clear about what it collects and why and has recognized benefits for users, many individuals agree to it. This allows people to feel more in charge and independent while playing. Users often feel more comfortable when they can choose if a specific feature is used or turned off, what privacy settings they use and who can see their achievements. People tend to cope with monitoring if they think it opposes others rather than themselves and promotes what matters most to them.

Still, many people do not accept surveillance and will soon lose trust if they feel they are being deceived, coerced or uninformed. They can lead to unease, mistrust and even resentment in people. It gets even worse if users believe their actions are being influenced not to help them but to benefit the business. Because of this, users often see themselves as being used only to benefit the system. Authors note that such cases may lead to exhaustion, stress or less independence, mainly when users are continually watched by the system and are criticized for going off script.

Surveillance gamification is affected by the social environment where it takes place. If being rewarded by others or compared to others plays a big role in a game, users may feel they have to act like others and achieve more than their peers. For a few, gaining recognition from others encourages them and lets them feel accepted and accomplished. For a different group, school sports can be upsetting and isolating and lead to stigma, when they find it hard to compete with those who are better. So, how people feel about surveillance in games is influenced by their personality, cultural background, past experience and so on.

It has been shown that people may feel both joy and accomplishment or else disappointment, unease and contempt if they are being watched in game environments. A number of users enjoy the game, believing that combining emotions and thought provokes in them a stronger sense of immersion. Some people, on the other hand, state that they feel annoyed or irritated by the surveillance, only when they believe the efforts are too much. Users can enjoy a better experience if they can switch off or adjust any annoying parts of the app. Whether a system offers clear explanations, options for pauses and is understanding of individuals, it will more often lead to people staying pleased with it.

Being open and sharing information with people allows them to accept surveillance more easily. Those who learn how the system is governed, the purpose of its awards and what information is collected can judge whether to join in or not. When gamification is done ethically, appropriate privacy policies are available, monitoring methods are made clear and people can offer feedback at any time. Users trust and enjoy playing the system only if they believe it is fair and impartial.

Being concerned about inclusivity and accessibility can shape people's opinions about surveillance. Meaningful learning is possible for people who are not motivated by competition or fame, just as it is for those who simply feel better in groups or by themselves, as well as those who have different mental abilities.

The common discourse about surveillance influences public attitudes towards it. Some people in today's digital society may grow accustomed to being watched and treat this situation as unavoidable. Other groups, however, work hard to promote stricter rules and higher morals. Frequently monitoring user habits in games often encourages questions about the future consequences for independence, privacy and our society's morals. People in charge of technology should understand that the public's acceptance of surveillance might decrease over time if individuals become aware of risks, experience wounds from it or use other tools that protect their privacy.

Acceptance of system surveillance in gamified systems is affected by their design, the actions of users, how clear the information is, its level of acceptance by society and the unique environment. Experts should ensure that their systems allow users to choose freely, understand the choices they make and always inform about monitoring activities. Giving priority to ethics and focusing on the user can help keep the interests of people protected as gamification is applied. Games and platforms require continued interactions between players, programmers and authorities to address surveillance and satisfy everyone interested in them.

3.3 Comparison of Different Platforms

It, however, important to recall that surveillance practices may differ markedly from one gamified system to another, based on their goals or on user populations. For instance, the learning management systems are concerned with the academic achievements, the engagement, and interactions of learners, while the fitness and health applications are concerned with the physical activities as well as sharing information with others. Employee engagement and performance metrics may be used by corporate training programs to monitor retention through surveillance.

Table 3. Comparative analysis of surveillance practices across platforms

Platform Type	Data Collected	Purpose of Surveillance	Privacy Measures Implemented
Education	Participation, grades, behavior	Monitor student progress and engagement	Data anonymization, user consent
Fitness	Location, activity levels, goals	Encourage physical activity	Opt-out options, data encryption
Corporate Training	Performance metrics, engagement	Assess employee training effectiveness	Regular audits, transparency policies

By analyzing the diverse surveillance practices described in this paper one can find the advantages and disadvantages of monitoring of data in gamified systems. It is crucial for such constructs to distinguish between these differences to create better, more moral approaches to gamification strategies that embrace users' privacy along with intensifying the engagements.

Data security in gamified environments should be achieved by using both technical and organizational methods. Since game-based systems deal with sensitive details, systems using encryption are essential to make the information inaccessible to those who should not have it. Data is encrypted by transforming it and to read it, you need the right decryption key. This makes encryption one of the best ways to protect the privacy and accuracy of both stored and transmitted information. Currently, advanced encryption is implemented across the industry to shield databases, messages and copies of sensitive data in case physical servers are accessed by unauthorized users. To improve security, extra measures such as SSL, firewalls, intrusion detection systems and clean software updates are implemented along with encryption.

Encryption is not the only important method; in data security, anonymization and pseudonymization are vital. Doing this reduces the possibility that users can be recognized after a data breach. Doing this is particularly useful for organizations that base their decisions on understanding behavior and performance, since it ensures privacy is protected. Furthermore, roles and multi-factor authentication are used to check identities, so employees with the required permissions are the only ones who can use important information.

Technology will only be effective if the organization follows certain security procedures. Errors by employees are often responsible for data breaches, so it is crucial to regularly train workers in privacy and security when developing a data protection strategy. Generally, keeping up with skills in data protection covers talking about the need to protect user information, spotting tricky phishing schemes, preparing good passwords and acting as asked when handling sensitive information. The programs should be modified for every employee to make sure that developers and customer support both understand how they should safeguard data. These kinds of simulation exercises can make it easier for employees to respond if a genuine threat occurs.

Policies that explain the method for collecting, processing, storing and removing data over its entire life should be part of any organization's plan. These guidelines should be updated regularly as new dangers, innovations and rules emerge. Higher-ups in any organization should pay close attention to data security, offer suitable resources for updates and training and encourage workers to value privacy and safety. Company leaders should ensure that there are clear communication channels so that workers feel they can report suspicious activity without fearing punishment.

Regular security audits and risk assessments help discover any gaps in your organization's computer systems and procedures. As a result of these appraisals, outdated software, poorly arranged security settings or a shortage of knowledge in employees might be identified by malicious users. Addressing these problems orderly ensures organizations have protection and can reassure users, regulators and other interested individuals. Likewise, the organization ought to develop and frequently exercise incident response plans to act immediately, control negative consequences and talk clearly with those involved in any security-related event.

Tell your users about the information they are sending and the dangers of sharing it. If website or app users have transparent information about their privacy, data and security, they can pick what's best for them online. You can guide people by including tutorials, providing FAQs and using in-app notifications to introduce them to the idea of using two-factor authentication and refreshing their passwords.

In health, education and at work, it is particularly important to use both technical and organizational safeguards for gamification. Since these situations are more important, a privacy or reputation breach could greatly affect a person's privacy, character or health. As an example, when games are used in the health sector, information such as medical data must be protected through solid encryption and employees must receive training on acting in accordance with the rules. When it comes to student data in education, strong technology measures should be put in place, along with set procedures for how and with whom student data can be shared.

In addition, with most gamified systems now connected and using cloud services, companies should focus on protecting their third-party suppliers and service providers. Before working with a partner, focus on reviewing their security systems, details contained in contracts and ensure that they are regularly checked for proper compliance. Data transmitted to outside groups should be fully encrypted and access should permitting only the services needed.

Ensuring gamified environments are safe requires using technology as well as good organizational strategies. Strong security mainly relies on encryption, anonymization, access controls and regular tests, as well as ensuring all employees are properly prepared, policies are straightforward, top executives are dedicated and users are educated. Focusing on both the technology and the people in the process allows organizations to protect users' information, build trust and carry out what is right for game users. This strategy addresses existing risks and helps organizations respond to any future challenges that may arise in this field.

4. REGULATORY AND ETHICAL FRAMEWORKS

4.1 Current Regulations

Major legal frameworks regulating the gamefulness paradigm to enhance user protection and regulatory measures targeting data privacy are still important when defining the gamification landscape. The incorporation of gamified systems as part of the society's life therefore calls for enhanced formulation of legal frameworks to regulate them. These regulations seek to protect consumer while at the same time ensuring the developers are responsible for why and how they consume the users' data. Two of the most important global regulations in this field are General Data Protection Regulation (GDPR) in EU and Children's Online Privacy Protection Act (COPPA) in USA.

The GDPR that was adopted in 2018, defines one of the highest levels of protection of personal data in the world. It has been framed, therefore, as having the overriding objective of improving the ability of individuals to control their own data. To capture, process, and share data under GDPR, organisations have very strict rules to follow with regards to consent. The regulation making requires users to be informed in advance of the type of data that is collected from them and how this data will be utilised as well as the time that it will take before the data is discarded. Also, users are allowed to grant consent for their data to be processed only after which the consent can be revoked anytime. This is highly useful in gamified spaces where players are potentially unaware of how much data it is collecting. Thus, by using informed consent, the GDPR enhances users control over their data, thus giving users the power or managing their own information.

In the same way the Children's Online Privacy Protection Act or COPPA targets the protection of child and youths online. Created in 1998, COPPA puts strict rules for any website or service that would gather information on users aged below thirteen years. This law requires the developer to prove that he has received prior consent from the parents for the collection of data concerning the child. It also requires policies that explain to users what information is being gathered about them, how it will be used and what procedures are in place for a parent or caregiver to review information collected on a child with an account. Especially today when many applications and educational programs for children contain elements of gamification, COPPA becomes an important protection measure for children against potential abuse by companies and steal of their personal data.

GDPR as well as COPPA places many conditions with the developers. Some of the things that are supposed to be put in place include; they are supposed to observe lawful and robust measures of processing individuals' data besides being supposed to be transparent. This implies that developers have to constantly review their methods of collecting data, implement the use of RegTech to secure data and also provide procedures for notification of data infringements. Moreover, organisations must supply easily understandable privacy notices in order to give a notice to the users about their rights concerning the data. It is left to the developers to design the systems that should implement all these regulations besides promoting ethical use of data.

To the users, these regulations provide the necessary safeguards that might ensure that some of the risks related to data privacy violations and misuse are alleviated. Similarly, they also require the subject to be aware of the rights of how their data is processed in gamified contexts. Some customer rights need to be explained as follows; They need to know that the guidelines set under GDPR mean they have rights like the right to data access, correction of data that is incorrect, and the right to have their data erased subject to certain conditions. As it is seen in section 3, by giving parents specific rights of administration and deletion of their children's data, COPPA ensures parents have considerable control of information gathered from the minors.

However, as has been seen these regulation policies work well only if there is adequate user consciousness. A lack of awareness regarding the rights of users or the ways in which data can be kept secure means that the protections granted to the user are not optimally utilized. Consequently, there is a need for educational intervention to 'teach users more about data privacy, and the importance of consent and impacts of their behaviours within Gamified Spaces. This awareness is important in enabling users to fight for their rights and also to enable them to come up with right decisions on how to engage with the gamified applications.

The impact of gamification and the consequences of following GDPR and COPPA or not show the need for ethical practices in the online environment. These regulations not only assign important duties to developers but can also be seen for the purpose of availing reactions from the users especially the children and other needy groups. As the field of gamification advances, discussion and exchange between game developers, players, and governmental or regulatory bodies becomes crucial for adaptation of these frameworks to answer new questions and still protect users' rights and their privacy.

4.2 Proposed Ethical Guidelines

It is crucial for the further development of ethical gamified experiences that, developers and stakeholders alike ensure and incorporate set ethical standards governing gamification that encompasses those complexity in engagement, data privacy and behavior change. The first of those guidelines that can be derived should be the principle of informed consent. This means that users must be evidently informed on which kind of data will be gathered and processed, for what purpose, and what the consequences of participating in gamified systems would be? It is not enough to prompt the user to check a box during the registration process; users need to know what their rights are and what may happen to their data. This can be done by removing complexity at the content level by having simple and concise privacy policies, clear language and making available and accessible Education and communication materials on data practices.

Transparency is the other area that has been identified to be part of ethical gamification. It is therefore important for developers to effectively communicate with the users on how his or her data is useful in creating the game atmosphere. This includes explaining how the data is collected; how the data is processed to make aggregates; is it masked; and is the data shared with third parties. Through transparency, developers will be in a position to ensure that users interact squarely with gamified systems, hence promoting the cause of engagement. transparent practices also enable the user to as exercise their agency towards participation more sufficiently allowing the user control over data.

Meaningful control over personal information it is at least as important as providing such information. User input on their data manipulation should be active in a manner that consists of the choice on whether to access, change or delete data. This control should apply to cases where one is able to select options he or she does not want to be tracked and instead, only want certain data collected. For example, a fitness application based on the game might allow users to decide whether their location data will be broadcasted to others or used to provide some feedback to the corresponding user. Such options do not only recognize users' self-governance principles but also other principles concerning data protection and privacy.

Another key issue of the present research is to involve users in the design of gamification strategies to find out what means the most to them. When users are asked to share stories or talk about something they have gone through, there is a lot of data that can be gathered especially from the designers. Such feedback can be obtained through, the surveys, focus group, and usability testing among others.

According to the previous research, the users who are primary engaged to a system feel a constructive attachment towards the system when their inputs are considered, therefore making the built game feel more positive and accepted.

The standards of ethics need the collective action of different stakeholders, which include developers, policymakers, and users. All the groups have their own task in influencing the culture of responsibility and ethical practice in the essence of gamification. Since developers are measured on evaluations, they are the ones responsible for the performance and implementation of measures, while policymakers may establish a favorable legal framework that strengthens ethical norms. By being active stakeholders in gamified systems, users must seek change in order to respect their rights and input proper values on relevant conversations. It also assists in developing a program where everyone to practice good morale and everyone will want to protect user rights.

It is tangible to have an open, non-restrictive discussion on the practical application of gamification with significant focus on morality in the rationales and processes of establishing frameworks that accounts for both, morality and user satisfaction. Through encouraging conversations, developers, users, and policy makers, it is possible for stakeholders to pinpoint ethically sensitive issues that are relevant to stakeholders as these are discussed and resolved ahead of time. For example, some participants may state that current trends in game design that are not previously covered by this ethical framework are explored in the discussion, for example the use of artificial intelligence to influence players' behavior. When these challenges are met in a joint manner, appearing later to stakeholders, it creates an opportunity to set up novel best practices solutions that conform to equal standards of ethics.

Also, creating a place for the continuation of discussion can help managers and employees learn and update with the changes in technology and users' demands that happen rather fast. In this forum it would have been possible to share examples of best practices, examples of ethical gamification, and new studies on the topic. Through such stakeholders' community, people interested in the use of gamification can share new findings related to ethical issues when creating games and develop effective strategies for avoiding undesirable practices.

Lastly, there is an implementation of numerous ethical rules in the framework of gamification as a threat; however, it is also seen as an appreciation of user security and confidence. By valuing the principles of informed consent and transparency, control and feedback regarding the impact of games on the users, developers can create not only thoroughly entertaining games but also ethical ones. With the increase of gamification across different fields, it is easy to conclude that the requirements for those ethical frameworks will also increase. If everyone involved in the development, research, and application of gamification continues engaging in conversations with one another, we can perhaps shape the future of this field in a way that protects the best interests of the end users while simultaneously allowing for even greater motivation in the application of gamified systems for a variety of purposes.

4.3 Future Directions

Phenomenon of gamification is expanding further and new trends that appear along with them open both opportunities and ethical concerns. For instance, application of AI and machine learning can improve the personalisation agenda, but at the same time lead to the worsening of surveillance and data control. The use of gamification in such sensitive themes as mental state and learning increases the problem of user sensitivity and their ability to make their own decisions.

Figure 3. Graph of predicted trends in gamification and associated ethical concerns

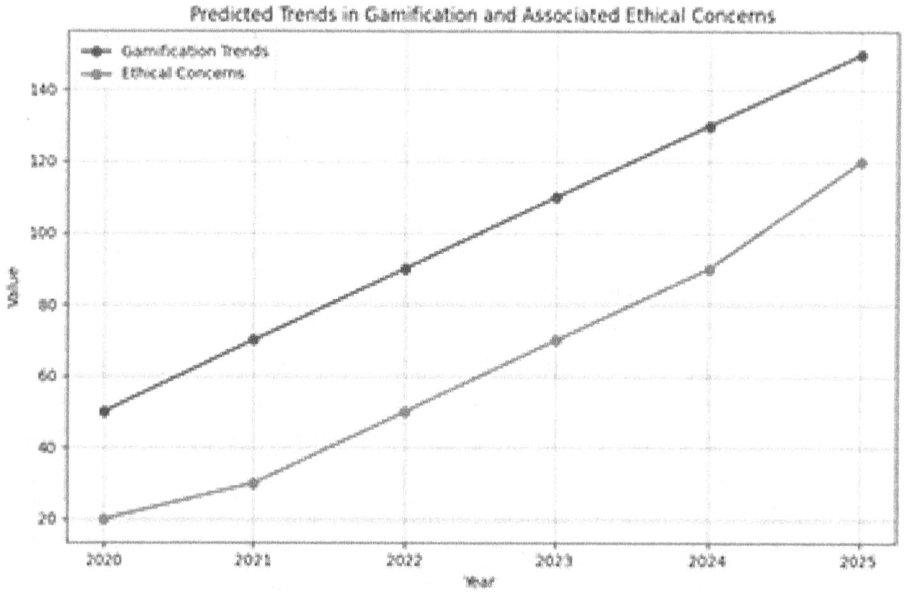

Looking ahead, it is crucial for developers and stakeholders to remain vigilant about the ethical implications of these trends. Proactively addressing these concerns will help ensure that gamification remains a positive force for engagement and motivation, rather than a source of ethical dilemmas. By fostering an ongoing conversation about the ethics of gamification, we can cultivate a more responsible and user-centered approach to its development and implementation.

AI-driven gamification is rapidly becoming very important, increasing the chances of good and bad outcomes from using gamified systems. Contrary to traditional ways, where challenges and rewards are fixed, AI systems adjust both challenges and rewards in real time using machine learning. Because of this, the way users interact with the system now becomes more responsive and often anticipates what they will do next. Using big data to offer so much personalization to students means we have to avoid facing new problems and come up with the best solutions.

Because of this, some worry that AI easily influences users by raising the user's game levels and thus getting them addicted to the game. They can shape how users interact with them by studying biometric information, user actions and their past behavior. Because of this, users can become so hooked that it's difficult for them to stop. Studies report that gamification in health and education apps may encourage users to act just like people addicted to behaviors, as they keep striving to achieve the next target. Sometimes, motivating someone through rewards for learning or fitness can backfire and transform into pressure and intimidation. Many of these models prevent people from leaving, as deciding to disengage can lead to social or work-related problems for them. Their influence on feelings and thought processes is usually overlooked and using them continually may have an impact on users' future efforts to become better or measure their achievements.

A significant problem occurs when the bias in AI algorithms appears in the field of gamification. If data labels from past years carry stereotypes, they can still create unfairness in AI systems designed to work justly. For instance such hiring platforms could accidentally make it easier for certain groups to pass the tests because the challenges are tailored to their culture. When tasks are designed in a gamified way, some of the strategies or ways people communicate may feel more comfortable to some groups and less so to others. Eventually, biases may increase unfairness in the workplace and damage the acceptance of gamified recruitment, resulting in a loss of diversity and orchestrating existing unequal situations. Since AI's reasoning can be difficult to understand, it raises more problems for those expected to take responsibility, as it is difficult for anyone to examine how certain decisions were made. If people cannot interpret the decisions made, they may have no option to challenge or know why certain opportunities such as taking part in education or getting employment, are taken from them.

Gamification with AI creates a major challenge involving the monitoring of people's behavior. Modern systems use eye movements and heart rate, together with behavior monitoring, to build in-depth profiles of their users. This category of surveillance uses emotions to uncover someone's stress levels, how closely they are paying attention and their mood. In such programs, AI keeps track of employees' performance as well as their emotions, using the data to change the lesson as it happens. Despite better learning results and matching of lessons with students' minds, the approach promotes regular surveillance practices that infringe on our personal freedom and right to privacy. Those who work with AI may become too fixated on the numbers produced by the software and creativity could decrease as a result. A teacher might feel more stress and less satisfied with their job due to being measured by metrics that are not fully clear. In the long run such a system can decrease our freedom by turning every decision into a list of computer-approved inputs, rewarding people for doing what predictive models expect rather than for trying other solutions and dismissing uniqueness as an annoyance.

Technology-backed tools should be included in the early stages of designing the project. Through federated learning, AI models train with decentralized data without sending people's raw data to a single location. Personal privacy is protected using this approach, while everyone can still learn from one another and participate in customized learning. If differential privacy is introduced into federated learning, it becomes less likely that someone will misuse user data during the personalization phase. For users to understand clearly, AI frameworks that explain the workings of algorithms can be used. As a result, a fitness app could remind users that their workout intensity has increased since their heart rate came back to normal more quickly in the past week, making their choices plain. It improves how users view the workings of AI and ensures that the company's developers take into account how ordinary users might interpret what AI does.

Yet, adopting new systems alone will not be enough unless others cooperate closely. Experts and policy makers should notice that the GDPR and COPPA regulations are not accurate enough for AI-driven gamification. These laws cope with usual data collection and get users' approval, but they are not designed for AI used in games. Managing accountable AI will require legislators to design laws that require checking AI systems for bias, how their data is handled and if they can be manipulated. Apps for learning could encounter tighter rules, as the data they collect sometimes comes from especially vulnerable users who are not fully grown. Cooperation at the global level could bring about standard ethics, but still allow locally accepted practices that suit the region.

Building AI-by-design should be guided by ethical principles in the industry. Fairness should be added at each stage in the development process, starting from selecting data to checking after the model is running in real time. Simulation tools for gamification can spot any unequal use of rewards in the software before it is used. Providing people with a way to define rules for AI functions often prevents it from going too far in personalization. As a result, users could set up their app so that there are not too many difficult challenges and disable any features designed to analyze their feelings, making the personalization feel less bothersome. Allowing people to alter the AI's influence helps them decide how involved they want to be in the application, instead of having decisions chosen for them by the AI.

Users and supporters are essential since AI-driven gameplay finds a home in significant realms such as healthcare, schools and jobs. We need more efforts aimed at teaching people to understand and examine the role of algorithms in their lives. Algorithms and AI could be made available through workshops, online supports and in classrooms, giving everyone the ability to ask questions about them. Organizations might be encouraged by grassroots movements to share how their models are trained and evaluated. If platforms ease reporting on their use of algorithms, it will help users better understand and trust them. With enough push from the public, those in charge may choose to reform or improve the ways systems work.

When AI gamification is not controlled, it can shape society in many significant and diverse ways. Personalizing lessons in schools can close off students to a variety of skills, due to AI prediction leading them down the same path. While effort is made to support students who require help, personalization sometimes leads them to remain at the same learning level for a long time. If engagement is given more importance than actual results, gamified apps in healthcare could prevent people from seeking professional treatment and increase the risks from continuing illness. While giving rewards for tracking their moods or doing mental exercises, assistive apps should be equipped to spot serious mental health concerns and avoid discouraging users by coercing them with negative results if they leave the app. Emotionally and financially, AI gamification at the workplace could increase the gap between high and low performers, as its supporting rules can restrict employees with brain-based conditions or disabilities. Due to these issues, some contributions may be excluded from a narrow definition of what makes a worker productive.

Having a holistic approach to governance will help cope with these issues. To ensure clear boundaries are set, experts from various fields work together on AI gamification. As an example, we could prevent apps created for children from improving user time to avoid exploitation, require independent tests for AI in major infrastructure and set up AI review boards that have users among their members, to monitor competitive online games. Just like ethics committees in universities, these boards could assess whether a system will have good or bad consequences before it becomes widespread. With blockchain and similar possibilities, it becomes possible to leave a permanent record of computer-based actions, allowing the outcomes to be checked and traced by people outside the company. Thanks to blockchain technology, users could share their achievements using badges instead of having their actions watched by others. Alternatively, adding AI to gamification could raise new issues related to ethics. Generated stories and challenges should never feature harmful stereotypes or make up incentives that play tricks on people's minds. Training generative models with unfiltered data could increase the presence of these problems in games.

If we view AI-driven gamification as part of a socio-technical system, it will shape its path in a positive way. Game developers should ask themselves: Can overpersonalized gamification help users or does it make users nothing more than academic studies? Should learning, work and growth always aim to be efficient and engaging, these activities would lack depth and human elements. Those who make public policy should be careful not to let progress in technology blind them to its effects on society. Highlighting human dignity can allow stakeholders to take advantage of AI's strengths without worrying about its dangers in altering, affecting and watching individuals.

Gamification is advancing rapidly, so everyone involved should regularly discuss and address new ethical problems that may emerge. Collaborating on these systems will ensure future game-based systems are fresh, enjoyable, respectful, clear and support user rights. When ethics are incorporated into all procedures, gamification might lead to social benefits without violating people's rights or causing unfairness.

CONCLUSION

In this chapter, we have turned the spotlight on the dark side of gaming together with the ethical implications, privacy and surveillance. We moved with defining and explaining what gamification means before expanding on how the fun aspects of the terminology can be effective in different areas including learning, exercises, and business training. But we also pointed at the dark side of applying the gaming techniques: manipulation, addictive behavior, and decreasing users' privacy. Based on the work accomplished in this paper, we were able to demonstrate that as helpful as gamification could be in increasing engagement it is replete with ethical hazards that require to be prevented in order to protect young users.

This is one of the main ideas touched: Ethical concerns are needed to be added before the creation and integration of a game into a system. Based on the examples of gamification constantly spreading in various spheres of life, the issue of user monitoring and data gathering becomes sensitive. Data protection legislation like GDPR and COPPA help codify a foundational level of protection for users and their data but they also show that developers need to put a strong emphasis on informed consent and the user's ability to shape her or his experience. In addition, describe and analyse the specific example of surveillance instruments that are beneficial for improving the users' experiences, while being unethical when they undermine users' privacy and control. Therefore, having ethical rules is important to determine the levels of interaction with respect to people's rights.

To build the future that will allow fair application of the gamification, everyone – developers, users, and policy-makers – must join forces. Creating an ethical based gamification is thus imperative for developers, this requires ensuring that the real use of data collected from the users is sane. Thus, the users themselves should fight for their rights and call for the truth concerning the specific use of data. Policy makers have a central function of defining laws that govern them with a purpose of safeguarding users while encouraging growth in application of game elements. All these stakeholders need to have an ongoing debate which involves discussion of the effects of gamification on the processes: the lessons learned about the field and the set of best practices have to be constantly discussed and updated. In this way, it can be possible to entice an atmosphere of fun that may improve motivation and prolonged usage while retaining ethical superiority and customers' confidence. In the long run, such synergy between all stakeholders would help in reaping the benefits of gamification while protecting the rights and benefits of a user in today's ever growing highly digitalized society.

REFERENCES

Acquisti, A., Brandimarte, L., & Loewenstein, G. (2015). Privacy and Human Behavior in the Age of Information. *Science*, *347*(6221), 509–514. DOI: 10.1126/science.aaa1465 PMID: 25635091

Adams, M. (2017). Big Data and Individual Privacy in the Age of the Internet of Things. *Technology Innovation Management Review*, *7*(4), 12–24. DOI: 10.22215/timreview/1067

Al-Msallam, S., Xi, N., & Hamari, J. (2023). Ethical considerations in gamified interactive marketing praxis. In *The Palgrave Handbook of Interactive Marketing* (pp. 963–985). Springer International Publishing. DOI: 10.1007/978-3-031-14961-0_41

Algashami, A. (2019). Gamification risks in collaborative information systems: identification and management method (Doctoral dissertation, Bournemouth University).

Algashami, A., Vuillier, L., Alrobai, A., Phalp, K., & Ali, R. (2019). Gamification risks to enterprise teamwork: Taxonomy, management strategies and modalities of application. *Systems*, *7*(1), 9. DOI: 10.3390/systems7010009

Arora, C., & Razavian, M. (2021). Ethics of gamification in health and fitness-tracking. *International Journal of Environmental Research and Public Health*, *18*(21), 11052. DOI: 10.3390/ijerph182111052 PMID: 34769570

Benjamin, G. (2019). Playing at control: Writing surveillance in/for gamified society. *Surveillance & Society*, *17*(5), 699–713. DOI: 10.24908/ss.v17i5.13204

Das, L., Poornachandrika, T. S., & Bhargava, D. (2024). Ethical Dilemmas in Gamified Marketing Approaches. In Marketing and Gamification (pp. 222-245). Routledge. DOI: 10.4324/9781032694238-16

Deterding, S., Dixon, D., Khaled, R., & Nacke, L. (2011). From game design elements to gamefulness: Defining “gamification”. *Proceedings of the 15th International Academic MindTrek Conference: Envisioning Future Media Environments*, 9-15. DOI: 10.1145/2181037.2181040

Fitria, T. N. (2022, December). Using game design techniques (gamification) in teaching and learning process: A review. *Prosiding Seminar Nasional & Call for Paper STIE AAS*, *5*(1), 1–18.

Gao, Z., Chen, S., Sun, H., & Wen, X. (2021). Impact of gamification on college students’ learning engagement. *Frontiers in Psychology*, *12*, 1185353.

Gupta, D. R. (2025). The Dark Side of Gamification: Ethics, Privacy, Surveillance, and Monitoring in the Use of Gamified Elements. In Gamification and Global Business Management: Mapping the Future (pp. 167-198).

Hamari, J., Koivisto, J., & Sarsa, H. (2014). Does gamification work?—A literature review of empirical studies on gamification. *Proceedings of the 47th Hawaii International Conference on System Sciences*, 3025-3034. DOI: 10.1109/HICSS.2014.377

Hyrynsalmi, S., Kimppa, K., Koskinen, J., Smed, J., & Hyrynsalmi, S. (2017). The Shades of Grey: Datenherrschaft in Data-Driven Gamification. DDGD@ MindTrek, 4-11.

Ibrahim, E. N. M., Jamali, N., & Suhaimi, A. I. H. (2021). Exploring gamification design elements for mental health support. *International Journal of Advanced Technology and Engineering Exploration*, *8*(74), 114–125. DOI: 10.19101/IJATEE.2020.S1762123

Jami Pour, M., & Binaei, H. (2024). The Ethical Challenges of Gamification in Iran: Uncovering the Dark Side. *Journal of Business and Management*, *16*(2), 415–446.

Kanat, M. (2019). The relationship between online game addiction and communication skills among college students. *Journal of Behavioral Addictions*, *8*(2), 213–221. PMID: 31120318

Kim, T. W., & Werbach, K. (2016). More than just a game: Ethical issues in gamification. *Ethics and Information Technology*, *18*(2), 157–173. DOI: 10.1007/s10676-016-9401-5

Kim, T. W., & Werbach, K. (2022). Excerpt from ethics of gamification. In *Ethics of Data and Analytics* (pp. 375–385). Auerbach Publications. DOI: 10.1201/9781003278290-55

Klock, A. C. T., Santana, B. S., & Hamari, J. (2023). Ethical Challenges in Gamified Education Research and Development: An Umbrella Review and Potential Directions. In Toda, A., Cristea, A. I., & Isotani, S. (Eds.), *Gamification Design for Educational Contexts* (pp. 37–48). Springer. DOI: 10.1007/978-3-031-31949-5_3

Lo, C. K., & To, W. M. (2023). Exploring the Impact of Gamification and AI on Personalized Learning: A Review. *International Journal of Research Publication and Reviews*, *6*(4), 5543–5548.

McCall, R., & Baillie, L. (2017). Ethics, Privacy, and Trust in Serious Games. In Handbook of Digital Games and Entertainment Technologies (p. 611).

Meral, M. (2019). The effect of online game addiction on academic performance and learning attitudes. *The Turkish Online Journal of Educational Technology, 18*(3), 45–52.

Mink, J., Yuile, A. R., Pal, U., Aviv, A. J., & Bates, A. (2022, April). Users Can Deduce Sensitive Locations Protected by Privacy Zones on Fitness Tracking Apps. *Proceedings Of The 2022 CHI Conference On Human Factors In Computing Systems*, 1-21. DOI: 10.1145/3491102.3502136

Nyström, T. (2021). Exploring the Darkness of Gamification: You Want It Darker? In Arai, K. (Ed.), *Intelligent Computing* (pp. 479–495). Springer. DOI: 10.1007/978-3-030-80129-8_35

Packin, N. G., & Chagal-Feferkorn, K. (2025). This Is Not a Game: The Addictive Allure of Digital Companions. *Seattle University Law Review, 48*(3), 693. DOI: 10.2139/ssrn.5133614

Raftopoulos, M. (2014). Towards gamification transparency: A conceptual framework for the development of responsible gamified enterprise systems. *Journal of Gaming & Virtual Worlds, 6*(2), 159–178. DOI: 10.1386/jgvw.6.2.159_1

Rivadeneira, J. E., Silva, J. S., Colomo-Palacios, R., Rodrigues, A., & Boavida, F. (2023). User-centric privacy preserving models for a new era of the Internet of Things. *Journal of Network and Computer Applications, 217*, 103695. DOI: 10.1016/j.jnca.2023.103695

Rowicka, M., & Postek, S. (2023). Who likes to learn new things? How Gamification User Types and Satisfaction but not the frustration of basic psychological needs explain the preference for learning new things. *Acta Psychologica, 236*, 103925. DOI: 10.1016/j.actpsy.2023.103925 PMID: 37116268

Rozalén, S. M. (2024). Gamification as a Persuasive Technology: Characteristics and Ethical Implications. *Journal of Ethics and Emerging Technologies, 34*(1), 1–19.

Ruggiu, D., Blok, V., Coenen, C., Kalloniatis, C., Kitsiou, A., Mavroeidi, A. G., Milani, S., & Sitzia, A. (2022). Responsible innovation at work: Gamification, public engagement, and privacy by design. *Journal of Responsible Innovation, 9*(3), 315–343. DOI: 10.1080/23299460.2022.2076985

Selinger, E., Sadowski, J., & Seager, T. (2015). Gamification and morality.

Sheetal, T., Tyagi, R., & Singh, G. (2023). Gamification and customer experience in online retail: A qualitative study focusing on ethical perspective. *Asian Journal of Business Ethics, 12*(1), 49–69. DOI: 10.1007/s13520-022-00162-1

Spanellis, A. (2023). Gamification for sustainable consumption: Ethical issues and future promises. In *Research Handbook on Ethical Consumption* (pp. 366–381). Edward Elgar Publishing. DOI: 10.4337/9781802202021.00031

Srivastava, G., Bag, S., Rahman, M. S., Pretorius, J. H. C., & Gani, M. O. (2023). Examining the dark side of using gamification elements in online community engagement: An application of PLS-SEM and ANN modeling. *Benchmarking*, *30*(9), 2921–2947. DOI: 10.1108/BIJ-03-2022-0160

Tomé Klock, A. C., Santana, B. S., & Hamari, J. (2023). Ethical Challenges in Gamified Education Research and Development: An Umbrella Review and Potential Directions. In Gamification Design for Educational Contexts (pp. 37-48). Springer.

Tsai, C. C., & Lin, S. S. (2020). The relationship between online game addiction and peer relationships among adolescents. *Computers & Education*, *148*, 103809.

Tyagi, S. (2023). Gamification and customer experience in online retail: A qualitative study focusing on ethical perspective. *Asian Journal of Business Ethics*, *12*(1), 49–69. DOI: 10.1007/s13520-022-00162-1

Vincent, B., Daniele, R., & Christopher, C. (2022). Responsible innovation at work: gamification, public engagement, and privacy by design.

Wang, Y., & Kosinski, M. (2018). Deep neural networks are more accurate than humans at detecting sexual orientation from facial images. *Journal of Personality and Social Psychology*, *114*(2), 246–257. DOI: 10.1037/pspa0000098 PMID: 29389215

Weiss, J. (2019, January). Gamification and Scholarly Ethical Perspectives on Industries, A Bibliometric Analysis. *Proceedings of the 52nd Hawaii International Conference on System Sciences*. DOI: 10.24251/HICSS.2019.827

Werbach, K., & Hunter, D. (2012). *For the win: How game thinking can revolutionize your business*. Wharton Digital Press.

White, M., & Shellenbarger, T. (2018). Gamification of nursing education with digital badges. *Nurse Educator*, *43*(2), 78–82. DOI: 10.1097/NNE.0000000000000434 PMID: 28817476

Xu, F., Buhalis, D., & Weber, J. (2017). Serious games and the gamification of tourism. *Tourism Management*, *60*, 244–256. DOI: 10.1016/j.tourman.2016.11.020

Xu, F., Weber, J., & Buhalis, D. (2013). Gamification in tourism. In *Information and Communication Technologies in Tourism 2014* (pp. 525–537). Springer. DOI: 10.1007/978-3-319-03973-2_38

Xu, Y. (2011). Literature review on web application gamification and analytics. CSDL Technical Report 11-05. Retrieved from https://csdl.ics.hawaii.edu/techreports/11-05/11-05.pdf

Yang, Y., Asaad, Y., & Dwivedi, Y. (2017). Examining the impact of gamification on consumer engagement. *Computers in Human Behavior*, *69*, 98–106.

Ye, S., & Lin, Y. (2023). The impact of short video addiction on students' behavioral engagement. *Computers in Human Behavior*, *137*, 107420.

Yonemura, K., Yajima, K., Komura, R., Sato, J., & Takeichi, Y. (2017). Practical Security Education on Operational Technology Using Gamification Method. 2017 7th IEEE International Conference on Control System, Computing and Engineering (ICCSCE), 284–88.

Zhang, L., Shao, Z., Benitez, J., & Zhang, R. (2023). How to improve user engagement and retention in mobile payment: A gamification affordance perspective. *Decision Support Systems*, *168*, 113941. DOI: 10.1016/j.dss.2023.113941

Chapter 10
The Rise of Digital Gaming in India a Comprehensive Study on User Engagement and Gamification:
Digital Gaming

Dharmendra Singh
https://orcid.org/0000-0003-0966-6530
Modern College of Business and Science, Oman

Garima Malik
https://orcid.org/0000-0002-3892-8299
Birla Institute of Management Technology, India

Swati Bhatnagar
New Delhi Institute of Management, India

ABSTRACT

Gamification and gaming have rapidly evolved as significant phenomena in India, with research on gamification gaining momentum since 2011. In recent years, this area has attracted increasing attention from practitioners, researchers, and policymakers alike, driven by the expanding size and influence of the gaming industry. This paper explores the current trends, challenges, and opportunities within the Indian gaming ecosystem, emphasizing the role of gamification in enhancing user engagement and driving industry growth. The study employs a mixed-methods approach, combining primary data collected through online surveys and interviews

DOI: 10.4018/979-8-3693-8886-0.ch010

with secondary data from scholarly articles and market reports. Findings reveal that factors such as game genre, platform preference, and graphic design quality significantly influence player engagement and the rising popularity of esports in India. The research highlights diverse gamer profiles and underscores the need for adaptive strategies in game development and marketing.

1. INTRODUCTION

The gaming industry in India is still at a relatively nascent stage, yet it is evolving at an unprecedented pace. It represents a paradigm shift in entertainment, reshaping the landscape of digital engagement and immersive experiences. This transformation is indicative of how technological advancements are deeply interwoven with the socio-cultural and economic fabric of society (KPMG, 2023). The proliferation of smartphones and mobile internet access has been instrumental in democratizing gaming, making it accessible across demographic and geographic boundaries. As a result, gaming has transcended its earlier perception as a generational fad or casual hobby to become a mainstream pursuit and a viable career option for many young Indians (RedSeer, 2022). The roots of the Indian gaming industry trace back to the early 2000s with the emergence of console and PC-based games. However, it was the advent of affordable mobile technology and increasing internet penetration that truly catalyzed the industry's explosive growth (EY–FICCI, 2024). Today, India is home to one of the world's fastest-growing gaming markets, attracting substantial investments from global technology giants such as Tencent, Alibaba, Nazara Technologies, and Microsoft Azure (Invest India, 2023). These strategic investments have expanded the gaming ecosystem, supporting both developers and consumers alike.

The Indian gaming market was valued at approximately USD 3.1 billion in 2023 and is projected to grow to USD 5.83 billion by 2034, with a compound annual growth rate (CAGR) of 16.2% (Mordor Intelligence, 2024). This rapid expansion is not just driven by mobile gaming but also by the rise of esports, casual and hyper-casual games, and the adoption of emerging technologies such as augmented reality (AR), virtual reality (VR), and blockchain-based Web3 platforms (NASSCOM, 2023). These innovations are transforming India into a hub for game-centric technological innovation and entrepreneurship. Moreover, the gaming industry's contribution goes beyond mere entertainment. It has emerged as a significant contributor to economic development through job creation, skill enhancement, and digital entrepreneurship. By 2034, the industry is expected to generate a considerable number of employment opportunities, particularly in game development, design, marketing, and esports management (Deloitte, 2023). This growth also necessitates specialized training and education programs to build the workforce required to sustain the industry's momentum, indicating its potential to impact India's broader digital economy and innovation ecosystem.

In this context, the dynamics of the Indian gaming ecosystem need to be understood. The one connotation of the "Digital Playground Paradigm" captures the asymmetrical nature of gaming, such that players play of various genres and across several different gaming devices. It starkly points out the need to see how gameplay systems and their classifications are connected with various types of players, and how such connections affect player experiences and preferences. The Indian gaming ecosystem is diversified: players play a plethora of game genres on various devices. Above all, mobile gaming rules the roost, with over 600 million smartphone users in India. This mobile-centric game strategy led to the provision of free-to-play and casual games, addressing broad audiences. But it represents only the other side of the ecosystem: console and PC gaming are alive and kicking, with their specific player preferences.

In close completed, however not restricted to, fitting the component considered or implementing mobile, console, and PC gaming, before thinking of any specific formats of a gaming platform for the games, study of these alliances could offer a decent instance of how players expect and use various gaming structures. Besides, examining such perceptions and experiences of individual players in relation to gaming systems is also of utmost importance. Certain aspects to be examined may include the psychological and social aspects of gaming, community-building-centric facets in terms of players' communal generation around certain genres and how that influences the game development and marketing strategy. The diversity of genres that players choose also molds the gaming milieu in terms of the demand for some games, which eventually fits the direction of game development. To sum up, the Indian gaming ecosystem is fast becoming one dynamic and multidimensional entity. Further, unraveling its further intricacy would matter more to its stakeholders with time, such as game developers, investors, and policymakers. With an aim to contribute to a further understanding of the links between mechanisms of gameplay, classifications of games, and the preferences of an audience in order to outline a solid course about the Indian gaming industry. The gaming industry in India is not an island, but rather an extension of world trends. The development of this sector draws its inspiration from some recent international events, technical developments, and changes in consumer behavior. While India participates in world esports competitions and hosts domestic tournaments, it is positioning itself as a crucial player in the universal gaming industry. This very integration with global gaming ecosystems adds a feather in the cap of the analysis of Indian gaming in a wider perspective.

The Indian gaming sector is slated to rank among the major GDP contributors in the next few years; this would also factor substantially into the rise of employment. Its positive effect would be felt in technology innovation, skills development, and cross-cultural exchange. In terms of its growth, the rising awareness among industry stakeholders has become more important to embrace its development dynamics and address its challenges. Looking at the positive spotlights from the gaming industry would also mean facing on the regulatory aspect towards sustainable growth.

The rise of esports in India is another important dimension within the gaming ecosystem. Esports have taken the gaming industry to the next level, with IPL franchises blending gaming with fan engagements and the government backing things like the WAVES Esports Championships. This meeting of traditional sports and esports is attracting new audiences and creating fresh avenues for players and investors alike.

To sum up, the Indian gaming sector is on the verge of a radical transformation led by technology, berate changing consumer behavior, and strategic investment. We are in an era where continued evolution will require a full understanding of the many complexities and dynamics that the Indian gaming sector churns out. One also needs to understand these dynamics if one is to grasp the potential that the Indian gaming sector holds for delivering sustainable, long-term growth. All the same, the Digital Playground Paradigm provides a useful lens for closely examining the Indian Gaming Sector, for viewing gameplay systems, game classifications, and gaming experiences through an analytical prism.

2. LITERATURE REVIEW

Kalyani (2017) mentioned the gaming industry as a multi-million-dollar industry worldwide which is growing rapidly even more than the movies and music industry. Beginning from the Mario to the latest games in PC, consoles or in mobile phones, there is a drastic change in graphics and animation. He specifically explored the area of smartphones gamers and smart generation users of schools and colleges due to availability of high end smartphones in different price ranges and thus causing the gaming market to boom.

Ryan and Deci (2000) used self-determination theory to explore what motivates people to play computer games and how gaming impacts their well-being. Across three studies, where participants played 1, 2, and 4 different games, they found that when players felt a sense of autonomy (freedom of choice) and competence (feeling capable), they tended to enjoy the games more, preferred certain games over others, and even experienced changes in well-being after playing. These feelings were often tied to how easy and intuitive the game controls were, as well as how immersed players felt during the experience. Overall, the study showed that the core psychological needs identified by SDT—autonomy, competence, and relatedness—each played a unique role in predicting how much people enjoyed games and whether they wanted to keep playing them.

The SDT model is also compared with Yee's (2005) motivation taxonomy of game play motivations. He gave an empirical model of player motivations in online games provides the foundation to understand and assess how players differ from one another and how motivations of play relate to age, gender, usage patterns, and in-game behaviors. In the current study, a factor analytic approach was used to create an empirical model of player motivations. The analysis revealed 10 motivation subcomponents that grouped into three overarching components (achievement, social, and immersion).

Piralova (2020) revealed in his research paper the modern understanding of the concept of the gaming industry while defining its priorities in the fields of education. He also established the structure and content of the classifier of functional posts in the gaming industry in the training of a new generation specialist in higher education.

Zackariasson (2010) identified, characterized, and discussed the paradigm shifts that have occurred in the video game industry with some emphasis on competition and competitiveness in his work. In order to do so, his research mainly relied upon the review of existing literature papers.

In a 2022 study, Palma Ruiz explored the growth of the gaming industry using a mix of descriptive, correlational, and forecasting analysis. The goal was to understand how key factors like market revenues, the number of players, Google Trends data, GDP per capita, and the size of the online population might be influencing the industry's expansion. Using predictive analytics in Microsoft Power BI, the study found some interesting patterns — particularly that in Europe and North America, higher GDP per capita was positively linked with both market revenues and player numbers. Interestingly, the trend was reversed in Asia, where higher GDP per capita didn't show the same kind of connection.

Marchand and Thurau (2013) developed a conceptual framework of value creation through video games, highlighting important findings from extant research in marketing and other disciplines, and applied the framework to derive future research opportunities.

However, Srivastava (2022) analyzed the gaming market conditions specifically in India. He wrote regarding the concept of responsible gaming and the adoption of models of responsible gaming, the various approaches to responsible gaming, origins of responsible gaming in India and drawings from Indian organizations on gaming, and the adoption of the smart-card approach in India. The author used a doctrinal method of study relying on case laws, articles, policy documents, reports, and opinions of the experts in the industry to suggest a way forward for the industry.

3. CONCEPTUAL FRAMEWORK

This study's conceptual framework aims to understand how various factors influence player engagement and the growing popularity of esports in India. It hypothesizes that specific game-related and user-driven attributes—such as game genre, gaming platform, visual design quality, and playing duration—play a significant role in shaping gamers' experiences. These independent variables are posited to influence intermediate factors like game ratings and in-game purchase behavior, which subsequently affect two primary outcomes: player engagement and the popularity of esports. By exploring this relationship, the framework illustrates a flow in which the core gaming characteristics drive user feedback and monetization behavior, which in turn contribute to wider patterns of engagement and esports growth. To account for contextual and individual variability, the study includes several control variables—such as player demographics (age, gender, education), monetization strategies employed by games (ads, subscriptions, microtransactions), and the level of internet speed and accessibility. These controls help isolate the effects of the key variables and ensure that the relationships examined are valid and reliable. Overall, the framework provides a structured lens through which to explore how the Indian gaming ecosystem is evolving, especially in terms of user behavior and the burgeoning esports landscape.

Figure 1. A pictorial representation of the IVs, DVs and CVs identified as per our research objectives.

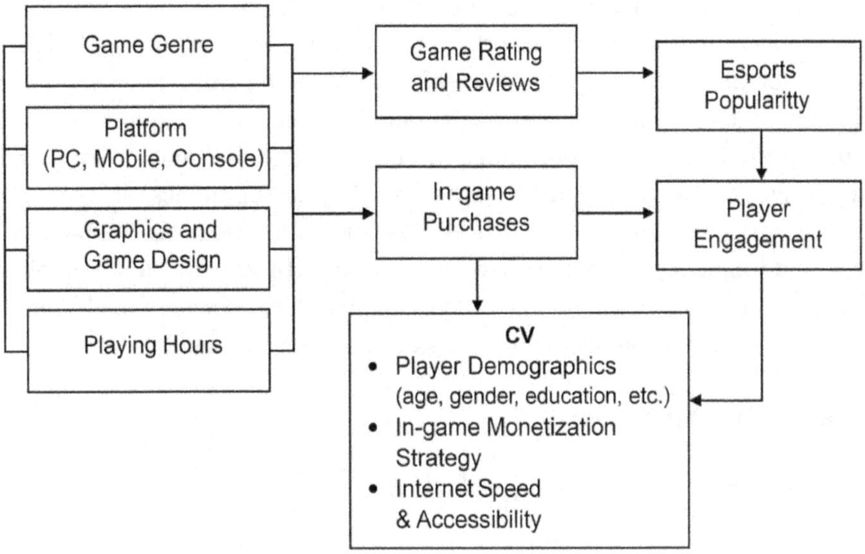

4. RESEARCH METHODOLOGY

This study adopts a **descriptive research design**, which is well-suited for exploring contemporary trends, preferences, and usage patterns within the Indian gaming community. The objective is to develop a comprehensive understanding of how the gaming ecosystem in India is evolving—especially in terms of platform choices, player motivations, and behavioral dynamics. Descriptive research allows for the systematic documentation and interpretation of gamers' experiences, offering actionable insights into the industry's growth. To achieve this, the study employed both **primary and secondary data collection methods**. Primary data was gathered through a structured online questionnaire administered to 32 individuals aged 16 or older, each of whom spends at least three hours per week playing video games. This survey included both closed- and open-ended questions addressing various aspects such as demographics, gaming habits, platform preferences, game genres, motivation to play, in-game spending, social interactions, and community involvement. Additionally, 12 semi-structured interviews were conducted with gamers representing different engagement levels casual players, competitive gamers, and content creators—to uncover deeper motivations and behavioral nuances. Secondary data was obtained through a thorough review of academic literature, gamer psychology studies, and industry reports from sources such as the new zoo Global Games Market Report, SuperData Research, and Game Developer Research. These sources provided theoretical frameworks and contextual understanding of market dynamics, including case studies of successful gaming companies. For sampling, a mixed-methods approach was adopted, combining convenience sampling to recruit participants from accessible platforms like Discord, Reddit, and Instagram with quota sampling to ensure adequate representation across key demographics. These quotas were based on age groups (16–24, 25–34, 35+), gaming platforms (mobile, PC, console), and frequency of gameplay (casual vs. competitive). This dual sampling strategy ensured both accessibility and representativeness, allowing for a balanced collection of data that captures the diversity of the Indian gaming landscape.

4.1 Research Objectives

The main goals of this research are to:

1. To establish connections between gameplay systems and game classifications and their connection to various types of game players.
2. To select different game types based on the type of gaming device they use
3. To investigate how gaming players think about and experience games in their connection with gaming systems together with preferred game genres.

4.2 Research Instrument

The questionnaire was thoughtfully structured and included both close-ended and Likert scale questions. It was organized into several key sections:

- Demographic Information
- Gaming Frequency and Platform Usage
- Game Genre Preferences
- Motivational Factors for Gaming (using SDT and Yee's framework)
- Views on Gaming as a Career
- Perceptions of Esports and Professional Gaming

    Hypothesis 1: Graphic Design Quality and Player Engagement
    Hypothesis 2: Heterogeneity in Game Genre and Mode Preferences
    Hypothesis 3: Sample Dominated by Dedicated Gamers

5. KEY FINDINGS

The statistical analysis conducted for this study indicates that the variable measuring graphic design quality demonstrates high internal reliability, with a Cronbach's Alpha of 0.731. This suggests that the set of items used to evaluate graphic design were cohesively aligned and measured the construct consistently. The mean score for graphic design quality among respondents was 15 out of a possible 21, and the median score stood at 16, reflecting a generally favorable perception of visual aesthetics and design elements in the games played. Additionally, the distribution of responses exhibited a strong negative skewness of -1.83, suggesting that a substantial proportion of respondents rated the graphic design quality higher than the average score. This implies that visual appeal continues to be a central component influencing gamers' perceptions and preferences in the Indian gaming context. Similarly, the construct measuring player engagement exhibited a moderate level of internal consistency, with a Cronbach's Alpha of 0.512, indicating acceptable but relatively lower reliability compared to graphic design. The mean engagement score reported by participants was 32.65, while the median was slightly higher at 34, supporting the presence of a negatively skewed distribution (-1.41). This pattern suggests that most gamers reported above-average levels of engagement, reinforcing the idea that gaming is not merely a casual activity but one in which users are deeply invested, both emotionally and behaviorally. This aligns well with the earlier findings regarding graphic design, suggesting a potential connection between visual quality and player immersion.

When analyzing the variable related to playing hours, the data reflected a mean of 14.21 hours of gameplay per week. The reliability of this measure was notably high, with a Cronbach's Alpha of 0.783, signifying a strong internal consistency in how respondents reported their weekly play duration. The distribution for this variable also revealed a negative skewness of -1.07, indicating that many participants reported higher-than-average gaming hours. Taken together, the consistent pattern of negative skewness observed across the three variables—graphic design quality, player engagement, and playing hours—suggests a potential interrelationship. Specifically, games perceived to have superior visual and design elements may not only promote greater emotional and behavioral engagement but also encourage longer and more frequent gaming sessions. These findings underscore the multifaceted role of aesthetic and experiential factors in shaping player behavior and the overall dynamics of the Indian gaming ecosystem.

The game genre preference analysis was problematically reliable with a negative Cronbach's Alpha of -0.125, which is a violation of reliability model assumptions. This was a surprising result indicating fundamental inconsistencies in participant answers to genre questions, possibly because of varying and sometimes conflicting preferences within the same players. Also, gaming mode preferences were extremely unreliable with Cronbach's Alpha of 0.022. Despite the low reliability, gaming mode scored a mean of 8.52 (on a scale of 14) with a standard deviation of 2.74, indicating a wide range of responses. The distribution was skewed to the left (-1.11) with high kurtosis (2.40), indicating bunched responses with extreme outliers.

The correlation of low reliability indices with fairly high means for all variables indicates a gaming population with diverse, perhaps situational tastes instead of consistent ones. This kind of diversity may be capable of accounting for the dynamic nature of modern gaming, where players engage in different genres and modalities depending on their situation.

In nearly all of the variables being measured, there is a negative skewness, meaning distributions in which the majority of the participants are providing values above the mean. This is especially common in graphic design (-1.83), player engagement (-1.41), and game mode (-1.11). These skewed distributions show a sample with a majority of participants who are reporting high game engagement. The variable playing hours reflects a mean of 14.21 hours and a median of 15 hours, indicating significant investment in gaming activities by the majority of respondents. Although the lowest value recorded is 0 hours, the highest value recorded is 21 hours, and the interquartile range is 6 hours, with a highly skewed distribution towards the upper end.

Player interest has a mean of 32.65 and a median of 34 on a theoretical maximum of 41 and indicates the majority of participants were very interested. The theoretical minimum of 0 is greater than the actual minimum value reported of 11 and indicates the least interested participants still have some interest in gaming.

6. RESULTS

The findings yielded support the contention that there is a positive correlation between graphic design quality and player involvement. The findings suggest that players who rate highly for graphic design quality will also report high levels of involvement coupled with more gameplay hours. Statistical strength in measurement increases the legitimacy of this relationship; nevertheless, correlation analysis should be carried out to definitely determine the size of this relationship.

The findings confirm firmly the hypothesis of gaming tastes being highly heterogeneous. The obtained negative and close to zero estimates of Cronbach's Alpha by both genre and mode suggest that the constructs fail to be accurately measured as one-dimensional variables. This suggests that the players most likely possess comprehensive preference profiles sensitive to situational cues, social situations, and personal gaming history. Therefore, the traditional identification of players through the preferred mode or genre may be becoming irrelevant in contemporary game context.

The persistent pattern of negative skewness across the variables is consistent with the hypothesis that the sample is dominated by committed players. The comparatively high means and medians for all measures, especially playing time and participation, provide additional evidence for this assertion. The evidence from the data is of a sample in which casual or occasional players are underrepresented, and this has profound implications for the interpretation of findings and the extrapolation of findings to larger gaming populations.

7. CONCLUSION

The statistical treatment of game playing behavior data reveals three significant and recurring trends: (1) a strong positive correlation between the quality of graphic design and player interest and engagement, (2) high heterogeneity in game genre and mode preferences, and (3) a sample population dominated by hardcore gamers rather than casual players. These findings bear important implications for game developers, marketers, and academic researchers alike, especially in the rapidly evolving Indian gaming ecosystem (KPMG, 2023; EY–FICCI, 2024).For game designers, the interdependence of visual quality and user engagement underlines the necessity for continued investments in visual aesthetics, user interface (UI), and immersive graphic environments (Ryan & Deci, 2000; Yee, 2005). Since players appear to be significantly influenced by the visual and structural design of games, future development efforts should incorporate advanced design elements such as adaptive rendering, dynamic environments, and immersive UI/UX features to maintain engagement. Simultaneously, the evident heterogeneity of user preferences points to the need for multi-modal design strategies—games should offer diversified game modes and customizable experiences to cater to a broad spectrum of player expectations (Deloitte, 2023; Palma Ruiz, 2022).

For researchers, the current sample's composition—being largely composed of serious or hardcore gamers—raises a concern about the representativeness of the findings. It suggests a sampling bias that could limit the generalizability of results to the broader population, particularly casual gamers who may have different motivations and constraints (Observer Research Foundation, 2024). As such, future studies should adopt stratified or purposive sampling strategies to ensure more inclusive representation. Moreover, these studies should employ more robust analytical tools, including correlation analysis, exploratory factor analysis, and cluster analysis, to test underlying hypotheses and identify distinct gamer archetypes within the diverse Indian gaming community (Mordor Intelligence, 2024; NASSCOM, 2023). These tools would allow researchers to segment players by behavioral patterns, platform usage, and psychological motivations—offering a more granular and actionable understanding of gaming behavior in emerging markets like India.

8. LIMITATIONS OF THE STUDY

This study has several limitations that should be considered when interpreting the findings. First, the relatively small sample size of 32 survey respondents and 12 interviewees limits the generalizability of the results to the wider Indian gaming population, which is vast and diverse (NASSCOM, 2023). Moreover, the use of convenience and quota sampling may introduce selection bias, especially given the predominance of hardcore gamers in the sample compared to casual players. This imbalance suggests that future research should aim for larger, more randomized samples to better capture the varied gaming behaviors and preferences across different segments of Indian gamers. Additionally, while key variables such as game genre, platform, graphic design quality, and playing hours were studied, other important factors like socioeconomic status, cultural influences, psychological well-being, and peer effects were not included and may play a significant role in shaping gaming engagement and esports popularity.

Another limitation arises from the study's cross-sectional and descriptive design, which restricts the ability to draw causal inferences about the relationships between variables. Longitudinal studies are necessary to understand how gaming behaviors and industry dynamics evolve over time, especially given the rapid technological advancements such as Web3, virtual reality, and augmented reality emerging in the Indian gaming ecosystem. Furthermore, the reliance on self-reported data introduces the risk of response biases, including inaccurate recall and social desirability, potentially skewing results related to playing hours, spending, and engagement levels. Finally, regional disparities in internet accessibility and technology availability may have excluded participants from less connected areas, thereby limiting the study's ability to fully represent the diverse realities of gaming across urban and rural India.

REFERENCES

Business Today. (2023). *IPL franchise investments create 1.8M viewership milestone for BGMI Masters Series*. https://www.businesstoday.in/

Deloitte. (2023). *Gaming: The next level*. Deloitte Insights. https://www2.deloitte.com/

Digra Conference. (2024). *Digital playgrounds and cognitive development: Implications for India's edutainment strategies* [Conference preprint]. *Digital Games Research Association*. https://www.digra.org/

EY–FICCI. (2024). *Tuning into consumer: Indian media & entertainment report 2024*. Ernst & Young. https://www.ey.com/

Financial Express. (2023). *India's 442M gamers embracing play-to-earn models via Web3 integration*. https://www.financialexpress.com/

Games India, E. P. I. C. (2024). *Case study: Virtual concert engagement and experiential marketing in India*. EPIC Games.

IDGS-MIB WAVES Initiative. (2025). *GameForge: Bridging academia and industry in gaming through Chitkara and NorthCap universities*. Ministry of Information and Broadcasting.

Invest India. (2023). *Gaming industry in India: Market overview & investment opportunities*. https://www.investindia.gov.in/

Jetir. (2023). *Esports and its 100B impact on India's digital economy: A study from Hyderabad's competitive scene. Journal of Emerging Technologies and Innovative Research (JETIR), 10*(6), 1002–1015. https://www.jetir.org/

Kalyani, P. (2017). Study on smartphone gaming adoption patterns among India's youth demographic, highlighting correlations between affordable device penetration and gaming market expansion. *International Journal of Research in Finance and Marketing*, *7*(11), 112–126.

KPMG. (2023). *India's media and entertainment sector: The digital reset*. https://home.kpmg/in • Lumikai & Google. (2024). *State of India interactive media report*. https://www.lumikai.com/

Mordor Intelligence. (2024). *India gaming market - Growth, trends, and forecasts (2024–2034)*. https://www.mordorintelligence.com/

NASSCOM. (2023). *Gaming: The emerging frontier in India's digital economy.* https://nasscom.in/

Observer Research Foundation. (2024). *Harnessing gaming potential: Policy proposals for India's gaming economy.* https://www.orfonline.org/

Palma Ruiz, J. M. (2022). Gaming revenue dynamics: A cross-continental analysis with Asia-specific implications. *International Journal of Interactive Media and Gaming*, *5*(2), 89–104.

PwC & Ministry of Information and Broadcasting. (2024). *From sunrise to sunshine: The growth trajectory of India's gaming sector.* https://www.pwc.in/

RedSeer. (2022). *Online gaming in India: The next wave.* https://redseer.com/

Ryan, R. M., & Deci, E. L. (2000). Self-determination theory and the facilitation of intrinsic motivation, social development, and well-being. *The American Psychologist*, *55*(1), 68–78. DOI: 10.1037/0003-066X.55.1.68 PMID: 11392867

Venly. (2025). *Web3 gaming white paper: Blockchain and NFT innovation in India's AVGC-XR sector.* https://www.venly.io/

Yee, N. (2005). Motivations for play in online games. *Cyberpsychology & Behavior*, *9*(6), 772–775. DOI: 10.1089/cpb.2006.9.772 PMID: 17201605

Chapter 11 Gamification and Retention in Mental Health Apps: Exploring the Role of User Engagement

Sarita Nagvanshi
https://orcid.org/0009-0007-0442-4213
New Delhi Institute of Management, India

Angad Munshi
New Delhi Institute of Management, India

Swati Bhatnagar
New Delhi Institute of Management, India

ABSTRACT

User retention is a key indicator of digital platform performance in the digital era. This study examines how gamification improves user retention by applying game-design principles to non-game contexts. The research uses psychology, user experience design, and behavioral economics to examine how rewards, points, badges, levels, and leaderboards affect user engagement and retention. Gamification increases intrinsic motivation and regular usage patterns, according to literature analysis and case analyses of platforms in education, fitness, and productivity. It admits constraints like over-reliance on extrinsic motivators and user fatigue. The findings emphasize the need for user-centered, entertaining, and meaningful gamification design. Gamification can boost user loyalty and platform sustainability done ethically and psychologically, the report suggests. This study adds to the digital

DOI: 10.4018/979-8-3693-8886-0.ch011

behavior management debate and helps developers, marketers, and policymakers improve user experience in the competitive digital economy.

INTRODUCTION

Gamification, though first formally evidenced in 2008, found extensive application beginning in 2010 (Edwards et al., 2016; Sardi et al., 2017). Since then, it has emerged as a transformative approach to enhance motivation, engagement, and user satisfaction, especially within sectors like education and healthcare, where sustaining attention and adherence can be challenging (Hamari et al., 2014; Seaborn & Fels, 2015). Defined as the use of game design elements in non-game contexts—such as educational systems, corporate training, or digital health platforms—gamification is designed to improve user interaction and overall experience (Deterding et al., 2011; Zichermann & Cunningham, 2011). By incorporating game-based elements such as points, badges, leaderboards, levels, and reward systems, it transforms mundane or difficult tasks into interactive and enjoyable experiences that stimulate user participation and long-term commitment (Health, 2022; Hoeppner et al., 2016). Within digital health, gamification extends beyond mere engagement tools; it actively supports users' behavioral and emotional needs. This makes it a potentially powerful agent for positive change in areas such as mental health, physical activity, and dietary behavior (Khaddage et al., 2014). Theories of health behavior change underline that gamification elements, especially those enabling self-monitoring—like real-time feedback, tracking progress, and enabling social comparison—can significantly influence users to adopt and sustain healthy behaviors. These mechanisms provide users with a sense of control, achievement, and belonging, thereby increasing the likelihood of behavioral shifts (Edwards et al., 2016; Michie et al., 2013). Prior studies also reveal that in-app reward systems encourage sustained engagement with health-promoting activities, such as regular exercise or mindfulness practices, which can lead to meaningful behavioral change (Orji et al., 2012).

Chan et al. (2017) observed that while reward systems play a critical role in encouraging the initial adoption of such apps among young users, there is a delicate balance to be maintained. Rewards linked to sensitive aspects like calorie counting or weight tracking can sometimes lead to negative emotional responses, underscoring the need for careful design that fosters empowerment rather than judgment (Garrido et al., 2022). As research suggests, intrinsic motivation—where individuals engage in activities for their own satisfaction or personal growth—tends to produce more sustainable outcomes than extrinsic motivators based on rewards or punishments (Garrido et al., 2022). Since the onset of the COVID-19 pandemic, the landscape of digital health has dramatically shifted, with the adoption of Health and Fitness

Apps (HFAs) skyrocketing (Wu et al., 2022; Yang & Koenigstorfer, 2020). Reports indicate up to a 330% surge in usage over recent years, as people turned to digital tools to manage both physical and mental wellbeing during lockdowns and social distancing measures (Yan et al., 2021). Projections now suggest that the global HFA market will reach $2,983 million by 2029, with India alone expected to contribute $364.5 million (Statista, 2024). However, despite this growth trajectory, India's market ranking is projected to fall from fifth to seventh globally by 2029 (Gough, 2024; Statista, 2024). This projected decline signals deeper challenges around user retention and sustained engagement, especially in the context of mental health and behavioral adherence (Sharma et al., 2024).

A critical issue contributing to low engagement, particularly with mental health-focused apps, is the persistent stigma and societal discomfort surrounding mental illness. Barriers such as fear of discrimination, embarrassment, and negative perceptions of mental health services continue to deter individuals—especially young people—from seeking professional help (Aguirre Velasco et al., 2020). This is particularly troubling given that suicide remains one of the leading causes of death among youth globally (Al Omari et al., 2020; Arensman et al., 2020). Encouraging help-seeking behavior, therefore, becomes not just a matter of individual wellbeing but a public health imperative. Reducing stigma is central to this goal, and while cultural attitudes are slowly evolving, targeted programs and interventions must be designed to address the unique concerns and hesitations young people face (Garrido et al., 2022). Digital mental health interventions, particularly those accessible via smartphone apps, provide a promising pathway. These platforms offer anonymity, flexibility, and user control, all of which align with the preferences of younger generations. In fact, many young users express a preference for digital tools over traditional face-to-face therapy, particularly when initial help-seeking feels intimidating or stigmatized (Burns et al., 2010; Marques et al., 2021). In this context, gamification, when thoughtfully integrated, can create non-threatening, engaging environments that encourage self-reflection, emotional resilience, and eventually, connection with professional resources.

While existing literature confirms the positive impact of gamification in digital health, few studies have examined its relationship with distinct user engagement dimensions—cognitive, emotional, and behavioral. Most past research treats engagement as a single, undifferentiated construct. Moreover, although gamification has been linked to improved adherence, limited work has systematically connected engagement to long-term user retention. Another gap lies in the lack of regional insights, particularly how Indian users interact with gamified mental health apps, despite India's growing relevance in the digital health space.

This study aims to examine how gamification enhances user engagement in mental health and fitness applications. It specifically investigates how various game elements—such as rewards, leaderboards, feedback loops, and social features—influence cognitive, emotional, and behavioral user engagement. Furthermore, it explores how these engagement forms contribute to sustained user retention, a critical factor in app success. A key objective is to generate empirical evidence that can guide developers and mental health professionals in crafting digital interventions that support not just app adoption, but ongoing usage—particularly within the Indian market where user dropout remains high.

LITERATURE REVIEW

Empirical studies show that gamification can significantly reduce symptoms of anxiety and depression, suggesting its powerful role in mental health interventions (Damaševičius et al., 2023; Sinha, 2021). By activating reward-related brain pathways, gamification may elicit pleasurable emotions that counter depressive tendencies5. It has also been effective in customer relationship management, where it enhances loyalty, app participation, and download intent (Hwang & Choi, 2020). Other benefits include greater marketing efficiency, higher user commitment, increased willingness to pay, product adoption, and improved brand equity (Müller-Stewens et al., 2017; Wolf et al., 2020; Xi & Hamari, 2020).

Gamification Elements

Common gamification elements include goals, rewards or scores, achievement badges, feedback systems, and leaderboards. These components foster competition and social interaction, encouraging users to perform specific tasks or adopt targeted behaviors (Zolfaghari et al., 2021). Many health apps deploy a mix of these elements to encourage behavioral change and long-term user involvement (Zolfaghari et al., 2021). Studies consistently find positive associations between gamification and behavior modification in health contexts (Cugelman, 2013; Johnson et al., 2016).

"H1: Gamification has a significant direct positive impact on Retention."

Engagement

Customer engagement refers to a user's motivational and contextual interaction with a brand, spanning cognitive, emotional, and behavioral domains (Hollebeek, 2011). It has become a central outcome of gamified experiences. Marketing and digital experience scholars explore engagement through components like attention, emotional resonance, and user activity (Brodie et al., 2011). Engagement here is defined as the depth of cognitive, affective, temporal, and behavioral investment during interactions with a digital system (O'Brien, 2018).

> "H2: Gamification has a significant positive impact on Cognitive Engagement."
> "H3: Gamification has a significant positive impact on Emotional Engagement."
> "H4: Gamification has a significant positive impact on Behavioural Engagement."
> "H8: Cognitive Engagement mediates the impact of Gamification on Retention."
> "H9: Emotional Engagement mediates the impact of Gamification on Retention."
> "H10: Behavioural Engagement mediates the impact of Gamification on Retention."

Retention

Retention is especially crucial for mental health apps, where ongoing use is linked to therapeutic success. User engagement is evaluated through attention, affect, and involvement which strongly influences retention (O'Brien, 2018). Gamification has been shown to improve participation, loyalty, action, and app downloads (Hwang & Choi, 2020), drive innovation adoption (Müller-Stewens et al., 2017), and enhance brand perception (Xi & Hamari, 2020). According to Wu et al., 2022, in the post-pandemic era, sustained engagement has been a core success metric for digital health platforms.

> "H5: Cognitive Engagement has a significant positive impact on Retention."
> "H6: Emotional Engagement has a significant positive impact on Retention."
> "H7: Behavioural Engagement has a significant positive impact on Retention."

Figure 1 depicts the research framework of the hypothetical relationships.

Figure 1. Research framework

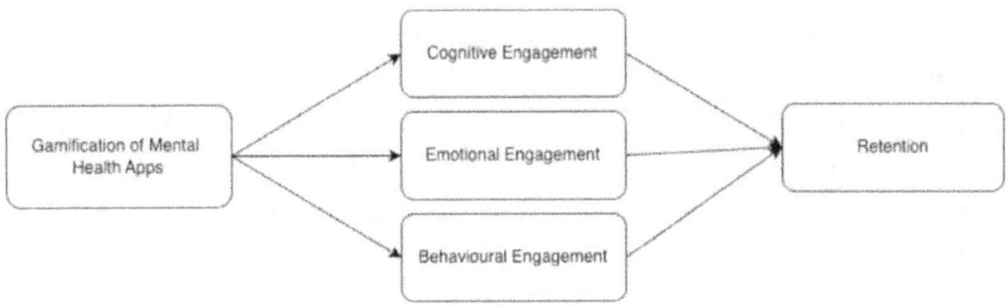

1. METHODOLOGY

This research analysed user retention in gamified mental health apps by assessing the mediating role of different types of engagement such as cognitive engagement, emotional engagement and behavioural engagement. Data was collected using purposive sampling from different age groups starting from Gen Z to Gen X. A structured questionnaire featuring closed-ended items and a 5-point Likert scale was employed to gather primary data. The questionnaire comprised two main sections: the first captured demographic details such as age, gender, and other personal characteristics, while the second measured latent constructs related to engagement and retention. To maintain the study's validity and reliability, the measurement items were adapted from well-established sources, focusing specifically on young users' adoption of AI-driven mental health technologies. The final dataset comprised 168 responses.

2. RESULTS

Descriptive Statistics

The descriptive analysis provides a comprehensive overview of the demographic profile of the participants, offering valuable context for interpreting the study's findings (Table 1). The sample reflected an equal gender distribution, with males and females each comprising 50% of the respondents, ensuring balanced representation. A significant portion of the participants belonged to Generation Z (73.21%), indicating that the primary user base for AI-based mental health applications is composed of younger, digitally native individuals. This was followed by Millennials (14.28%) and Generation X (12.5%), suggesting a gradually decreasing engagement with older age groups. In terms of socioeconomic background, over half of the respondents (51.78%) reported annual household incomes exceeding 10 lakhs, reflecting a relatively affluent demographic likely to have access to premium digital mental health services. Educational qualifications were notably high, with 59.52% holding a Master's degree, 26.19% possessing a Bachelor's degree, and 11.9% having earned a Doctoral degree, which suggests a well-educated participant base. Employment status further illustrated the sample's diversity: the majority were employed (53.57%), a significant number were students (34.52%), while the remaining participants were either self-employed (7.14%) or unemployed (4.76%). These demographics help in understanding the preferences and usage patterns of different user segments.

Table 1. Descriptive statistics

Variable	Frequency (n)	Percentage (%)
Gender		
Male	84	50
Female	84	50
Others	-	-
Age		
Gen Z (Born 1997-2012)	123	73.21
Millennial (Born 1981-1996)	24	14.28
Gen X (Born 1965-1980)	21	12.5
Annual household income		
Below 2.5 lakhs	8	4.76
2.5-5 lakhs	12	7.14
5-7.5 lakhs	36	21.42
7.5-10 lakhs	24	14.28
Above 10 lakhs	87	51.78
Education		
High school, diploma or less	4	2.38
Bachelor's degree	44	26.19
Master's degree	100	59.52
Doctoral degree	20	11.9
Employment		
Student	58	34.52
Working	90	53.57
Unemployed	8	4.76
Self employed	12	7.14

The reliability and validity of the measurement model were confirmed through various statistical indicators (Table 2), affirming the robustness of the constructs used in the study. Cronbach's alpha values ranged from 0.785 to 0.909, demonstrating high internal consistency among the indicators within each construct. Composite reliability (CR) values ranged from 0.862 to 0.943, further supporting the reliability of the measurement items. The Average Variance Extracted (AVE) values, which ranged from 0.565 to 0.846, confirmed convergent validity, suggesting that the items sufficiently captured the variance of their respective latent constructs. All factor loadings exceeded the minimum threshold of 0.6, falling between 0.662 and 0.933, indicating that each item had a strong association with its underlying construct. Additionally, Variance Inflation Factor (VIF) values ranged from 1.275 to 2.71, all well below the conservative cut-off of 5.0, signifying the absence of multicollinearity among the indicators. These results collectively underscore that the measurement model is both statistically sound and theoretically coherent, providing a strong foundation for testing the structural relationships in the model. The robust reliability and validity support the accuracy of subsequent analyses related to gamification, user engagement, and retention in AI-based mental health applications.

Table 2. Reliability and validity assessment

Paths	Factor Loading	Cronbach Alpha	Composite Reliability	AVE	VIF
Gamification		0.807	0.866	0.565	
GMF1 → GMF	0.695				1.463
GMF2 → GMF	0.662				1.425
GMF3 → GMF	0.833				2.354
GMF4 → GMF	0.763				1.561
GMF5 → GMF	0.794				2.171
Cognitive Engagement		0.806	0.885	0.722	
CEG1 → CEG	0.869				1.992
CEG2 → CEG	0.914				2.402
CEG3 → CEG	0.757				1.529
Emotional Engagement		0.843	0.892	0.675	
EEG1 → EEG	0.873				2.71
EEG2 → EEG	0.85				2.156
EEG3 → EEG	0.77				2.052
EEG4 → EEG	0.788				1.604
Behavioural Engagement		0.785	0.862	0.612	
BEG1 → BEG	0.792				1.548
BEG2 → BEG	0.668				1.275
BEG3 → BEG	0.823				2.151
BEG4 → BEG	0.835				2.244
Retention		0.909	0.943	0.846	
RTN1 → RTN	0.893				2.551
RTN2 → RTN	0.932				2.404
RTN3 → RTN	0.933				2.518

The discriminant validity of the research framework was measured using the Fornell-Larcker Criterion and the Heterotrait-Monotrait Ratio (HTMT) (Table 3). As per the Fornell-Larcker Criterion results, the square roots of the Average Variance Extracted (AVE) for each construct (diagonal values) were higher than their correlations with other constructs, confirming that each construct was empirically distinct from the others. This suggests that the latent variables in the model were capturing phenomena unique to their own domains. Similarly, HTMT values remained below the recommended threshold of 0.85, further supporting discriminant validity. This indicates that the constructs demonstrated acceptable levels of distinctiveness even under more stringent testing. These dual assessments strengthen the credibility of the structural model by ensuring that overlap between constructs is minimal and that the measured variables represent clearly defined concepts. Establishing discriminant validity is particularly important in complex models involving multiple types of user engagement, as it ensures that emotional, cognitive, and behavioral dimensions are being accurately differentiated. This robustness enhances the overall validity of the research findings, enabling more confident interpretation of relationships among constructs within the gamification-retention framework.

Table 3. Discriminant validity analysis

	BEG	CEG	EEG	GMF	RTN
Heterotrait Monotrait Ratio (HTMT)					
BEG					
CEG	0.783				
EEG	0.832	0.852			
GMF	0.803	0.421	0.52		
RTN	0.861	0.413	0.729	0.587	
Fornell-Larcker Criterion (FLC)					
BEG	0.782				
CEG	0.625	0.849			
EEG	0.761	0.763	0.821		
GMF	0.646	0.323	0.459	0.752	
RTN	0.729	0.358	0.679	0.522	0.92

HYPOTHESIS EVALUATION

The structural equation modeling (PLS-SEM) results provided valuable insights into how gamification and different types of user engagement influence retention in AI-based mental health applications (Table 4). The direct effects showed that gamification significantly enhanced emotional engagement ($\beta = 0.459$, $p < 0.01$) and behavioral engagement ($\beta = 0.646$, $p < 0.01$), suggesting that gamified features are effective in fostering deeper emotional connection and actionable participation among users. However, gamification did not have a statistically significant direct impact on cognitive engagement ($\beta = 0.323$, $p > 0.05$) or on retention itself ($\beta = 0.06$, $p > 0.05$), indicating that its influence on retention might be indirect.

Further, cognitive engagement ($\beta = 0.433$, $p < 0.05$), emotional engagement ($\beta = 0.596$, $p < 0.01$), and behavioral engagement ($\beta = 0.508$, $p < 0.05$) were all found to have significant positive effects on user retention. This confirms that all forms of engagement contribute meaningfully to sustained app usage. The mediation analysis revealed that both emotional and behavioral engagement significantly mediated the relationship between gamification and retention ($\beta = 0.273$ and $\beta = 0.328$, respectively), while cognitive engagement did not show a significant mediating role ($\beta = 0.14$, $p > 0.05$).

These findings offer crucial theoretical and practical implications. From a theoretical standpoint, they validate the multidimensional nature of user engagement—highlighting how emotional and behavioral components play a more central role in influencing long-term usage of mental health apps than cognitive engagement. This could be due to the emotionally sensitive context of mental health, where users seek comfort, motivation, and tangible actions more than cognitive stimulation. On a practical level, developers and mental health professionals should consider embedding emotionally resonant narratives, rewards, and feedback systems that foster both emotional affinity and active user behavior. Gamified elements like mood-tracking streaks, interactive journaling, or progress-based avatars may serve as powerful tools in driving consistent engagement.

Interestingly, the non-significant direct relationship between gamification and retention suggests that users do not remain committed to the app purely because of gamified elements in isolation. Instead, the experience these features create—specifically how they emotionally connect with users and motivate them to act—serves as the true driver of retention. This highlights the necessity of a thoughtful, user-centered design approach when implementing gamification. Finally, the total effect of gamification on retention was significant ($\beta = 0.462$, $p < 0.01$), reinforcing the idea that although gamification may not directly result in higher retention, its influence operates effectively through emotional and behavioral pathways. These findings underscore the importance of designing emotionally resonant and behaviorally engaging gamified experiences to drive long-term user commitment in mental health applications. Figure 2 presents the diagrammatic representation of the structural model and its analysis.

Table 4. Hypothesis evaluation and SEM analysis

HN	Hypothesised Paths	β	M	SD	t value	p values	Results
Direct Effect							
H1	GMF → RTN	0.06	0.057	0.211	0.283	0.389	Not-Supported
H2	GMF → CEG	0.323	0.344	0.213	1.511	0.065	Not-Supported
H3	GMF → EEG	0.459	0.472	0.166	2.763	0.003	Supported
H4	GMF → BEG	0.646	0.65	0.12	5.38	0	Supported
H5	CEG → RTN	0.433	0.386	0.188	2.304	0.011	Supported
H6	EEG → RTN	0.596	0.56	0.198	3.01	0.001	Supported
H7	BEG → RTN	0.508	0.517	0.255	1.995	0.023	Supported
Mediating Effect							
H8	GMF → CEG → RTN	0.14	0.137	0.107	1.311	0.095	Not-Supported
H9	GMF → EEG → RTN	0.273	0.263	0.134	2.041	0.021	Supported
H10	GMF → BEG → RTN	0.328	0.344	0.198	1.66	0.049	Supported
Total Effect							
	GMF → RTN	0.462	0.47	0.185	2.5	0.006	Supported

Figure 2. Hypothesis evaluation and SEM analysis

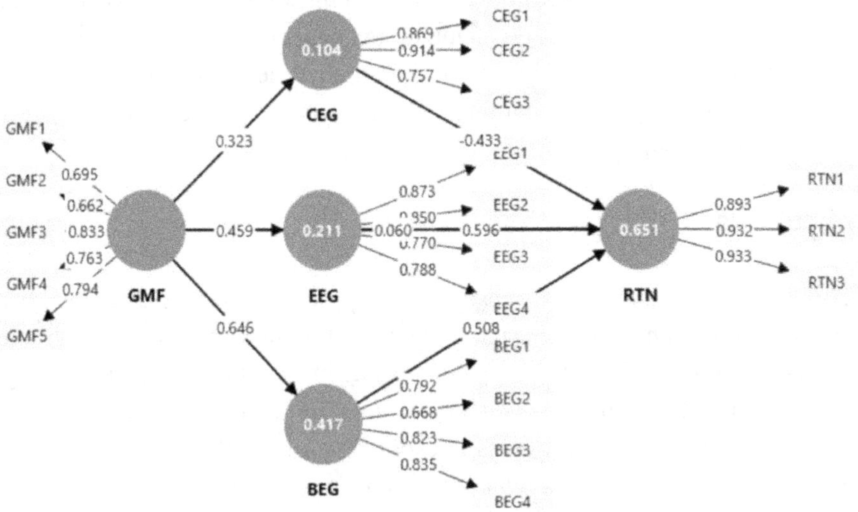

DISCUSSION

This study highlights the role of gamification in enhancing user engagement and retention in mental health apps. This study reinforces the growing application of gamification in mental health interventions, where the strategic integration of game-based elements such as points, rewards, badges, and challenges has been shown to significantly enhance client motivation, participation, and overall engagement within therapeutic environments (Bell et al., 2020; Ebrahimi et al., 2019; Kothgassner et al., 2022; Sweileh, 2023). Empirical research also suggests that mobile applications offering a greater range of customization features tend to foster higher levels of user engagement and long-term usage compared to those with fewer customization options (Alqahtani et al., 2019). In turn, these dimensions of engagement positively influence user retention. Among the user engagement types, emotional and behavioral engagement showed strong mediation between gamification and retention. This indicates that users not only enjoy using gamified apps but are also more likely to continue using them when emotionally invested and actively involved. To tackle the issue of low engagement and reduce dropout rates, gamification has frequently been employed across different settings, including mental health interventions (Kim et al., 2012; Litvin et al., 2020). However, gamification did not have a direct effect on retention; instead, its impact was channeled through engagement. This suggests that only adding gamified features is not sufficient, how users connect and respond to the features is a major determinant of effectiveness.

Not all gamification strategies are equally effective. But, irrelevant features or overuse can distract users, especially in the mental health context where trust and sensitivity are essential. Therefore, gamification must be designed with a balance, supporting therapeutic goals while maintaining engagement. The study emphasizes the need for thoughtful, user-centric gamification. When aligned with user needs and mental health objectives, gamified elements can significantly improve user experience and sustained app use.

Implications

This study provides valuable insights for app developers, mental health professionals, and designers, emphasizing the role of gamification in improving user engagement. In areas like mental health management, where sustained usage is essential, gamification can be a powerful tool. For developers, incorporating thoughtful gamified features—like progress trackers, rewards, and challenges—can help motivate users, making the experience feel more engaging and rewarding. However, it's important that these features remain subtle and non-intrusive, aligning with therapeutic goals to avoid overwhelming users. Mental health professionals can play a key role in working with design teams to ensure that gamification enhances emotional well-being, rather than just pushing for increased usage. This collaborative effort helps create an experience that is both ethical and truly beneficial to the user. By integrating gamification thoughtfully, we can bridge the gap between clinical effectiveness and user engagement, making mental health apps not only more effective but also more sustainable in the long term.

LIMITATIONS, CONCLUSION, AND FUTURE SCOPE

The study has some limitations. It relied on self-reported data, which may involve bias. The sample was also relatively limited in scope, potentially affecting generalizability. Moreover, the study was cross-sectional, so long-term retention and engagement patterns couldn't be assessed. Despite these limitations, the study clearly shows that gamification enhances user engagement, which in turn supports user retention. Emotional and behavioral engagement emerged as key mediators, reinforcing the idea that users must feel connected and involved for gamification to be effective. Simply adding game features is not enough—these features must resonate with users and support their mental health journey.

In conclusion, gamification has strong potential to make mental health apps more engaging and effective. However, its use must be intentional and user-sensitive, especially given the vulnerable nature of the target audience. Future research should adopt longitudinal designs to explore sustained engagement and its mental health outcomes. There is also scope to examine more diverse gamification techniques and user groups. Integrating AI and adaptive design could personalize gamified experiences, improving both relevance and effectiveness. Ultimately, collaboration between tech and mental health professionals will be key to designing impactful digital interventions.

REFERENCES

Aguirre Velasco, A., Cruz, I. S. S., Billings, J., Jimenez, M., & Rowe, S. (2020). What are the barriers, facilitators and interventions targeting help-seeking behaviours for common mental health problems in adolescents? A systematic review. *BMC Psychiatry*, *20*(1), 293. DOI: 10.1186/s12888-020-02659-0 PMID: 32527236

Al Omari, O., Al Sabei, S., Al Rawajfah, O., Abu Sharour, L., Aljohani, K., Alomari, K., Shkman, L., Al Dameery, K., Saifan, A., Al Zubidi, B., Anwar, S., & Alhalaiqa, F. (2020). Prevalence and Predictors of Depression, Anxiety, and Stress among Youth at the Time of COVID-19: An Online Cross-Sectional Multicountry Study. *Depression Research and Treatment*, *8887727*, 1–9. Advance online publication. DOI: 10.1155/2020/8887727 PMID: 33062331

Alqahtani, F., Al Khalifah, G., Oyebode, O., & Orji, R. (2019). Apps for Mental Health: An Evaluation of Behavior Change Strategies and Recommendations for Future Development. *Frontiers in Artificial Intelligence*, *2*, 30. Advance online publication. DOI: 10.3389/frai.2019.00030 PMID: 33733119

Arensman, E., Scott, V., De Leo, D., & Pirkis, J. (2020). Suicide and Suicide Prevention From a Global Perspective. *Crisis*, *41*(Suppl 1), S3–S7. DOI: 10.1027/0227-5910/a000664 PMID: 32208759

Bell, I. H., Nicholas, J., Alvarez-Jimenez, M., Thompson, A., & Valmaggia, L. (2020). Virtual reality as a clinical tool in mental health research and practice. *Dialogues in Clinical Neuroscience*, *22*(2), 169–177. DOI: 10.31887/DCNS.2020.22.2/lvalmaggia PMID: 32699517

Brodie, R. J., Hollebeek, L., Juric, B., & Ilic, A. (2011). Customer engagement: Conceptual domain, fundamental propositions, and implications for research. *Journal of Service Research*, *17*(3), 1–20. DOI: 10.1177/1094670511411703

Burns, J. M., Davenport, T. A., Durkin, L. A., Luscombe, G. M., & Hickie, I. B. (2010). The internet as a setting for mental health service utilisation by young people. *The Medical Journal of Australia*, *192*(11). Advance online publication. https://www.mja.com.au/journal/2010/192/11/internet-setting-mental-health-service-utilisation-young-people. DOI: 10.5694/j.1326-5377.2010.tb03688.x PMID: 20528703

Chan, A., Kow, R., & Cheng, J. (2017). Adolescents' Perceptions on Smartphone Applications (Apps) for Health Management. *Journal of Mobile Technology in Medicine*, *6*(2), 47–55. DOI: 10.7309/jmtm.6.2.6

Cugelman, B. (2013). Gamification: What It Is and Why It Matters to Digital Health Behavior Change Developers. *JMIR Serious Games*, *1*(1), e3139. DOI: 10.2196/games.3139 PMID: 25658754

Damaševičius, R., Maskeliūnas, R., & Blažauskas, T. (2023). Serious Games and Gamification in Healthcare: A Meta-Review. *Information (Basel)*, *14*(2), 2. Advance online publication. DOI: 10.3390/info14020105

Deterding, S., Dixon, D., Khaled, R., & Nacke, L. (2011). From Game Design Elements to Gamefulness: Defining Gamification. In *Proceedings of the 15th International Academic MindTrek Conference: Envisioning Future Media Environments, MindTrek 2011* (Vol. 11, p. 15). DOI: 10.1145/2181037.2181040

Ebrahimi, O. V., Pallesen, S., Kenter, R. M. F., & Nordgreen, T. (2019). Psychological Interventions for the Fear of Public Speaking: A Meta-Analysis. *Frontiers in Psychology*, *10*, 488. Advance online publication. DOI: 10.3389/fpsyg.2019.00488 PMID: 30930813

Edwards, E. A., Lumsden, J., Rivas, C., Steed, L., Edwards, L. A., Thiyagarajan, A., Sohanpal, R., Caton, H., Griffiths, C. J., Munafò, M. R., Taylor, S., & Walton, R. T. (2016). Gamification for health promotion: Systematic review of behaviour change techniques in smartphone apps. *BMJ Open*, *6*(10), e012447. DOI: 10.1136/bmjopen-2016-012447 PMID: 27707829

Garrido, S., Oliver, E., Chmiel, A., Doran, B., & Boydell, K. (2022). Encouraging help-seeking and engagement in a mental health app: What young people want. *Frontiers in Digital Health*, *4*, 1045765. Advance online publication. DOI: 10.3389/fdgth.2022.1045765 PMID: 36620186

Gough, C. (2024). Health & fitness clubs. Statista. https://www.statista.com/topics/1141/health-and-fitness-clubs/

Hamari, J., Koivisto, J., & Sarsa, H. (2014). Does Gamification Work? – A Literature Review of Empirical Studies on Gamification. 2014 47th Hawaii International Conference on System Sciences, 3025–3034. DOI: 10.1109/HICSS.2014.377

Health, C. for D. and R. (2022, September 29). Device Software Functions Including Mobile Medical Applications. FDA; FDA. https://www.fda.gov/medical-devices/digital-health-center-excellence/device-software-functions-including-mobile-medical-applications

Hoeppner, B. B., Hoeppner, S. S., Seaboyer, L., Schick, M. R., Wu, G. W. Y., Bergman, B. G., & Kelly, J. F. (2016). How Smart are Smartphone Apps for Smoking Cessation? A Content Analysis. *Nicotine & Tobacco Research: Official Journal of the Society for Research on Nicotine and Tobacco*, *18*(5), 1025–1031. DOI: 10.1093/ntr/ntv117 PMID: 26045249

Hollebeek, L. (2011). Demystifying Customer Brand Engagement: Exploring the Loyalty Nexus. *Journal of Marketing Management*, *27*(7-8), 785–807. DOI: 10.1080/0267257X.2010.500132

Hwang, J., & Choi, L. (2020). Having fun while receiving rewards?: Exploration of gamification in loyalty programs for consumer loyalty. *Journal of Business Research*, *106*, 365–376. DOI: 10.1016/j.jbusres.2019.01.031

Johnson, D., Deterding, S., Kuhn, K.-A., Staneva, A., Stoyanov, S., & Hides, L. (2016). Gamification for health and wellbeing: A systematic review of the literature. *Internet Interventions : the Application of Information Technology in Mental and Behavioural Health*, *6*, 89–106. DOI: 10.1016/j.invent.2016.10.002 PMID: 30135818

Khaddage, F., Lattemann, C., & Acosta-Díaz, R. (2014). Mobile Gamification in Education Engage, Educate and Entertain via Gamified Mobile Apps.

Kim, H., Munson, M. R., & McKay, M. M. (2012). Engagement in Mental Health Treatment Among Adolescents and Young Adults: A Systematic Review. *Child & Adolescent Social Work Journal*, *29*(3), 241–266. DOI: 10.1007/s10560-012-0256-2

Kothgassner, O. D., Goreis, A., Bauda, I., Ziegenaus, A., Glenk, L. M., & Felnhofer, A. (2022). Virtual reality biofeedback interventions for treating anxiety: A systematic review, meta-analysis and future perspective. *Wiener Klinische Wochenschrift*, *134*(S1, Suppl 1), 49–59. DOI: 10.1007/s00508-021-01991-z PMID: 34989862

Litvin, S., Saunders, R., Maier, M. A., & Lüttke, S. (2020). Gamification as an approach to improve resilience and reduce attrition in mobile mental health interventions: A randomized controlled trial. *PLoS One*, *15*(9), e0237220. DOI: 10.1371/journal.pone.0237220 PMID: 32877425

Marques, G., Drissi, N., Díez, I. de la T., de Abajo, B. S., & Ouhbi, S. (2021). Impact of COVID-19 on the psychological health of university students in Spain and their attitudes toward Mobile mental health solutions. *International Journal of Medical Informatics*, *147*, 104369. DOI: 10.1016/j.ijmedinf.2020.104369 PMID: 33388481

Michie, S., Richardson, M., Johnston, M., Abraham, C., Francis, J., Hardeman, W., Eccles, M. P., Cane, J., & Wood, C. E. (2013). The behavior change technique taxonomy (v1) of 93 hierarchically clustered techniques: Building an international consensus for the reporting of behavior change interventions. Annals of Behavioral Medicine: A Publication of the Society of Behavioral Medicine, 46(1), 81–95. DOI: 10.1007/s12160-013-9486-6

Müller-Stewens, J., Schlager, T., Häubl, G., & Herrmann, A. (2017). Gamified Information Presentation and Consumer Adoption of Product Innovations. *Journal of Marketing*, *81*(2), 8–24. DOI: 10.1509/jm.15.0396

O'Brien, H. (2018). *A Holistic Approach to Measuring User Engagement.*, DOI: 10.1007/978-3-319-73374-6_6

Orji, R., Vassileva, J., & Mandryk, R. (2012). LunchTime: A slow-casual game for long-term dietary behavior change. *Personal and Ubiquitous Computing*, *17*(6), 1211–1221. Advance online publication. DOI: 10.1007/s00779-012-0590-6

Sardi, L., Idri, A., & Fernández-Alemán, J. L. (2017). A systematic review of gamification in e-Health. *Journal of Biomedical Informatics*, *71*, 31–48. DOI: 10.1016/j.jbi.2017.05.011 PMID: 28536062

Seaborn, K., & Fels, D. I. (2015). Gamification in theory and action: A survey. *International Journal of Human-Computer Studies*, *74*, 14–31. DOI: 10.1016/j.ijhcs.2014.09.006

Sharma, V., Payal, R., Dutta, K., Poulose, J., & Kapse, M. (2024). A comprehensive examination of factors influencing intention to continue usage of health and fitness apps: A two-stage hybrid SEM-ML analysis. *Cogent Business & Management*, *11*(1), 2391124. Advance online publication. DOI: 10.1080/23311975.2024.2391124

Sinha, N. (2021). *Introducing Gamification for Advancing Current Mental Healthcare and Treatment Practices.*, DOI: 10.1007/978-981-15-9897-5_11

Statista. (2024). Biggest social media platforms. Statista. https://www.statista.com/statistics/272014/global-social-networks-ranked-by-number-of-users/

Sweileh, W. (2023). Analysis and mapping of scientific literature on virtual and augmented reality technologies used in the context of mental health disorders (1980 – 2021). *The Journal of Mental Health Training, Education and Practice*, *18*(4), 288–305. Advance online publication. DOI: 10.1108/JMHTEP-04-2022-0019

Wolf, T., Weiger, W. H., & Hammerschmidt, M. (2020). Experiences that matter? The motivational experiences and business outcomes of gamified services. *Journal of Business Research*, *106*, 353–364. DOI: 10.1016/j.jbusres.2018.12.058

Wu, C., Zhou, Y., Wang, R., Huang, S., & Yuan, Q. (2022). Understanding the Mechanism Between IT Identity, IT Mindfulness and Mobile Health Technology Continuance Intention: An Extended Expectation Confirmation Model. *Technological Forecasting and Social Change*, *176*(C), 121449. https://ideas.repec.org//a/eee/tefoso/v176y2022ics0040162521008805.html. DOI: 10.1016/j.techfore.2021.121449

Xi, N., & Hamari, J. (2020). Does gamification affect brand engagement and equity? A study in online brand communities. *Journal of Business Research*, *109*, 449–460. DOI: 10.1016/j.jbusres.2019.11.058

Yan, M., Filieri, R., Raguseo, E., & Gorton, M. (2021). Mobile apps for healthy living: Factors influencing continuance intention for health apps. *Technological Forecasting and Social Change*, *166*, 120644. DOI: 10.1016/j.techfore.2021.120644

Yang, Y., & Koenigstorfer, J. (2020). Determinants of physical activity maintenance during the Covid-19 pandemic: A focus on fitness apps. *Translational Behavioral Medicine*, *10*(4), 835–842. DOI: 10.1093/tbm/ibaa086 PMID: 32926160

Zichermann, G., & Cunningham, C. (2011). *Gamifcation by Design: Implementing Game Mechanics in Web and Mobile Apps*. O'Reilly Media, Inc.

Zolfaghari, M., Shirmohammadi, M., Shahhosseini, H., Mokhtaran, M., & Mohebbi, S. Z. (2021). Development and evaluation of a gamified smart phone mobile health application for oral health promotion in early childhood: A randomized controlled trial. *BMC Oral Health*, *21*(1), 18. DOI: 10.1186/s12903-020-01374-2 PMID: 33413304

Chapter 12
Enhancing Brand Awareness and Loyalty Through Gamification in the Metaverse

Ritesh Dwivedi
https://orcid.org/0000-0003-3921-5458
Symbiosis Institute of Business Management, Noida, India

Nazia Hasan
https://orcid.org/0000-0002-6666-5473
Teerthanker Mahaveer Institute of Management and Technology, India

ABSTRACT

Objective of the study This study aims to understand how gamification when integrated with metaverse serves as a powerful tool for marketing and fostering brand loyalty of customers. This chapter explores how gamification in metaverse offers brand new opportunities to engage customers and win their loyalty with specific study on sports industry automobile industry, education industry and fashion industry. The ethical considerations and potential challenges are also discussed. Methodology The study is based basically on secondary data, whereby the study is done already existing data pertaining to a company or organization and sources which are internal to a company. The study also takes into account various research papers, magazines, newspapers, etc. for in-depth analysis. Conclusion The Metaverse is a real digital world where individuals may communicate, work, and play; it is no longer science fiction. It's a future where virtual and physical worlds coexist together, providing countless opportunities for companies.

DOI: 10.4018/979-8-3693-8886-0.ch012

1. INTRODUCTION

The term "gamification" describes a design that aims to replicate the beneficial effects of games and so influence user behaviour and cognitive processes (Xi, 2019). Game mechanics are frequently used in gamification as games serve as its primary source of inspiration. For example, in a commercial setting, various gamification elements can be used in websites for services, products, advertisements, etc., to boost engagement. Features connected to immersion, which include gaming mechanisms like avatars, storytelling, narrative frameworks, role-play mechanics, etc., are primarily designed to immerse the player in self-directed, inquiring action (Huotari & Hamari, 2017)

The metaverse has ushered in a new age of possibilities in the rapidly evolving field of digital technology (Wang et al., 2022). The metaverse, which is defined as a communal virtual shared world created by the fusion of persistent virtual reality with augmented physical reality, offers businesses previously unheard-of chances to interact creatively with their clientele. Companies are looking for innovative ways to improve customer loyalty in an increasingly connected environment because they understand how important it is to long-term success in the cutthroat marketplaces of today (Xi, Chen, Gama, Riar, & Hamari, 2023). Before being extended to online platforms, client involvement was limited to in-person encounters. But the metaverse represents a paradigm change, making it harder to distinguish between the real and virtual worlds. It enables companies to design individualized, immersive, and interactive experiences that give clients a feeling of community and connection. Cha et al. (2024) highlight the importance of the metaverse in redefining these interactions by comprehending the evolution of consumer involvement. Understanding the underlying technology is essential to understanding how the metaverse affects client loyalty.

Recent research (Abou-Shouk & Soliman, 2021) has looked at the relationship between gamification-based marketing and several brand outcomes, including awareness, love, involvement, loyalty, experience, attitude, engagement, engagement, and impulsive buying. Although the majority of study has concentrated on the effects of gamification on consumer engagement and associated results, little is known about how metaverse gamification affects marketing, brand love, and consumer engagement (Arya et al.,2024; Xi & Hamari,2020). Still, not enough research has been done on the application of gamification marketing initiatives and virtual retail experiences in the field of sports, automobile, fashion and education in the metaverse. The current study has tried to cover before mentioned gaps.

2. EFFECTIVE STRATEGIES FOR GAMIFICATION MARKETING

For reaping the rewards of gamification marketing. All you have to do is include game principles into your marketing plan to provide entertaining, engaging, and lucrative consumer experiences. (Arya, Sambyal, Sharma, & Dwivedi, 2024)

1) Enhance Loyalty Incentive Schemes by Adding Gamified Components

The secret to developing loyalty reward systems that entice users to return for more chances to earn special prizes and perks is gamification. Start by developing the points system. Your gamified loyalty rewards program is built on this. Clearly state which purchases or interactions are worth points and how many points should be awarded for each. For instance, you might give out 25 points for each referral and 1 point for every $1 spent. Create a mobile app or incorporate the loyalty program into your website. This is essential to giving your clients a smooth and convenient experience. Then, to encourage individuals to join up, promote your rewards program with a unique beginning event, such as a bonus point promotion.

2) Incorporate Interactive Tests Into Your Gamification Marketing Initiative

One of the most effective gamification marketing tools is an interactive quiz. They may engage your audience by providing them with value and enjoyment while strengthening their bond with your company. Additionally, they're a great approach to learn more about your clients so that you can consistently provide the greatest experience. Make use of what you already know about your target audience when developing online tests to make them engaging. Consider what would be interesting to them and pertinent to their hobbies

3) Upgrade Website With Gamified Content

Everyone enjoys a good bargain, and the excitement is increased when the discount is unexpected. Adding a spin-to-win discount game to your website is a simple way to do that. By allowing users to spin the wheel for exclusive deals, freebies, and incentives, this gamified feature makes shopping enjoyable. Making a spin-to-win widget that complements the aesthetic of your company will be the first step in this process. Rewards on the wheel should be varied and alluring, ranging from little savings and free delivery to premium goods and time-limited deals..

4) Use Augmented Reality to Run A Virtual Treasure Hunt to Increase Sales

The next big thing in marketing is augmented reality, or AR. It provides a distinctive and engaging brand experience that may help you establish a long-lasting relationship with your clients. Although it is already quite engaging, its efficacy may be increased by including a gamified marketing experience, such as a virtual treasure hunt. Select an AR platform based on your goals and budget to create your own customized treasure hunt. Choose a platform that lets you give your clients a completely personalized experience.

5) Establish a Mechanism for Collecting Badges to Honor Brand Interactions

People's need for accomplishment, acknowledgment, and social acceptance is satiated by badge collecting. Customers feel more accomplished after earning a badge, which encourages them to keep interacting with your business. Additionally, they can be motivated to showcase their collection and perhaps invite their friends and family to a friendly competition. Consider which interactions, such leaving a review, sharing your content, or making a purchase, you would like to reward in order to create the conditions for customer success. Make a variety of badges that recognize a variety of accomplishments, such as doing easy tasks or multistep challenges. Start the design process on your own or with a graphic designer's assistance, keeping your accomplishments in mind. Utilize the character and aesthetic of your brand to design eye-catching badges with a distinctive flare.

6) Create a Smartphone Application With Virtual Worlds and Customized Avatars

People are more eager than ever to establish their online persona and stake a claim to the virtual world. By creating a mobile application for your brand, you can satisfy this increasing need. For users to fully express their individuality, style, and preferences, the app should offer a wide range of personalization possibilities. They should be able to switch up their accessories, clothes, and haircuts, for example. Additionally, whenever possible, include your items within the app.

3. METAVERSE: COMPONENTS AND CAPABILITIES

In his 1992 novel Neal Stephenson first used the term "metaverse" to refer to a world which is virtualized world in which status of people was partly determined by the technological prowess of their avatars.

In the metaverse, people engage with one another as avatars in a three-dimensional environment that simulates the actual world. In addition to being online, the metaverse is three-dimensional and malleable. The future's spatialized Net is called the Metaverse. The term "metaverse" is a world where the real world and virtual world are merged, which can be accessed through computers with the help of immersive technologies like augmented reality, mixed reality, and virtual reality. Experts have referred to this 3D world as the next evolution of the internet, as a permanent, collective, shared platform where digital avatars, or facsimiles of human beings themselves, may freely roam between experiences, bringing our identities and financial resources with them.

Though they precede the internet, visions of an equivalent digital world where people experience life in ways that are both similar to and impossible in the real world are not new. However, in recent decades, the idea of a mixed digital and physical world became increasingly plausible as technological advancements—from the widespread use high-speed internet and mobile phones games made the metaverse appear less unrealistic.

3.1 How Can One Reach the Metaverse?

Metaverse is created and expanded with the help of two technologies. These are:

1) Virtual Reality
2) Augmented Reality

1) Virtual reality (VR) can be defined as an environment that has 3D simulation that users can experience for interaction in a virtual world in a way similar to the real world. VR headset is used to access approximation of reality.

2) Augmented Reality (AR) Using digital rendering technologies, it overlays the actual environment with digital images. Users are still able to interact with their physical environment. An early example of augmented reality is the video game "Pokémon Go". Two well-known AR devices are "Google Glass" and head-up displays on the windshields of automobiles. It remains to be seen if VR and AR experiences become the major metaverse interfaces. Currently, mobile devices or browsers with high internet connections can give metaverse experiences provided mostly by gaming platforms like Decentral, Minecraft, and Roblox.

3.2 Difference Between Metaverse and the Internet

Millions of servers, computers, and many other devices that are electrical make up the internet. Users of the internet may view and be involved with websites, purchase and trade products and services, and communicate with each other once they are on an online platform. The metaverse, on the other hand, operates on the internet. The experience provided by the metaverse is more immersive, where users may "live" to some extent in virtual places, whereas the internet is mostly used for surfing. The metaverse is being shaped by the numerous services that have emerged as a result of the internet's expansion. "In gaming, you see Roblox, Minecraft, and other immersive video games -- and even Zoom -- foreshadow what the metaverse is designed to offer," stated CEO Ben Bajarin. All the basic components of Metavesre are explained in Figure 1

Figure 1. Components of Metaverse

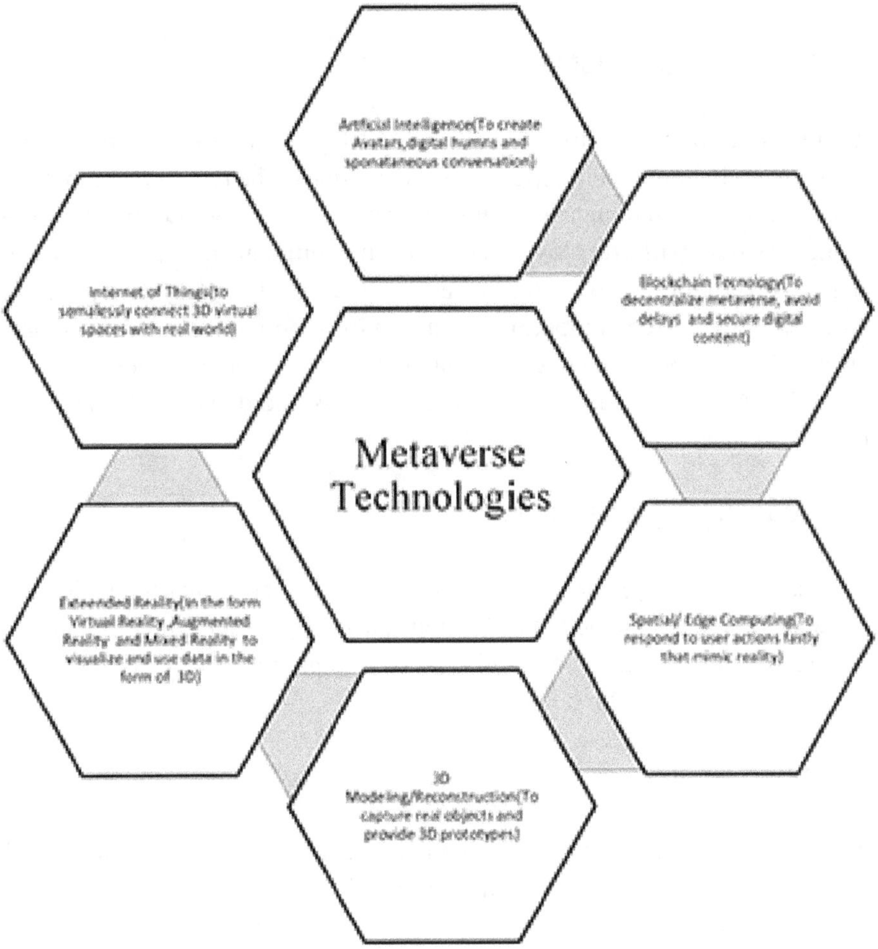

Source: Author compilation

3.3 Components of Metaverse

1) Blockchain Technology

In the metaverse, blockchain technology has two vital functions. On the one hand, users may store data anywhere in the metaverse by using blockchain technology, which acts as a repository. On the other hand, blockchain technology can offer a comprehensive economic framework that links the metaverse's virtual and physical worlds. Thus, blockchain connects the metaverse with the actual world(Jeon, Youn, Ko, & Kim, 2021)

2) Spatial/ Edge Computing

It will take a lot of data to be processed quickly for the Metaverse to provide people with a fully immersive experience. This is due to the requirement that every user be able to view and engage with real-time, high-quality 3D representations. Network providers will probably need to install additional fiber-to-the-home and other next-generation infrastructure to enable this. By bringing data processing closer to end users, edge computing can aid in overcoming this scale issue in the Metaverse. Much of this data might be handled at edge computing sites rather than networks having to send massive volumes of uplink and downlink traffic to centralized cloud locations.

3) 3D Modeling/Reconstruction

The metaverse will become a reality thanks to 3D reconstruction, which accurately depicts the form and look of actual items. In order to offer a three-dimensional framework and prototype of a particular process or product, the technology incorporates techniques like 3D modelling.

4) Extended Reality

By moving from 2D to 3D for more realistic experiences and digital displays that better correlate with head motions, AR, VR, and MR technologies will revolutionize how organizations see and use data, according to BCG. As AR glasses become popular, computer vision will be used to assist users find the information they need and comprehending their surroundings. For instance, Microsoft's HoloLens already uses extended reality (XR) to give users the impression that 3D holographic pictures are a part of their surroundings.

5) Internet of Things

IoT is described by the Blockchain Council as "an important pillar of the metaverse infrastructure." One example of how the metaverse and IoT might be used is to "unlock new opportunities for industrial domain, individual needs and social requirements," according to the council. The council refers to this as "a user-centered IoT and metaverse experience." IoT would enable virtual spaces to easily access and interact with the real world, while the metaverse would supply the 3D user interface for the IoT device cluster.

6) Artificial Intelligence

AI contributes intelligence to real-world computer vision and is essential to the development of chatbots and bots. However, just 10% of businesses say their AI implementations have produced meaningful advantages, according to BCG. The processing power of AI might be used to produce metaverse avatars, improve the features of digital people to make them more realistic, and be used to construct non-player characters that interact with players in virtual worlds.

4.GAMIFICATION IN THE METAVERSE: TANSFORMATION OF BRAND EXPERIENCE

Gamification, or the use of game features outside of gaming, has become more and more popular in recent years due to consumers' increasing need for immersive, fascinating, and engaging brand experiences. Gamified marketing efforts that include motivation-driven games, reward-based systems, and community-building elements have become increasingly common in the metaverse. Marketers may increase customer loyalty, reach a larger audience, and promote certain consumer behaviors using this method (Mattke & Maier, 2021). Gamification may help businesses increase sales, create visually appealing marketing campaigns, and promote user-generated content (UGC) through customer advocacy.

Integrating in-game features, mechanics, and signs into non-gaming environments is known as gamification. Motivating individuals to meet goals, finish activities, or develop new abilities, it fosters a competitive atmosphere that increases user engagement and keeps people engaged for longer. Therefore, the metaverse offers a variety of opportunities, and each organization does not need to adopt the same approach to reap its benefits. Gaming may be used in a variety of metaverse industry activations, including e-commerce, learning and development, entertainment, fitness, and more in the following ways:

1) **Systems that rely on rewards:** Gamification includes incentives such as badges, leaderboards, and point systems. Leaderboards provide competitive rankings, badges show reaching a milestone or denoting status, and points may be included in a brand's game-based campaign or activation to track progress. For example, Foursquare, a cloud-based location technology platform, incentivizes users to

keep using their app by rewarding them with points each time they check into a place.

2) **Engaging and motivating**: Gamification inspires users to perform certain tasks, increasing customer engagement rates and laying the groundwork for strong bonds. Based on the ubiquitous real-life habit of flipping an empty cup, Starbucks developed the smartphone game "Flip the Cup." The game increased total fan engagement by 90% by encouraging users to try their hand at the chore, receive points, and share the score with others.
3) **Community-driven**: By providing incentives for people to accomplish goals, game-based experiences may foster a feeling of community and purpose among those attempting to accomplish them. In order to overcome a problem or reach a goal, participants are urged to cooperate. By rewarding users who create content, gaming metaverses such as Roblox and Minecraft, for instance, engage users in the platform's growth and foster a thriving creative community.
4) **Better learning and retention**: Gamification may be a powerful technique for teaching people or customers about goods or ideas in novel ways that will help them remember them. To educate consumers about their new health-conscious formula, Emmi Good Day's, a lactose-free drink company, for example, introduced a game in which players had to gather milk without touching sugar cubes to get points

It's critical to keep ahead of the curve in the constantly changing field of digital marketing. Today, we explore two innovative trends—gamification and the metaverse—revolutionizing how companies interact with their customers. These breakthroughs have the power to completely transform your marketing approach; they are more than simply trendy terms.(Bogoslov, Stoica, Georgescu, & Lungu, 2023) The Metaverse is a digital world where individuals may communicate, work, and play; it is no longer science fiction.

5. THEORETICAL FRAMEWORK

A theoretical foundation for comprehending consumer behavior is provided by the Stimulus-Organism-Response (S-O-R) framework (Mehrabian & Russell, 1974), which is based on environmental psychology. In particular, the S-O-R framework is a psychological paradigm that aids in the analysis and understanding of the connections among behavioral reactions, internal psychological processes, and external stimuli. The Stimulus–Organism–Response (S-O-R) paradigm, which has been successfully used in recent research to investigate consumer behavior in immersive digital environments, may be used to methodically comprehend how gamification in the metaverse affects brand recognition and loyalty.

6. GAMIFICATION IN METAVERSE IN THE SPORTS INDUSTRY

A major measurable network of linked worlds, which are virtual working on reality interaction, the metaverse, also known as the 3D internet, allows users to work, socialize, play, conduct business, and even create. Virtual worlds are becoming a common way for businesses in a variety of sectors and industries to interact with their clientele, improve productivity, and develop new ideas. 85% of corporate executives believe that the 3D internet is "essential to success," according to research by Wunderman Thomson. When it comes to using the metaverse, the sports sector has far outperformed rivals. Several sportsmen and sports businesses utilize the internet with 3D for engaging with viewers and investigating unexplored avenues for generating income. These actions reflect the shifting preferences of Gen Z and Millennial consumers, who now want more engaging and immersed viewing experiences in sports. Traditional sports activities are broadcast into experiences where viewers may use augmented reality (AR) glasses to observe real-time statistics during a sporting event or view a match from the perspective of a virtual reality (VR) by using the metaverse.

6.1 Advantages of Gamification in Sports Industry

1) Engagement of Fans

With its unparalleled immersive and interactive experiences, the metaverse can transform how sports fans connect with their favorite teams and players completely. The 3D internet is changing how sports fans interact in the following ways:

a) **Virtual stadiums**: Fans may experience the thrill of live sports from the comfort of their homes by entering virtual stadiums and arenas using virtual reality (VR), augmented reality (AR), and other cutting-edge technology. Beyond conventional broadcasting, these immersive experiences let viewers experiment with interactive features like 360-degree panoramas, behind-the-scenes footage, and information that is customized according to viewers' tastes.
b) **Real-time statistics**: Sophisticated artificial intelligence algorithms are able to forecast the trajectory of a player and offer statistics for an event of a sports event. During a live game, AR devices may superimpose highlights, player statistics,

and other information straight onto the screen of a viewer, giving them a very engaging and thrilling experience.

c) **Interactive features**: Through the metaverse, fans may communicate with their favorite players' digital personas, go to virtual greetings and meeting, take part in live question and answers sessions, and train virtually with their heroes.
d) **Virtual competitions**: If the users want interactive gaming experiences where they can compete with each other or with athletes in tournament and matches metaverse serves as a best platform.
e) **Social viewing**: The metaverse, AR, and VR lead to social viewing experiences, giving experience to fans for watching games collectively in virtual environments, while interacting, and communicating in real time.

City of Manchester's intention to build a virtual version of the "Etihad Stadium" in the metaverse is a fantastic illustration of fan interaction in the metaverse. Fans will be able to watch games from the comfort of their homes in this virtual stadium, even selecting their favorite viewing angle, just like they would if they were actually on the field or in the stadium.

2) Analysis of Performance

Through virtual settings for skill development and performance monitoring, the metaverse provides athletes with a cutting-edge training aid. Athletes may practice and hone their talents without limitations by immersing themselves in realistic environments via the use of augmented reality (AR) and virtual reality (VR), and Geographical boundaries are broken down and performance is elevated to new levels through instant feedback, analysis, and collaborative training experiences.

Virtual reality simulations allow athletes to rehearse strategy and decision-making in safe settings. Basketball players may practice offensive moves by simulating game scenarios, while soccer players can enhance their positioning and passing tactics by simulating game scenarios. Major teams employ Rezzil Player 21, a virtual reality training tool, to help athletes practice abilities and maneuvers, including headers, rondo drills, and soccer shooting. Biometric sensors and motion monitoring are also essential for gathering information on athletic performance. During workouts or virtual games, heart rate, muscle activity, motions, and various other physiological markers can be monitored by these sensors. This information offers insightful information on areas that require work, such as technique refinement, movement efficiency optimization, or fatigue management. Coaches and athletes may modify training plans to target certain areas of weakness, improve performance, and lower the chance of injury by evaluating this data.

3) Collectibles and Merchandise

Metaverse provides a distinctive platform for producing, selling, and distributing digital treasures and sports memorabilia. The creation of virtual products as " non-fungible tokens (NFTs)" that may be purchased, sold, and exchanged on niche online markets created especially for digital commodities is made possible by the use of cutting-edge blockchain technology. (Liboriussen, 2011)This structure appeals to a worldwide audience of collectors and enthusiasts by promoting safe transactions as well as pleasing to the eye, the authenticity and uniqueness of collectibles.

4) The Branding of Athletes

With the creative enhanced fan interaction and content production, and tactical sponsorship partnerships, athletes in the metaverse have the scope to strengthen their brands. Athletes can be connected with the audience worldwide and overcome geographical boundaries with the help of the 3D internet, which increases brand awareness and facilitates creative fan interaction. Through collaborations and endorsements, the 3D internet offers athletes creative opportunities to make money off their online presence. The following are some ways that athletes might make money in the metaverse:

a) **Virtual endorsements**: Brands may reach fans in immersive environments by having athletes wear or utilize branded virtual merchandise during online performances.
b) **Collaborations with virtual experiences and platforms:** Athletes may work with platforms on metaverse to arrange virtual meeting-and-greeting that provide fans 3D engagements, such as live mentorship and Q&A sessions. By selling tickets or releasing limited-edition digital items, these events may raise money while improving fan interaction in a special and intimate environment. LeBron James, for example, met and coached community members in the Roblox NIKELAND metaverse during NBA All-Star Week. Additionally, visitors had the chance to win a Roblox-exclusive "LeBron 19" digital sneaker.
c) **Digital collectibles**: To create a devoted fan base and generate extra income, athletes might start their NFT collections. For example, the seven-time Super Bowl winner Tom Brady introduced the "Tom Brady Origins Collection," which featured NFTs such as his NFL Draft combine jersey and college résumé.
d) **Sponsored virtual events:** Athletes may draw sizable virtual audiences, establish their brands, and generate income by organizing or taking part in metaverse events with brand sponsorships.

e) **Fan-generated content production:** By turning sports fans from passive viewers into active content producers who can create and distribute virtual stories and experiences, the 3D internet has completely changed how fans interact with sports. Fans may develop unique arenas, model matches, and sell digital items thanks to this empowerment. The transition to fan-driven content production adds a variety of stories to the sports ecosystem. Stages like Fortnite, where users have welcomed the chance to make their own tournaments and games using the platform's "Creative Mode," provide a real-world example of fan-driven content production in the metaverse. With personalized avatars that reflect themselves or their favorite sportsmen and exclusive game rules, fans create their own tournaments in these virtual environments

7. BRAND AWARENESS AND LOYALTY THROUGH GAMIFICATION IN THE METAVERSE IN SPORTS INDUSTRY

With the changing times, Sports marketing has emerged, and companies are seeking ways for new and creative methods for getting connected to customers. Brands are doing everything in their capacity to attract sports fans, from sponsoring athletes and teams to running ads during games. However, marketers now have a new way to promote their businesses to their followers thanks to the Metaverse.

Brands have an occasional chance to interact with their audience in an immersive setting through the Metaverse. Virtual experiences can be designed by Brands Metaverse that are specific to their target interests of the audience. For instance, a company that sells cricket gear may develop a virtual game where customers can interact with the brand and test out their wares(Sharma et al., 2024). This gives customers a memorable experience in addition to enabling organizations to display their products interactively.

One of the main benefits of advertising in the Metaverse is the capacity to target a particular audience because brands have not much control over who can see their promotional ads when adopting traditional methods of advertising. Brands may, however, target people in the Metaverse according to their interests, habits, and demographics. As a result, advertising is more successful and firms are certain to reach their target demographic. The capability to monitor activities of the user and participation is another advantage of advertising in the Metaverse. Organizations may collect information about how customers engage with their worlds virtually and use it to enhance their tactics of marketing tactics. Traditional means of advertising make it difficult to measure the involvement of the customer.

7. GAMIFICATION IN METAVERSE IN THE AUTOMOBILE INDUSTRY

At a compound annual growth rate (CAGR) of 31.4%, the global market in metaverse for automotive size is estimated to grow from its 2022 valuation of USD 1.9 billion to USD 16.5 billion by 2030 (Markets and Markets, 2022) From creating to exhibiting goods on the metaverse space, automakers, hardware manufacturers, and software developers have demonstrated a strong interest in utilizing metaverse-related solutions in their industrial pipeline. With the use of virtual showrooms and other XR-based technologies, such as VR simulation, several automakers and dealers are offering users and consumers immersive experiences. Customers and users are expressing interest in using NFTs and cryptocurrency in the virtual asset marketplace. The field of simulation has become considerably more convenient due to metaverse technology.

8.1. During the Projected Period (from 2022 to 2030), the Software Sector is Anticipated to Lead the Market

Avatars, digital twins, online auto design, AR-based virtual showrooms, and metaverse platforms are among the software's features. A game engine is an environment or software development package that was first used for the creation of video games (Tena Ochoa, 2023). These days, a gaming engine may be utilized for visualization, collaboration (as in the creation of digital twins), and more. A gaming engine may have physics and collision engines, AI, animation tools, audio engines, and more. Given that many corporations currently use metaverse platforms to facilitate collaboration between the actual and virtual worlds, these platforms are probably going to dominate the software market. Numerous game developers, including Epic Games, Roblox, Decentral, Infinite World, and Upland, have created their metaverse games that feature the introduction of new cars from various automakers.

8.2. During the Projection Period (from 2022 to 2030), AR is Anticipated to be the Biggest Market

There are several uses for AR in the automotive sector. For example, it is utilized to enhance production and inspection procedures in factories by utilizing a variety of AR hardware and software items. Along with helping to construct different kinds of HUDs, it is also utilized in car maintenance. With the use of a device called a Head-Up Display (HUD), drivers may view vital driving information on the windshield without taking their eyes off the road. Among other things, it is utilized for online automobile sales and advertising through virtual showrooms, virtual simulation rides, and online car designs. Modern augmented reality technologies are being used by automakers and dealers to offer unmatched services and car safety.

8.3 Dynamics of the Marketing in the Automobile Industry

1) Driver: Gamification-Based Brand Marketing for Automakers

The game aspect of the metaverse is being exploited by several automakers to raise brand recognition. They are carefully utilizing the metaverse to carry out sponsorships and marketing based on the metaverse. These businesses profit by using virtual world simulators and immersive internet experiences to gamify their brands. Moving Platform by Microsoft and Volkswagen AG, and Mobility Adventure by Hyundai Motor Company, Roblox are a few examples of metaverse initiatives that gamify brand awareness. These 3D environments are used by users to play mini-games, interact with other players, communicate, create friendships, and obtain product information via chatbots, virtual AI agents, or salesmen. For young consumers, the metaverse adds interest and engagement to brand advertising. The chances in areas like virtual reality, augmented reality, XR, cloud gaming, artificial intelligence in social media, virtual fitting rooms, and AR/VR gear and accessories are generating new income opportunities for metaverse businesses. The market sizes and CAGRs of these nearby markets are shown in the following table.

2) Opportunity: Including the Metaverse in Car Infotainment

In the upcoming years, it is anticipated that VR, AR, and MR will find use in the car infotainment industry. From creating to exhibiting goods on the metaverse space, automakers, hardware manufacturers, and software developers have demonstrated a strong interest in utilizing metaverse-related solutions in their industrial pipeline. With the use of virtual showrooms and other XR-based technologies, such as VR simulation, several automakers and dealers are offering users and consumers immersive experiences. Customers and users are expressing interest in using NFTs and cryptocurrency in the virtual asset marketplace. (Arumugam & Tyagi, 2023) The field of simulation has become considerably more convenient because of metaverse technology. Below are some of the key aspects forming part of gamification in the metaverse in the sports industry

a) Software Segment in the Automobile Industry

Avatars, digital twins, online auto design, AR-based virtual showrooms, and metaverse platforms are among the software's features. A game engine is an environment or software development package that was first used for the creation of video games. These days, a gaming engine can be utilized for visualization, collaboration (as in the creation of digital twins), and more. (Rane, Choudhary, & Rane, 2023) A gaming engine may have physics and collision engines, AI, animation tools, audio engines, and more. Given that many corporations currently use metaverse platforms to facilitate collaboration between the actual and virtual worlds, these platforms are probably going to dominate the software market. Numerous companies are creating their own metaverse spaces, such as NVIDIA's Omniverse and Tech Mahindra's Tech Verse, and many gaming companies, including Epic Games, Roblox, Decentral, Infinite World, and Upland, have created their metaverse games that have featured the introduction of new cars from numerous automakers.

b) AR in the Automobile Industry

From holding the steering wheel to depressing the gas pedal to experiencing a jolt if the car stops abruptly, driving is an extremely physical experience. In the future, taking a virtual ride in the metaverse—the next version of the internet that allows users to immerse themselves in a digital environment that closely resembles the actual world—may allow users to feel these same emotions. There are numerous uses for AR in the automotive sector. For example, it is utilized to enhance manufacturing and inspection procedures in factories by utilizing a variety of AR hardware and software items. (Rauschnabel, Felix, & Hinsch, 2019) Along with helping to construct different kinds of HUDs, it is also utilized in car maintenance. Among other things, it is utilized for online automobile sales and advertising through virtual showrooms, virtual simulation drives, and online car designs. Modern augmented reality technologies are being used by automakers and dealers to offer unmatched services and car safety. The automotive sector has persisted in experimenting with augmented reality (AR) technology to optimize the value chain, from research and development to manufacturing, as well as in product sales and marketing, despite COVID-19 in the past. AR applications are widely used in the automotive industry. For example, Nissan offers test drives and an augmented reality (AR)-based virtual showroom to potential customers who visit its website to purchase vehicles. This came about as a result of a decline in sales during COVID-19, as a result of consumers avoiding showroom visits. As this application grew in popularity over time, Nissan was able to obtain a competitive edge in the early stages of the system's rollout. By creating digital twins of its plants, BMW has also used augmented reality in its operations. Before utilizing each tool, the technicians can obtain relevant information about it via the AR app. With AR pictures of cars and technical details regarding AR glasses, it streamlines the assembly process. Additionally, BMW unveiled its first-ever augmented reality tool, Virtual Viewer. It will give users and customers a completely new method to personalize a BMW car. Hyundai also invested in

WayRay in September 2018 to create a holographic augmented reality navigation system for its upcoming automobiles.

c) Role of Metaverse in Repair and Maintenance

OEMs (Original Equipment Manufacturers) can instruct auto technicians and walk them through a vehicle's repair process by using metaverse tools. For instance, Daimler Trucks North America recently tested a pilot program to deploy augmented reality (AR) technology at its dealerships to give service personnel step-by-step instructions and training (Abrar, 2018). In a similar vein, all BMW dealerships in the US currently use wearable XR technology. By facilitating the training and licensing of third-party technicians in remote areas and enabling OEMS to better interact with consumers throughout a vehicle's life cycle, the metaverse can also assist OEMs in growing their service networks. Given the growing scarcity of skilled technicians, this competency might become even more important in the future. Cars may gather and share more data throughout their life cycle as technology advances. After examining a car's onboard data using these new technologies, technicians might digitally connect with an AI-based avatar to do collaborative diagnostics.

d) Gamification-Based Brand Promotions for Automakers

The game aspect of the metaverse is being exploited by numerous automakers to raise brand recognition. They are strategically exploiting the metaverse to engage in sponsorships and promotions based on the metaverse. The 3D environments are used by users to play mini-games, interact with other players, communicate, create friendships, and obtain product information via chatbots, virtual AI agents, or salesmen. For young consumers, the metaverse adds interest and engagement to brand advertising.

9. GAMIFICATION IN METAVERSE IN THE FASHION INDUSTRY

The fashion industry is taking video games seriously due to their growing popularity and the opportunities they present for influencer marketing, partnerships, and virtual commerce. Due to the opportunity to interact with interested audience, customize avatars, and display of personalized style, there is currently a growing demand for fashionable virtual clothing and accessories (Wanick & Stall wood, 2023). Thanks to the expansion of e-commerce, the fashion industry now has access to new revenue sources, and the gaming industry is worth billions of dollars. Using wildly successful game franchises, from Roblox and other metaverse gaming platforms to The Sims and League of Legends, well-known fashion companies like Prada, Gucci, Louis Vuitton, and Moschino have entered the virtual fashion space.

Fashion has always had a close association with identity. Consumers express their uniqueness and sense of style through clothing, fashion trends, and labels. In many ways, gaming is no different. Because both fashion and gaming seek to provide fans with a world of fantastical, aspirational experiences, they also go hand in hand. (Kim, Kim, & Mattila, 2012) Players are represented virtually by avatars, which look and dress like the real players. A player's avatar and the "skins" they select to wear in the online shooting game Fortnite may reveal both their gaming experience and personal flair. Similar to clothing, most skins are purchased, and some have a short shelf life.

9.1 Important Domains for Metaverse Fashion Brand Development

1) **Branding**: Increasing a brand's visibility in the real world, introducing it into a new virtual setting that enables a fresh understanding of its advantages, and engaging with generating synergies between the virtual and real worlds, gamifying brand equity, engaging consumers with virtual products, and attracting new and existing clients
2) **Product:** NFTs make it possible to purchase, own, and exchange distinct virtual artifacts that are recognized by blockchain technology. NFTs enhance interaction between the virtual and physical worlds and add virtual offerings to brands' product catalogs. In the battle against counterfeits, NFTs serve as digital twins that record data about the provenance, ownership, and history of physical or digital goods. This is particularly crucial for the luxury market. NFTs as "loyalty tokens" that provide users with extra advantages, including access to physical goods and new NFT releases
3) **Channels of distribution and logistics**: Using NFTs to dissolve the distinctions between the real and virtual worlds
4) **Communication with customers**: Artificial intelligence interaction that uses repetition to learn from encounters with customers. Customized consumer interactions with holograms in augmented reality or virtual 3D artificial intelligence agents in virtual reality.
5) **Details about the customer**: Availability of consumer data, both in terms of quantity and quality. Large-scale chances for experimentation to gather data on how customers respond to novel ideas or product concepts.

9.2 Integration of Gamification and Fashion

Fashion firms can use gaming as a way to interact with their clientele, particularly Gen Z and other young, tech-savvy consumers. Fashion brands may display their products, share their stories, and provide unique experiences by developing their games or collaborating with already-existing ones. (Sharma, Lim, Kumar, Verma, & Kumra, 2024) Additionally, fashion firms can reach out to the current influencer and gaming communities, who can serve as brand ambassadors and advocates. From casual smartphone users to avid PC and console owners, more than 3.2 billion people play video games worldwide. The huge number of younger audience choose gamification over more traditional media as their main foundation of enjoyment and socialization, even though gamers come in all various age groups. During the coronavirus outbreak, fashion designers had to quickly think creatively to reach consumers. The traditional "shop window" out-of-home approach had to give way to the digital sphere. High-end fashion brand Balenciaga collaborated with the popular battle royale game Fortnite to display its apparel lines using in-game different skins. Compared to earlier times, fashion companies are using gaming in more clever ways.

10. Gamification in Metaverse in the Education Industry

Metaverse games are becoming more popular. Names like Fortnite and Roblox can be found everywhere. Educational technology in the future will be greatly affected by the metaverse, with the integration of artificial intelligence, augmented reality, and virtual reality, creating an immersive imaginary environment. Social interactions within the Metaverse, AI-guided personal instructors, and real-time simulations all increase engagement and learning. This invention promotes universal access to education by overcoming regional limitations. Traditional classrooms transform into dynamic centers of information exchange when educational institutions integrate Metaverse technologies, critical thinking, encourage students' creativity, and flexibility. This revolutionary change has the potential to completely change the education sector and create an environment that is more influential and interconnected.

10.1. Transformation of Training and Educational Settings by the Metaverse

1) Classrooms on the Cloud

Students will be able to access virtual learning environments from any location, and instructors will be able to personalize their online classrooms to fit their lesson plans. Beyond conventional classroom settings, the metaverse can provide engaging and dynamic learning experiences. Students can investigate historical events, carry out virtual experiments, or even visit locations that would not be possible without the use of virtual reality (VR) and augmented reality (AR) technologies, which can provide lifelike simulations. Deeper comprehension and increased engagement are the results of this immersive experience.

2) Immersion-Based Learning Settings

The metaverse's immersive and interactive learning environments can be advantageous for cloud-based schools. Teachers and students may use these online spaces, which enhance collaboration and communication.

3) Audio and Presence in Space

Through the use of lifelike avatars and spatial audio, the metaverse may simulate people's physical presence in a shared space. The more engaging and natural collaborative experience that online learning creates makes it more like conventional in-person classrooms.

4) Education with Augmented Reality (AR)

We can construct digital overlays over real-world things in the classroom by utilizing augmented reality (AR) technology in the metaverse. This allows us to transform a variety of settings into chances for students to get more involved and connect with the content they are studying.

5) Information Overlay in Real Time

Students can get real-time information overlays on their physical surroundings by incorporating augmented reality (AR) into the metaverse. In disciplines like medicine, where students can visualize 3D models superimposed on real items to learn about anatomy, this can be especially helpful

6) Virtual Objects and Field Trips

AR-enhanced field trips or activities can be made possible by the metaverse. A dynamic and interactive learning environment can be created by allowing students to explore historical locations or virtual objects superimposed on the actual world using augmented reality devices.

7) Education with Virtual Reality (VR)

Theoretically, immersive training can improve any abilities learned through practical experience, hence, VR in the metaverse has enormous educational potential.

8) Experiences of Immersion Learning

VR and the metaverse can work together harmoniously to provide more immersive and lifelike learning environments. Without physically leaving their location, students can perform virtual science experiments, investigate historical events, or even take virtual trips to different parts of the world.

9) Engaging Simulations

Students can use their academic knowledge in real-world conditions through interactive simulations and scenarios that can be accessed within the metaverse. This practical method helps students better understand and remember difficult ideas.

10) International Cooperation

Students and teachers can work together globally thanks to the metaverse. People from all over the world may communicate, exchange ideas, and collaborate on projects thanks to virtual classrooms and collaborative spaces. This can promote a more worldwide approach to education, cultural exchange, and a diversity of viewpoints.

11) Customized Education

With the use of metaverse technology, learning experiences may be customized to fit the tastes and learning styles of each individual. Educational platforms in the metaverse can modify content and instructional strategies to match the exceptional needs of every student by utilizing data analytics and AI-powered technologies. By targeting each person's unique strengths and shortcomings, this personalization can improve learning outcomes.

11. POTENTIAL RISKS ABOUT GAMIFICATION IN METAVERSE

The metaverse holds great potential, and numerous businesses are creating apps, goods, and services to support its growth and provide its users with a more engaging virtual environment. However, the metaverse also has a darker side, so we must consider some of the difficulties this amazing technology will present.

1) Privacy Issues

The metaverse is the next internet, and we use technologies like virtual reality and augmented reality to immerse ourselves in the digital world. As a result of all this digitization, we already have privacy apprehensions when we browse the web, and the technology that is continuously tracking our digital behavior currently will also be present in the metaverse, where the tracking is probably going to get even more intense and intrusive. For example, VR headsets will come equipped with eye-tracking technology, which may let marketers and advertisers know where and how long we gaze throughout our immersive experience. Naturally, this is a marketer's dream, but anyone worried about their privacy would be quite concerned.

2) Regulatory Challenges

Entering the Metaverse will raise issues of jurisdiction and regulation, necessitating further research into virtual legal realms by nations. Finding the mechanism by which the subject of jurisdiction will be relevant will be crucial given the expanding virtual area that is available to users globally. Major user groups will unavoidably collect in the metaverse, providing a wealth of opportunities for interaction and commerce. On the other hand, users are exposed if there are no regulations governing the borders. Regulatory laws and Jurisdiction are therefore included for issues in the Metaverse. Finding a set of laws and jurisdiction that can guarantee the virtual environment is safe and secure for its users will be extremely difficult.

3)Challenges of Property Metaverse and Ownership

Property and ownership are among the problems of the Metaverse. When we talk about a unified, coherent virtual environment where you can interact with the outside world and other people much as in the real world, we may presume that there will be the opportunity to purchase and own a range of products and assets. In 2021, Non-Fungible Tokens, or NFTs, have been attracting more users and investors to the digital assets and tokens as a result of their growing popularity and media coverage.

In the same way that NFTs now represent real-world objects, the challenge will be creating a single system that may be used to authenticate the owners of virtual assets in the Metaverse, granting and confirming the ownership rights for music, movies, art, and much more.

4) Challenges in the Community and Network Metaverse

Without a question, the Metaverse will bring people from all over the world together in a single virtual setting, bringing a diverse civilization together and posing a unique challenge to Metaverse communities. One of society's needs, as seen in recent years, is connection, which might lead to the growth of a strong network in the Metaverse for both personal and professional purposes. (Thomason, 2022)

5) Challenges in the Time and Space Metaverse

Time and space are two of the Metaverse's difficulties. When comparing the actual world with a virtual one, we may find that people perceive time differently since they are less conscious of their bodies in the setting for virtual reality setting. More time can be spent by viewers in the metaverse, unintentionally spend more time in the Metaverse as a result of the complete immersion. It is vital to put in place systems that will keep users grounded in reality because of the potential for a warped sense of time. The idea of space is the second idea in the Metaverse that has to be examined. Customers may first find it difficult to immerse themselves in such a massive space, trying to understand the quantity and variety of information at once, because the Metaverse presupposes an unlimited space. For a guarantee that customers are conscious and at ease in the virtual world, space and time perception in the Metaverse will need to be guided during the preliminary stages of submersion.

12. CONCLUSION

Marketing through gamification, particularly in the metaverse, gives companies new ways to interact with consumers. Brands may provide engaging experiences that increase consumer loyalty and improve brand impression by utilizing virtual worlds and integrating gaming elements into marketing campaigns. The use of gamification and the metaverse will probably become more and more essential to successful marketing tactics as technology advances. By increasing user involvement and changing conventional experiences, the incorporation of gamification into the metaverse is reshaping several businesses. Gamified metaverse systems provide immersive learning environments in the educational field that boost student engagement and motivation. Customers may interact with digital clothing and events thanks to the fashion industry's use of virtual environments to create interactive brand experiences. Metaverse simulations are used by automakers to give customers interactive product explorations through virtual showrooms and test drives. When taken as a whole, these developments represent a paradigm shift in several sectors toward more customized and engaging user experiences.

13. IMPLICATIONS AND FUTURE RECOMMENDATIONS

The study provides particular implication strategies and several important practical implications for brand loyalty in the metaverse setting. Through a variety of methods, the consistent use of metaverse-based marketing initiatives can stimulate the growth of brand loyalty. The study shows that marketers have never-before-seen chances to create deep relationships with customers through multisensory interaction through immersive, gamified experiences in the metaverse. As the current study is done on four sectors: fashion, automobile, education, and sports, the future research can be done on more unexplored sectors

REFERENCES

Abou-Shouk, M., & Soliman, M. (2021). The impact of gamification adoption intention on brand awareness and loyalty in tourism: The mediating effect of customer engagement. *Tourism and Hospitality Research*, *21*(3), 261–276. DOI: 10.1177/1467358420988048

Abrar, K. (2018). Impact of augmented reality on consumer purchase intention with the mediating role of customer brand engagement: Moderating role of interactivity in online shopping. Bahria University. *Journal of Management & Technology*, *1*(2), 64–80.

Arumugam, S. K., & Tyagi, A. K. (2023). Gamification for Industry 5.0 at the Core of Society 5.0. In *Concepts, Technologies, Challenges, and the Future of Web 3* (pp. 307–336). IGI Global. DOI: 10.4018/978-1-6684-9919-1.ch016

Arya, V., Sambyal, R., Sharma, A., & Dwivedi, Y. K. (2024). Brands are calling your AVATAR in Metaverse–A study to explore XR-based gamification marketing activities & consumer-based brand equity in virtual world. *Journal of Consumer Behaviour*, *23*(2), 556–585. DOI: 10.1002/cb.2214

Bathla, D., & Ahuja, R. (2024). Leveraging Big Data Analytics for Customer Experience Excellence in Metaverse. In *Entrepreneurship and Creativity in the Metaverse* (pp. 128–142). IGI Global. DOI: 10.4018/979-8-3693-1734-1.ch010

Bogoslov, I. A., Stoica, E. A., Georgescu, M. R., & Lungu, A. E. (2023). Gamification In E-Commerce: Advantages, Challenges, And Future Trends. *Revista Economica (Sibiu)*, *75*(2), 17–33. DOI: 10.56043/reveco-2023-0012

Chakraborty, U., & Biswal, S. K. (2024). Diffusion of Innovation in Direct-to-Avatar (D2A): A Study of Immersive Communication and Branding in the Metaverse. *Computers in Human Behavior*, *158*, 108318. DOI: 10.1016/j.chb.2024.108318

Chen, S. S., & Zhang, J. J. (2024). Market demand for metaverse-based sporting events: A mixed-methods approach. *Sport Management Review*, •••, 1–27. DOI: 10.1080/14413523.2024.2401640

Chu, S. C., & Seock, Y. K. (2020). The power of social media in fashion advertising. *Journal of Interactive Advertising*, *20*(2), 93–94. DOI: 10.1080/15252019.2020.1802955

Gamayanto, I., Wibowo, S., & Prayitno, A. (2024). The Concept of gamification, metaverse & AI to develop hybrid learning systems inside education. [International Journal of Information System and Technology]. *IJISTECH*, *7*(6), 370–378.

Ho, X. N. L. (2024). *Exploring Factors That Influence Gen Z Consumers' Adoption of Metaverse and Brand Experience through Metaverse* (Master's thesis, Illinois State University).

Huotari, K., & Hamari, J. (2017). A definition for gamification: Anchoring gamification in the service marketing literature. *Electronic Markets*, *27*(1), 21–31. DOI: 10.1007/s12525-015-0212-z

Jeon, H.-J., Youn, H.-C., Ko, S.-M., & Kim, T.-H. (2021). Blockchain and AI meet in the metaverse. In Fernández-Caramés, T. M., & Fraga-Lamas, P. (Eds.), *Advances in the convergence of blockchain and artificial intelligence* (pp. 73–82). Intech Open., DOI: 10.5772/intechopen.99114

Kim, S. J., Kim, K. H., & Mattila, P. (2012). The role of fashion in the characters of online games. *Journal of Global Fashion Marketing*, *3*(2), 81–88. DOI: 10.1080/20932685.2012.10593110

Koster, R. (2021). *Online world or metaverse?* Raph's Website. https://www.raphkoster.com/2021/09/02/online-world-or-metaverse/

Kulkarni, K., Adithya, V. V., Hitesh, K., & Kumari, N. (2023). Brand Management in the Metaverse. In *The Business of the Metaverse* (pp. 95–112). Productivity Press. DOI: 10.4324/b23404-6

Kumar, G., Singh, R. K., Arya, V., & Mishra, S. K. (2024). Analyzing barriers in adoption of artificial intelligence for resilient health care services to society. *Global Journal of Flexible Systems Managment*, *25*(1), 179–197. DOI: 10.1007/s40171-024-00373-4

Kumar, J., Arora, M., & Erkol Bayram, G. (Eds.). (2024). *Exploring the Use of Metaverse in Business and Education*. IGI Global. DOI: 10.4018/979-8-3693-5868-9

Liboriussen, B. (2011). Collective building projects in second life: User motives and strategies explained from an architectural and ethnographic perspective. In Zagalo, N., Morgado, L., & Boa-Ventura, A. (Eds.), *Virtual worlds and metaverse platforms: New communication and identity paradigms* (pp. 33–46). IGI Global., DOI: 10.4018/978-1-60960-854-5.ch003

Liu, C. C., Lin, Y. Y., & Lo, F.. (2024). From readers to players: Exploring student engagement in a gamified metaverse and its effect on reading interest. *Education and Information Technologies*. Advance online publication. DOI: 10.1007/s10639-024-13068-1

Loijas, J. (2024). How Gamification Shapes Learning And Interaction In Virtual Educational Events.

Markets and Markets. (2022). *Metaverse Market for Automotive worth $16.5 billion by 2030.* https://www.marketsandmarkets.com/PressReleases/automotive-metaverse.asp

Mattke, J., & Maier, C. (2021). Gamification: Explaining brand loyalty in mobile applications. *AIS Transactions on Human-Computer Interaction, 13*(1), 62–81. DOI: 10.17705/1thci.00142

Mehrabian, A., & Russell, J. A. (1974). An approach to environmental psychology. 'e MIT Press

Newzoo. (2021). Global games market report 2021. https://newzoo.com/ insights/trend-reports/newzoo-global-games-market-report-2021-freeversion

Rane, N., Choudhary, S., & Rane, J. (2023, November 1). *Metaverse for enhancing customer loyalty: Effective strategies to improve customer relationship, service, engagement, satisfaction, and experience. SSRN.* https://ssrn.com/abstract=4624197 or DOI: 10.2139/ssrn.4624197

Rauschnabel, P. A., Felix, R., & Hinsch, C. (2019). Augmented reality marketing: How mobile AR-apps can improve brands through inspiration. *Journal of Retailing and Consumer Services, 49*, 43–53. DOI: 10.1016/j.jretconser.2019.03.004

Robertson, A., & Peters, J. (2021). *What is the metaverse, and do I have to care?* The Verge. https://www.theverge.com/22701104/metaverse-explained-fortnite-roblox-facebook-horizon

Rosário, A. T., Lopes, P. R., & Rosário, F. S. (2023). Metaverse in Marketing: Challenges and Opportunities. *Handbook of Research on AI-Based Technologies and Applications in the Era of the Metaverse*, 204-227.

Sharma, W., Lim, W. M., Kumar, S., Verma, A., & Kumra, R. (2024). Game on! A state-of-the-art overview of doing business with gamification. *Technological Forecasting and Social Change, 198*, 122988. DOI: 10.1016/j.techfore.2023.122988

Tena Ochoa, K. A. (2023). *An explorative Impact Analysis of Digitalization in Automotive Customer Journey and Retail Experience* (Doctoral dissertation, Wien).

Thomason, J. (2022). Metaverse, token economies, and non-communicable diseases. *Global Health Journal (Amsterdam, Netherlands), 6*(3), 164–167.

Wang, Y., Su, Z., Zhang, N., Xing, R., Liu, D., Luan, T. H., & Shen, X. (2022). A survey on metaverse: Fundamentals, security, and privacy. *IEEE Communications Surveys and Tutorials.*

Wanick, V., & Stallwood, J. (2023). Brand storytelling, gamification and social media marketing in the "metaverse": A case study of the Ralph Lauren winter escape. In *Reinventing fashion retailing: Digitalising, gamifying, entrepreneuring* (pp. 35–54). Springer International Publishing. DOI: 10.1007/978-3-031-11185-3_3

Woo, A., & Forbes Agency Council. (2021). *Mapping the metaverse: How can brands make the most of this new world?* https://www.forbes.com/sites/forbesagencycouncil/2021/11/30/mapping-the-metaverse-how-can-brands-make-the-most-of-this-new-world/?sh=3edd3fdb6534

Xi, N., & Hamari, J. (2020). The relationship between gamification, brand engagement and brand equity. *Journal of Business Research, 109*, 449–460. DOI: 10.1016/j.jbusres.2019.11.058

Yee, N. (2014). *The Proteus paradox: How online games and virtual worlds change us—And how they don't.* Yale Univeristy Press.

Zeiser, A. (2015). Transmedia marketing: From film and TV to games and digital media. In *Transmedia marketing*. https://www.proquest.com/books/transmedia-marketing/docview/2148110801/se-2?accountid=11526%0Ahttps://hud.alma.exlibrisgroup.com/discovery/openurl?institution=44HUD_INST&vid=44HUD_INST:Services&sid=ProQ%3Aebookcentral1&genre=book&issn=&volume=&issue=&spag

Chapter 13
Incentivizing Sustainability a Gamified Approach to Plastic Waste and Pollution Challenges

Sunetra Saha
https://orcid.org/0000-0003-0879-774X
Amity Business School, Amity University, Noida, India

Arpita Srivastava
https://orcid.org/0000-0002-9734-8008
G.L. Bajaj Institute of Management and Research, Greater Noida, India

Nidhi Srivastava
https://orcid.org/0000-0002-3350-0728
G.L. Bajaj Institute of Management and Research, Greater Noida, India

ABSTRACT

This study looks at how well gamified incentive models work in India to encourage recycling, responsible plastic disposal, and a decrease in plastic use. The study investigates user motivations, preferences, and barriers to using gamified waste management systems using a mixed-methods research technique. The qualitative interviews offer detailed insights into the elements—like personal accountability, environmental concerns, and the requirement for an easily navigable platform—that motivate consumer engagement. The impact of gamified incentive models on behaviour change is further demonstrated by the quantitative survey data, which also shows how their efficacy is influenced by age, education level, and past environmental awareness. The results of this study highlights key design dimensions for creating

DOI: 10.4018/979-8-3693-8886-0.ch013

effective gamified incentive models including balanced reward systems, user-centric design, tailored experience and smooth interaction with the trash management infrastructure. It also suggest ways to encourage long term behavioural changes and enhance consumer involvement.

INTRODUCTION

The adverse impact of plastic pollution on environment has become a major concern when it comes to public health and sustainable development. The fast consumption and urbanization in last two decades have given rise to increased plastic usage resulting in more and more plastic garbage. The absence of effective recycling of this garbage has crated severe consequences. As per Central Pollution Control Board (CPCB, 2021) only 60 percent of the plastic garbage is recycled, remining 40 percent still landfilled, littered or pollutes water bodies. The incorrect disposal of plastic waste pollutes streams, soil, and put aquatic ecosystem at risk (Jayasiri, 2013). The air quality is also contaminated with harmful compounds when plastic is burnt outdoor, leading to negative impact on human health (Verma et al, 2016). Economic point of view also suggests that loss of available resources and income from recycling programmes do not help any economy when plastic waste is not handled correctly (Nandy et al, 2015). Despite introduction of several laws and programmes to control plastic pollution in India such as Plastic Waste Management Rules (2016) and National ban on single use plastics (2022) a lot is still desired to create public awareness, behavioral change for sustainable development.

This study is and effort to acknowledge the need for strategies that address the problem of plastic pollution through Gamified incentive model. The Gamified incentive model is proposed to promote environment friendly behaviour by integrating reward systems and game like behaviour (Deterding et al., 2011; Ouariachi et al., 2017). The study examines that responsible plastic disposal in Indian context may be stimulated by gamification and incentive modeling. The study will give valuable insights to policymakers, communities and corporations to raise awareness, increase consumer involvement and control plastic trash.

Research Objectives

This study's main goal is to evaluate how well gamified incentive models work in India to promote recycling, cut down on plastic use, and dispose of plastic waste responsibly. The study's specific objectives are to:

- Examine user preferences, issues, and motives in relation to gamified waste management systems.
- Determine which aspects of the design and which engagement techniques can improve the effectiveness of gamified incentive schemes.
- Recognize the variables affecting how people manage their plastic trash and the possible impact of incentives and gamification on changing behaviour.

Literature Review

According to mandate given by Ministry of Environment, Forest and climate Change in the year 2016 the plastic trash handling rules set obligations of local authorities, producers to supervise the proper disposal of plastic waste in India. The mandate also lay foundation for development of infrastructure for collection, recycling and disposal of plastic waste by giving due weightage to principle of extended producer responsibility (EPR). The launch of Swachh Bharat Abhiyan (Clean Indian Mission 2014) and Garbage segregation programme in India the efforts are made to develop formal system for managing plastic waste (Chaturvedi et al, 2021). The vastness of geographic area and heterogenous social landscape of India has made it difficult to implement consistent and efficient waste management systems. Some of the major challenges faced in India in plastic waste disposal are: A) Inadequate Infrastructure and Resources due to rural and urban diversity (Bhardwaj et al, 2017) B) Lower level of recycling (15%-30%) due to technological factors, lower incentives and mixture of multilayers plastic (CPCB, 2019), C) Lack of Public Engagement and Awareness efforts due to inadequate public knowledge and participation in segregation and disposal practices (Arora & Agarwal, 2022).

It is examined that use of game design and concepts and components outside of games helps to improvise the user motivation, engagement and behaviour modification, this technique is known as gamification (Deterding et al, 2011). The theory is based on pillars of Self Determination theory (Ryan & Deci, 2000), Goal Setting theory (Locke & Latham, 2002). The incentive model requires incentive system to be in place to encourage reward desired action (Zichermann & Cunningham, 2011). To address the issues of resource management, energy conservation, garbage reduction and to encourage environment friendly behaviour gamification is used (Ouariachi et al., 2017). Monetary and non-monetary such as cash discounts, recognition, etc are introduced in the system and policies to ensure long term behaviour change (Hassen & El-Amine, 2021).

In case of plastic waste disposal and management incentive model can encourage recycling and appropriate disposal by offering incentives such as loyalty bonus, cash discount (Anixter & Kohn, 2022). Some of the existing incentive models for gamifying plastic waste management in India are Recycle Mate (Ganesan, 2020),

Plastic Bank (Plastic Bank, 2023), Litterati (Global) (Litterati, 2023) and Garbage Free World (India) (Waste-Free World, 2023). It is observed that following are the gaps when in comes to literature about gamification and incentive model on environmental context in India:

1. Lack of data on effectiveness of gamification strategies to incentivise management of plastic trash in India
2. Lack of understanding of limitations faced by users with respect to gamified waste management system in India
3. Limited research on engagement tactics used for gamified reward model
4. Lack of information available on how India's current waste management processes and laws integrate gamification incentive modelling.

Current study makes an effort to address these gaps and would help us to acknowledge:

1. How effective are gamified waste management incentive models in India?
2. What motivates consumers to get engaged with gamified waste management systems in India and what limitations they face?
3. What improvement can be suggested to encourage and incentivised desired waste management behaviour?
4. How effectively the incentive model is supported by laws and regulations of the country?

RESEARCH METHODOLOGY

Research Questions

1. In the Indian context, how effective are gamified incentive models in promoting responsible plastic disposal, recycling, and cutting down on plastic use?
2. What drives consumers to interact with gamified waste management systems in India? What are their preferences? What are the obstacles they face?
3. What aspects of the design and methods of interaction can improve the way that gamified incentive models encourage environmentally friendly practises in the area of managing plastic waste?
4. In order to promote structural change in India's plastic waste management practices, how might gamified incentive models be successfully incorporated with the country's current waste management laws and regulations?

Qualitative Research: In-Depth Interviews

The study's qualitative component entails interviewing consumers of gamified trash management programmes or platforms in India in-depth. The purpose of this approach is to get deep insights into their motivations, problems, and lived experiences with respect to the use of gamified incentive models for the management of plastic trash.

Participant Selection and Sampling

To find volunteers who have actively participated in gamified waste management programmes or platforms in India, purposeful sampling has been used. To guarantee variety in the sample, participants were chosen based on factors including their degree of participation, demographics (e.g., age, gender, socioeconomic position), and geography.

Data Collection and Analysis

Semi-structured interviews were conducted based on the convenience and preferences of the participants.

Survey Design and Distribution

The purpose of the survey is to gather data on demographics, user experiences, engagement levels, motives, and opinions of gamified incentive models for the management of plastic trash. In order to facilitate more in-depth answers, the survey combined closed-ended questions (such as multiple-choice and rating scales) with open-ended ones. The questionnaire was disseminated via a number of online means, including social media sites, email lists, and pertinent discussion boards or communities about waste management and environmental sustainability in India. Targeting a range of age groups, regions, and socioeconomic backgrounds helped create a representative and varied sample.

Data Collection and Analysis

Online survey platforms or suitable software were used to compile and arrange survey responses. In order to find patterns, correlations, and trends in the quantitative data, descriptive and inferential statistical analysis were carried out. The survey participants' demographics, levels of participation, and perceptions were compiled and presented using descriptive statistics. The study utilizes inferential statistics, including regression analysis, correlation analysis, and suitable parametric and non-parametric tests, to investigate the associations among variables and pinpoint the elements affecting plastic waste management practices and the efficacy of incentive models with gamification.

Using content analysis approaches, open-ended survey questions gave qualitative data from which recurrent themes and patterns were found and categorized (Vaismoradi et al., 2013).

Reliability Statistics

Table 1. CronBach Alpha

Cronbach's Alpha	N of Items
0.045	20

It is important to note that the relatively low Cronbach's alpha value (0.045) indicates low internal consistency among the survey items, suggesting that the questionnaire may not have adequately captured the underlying constructs related to gamified approaches and plastic waste management. Additional validation and refinement of the survey instrument could be beneficial for future studies in this area.

Ethical Considerations

The study approach will prioritise ethical issues above anything else. All participants will be asked to provide informed permission, which guarantees they understand the aim of the study, that their participation is voluntary, and that confidentiality and anonymity procedures are in place.

FINDINGS AND ANALYSIS

Table 2. Anova

Model	Sum of Squares	df	Mean Square	F	Sig.
1	2381.912	20	119.096	0.666	.853b
Regression	23068.92	129	178.829		
Residual	25450.83	149			
Total					
---					

a. Dependant Variable: Age

b. Predictors: (Constant), Would you be more likely to actively participate in plastic waste reduction if there were competitive gamified challenges with rewards?, Rate your satisfaction with existing gamified initiatives related to plastic waste management, How well do you think gamified models align with environmental sustainability goals?, Do you believe that gamification can positively impact recycling rates for plastic materials?, How likely are you to recommend gamified plastic waste reduction programs to others?, Do you think gamified incentives can encourage community participation in plastic cleanup drives and awareness campaigns?, To what extent do you agree with the statement: "Gamified incentives encourage individuals to reduce their plastic waste"?, Rate your confidence in the effectiveness of gamified approaches to reduce plastic pollution:, Do you believe that gamified approaches can lead to long-term behavior change regarding plastic waste management?, How effective do you think gamified reward systems are in promoting proper plastic disposal practices?, Rate the overall effectiveness of gamified incentive modeling in reducing plastic waste:, Do you think gamified Incentives can encourage businesses and industries to adopt more sustainable plastic packaging practices?, Would you be more likely to participate in plastic waste reduction efforts if they were integrated into a garnified mobile app?, How well do you think gamified models address the psychological factors influencing plastic waste behavior?, How aware are you of existing gamified initiatives related to plastic waste management?, Rate the effectiveness of gamified challenges (e.g., recycling competitions, point-based rewards) in potivating plastic waste reduction:, In your opinion, how important is it to incorporate gamified elements into plastic waste management programs?, Rate the impact of gamified incentives on your personal plastic consumption habits:,

Have you personally participated in any gamified initiatives related to plastic waste reduction?, How likely are you to engage in plastic waste reduction activities if they were part of a gamified system?

A multiple regression analysis was conducted to find whether age had a significant impact on affecting perception and attitudes towards gamification and plastic waste reduction. The model sum of squares (2381.912) is tiny in comparison to the residual (25450.83) and total (about 48519.75), indicating that age is mostly irrelevant to the attitudes and perceptions presented. As a result, we may infer that age is not a major predictor of an individual's response to gamified plastic waste reduction measures.

Table 3. Constructs

Items	Mean	Std. Dev.	Skewness	Kurtosis
Gamified incentives encourage reduction of plastic waste	3.07	1.419	-0.045	-1.311
Effectiveness of gamified reward systems	2.78	1.37	0.231	-1.194
Gamification's impact on recycling rates	2.94	1.362	0.094	-1.204
Importance of gamified elements in programs	2.89	1.396	0.073	-1.256
Personal participation in gamified initiatives	3.12	1.4	-0.098	-1.226
Effectiveness of gamified challenges	3.05	1.358	-0.053	-1.213
Likelihood to engage if part of gamified system	3.11	1.443	-0.067	-1.355
Gamified incentives for sustainable packaging	3.04	1.492	-0.032	-1.427
Confidence in gamified approaches	2.85	1.373	0.063	-1.295
Awareness of gamified initiatives	2.91	1.377	0.092	-1.279
Likelihood to participate via mobile app	2.93	1.441	0.104	-1.327
Impact on personal plastic consumption	2.84	1.395	0.11	-1.312
Gamified models and psychological factors	2.85	1.392	0.206	-1.249
Long-term behavior change via gamification	2.89	1.342	0.096	-1.195
Overall effectiveness of gamified incentive modeling	3.05	1.437	0.002	-1.286
Likelihood to recommend gamified programs	3.03	1.378	-0.061	-1.207
Gamified incentives and community participation	2.87	1.389	0.013	-1.329
Satisfaction with existing gamified initiatives	2.87	1.467	0.196	-1.355
Gamified models' alignment with sustainability goals	3.03	1.444	-0.005	-1.37
Likelihood to participate in competitive gamified challenges	2.84	1.424	0.131	-1.275

Interpretation and Implications

General Attitudes: Respondents are moderately receptive to the idea that gamified incentives can encourage plastic waste reduction, but there is no strong consensus. The means hovering around 3 suggest that while there is interest, there is also caution or uncertainty about the effectiveness of gamification in this context.

Variability: The high variability in responses underscores the need for targeted communication and program design, as different segments of the population may respond differently to gamified interventions.

Distribution Shape: The near-symmetrical and platykurtic distributions indicate that most respondents fall in the middle of the scale, with relatively few expressing extreme agreement or disagreement

Figure 1. Scree plot

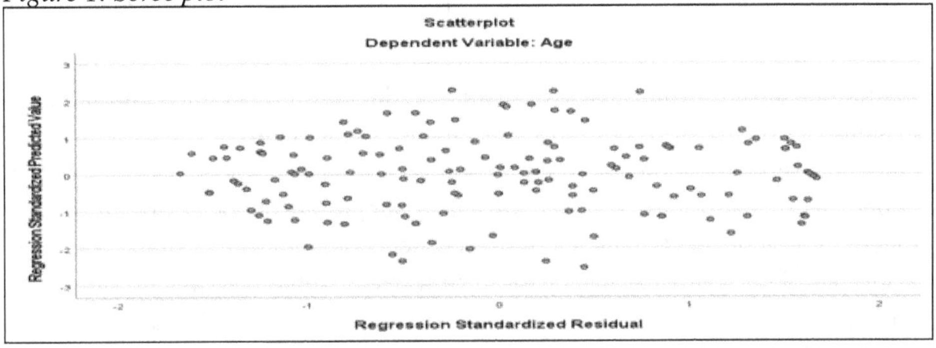

Table 4. Principle component analysis

Component	Total	% of Variance	Cumulative %	Total	% of Variance	Cumulative %
1	1.725	8.626	8.626	1.725	8.626	8.626
2	1.525	7.625	16.251	1.525	7.625	16.251
3	1.446	7.231	23.482	1.446	7.231	23.482
4	1.433	7.166	30.647	1.433	7.166	30.647
5	1.254	6.269	36.916	1.254	6.269	36.916
6	1.242	6.208	43.124	1.242	6.208	43.124
7	1.159	5.793	48.916	1.159	5.793	48.916
8	1.123	5.616	54.532	1.123	5.616	54.532
9	1.036	5.179	59.711	1.036	5.179	59.711

continued on following page

Table 4. Continued

Component	Total	% of Variance	Cumulative %	Total	% of Variance	Cumulative %
10	1.007	5.037	64.749	1.007	5.037	64.749
11	0.933	4.663	69.412			
12	0.874	4.368	73.78			
13	0.828	4.138	77.918			
14	0.778	3.891	81.809			
15	0.716	3.581	85.391			
16	0.678	3.39	88.78			
17	0.64	3.202	91.982			
18	0.587	2.935	94.917			
19	0.563	2.814	97.731			
20	0.454	2.269	100			
Extraction Method: Principal Component Analysis.						

Attitudes towards gamified plastic waste reduction are complex and multidimensional, as revealed in the study. The first 10 components account for 64.75% of the total variance, with the first component accounting for 8.63%. The first 5 components explain 36.92% of the variance, suggesting moderate clustering of attitudes. A gradual decline in eigenvalues reflects the multidimensional nature of perceptions about gamified incentives. The low explanatory power of individual components aligns with the high response variability observed in the descriptive statistics. Many distinctive factors like personal engagement, skepticism about effectiveness, and belief in long-term impact may affect attitude. It is suggested that targeted interventions, survey refinement, and segmented communication may be used to address these factors.

Qualitative Research Findings

- **User motivations and challenges** - The reasons given by participants for participating in gamified programmes pertaining to the management of plastic trash varied. Key motivators were the need to contribute to a cleaner,more sustainable future and environmental concerns. Many people showed a readiness to embrace eco-friendly habits and a sense of personal responsibility. Participants did, however, also identify a number of obstacles that restricted the efforts' efficacy or prevented them from being fully engaged. One recurrent problem was ignorance of the characteristics of the gamified platforms already in place. The intricacy or user-friendliness of some systems worried several participants, which highlighted the necessity for accessible and user-friendly design.

• **Customised and personalised experiences –** Participants also underlined the importance of customised and personalised experiences on gamified platforms. Individual preferences and circumstances were taken into account when creating objectives, challenges, and incentives; they were shown to be more effective and engaging.

• **Preferred gamification elements and incentives-** Participants gave a variety of answers when asked which gamification features and rewards they liked. Point-based incentive schemes, leaderboards, and challenges that promoted success and competitiveness were popular.

• **Perceived effectiveness of existing platforms-** The participants' opinions on the success of the current gamified programmes for managing plastic trash were divided. Some raised doubts about these platforms' practical effects, while others acknowledged their ability to increase awareness and promote beneficial actions.

Quantitative Research Findings

Based on an online survey, the study's quantitative component offered insightful information on user demographics, engagement levels, and the effects of gamified incentive models on behaviours related to the management of plastic trash.

- **User Demographics and Engagement Levels**

The online survey's results showed a wide variety of participant demographics. The respondents' ages ranged widely: 40% were between the ages of 36 and 55, 15% were above 55, and 45% were between the ages of 18 and 35. The sample had a reasonably equal gender distribution, with 52% of the participants being female and 48% being male.

With respect to educational background, sixty-one percent of respondents had earned a bachelor's or master's degree, twenty-one percent had just completed high school or some college, and eighteen percent had a doctorate or professional degree. Participants' backgrounds in terms of occupation were equally varied; among them were students (18%), professionals (43%), stay-at-home parents (12%), and retirees (9%).

The poll gathered responses from all over India in terms of geographic distribution, with 35% of participants living in big cities, 30% in smaller urban centres, and 25% in rural or semi-urban regions. Ten percent of the population came from semi-urban areas.

Mixed results were found regarding the degrees of participation with gamified waste management solutions. Although 42% of participants said they have previously used these kinds of systems, a sizable majority (58%) said they had either little or no exposure to these programmes. This shows that a larger audience has to be made more aware of and able to use gamified options for managing plastic waste.

- **Factors influencing plastic waste management behaviours**

Peer pressure and social impact were also found to be significant determinants, especially for the younger respondents. The perception of rewards and gamified components was found to be a motivating factor; however, the degree of this impact differed among various demographic groups.

- **Impact of gamified incentive models on behaviour change**

According to the survey results, gamified incentive schemes are typically seen favourably when it comes to encouraging proper disposal behaviours and a decrease in plastic waste. Users of gamified platforms reported greater levels of engagement and were more likely to maintain environmentally friendly behaviors.

Integration of Qualitative and Quantitative Findings -

By integrating the qualitative and quantitative findings, several key themes and patterns emerged:

- **Knowledge and accessibility**: The survey and interview results underscored the importance of increasing public knowledge of existing gamified initiatives and ensuring their accessibility for a wider user base.
- **Customized and personalised experiences:** The participants show a high demand for personalized experience on gamified platforms. It clearly shown in quantitative data showing difference in effectiveness at various groups.
- As the research result clearly indicates that designing incentives that are appropriately tailored to each individual's tastes and motives are very important. The quantitative data, clearly shows that thoughtfully created incentives may have a favourable impact on how people manage their plastic trash.

DISCUSSION OF KEY THEMES AND PATTERNS

The study's conclude a number of important themes and trends about how well gamified incentive schemes works to reduce pollution and manage plastic waste in India.

1. Awareness and accessibility: Raising awareness is a key element in boosting engagement and involvement of large audience.
2. Customized and personalized experiences: The study emphasized the significance of customized and personalised experiences in gamified platforms.
3. The results advocates the need of meticulous incentive design and matching with personal preferences and motives. R
4. Rewards that align with users' beliefs, objectives and desired results have a higher chance of successfully influencing how they manage plastic trash.
5. Although gamified incentive models have the potential to promote positive behaviors and short-term engagement, questions have been raised about their ability to sustain long-term behavior change.
6. Integration with current systems: The study emphasized how important it is to incorporate gamified incentive models into the rules and practices currently in place for trash management. If there is collaboration with policymakers, companies and communities it will make integration easier.

Recommendations and Implications

Design principles for effective gamified incentive models – Based on the results of the study, several design ideas could be suggested for creating successful gamified incentive models to address plastic waste management and pollution in India.

User-centric design: Gamified platforms should be designed keeping in mind understanding of user preferences and motivations

Customised and personalised experiences: Maintaining consumers' motivation and interest on gamified platforms requires offering individualized and customized experiences. These programs can appear more relevant and successful if they have objectives, challenges, and rewards that can be customized to each person's preferences and circumstances (Deterding et al., 2011).

A **well-balanced incentive system** should incorporate both extrinsic (such as discounts and financial prizes) and intrinsic (such as motivation) rewards (e.g., recognition, social status).

Clear goal-setting, progress tracking and feedback mechanism like: Gamified platforms should give users simple, user-friendly ways to monitor their progress and get performance feedback.
Community building and social elements: Including social features like leaderboards, challenges and sharing options can help to create a feeling of community and promote peer-to-peer influence.
Smooth connection with current systems: Gamified incentive programmes have to be created in a way that allows them to easily interact with the infrastructure and waste management systems already in place. Working together with waste management companies, local government agencies, and other interested parties may help ensure that implementation is done well and that it is in line with larger sustainability objectives.

Potential Impact on Plastic Waste Management and Pollution Reduction

The effective implementation of gamified incentive models, informed by the design principles and strategies outlined in this study, has the potential to significantly impact plastic waste management and pollution reduction in India. Some potential impacts include:

1. Enhanced public involvement and engagement: By making plastic waste management more approachable, entertaining, and fulfilling, gamified programmes can encourage more public involvement in recycling, appropriate disposal, and trash reduction activities.
2. Behavioural modification and habit development: These strategies can support long- term habit formation linked to plastic waste management by utilising the concepts of gamification and reward modelling.
3. Reducing the demand for virgin plastics and the related environmental effects can help with resource recovery and the growth of a more circular economy by providing incentives for the collection and recycling of plastic trash.
4. Decreased plastic pollution: By encouraging appropriate disposal methods, cutting back on plastic use, and fostering an environmental stewardship culture, effective gamified incentive models may dramatically reduce plastic pollution.
5. Job creation and economic opportunities: The use of gamified initiatives has the potential to provide jobs in the waste management, recycling, and environmental services sectors.
6. Alignment with sustainability goals: Gamified incentive models can help achieve a number of sustainability goals, such as those outlined in the United Nations Sustainable Development Goals (SDGs) and India's nationally determined con-

tributions (NDCs) under the Paris Agreement, by addressing plastic pollution and encouraging pro-environmental behaviours.

Overall, this study's recommendations and consequences show how gamified incentive models might encourage improved plastic waste management procedures and lower plastic pollution levels in India. But for them to be successful, governments, corporations, communities, and individuals must work together in an integrated and cooperative manner to create a future that is more ecologically sensitive and sustainable.

Table 5. Hypothesis testing

	N	Minimum	Maximum	Sum	Mean	Std. Deviation
To what extent do you agree with the statement: "Gamified incentives encourage individuals to reduce their plastic waste"?	150	1	5	461	3.07	1.419
How effective do you think gamified reward systems are in promoting proper plastic disposal practices?	150	1	5	417	2.78	1.37
Do you believe that gamification can positively impact recycling rates for plastic materials?	150	1	5	441	2.94	1.362

Hypothesis 1, the results indicate a neutral to slightly positive response (mean = 3.07, SD = 1.419) when asked about the extent to which gamified incentives encourage individuals to reduce their plastic waste. This suggests that there is potential for gamified approaches to influence plastic waste reduction behaviour, but the perceived effectiveness may not be overwhelming.

For Hypothesis 2, the data shows a similar neutral to slightly positive response (mean = 2.78,SD = 1.370) when evaluating the effectiveness of gamified reward systems in promoting proper plastic disposal practices. This implies that while gamified reward systems may have some influence, their overall effectiveness in this area is not strongly perceived by the respondents.

Hypothesis 3, which examines the belief that gamification can positively impact recycling rates for plastic materials, also received a neutral to slightly positive response (mean = 2.94,SD = 1.362). This indicates that there is some optimism about the potential of gamification to improve recycling rates, but the respondents do not overwhelmingly believe in its effectiveness.

Overall, the survey results suggest a moderately positive perception of the role of gamified incentives and approaches in plastic waste reduction efforts. However, the data also highlights the need for further research and refinement of these strategies to enhance their perceived effectiveness and impact.

It is important to note that the relatively low Cronbach's alpha value (0.045) indicates low internal consistency among the survey items, suggesting that the questionnaire may not have adequately captured the underlying constructs related to gamified approaches and plastic waste management. Additional validation and refinement of the survey instrument could be beneficial for future studies in this area.

CONCLUSION

This study looked into how well gamified incentive schemes worked in India to improve the way plastic trash is managed and to cut down on pollution. The main conclusions show how gamified incentive models may be used to promote appropriate disposal methods, discourage plastic consumption, and boost recycling.

Preferences for customised experiences, customised incentives, and interesting gamification components like leaderboards, challenges, and point-based prizes were shown by the qualitative data.

However, the study also identified challenges and limitations, including concerns about long-term behavior change, awareness and accessibility barriers, and the need for seamless integration with existing waste management systems and policies.

Contributions to the Field

With a particular focus on plastic waste management in India, this study adds to the expanding corpus of research on gamification and incentive modelling in environmental contexts. The study offers a thorough grasp of user viewpoints, preferences, and the variables affecting how successful gamified projects are.

To create and execute efficient gamified incentive models for plastic waste management and pollution reduction, enterprises, and organisations can benefit from the design ideas and tactics discussed in this paper.

The results also add to the larger conversation on sustainable waste management techniques by emphasising the power of creative and captivating methods to encourage environmental stewardship and behaviour modification.

Limitations and Future Research Directions

- Although this study offers insightful information it also shares some limitations also. Future studies should look at the long-term effects of gamified incentive models, as well as the efficacy of these strategies in various socio-economic and cultural contexts in India.

- Coming studies can also investigate how to improve the design and execution of these projects by using cutting-edge technology like blockchain, artificial intelligence and VR/AR. As the fields of gamification and incentive modelling is evolving.
- As a result, this study advances knowledge on the possibilities and difficulties of gamified incentive models for tackling India's pressing problems with pollution and the management of plastic trash. The study's conclusions, suggestions, and recommendations for further research can help shape practical, long-term plans for encouraging pro-environmental behaviour and bringing about the kind of positive change that will lead to a more sustainable future.

REFERENCES

Anixter, K., & Kohn, D. (2022). Incentive-based waste management and recycling systems: A review. *Waste Management (New York, N.Y.), 147*, 293–317. DOI: 10.1016/j.wasman.2022.04.027

Arora, S., & Agarwal, R. (2022). Plastic pollution: A review of challenges, policies, and strategies for managing plastic waste in India. *Journal of Environmental Management, 319*, 115740. DOI: 10.1016/j.jenvman.2022.115740

Bharadwaj, A., Yadav, D., & Varshney, S. (2017). Non-hazardous solid waste management in Indian cities – A review. *Management of Environmental Quality, 28*(2), 163–178. DOI: 10.1108/MEQ-06-2015-0119

Braun, V., & Clarke, V. (2006). Using thematic analysis in psychology. *Qualitative Research in Psychology, 3*(2), 77–101. DOI: 10.1191/1478088706qp063oa

Central Pollution Control Board (CPCB). (2019). Annual report for the year 2018-19 on implementation of Plastic Waste Management Rules. https://cpcb.nic.in/uploads/plasticwaste/Annual_Report_2018-19_PWM.pdf

Central Pollution Control Board (CPCB). (2019). Annual report for the year 2018-19 on implementation of Plastic Waste Management Rules. https://cpcb.nic.in/uploads/plasticwaste/Annual_Report_2018-19_PWM.pdf

Chaturvedi, A., Arora, R., & Ahmed, S. (2021). Challenges in municipal solid waste management: A case study of Delhi. *Waste Disposal & Sustainable Energy, 3*(2), 123–136. DOI: 10.1007/s42768-021-00063-6

Deterding, S., Dixon, D., Khaled, R., & Nacke, L. (2011). From game design elements to gamefulness: Defining "gamification". *Proceedings of the 15th International Academic MindTrek Conference: Envisioning Future Media Environments*, 9-15. https://doi.org/DOI: 10.1145/2181037.2181040

Ganesan, S. (2020). Recycle Mate: A gamified recycling app to promote waste segregation. https://www.recyclemate.co/ 10.

Hassen, D. E., & El-Amine, S. (2021). Incentive model designs for crowdsourcing: Review and research directions. *Computer Science Review, 39*, 100350. https://doi.org/doi:10.1016/j.cosrev.2020.100350

Hassen, D. E., & El-Amine, S. (2021). Incentive model designs for crowdsourcing: Review and research directions. *Computer Science Review, 39*, 100350. DOI: 10.1016/j.cosrev.2020.100350

Jayasiri, H. B., Purushothaman, C. S., & Vennila, A. (2013). Plastic litter accumulation on high-water strandline of urban beaches in Mumbai, India. *Environmental Monitoring and Assessment*, *185*(9), 7709–7719. DOI: 10.1007/s10661-013-3129-z PMID: 23430068

Litterati. (2023). Litterati: A global community cleaning the planet one piece at a time. https://www.litterati.org/

Locke, E. A., & Latham, G. P. (2002). Building a practically useful theory of goal setting and task motivation: A 35-year odyssey. *The American Psychologist*, *57*(9), 705–717. DOI: 10.1037/0003-066X.57.9.705 PMID: 12237980

Ministry of Environment. Forest and Climate Change. (2016). Plastic Waste Management Rules, 2016. https://cpcb.nic.in/uploads/plasticwaste/PWM_Rules_2016.pdf

Nandy, B., Sharma, G., Garg, S., Kumari, S., George, T., Sunanda, Y., & Sinha, B. (2015). Recovery of hydrocarbons from waste plastics by thermal pyrolysis and catalytic pyrolysis. *Energy & Fuels*, *29*(6), 3544–3557. DOI: 10.1021/acs.energyfuels.5b00472

Ouariachi, T., Elving, W. J., & Pierie, F. (2017). Playing for a sustainable future: Games to model and appraise paths towards sustainable behavior change. *Proceedings of the 11th European Conference on Games Based Learning*, 492-499.

Plastic Bank. (2023). Plastic Bank: A global network of ethical Plastic Collectors and recyclers. https://plasticbank.com/

Ryan, R. M., & Deci, E. L. (2000). Self-determination theory and the facilitation of intrinsic motivation, social development, and well-being. *The American Psychologist*, *55*(1), 68–78. DOI: 10.1037/0003-066X.55.1.68 PMID: 11392867

Sharholy, M., Ahmad, K., Mahmood, G., & Trivedi, R. C. (2008). Municipal solid waste management in Indian cities – A review. *Waste Management (New York, N.Y.)*, *28*(2), 459–467. DOI: 10.1016/j.wasman.2007.02.008 PMID: 17433664

Shi, Y., Qian, Y., & Cao, L. (2019). Gamification recycling: Study into the factors influencing the continuation intention of the use of a gamified recycling system. *Sustainability*, *11*(6), 1532. DOI: 10.3390/su11061532

Thaler, R. H., & Sunstein, C. R. (2008). *Nudge: Improving decisions about health,wealth, and happiness*. Yale University Press.

Vaismoradi, M., Turunen, H., & Bondas, T. (2013). Content analysis and thematic analysis: Implications for conducting a qualitative descriptive study. *Nursing & Health Sciences*, *15*(3), 398–405. DOI: 10.1111/nhs.12048 PMID: 23480423

Verma, R., Vinoda, K. S., Papireddy, M., & Gowda, A. N. S. (2016). Toxic pollutants from plastic waste- A review. *Procedia Environmental Sciences*, *35*, 701–708. DOI: 10.1016/j.proenv.2016.07.069

Waste-Free World. (2023). Waste-Free World: Incentivizing communities to recycle. https://wastefreeworld.org/

Zichermann, G., & Cunningham, C. (2011). *Gamification by design: Implementing game mechanics in web and mobile apps*. O'Reilly Media, Inc.

Chapter 14
The Moderating Effect of Demographic Profiles of Indian Consumers on the Impact of Different Website Attributes on the Purchase Intentions of Buyers

Aanchal Aggarwal
https://orcid.org/0000-0002-2072-9806
Vivekananda Institute of Professional Studies, India

Nupur Arora
https://orcid.org/0000-0003-2297-6912
Vivekananda Institute of Professional Studies, India

Parul Manchanda
Netaji Subhas University of Technology, New Delhi, India

Rajesh Verma
https://orcid.org/0000-0002-0195-8988
Christ University, Bangalore, India

ABSTRACT

The aim of the paper is to provide a thorough model that explains how Indian con-

DOI: 10.4018/979-8-3693-8886-0.ch014

sumers' demographic profiles moderate the impact of various website attributes on their purchase intentions and how this helps e-retailers in the context of online shopping. We identified eight online interface features—site design, site convenience, transaction security, payment system, customer communication, delivery information, product information, and special content information—after conducting a in depth literature review. Therefore, we made an effort to ascertain the connections between age, gender, wealth, and online interface elements. 500 Delhi NCR online shoppers took part in the poll. We used structural equation modelling and AMOS to explore the hypothesized correlations between web interface elements, age, gender, income, and purchase intentions. The findings indicated that while income has no discernible influence, age and gender have a major moderating effect on the impact of web interface elements on purchase intentions.

INTRODUCTION

India is a country where e-commerce and internet purchasing are very evident. Both people in cities and rural areas use the internet. E-commerce, or online business transactions between buyers and sellers, opens up new business opportunities and a new economic climate. Banerjee, N. (2017, Jan 9) stated that "demonetization and a reduction in cash transaction, along with improvement of net banking facilities, can be opportunities for the Indian e-commerce sector. The study suggested that in 2016, about 69 million consumers purchased online which has crossed 100 million by 2017 with the rise of digital natives, better infrastructure in terms of logistics, broadband and Internet-ready devices to fuel the demand". For e-firms and researchers alike, acquiring and keeping clients has become more dependent on the growth of business-to-consumer (B2C) online transactions on large e-retailing platforms (Katta & Patro, 2021). The increasing prevalence of e-commerce platforms for the exchange of products and services presents a challenge for e-vendors in attracting new clients and holding on to their existing clientele (Hiranrithikorn & Banjongprasert, 2022). It is exciting to observe that "transactions of online shopping malls constitute 66.5% of total B2C marketplace transactions and offline mall transactions account for 33.5% of the whole". "The number of consumers who purchase online is has crossed 100 million by 2020 end with e-retail market likely jumping 65% on year in 2022, an ASSOCHAM-Resurgent India study.

LITERATURE REVIEW

Shopping Convenience

Shopping convenience refers to the factors that reduces the customers time and effort in the online shopping transaction (Aggarwal & Rahul, 2017). Convenience to use any website reduces the efforts a consumer puts in while searching through a website and hence increases consumer purchase intentions and payment options (Liang and Lai, 2002). Website personality has been evaluated to have a positive significant correlation with the consumer purchase intentions. Also, shopping convenience in regard to perceived usability intends the customer to purchase online (Yoo and Donthu (2001) ; Fink and Nyaga (2009). Previous researches have also suggested that higher perceived value of website personality and higher values of perceived usability leads to higher levels of profitability (Cristobal et al., 2007. Bauer et al. (2006) stated that reliability, process, enjoyment, convenience affect online purchase intentions positively.

Site Design

E-vendors must make the users feel comfortable, give them an enjoyable shopping experience, entice the customers to purchase and revisit the site and increase purchase intentions (Longstreet et al., 2022). Information quality plays a very crucial role in increasing consumer purchase intentions because it serves as a physical store environment for the customers as they search for product information before purchase of any product. Yoon (2002) suggested that, this idea comprises technical experience of the web site designer, complete operational potency, utility of facilitate functions, and also the speed with that navigation is directed on-line as necessary approaches of the efficiency of web site performance. Ranganathan and Ganapathy (2002) also argued that concluded that privacy, security, information content and website design are vital for B2C platforms.

Transaction Security

Consumers are very specific about the privacy of their data and its security. If the level protection guaranteed by e-retailer meets expectations of the consumers, then a consumer is willing to share his or her private information for purchase of product from the website (Liu et al., 2008). If the users are satisfied with the transaction security and payment procedures they will inculcate degree of trust with the e-retailer leading to increase in the purchase intentions (Park and Kim 2003; Grewal et al. 2004). If there is lack of trust and satisfaction towards the e-retailer, it may result in loss of sales for the e-retailers (Grewal et al. 2004).

Payment System

Consumers are more comfortable with web portals that have smooth payment mechanisms that will inculcate trust and satisfaction to process their purchase from the shopping cart (Aggarwal & Rahul, 2018). If the procedure to process transaction and payment is convenient, the consumer is more willing to purchase from that website and created a sense if trust and satisfaction towards the e-retailer (Shin et al., 2013). A higher level of trust and satisfaction is achieved if the website has strong and efficient payment system (Ozkan et al. 2010).

Product Value

Chen et al. (2010) suggested that product value signifies apparent product and information quality as expected by the consumers about the products. Turban et al. (2006) suggested that reasonably priced products and good quality are important factors to product value. Boyer and Hult, (2006) concluded that features of the product should match consumer expectation is significant to product value. Product catalogue to compare products and their prices and reasonable pricing are crucial to product value Brucks et al., 2000 and Turban et al., 2002 . E- vendors should offer wide variety of products to choose from (Brucks et al., 2000, Anand, 2007).

Delivery

Delivery denotes to the overall time spent in shipping and logistics. Chen et al. (2010) suggested that reliable and timely delivery of product plays a vital role in consumer satisfaction. (Anand, 2007) suggested that if the delivery mechanism of a web portal are efficient and quick, the customer tends to develop a feeling of trust and satisfaction which reduces consumer anxiety.

Special Content Information

The specific information on a website consisting of contact information of website, firm's general information, customer policies, customer support, and details about products and facilities is referred to as Special Content Information (Al-Qeisi et al 2014). It has been identified as a significant factor in determining the information quality of e-vendor (Al-Qeisi et al 2014).

Customer Communication

Customer communication refers to the freedom of consumers to share their opinions about the product or the services provided by the e-retailer. Customer communication is considered a very significant factor in determining the quality of information provided by the e-retailer (Shin et al. 2013).

Purchase Intentions

Quality information on a website facilitates consumers to assess valuable aspects and attributes regarding product value and also convey customised, value-added and innovative products and services to customers leading to development of purchase intension amongst the customers (Chiu et al. 2005). Detailed information provided by an e-retailer increases the likelihood to retain and attract customers towards an e-vendor site (Honeycutt et al. 1998). Also, relevant updated and well-organized information plays a significant role in increasing consumer's behavioural intensions Chiu et al. (2005). Purchase intensions of consumer towards an e-retailer is predicted by the quality of information provided by that e-vendor in the form of information search and evaluation of product (Poddar et al., 2009; Hausman and Siekpe, 2009). Conjointly web site design affects on-line purchase intentions

Moderation Effect

Researchers have examined the effects of gender, age, income, education, and culture of consumers on online shopping behavior (Bellman et al. 1999; Jarvenpaa and Tractinsky 1999; Swaminathan et al. 1999). There has always been a gender gap in the way male and females use the technology and indulge themselves in online shopping. Prior research studies conclude that women were less likely than men to use personal computers during the 1980s but that the gender gap in computer usage has since disappeared (Kominski and Newburger, 1999)

Females have traditionally been and continue to be the principle buying agents for households; therefore females are more likely to have greater satisfaction with shopping (Allreck and Settle, 2002). Trocchia and Janda (2000) consider that the principal obstacles to the evolution of e-commerce, which make older consumers more reluctant to shop online, are:

- Less IT experience
- Resistance to change
- Their firmness on using the product before purchase

An important variable that may encourage or check the use of e-commerce, income is another attribute that has fascinated many researchers in the field of technology acceptance (Serenko et al., 2006; Shin, 2009). Numerous research studies have included income as an explanatory variable of shopping behaviour, yet the results concerning its significance are conflicting (Miyazaki and Ferna´ndez, 2001; Raijas and Tuunainem, 2001; Lu et al., 2003; Al-Somali et al., 2009).

Higher income cause internet users to perceive lower implicit risks in undertaking online purchases and thereby affects their demand for internet products and services. Low income discourages online transactions, and perceptions of self-efficacy, ease of use and usefulness should improve with rising incomes, due to the ability to withstand possible financial losses. Usually, income is reflected in the professional status or social class of the individual – different professional categories are accompanied by different incomes and by different levels of IT knowledge and experience. Thus, such categories may produce different user attitudes and behaviour regarding information systems (Hubona and Kennick, 1996; Chau and Hu, 2002).

The year 2018 will see large scale growth in the Indian e-commerce sector with increased participation from people across the country. This industry will continue to drive more employment opportunities and contribute towards creating more entrepreneurs through the e-commerce marketplace model. The report also added that demonetization and a reduction in cash transaction, along with improvement of net banking facilities, can be opportunities for the Indian e-commerce sector". Prospective customers may not be inferred from the results of earlier research conducted on current customers since they may not have the necessary knowledge or experience purchasing online. Thus, it is important to use a strong approach while analysing the moderating role that Indian customer demographic profiles have over web interface elements and consumer purchase intentions (Schaupp and Belanger, 2005).

Research Gap & Research Problem

With respect to literature review, there is a dearth of research elucidating the moderating influence of Indian consumers' age, gender, and income group demographic characteristics on the influence of various website qualities on their purchase inclinations. Furthermore, there is a dearth of study on the online interface components that include unique content information paired with site design, ease of shopping, payment options, transaction security, delivery, and product value.

In the current environment, internet shopping has emerged as a new face that is both incredibly easy for consumers and a time-saver. It is a very practical method of purchasing a wide range of products from various manufacturers online. Customers can take use of an extensive assortment of goods and products from various stores as well as a diverse storage that contains a variety of stuff. The focus of this study is on variables influencing consumers' online purchasing decisions, specifically in relation to web interface elements. This study aims to investigate the moderating effect of Indian consumers' age, gender, and income group demographic characteristics on the influence of various website qualities on consumers' purchase intentions. Online marketers may find the anticipated study results useful in understanding how to boost sales by keeping customers happy.

In this work, we used previous research to identify eight online interface characteristics that influence consumer purchase intentions, using Indian consumer demographic profiles as moderating factors. With the assistance of a questionnaire completed by 500 respondents who had previously shopped online, we performed a survey to explain the influence of these variables on the purchase intentions with the moderation of consumer demographic profiles. With the use of this survey, the study will be able to assess the moderating effects of age, gender, and income on the influence of various website features on customers' purchase intentions. The research's conclusions have implications for practitioners and researchers alike.

Conceptual Model for the Study

Figure 1. Conceptual model for the study

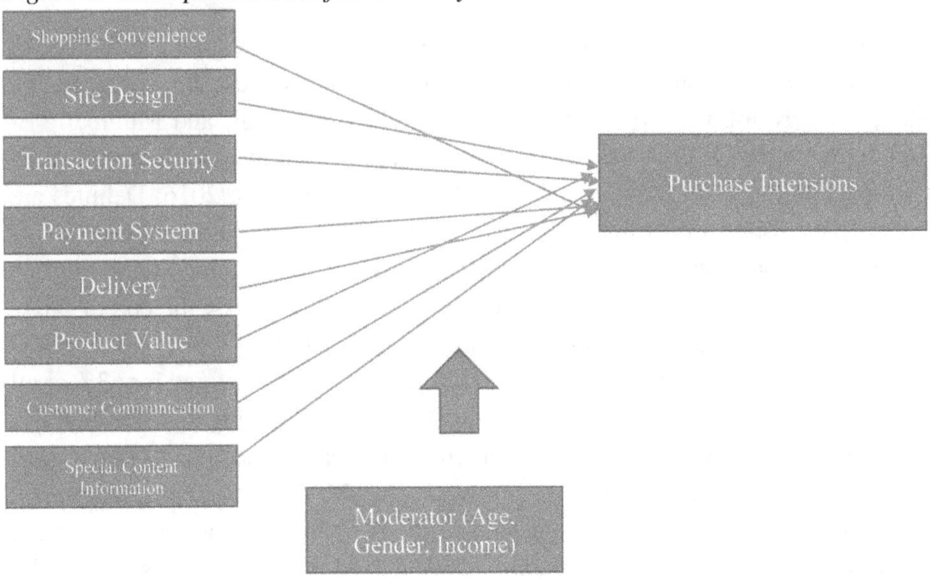

Objectives of the Study

The aim of the paper is to provide a in-depth model that explains how the age, gender, and income groups of Indian consumers moderate the impact of various website attributes on consumers' purchase intentions and how this helps e-retailers in the context of online shopping. We identified eight online interface features—site design, site convenience, transaction security, payment system, customer communication, delivery information, product information, and special content information—after conducting a thorough literature review. Thus, we made an effort to ascertain the connections between Indian consumers' demographic characteristics, buying intentions, and online interface elemnts.

Hypothesis

H1: There exists a significant moderation effect of demographic profiles of Indian consumers (age group, gender, income group) on the impact of different website attributes on the purchase intentions of consumers.

RESEARCH METHODOLOGY

Delhi-based online buyers took part in the poll. With the greatest number of consumers using e-commerce, the National Capital has once again surpassed all others, closely followed by Bengaluru. Hyderabad, Chennai, and Mumbai. "E-commerce major Flipkart has said it saw the highest number of shoppers on its platform coming from the national capital region this year" ("2016: Delhites are the biggest shoppers on Flipkart", 2016). Delhi NCR is the most internet-savvy city in India for shopping, accounting for 60% of all traffic generated by online shoppers ("NCR had highest number for e-shoppers, 2016"). By the end of 2016, there were over 63 million Indians shopping online, with the majority of these visitors originating from the National Capital Region, which accounted for 63% of all Indian online shoppers ("Online sales: Tier-II/III cities catching up with metros", 2014). 40 million Indians will be e-commerce shoppers by the end of 2016 (Accel estimates, Accel Portfolio businesses, comscore & IAMAI, 2015). Using hyperlinks, the survey message outlining the purpose of the study was disseminated to online buyers via e-mails, Facebook, LinkedIn, and WhatsApp, among other social media platforms and mobile applications. The link's validity was available to respondents for a duration of one month. The participants answered the online survey voluntarily. The data irregularities, such as duplicate IP addresses, email accounts, and incomplete responses, were eliminated after a month to obtain useful response data.

Online shoppers received the survey message outlining the purpose of the study via emails, Facebook, LinkedIn, and WhatsApp. 500 respondents made up the sample size after 75 out of 575 responses were eliminated, yielding the operational data. The adoption of purposive non-probability sampling revealed a tendency among 500 online respondents with prior online retailing reviews. We completed structural equation modelling with the aid of AMOS in accordance with the anticipated inter-relationships among all contruct. Using SEM, we were able to examine the causal relationships between the concepts in the model and determine whether the model made sense in light of the new data.

In this section the effort is done in order to analyse the group moderation impact of selected demographic profiles of Indian consumers in the cause and effect relationship considered in the SEM Model. The first group moderation effect is tested using the gender of the consumers. It is assumed that the consumers of different genders may have different impact of website attributes on their intentions to buy. In other words the nature of cause and effect relationship between website attributes to the intentions to buy may be different for male and female consumers. The null hypothesis of moderation effect assumes that there is no significant difference in the cause and effect relationship between different attributes of website and buying intention of consumers. The different path diagrams of male and female consumers showing the impact of website personality attributes on the intentions to purchase is shown in Figure 2 and 3. This is followed by the results of group moderation effects in case of age and annual income as a demographic profile for the selected consumers.

RESULTS

Table 1. Research sample demographic profile

Measure	Items	Frequency	Percentage
Gender	Male	276	55.67
	Female	224	43.42
Age	Less than 20	80	16.5
	20-30	154	30.8
	30-40	136	27.2
	40 & above	123	24.6

continued on following page

Table 1. Continued

Measure	Items	Frequency	Percentage
Annual income	0-2 lac	100	19.2
	Above 2-5 lac	170	31.8
	Above 5-10 lac	150	29.8
	Above 10 lac	80	14.2

Table 2. Dimensionality, reliability and convergent validity statistics

Statement		Constructs	Standardized Beta	Standardized Estimates	Composite reliability	P-value
SC5	<---	Shopping Convenience	0.853			
SC4	<---		0.738	0.046	19.307	***
SC3	<---		0.828	0.041	23.117	***
SC2	<---		0.897	0.04	26.394	***
SC1	<---		0.834	0.045	23.356	***
SD5	<---	Site Design	0.739			
SD4	<---		0.778	0.059	17.556	***
SD1	<---		0.885	0.057	20.186	***
SD2	<---		0.806	0.061	18.229	***
SD6	<---		0.851	0.061	19.355	***
SD3	<---		0.816	0.061	18.487	***
TS6	<---		0.74	0.058	17.008	***
TS5	<---	Transaction Security	0.778			
TS4	<---		0.753	0.058	17.379	***
TS3	<---		0.701	0.059	15.984	***
TS2	<---		0.751	0.057	17.303	***
TS1	<---		0.77	0.059	17.814	***
PS5	<---	Payment System	0.882			
PS4	<---		0.84	0.039	24.596	***
PS3	<---		0.802	0.039	22.681	***
PS2	<---		0.766	0.039	21.024	***
PS1	<---		0.824	0.039	23.773	***
CC6	<---		0.723	0.054	16.819	***

continued on following page

Table 2. Continued

Statement		Constructs	Standardized Beta	Standardized Estimates	Composite reliability	P-value
CC5	<---	Customer Communication	0.777			
CC4	<---		0.833	0.052	19.944	***
CC3	<---		0.81	0.054	19.268	***
CC2	<---		0.767	0.055	18.056	***
CC1	<---		0.729	0.057	16.978	***
D5	<---	Delivery	0.813			
D4	<---		0.735	0.05	18.238	***
D3	<---		0.888	0.046	23.796	***
D2	<---		0.869	0.045	23.045	***
D1	<---		0.863	0.045	22.825	***
PV5	<---	Product Value	0.812			
PV4	<---		0.757	0.051	18.451	***
PV3	<---		0.804	0.047	19.973	***
PV2	<---		0.781	0.05	19.219	***
PV1	<---		0.819	0.046	20.461	***
SCI5	<---	Special Content Information	0.81			
SCI4	<--		0.704	0.053	16.665	***
SCI3	<---		0.818	0.046	20.158	***
SCI2	<---		0.751	0.05	18.076	***
SCI1	<---		0.806	0.047	19.773	***
PI6	<---	Purchase Intentions	0.755	0.074	16.264	***
PI7	<---		0.725	0.052	17.527	***
PI8	<---		0.735	0.813	14.71	***
PI5	<---		0.723			
PI4	<---		0.716	0.068	15.422	***
PI3	<---		0.827	0.063	14.273	***
PI2	<---		0.821	0.066	14.348	***
PI1	<---		0.714	0.067	14.371	***

Figure 2. Moderation effect of male

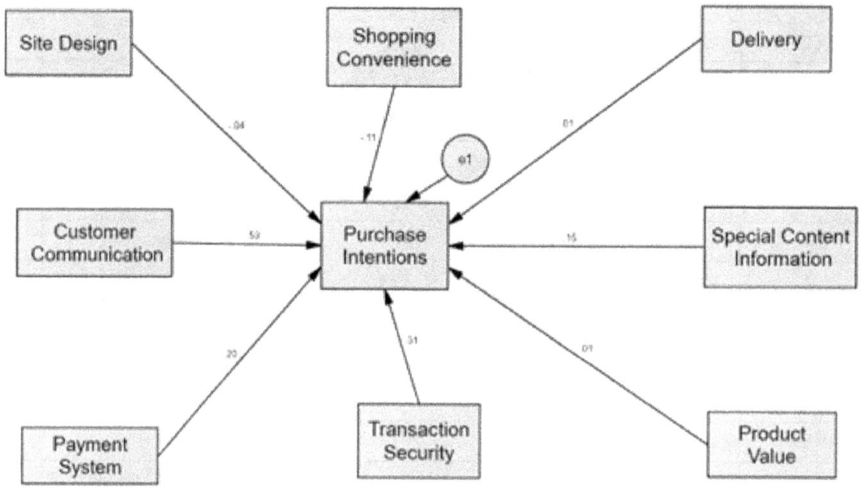

Figure 3. Moderation effect of female

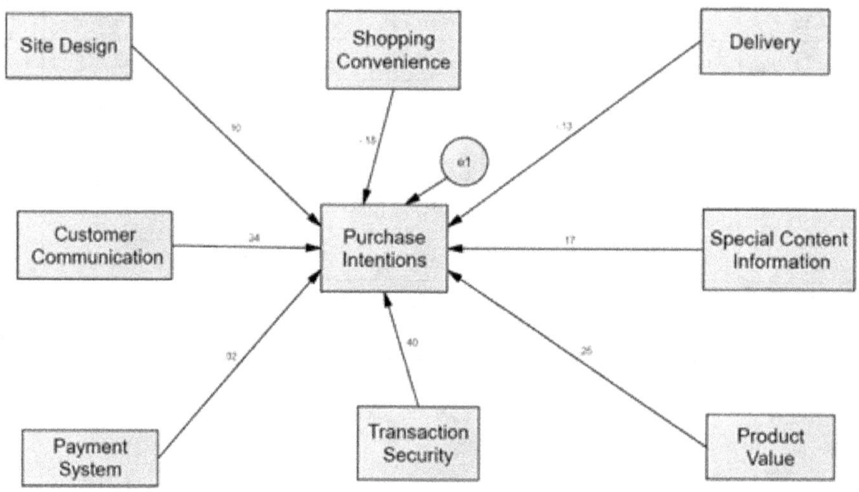

Table 3. Results of gender group moderation effect

Endogenous Construct		Exogenous Construct	Male		Female		z-score
			Regression Coefficient	P Value	Regression Coefficient	P Value	
Purchase Intention	<---	Site Design	-0.021	0.410	0.060	0.056	1.993**
Purchase Intention	<---	Customer Communication	**0.325**	0.000	0.221	0.000	-2.409**
Purchase Intention	<---	Payment System	0.113	0.000	0.012	0.664	-2.718***
Purchase Intention	<---	Transaction Security	0.215	0.000	0.258	0.000	0.953
Purchase Intention	<---	Product Value	0.008	0.743	0.129	0.000	3.322***
Purchase Intention	<---	Special Content Information	0.089	0.000	0.089	0.000	-0.016
Purchase Intention	<---	Delivery	0.007	0.763	-0.065	0.012	**-2.023****
Purchase Intention	<---	Shopping Convenience	-0.060	0.016	-0.104	0.000	-1.160

Notes: *** p-value < 0.01; ** p-value < 0.05; * p-value < 0.10

The result of group moderation effect indicates that the z scores of all the cause and effect relationship (except for TS, SCI and SC) is found to be statistically significant at 5 percent level of significance. Hence, it can be concluded that there exists significant moderation effect of male and female customers in case of cause and effect relationships considered in the path diagram.

In case of cause and effect relationship from the site design on the intention to buy, the z score is found to be 1.993 which is also statistically significant. The results indicate that the female customers are found to have more positive influence of the site design on the intention to buy as compared to male customers. In fact the male customers are mot found to be influenced by the site design.

In case of cause and effect relationship from the payment system on the intention to buy, the z score is found to be 2.718 which is also statistically significant. The results indicate that the female customers are found to have more positive influence of the customer communication on the intention to buy as compared to male customers.

In case of cause and effect relationship from the product value on the intention to buy, the z score is found to be 3.322 which is also statistically significant. The results indicate that the female customers are found to have more positive influence of the product value on the intention to buy as compared to male customers.

Table 4. Results of age group moderation effect

Endogenous Construct		Exogenous Construct	Less than 35		More than 35		z-score
			Estimate	P Value	Estimate	P Value	
Purchase Intention	<---	Site Design	0.045	0.106	-0.003	0.919	-1.207
Purchase Intention	<---	Customer Communication	0.364	0.000	0.195	0.000	-4.02***
Purchase Intention	<---	Payment System	0.081	0.003	0.056	0.024	-0.690
Purchase Intention	<---	Transaction Security	0.123	0.000	0.350	0.000	5.1***
Purchase Intention	<---	Product Value	0.037	0.145	0.093	0.000	1.540
Purchase Intention	<---	Special Content Information	0.081	0.003	0.080	0.002	-0.038
Purchase Intention	<---	Delivery	-0.047	0.064	-0.009	0.722	1.088
Purchase Intention	<---	Shopping Convenience	-0.096	0.000	-0.058	0.021	0.996

Notes: *** p-value < 0.01; ** p-value < 0.05; * p-value < 0.10

Figure 4. Moderation effect of age less than 35 years showing the impact of website attributes on the purchase intentions.

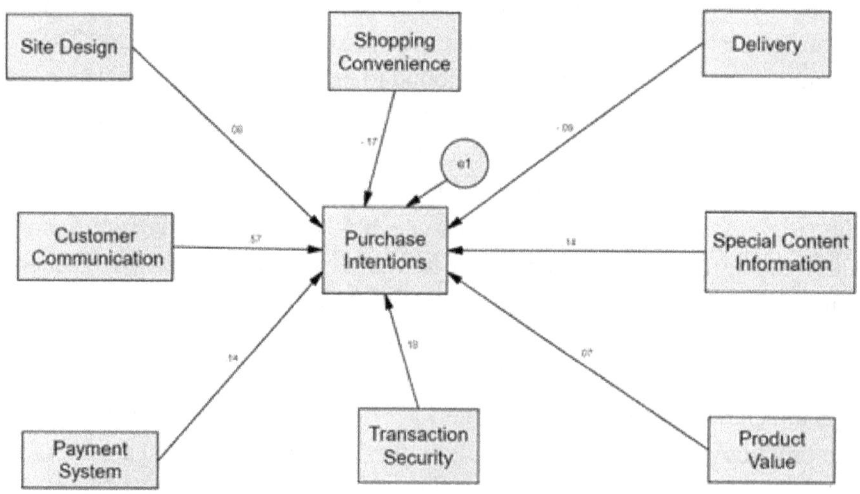

Figure 5. Moderation effect of age more than 35 years showing the impact of website attributes on the purchase intentions

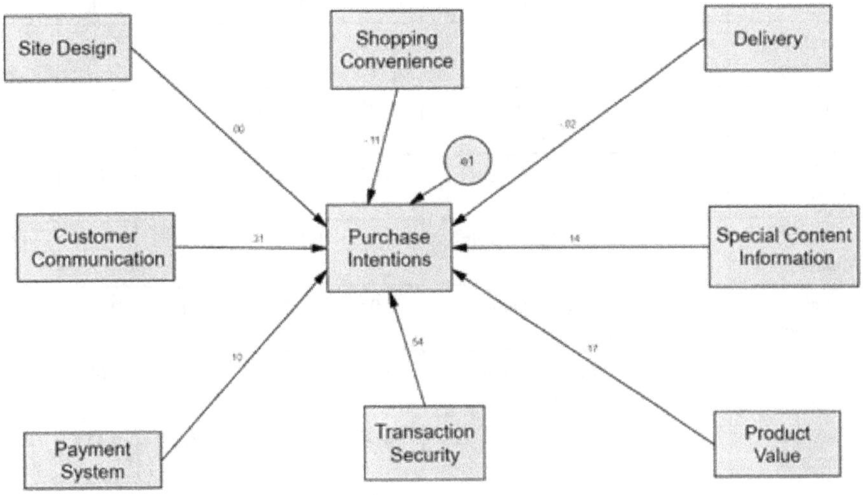

In case of cause and effect relationship from the customer communication on the intention to buy, the z score is found to be 4.02 which is also statistically significant. The results indicate that the customers with age less than 35 are found to have more positive influence of the customer communication on the intention to buy as compared to customers with age more than 35.

In case of cause and effect relationship from the transaction security on the intention to buy, the z score is found to be 5.2 which is also statistically significant. The results indicate that the customers with age more than 35 are found to have more positive influence of the transaction security on the intention to buy as compared to customers with age less than 35.

Table 5. Results of annual income moderation effect

Endogenous Construct		Exogenous Construct	Less than 5 lac		More than 5 lac		z-score
			Estimate	P Value	Estimate	P Value	
Purchase Intention	<---	Site Design	0.042	0.164	0.001	0.974	-1.012
Purchase Intention	<---	Customer Communication	0.270	0.000	0.312	0.000	0.973
Purchase Intention	<---	Payment System	0.080	0.003	0.058	0.026	-0.577
Purchase Intention	<---	Transaction Security	0.215	0.000	0.243	0.000	0.623
Purchase Intention	<---	Product Value	0.043	0.094	0.084	0.001	1.138
Purchase Intention	<---	Special Content Information	0.090	0.000	0.083	0.002	-0.177
Purchase Intention	<---	Delivery	-0.032	0.211	-0.019	0.454	0.351
Purchase Intention	<---	Shopping Convenience	-0.102	0.000	-0.056	0.037	1.214

Notes: *** p-value < 0.01; ** p-value < 0.05; * p-value <0.10

Figure 6. Moderation effect of annual income less than 5 lacs showing the impact of website attributes on the purchase intentions

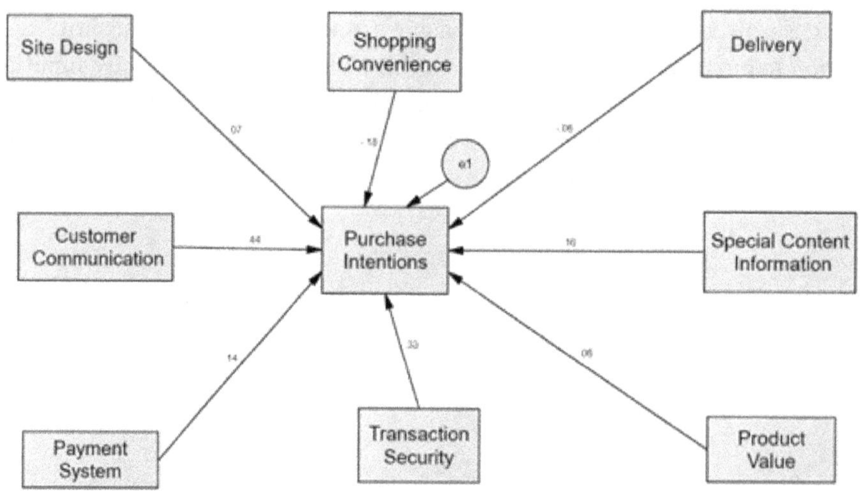

Figure 7. Moderation effect of annual income more than 5 lacs showing the impact of website attributes on the purchase intentions

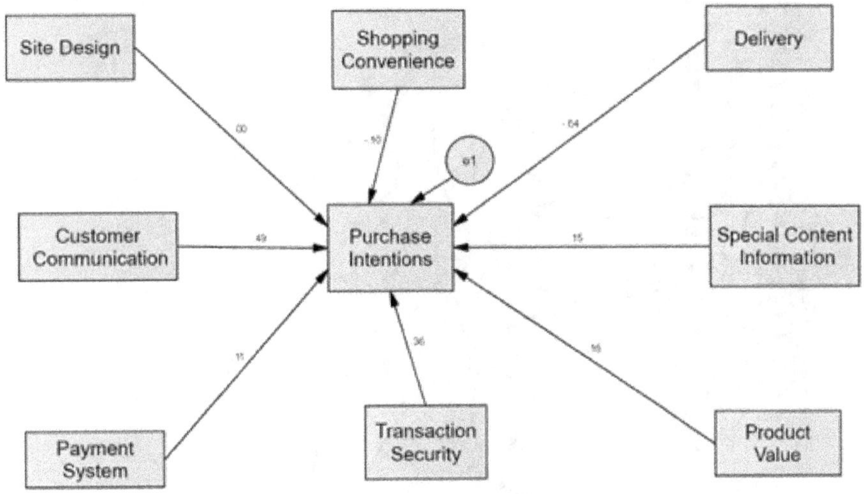

Figure 8. Confirmatory Factor Analysis

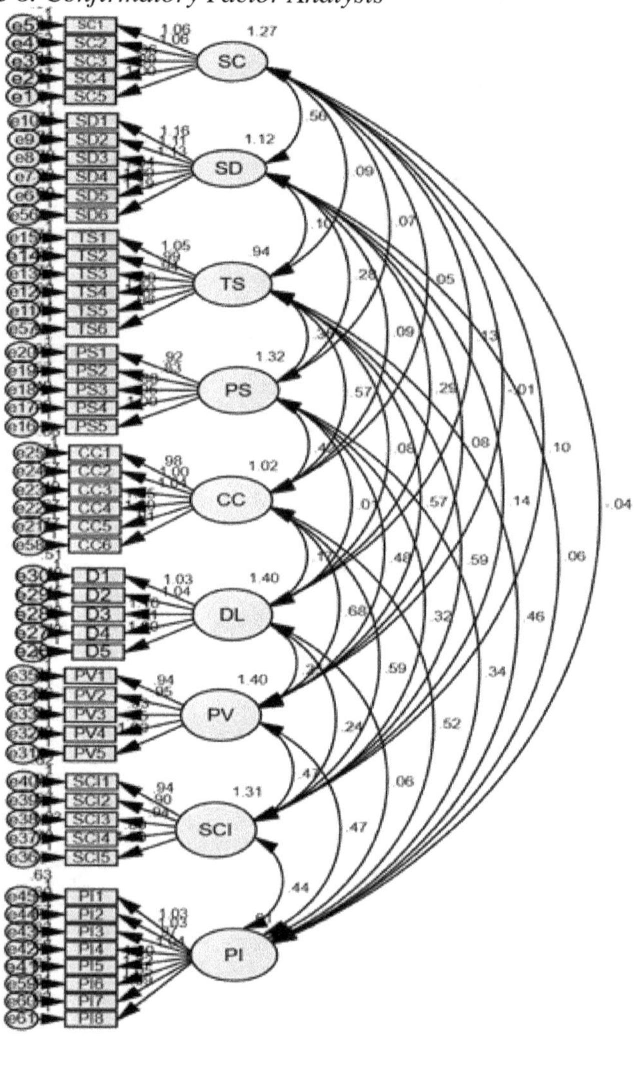

Table 6. Discriminant Validity

	CR	AVE	MSV	ASV	Shopping Convenience	Site Design	Transaction Security	Payment System	Customer Communication	Delivery	Product Value	Special Content Information	Purchase Intentions
Shopping Convenience	0.918	0.692	0.223	0.038	0.832								
Site Design	0.921	0.662	0.223	0.047	0.472	0.814							
Transaction Security	0.885	0.561	0.368	0.181	0.079	0.101	0.749						

continued on following page

Table 6. Continued

	CR	AVE	MSV	ASV	Shopping Convenience	Site Design	Transaction Security	Payment System	Customer Communication	Delivery	Product Value	Special Content Information	Purchase Intentions
Payment System	0.913	0.678	0.146	0.081	0.056	0.227	0.319	0.824					
Customer Communication	0.900	0.599	0.429	0.193	0.040	0.087	0.586	0.364	0.774				
Delivery	0.920	0.698	0.053	0.021	0.094	0.231	0.074	0.007	0.146	0.835			
Product Value	0.896	0.632	0.327	0.129	-0.006	0.066	0.499	0.352	0.572	0.175	0.795		
Special Content Information	0.885	0.607	0.285	0.147	0.075	0.120	0.532	0.246	0.514	0.176	0.351	0.779	
Purchase Intentions	0.89	0.525	0.429	0.185	-0.048	0.070	0.607	0.382	0.655	0.068	0.512	0.497	0.725

Table 7. Model fit for CFA

CMIN/DF	GFI	RMR	CFI	RMSEA
1.248	0.875	.057	0.977	.022

The results indicate that the measurement model is seems to be statistically fit.

FINDINGS OF THE STUDY

The results of this study also indicate that the gender has a significant moderating effect of attributes of website personality on consumer purchase intensions. The results indicate that the female customers are found to have more positive influence of the site design on the intention to buy as compared to male customers. In fact the male customers are mot found to be influenced by the site design. The results indicate that the female customers are found to have more positive influence of the customer communication on the intention to buy as compared to male customers. Also, females are more influenced by the product value which includes detailed description about the product as compared to their male counterparts. Consumers below the age group of 35 years are more influenced by the customer communication as compared to consumers more than 35 years of age group. Also, consumers with more than 35 years of age group are more influenced by the transaction security as compared to the group of consumers with age less than 35. The study also indicated that monthly income does not impact consumers purchase intensions.

Web interface elements are an essential tool that can lead to incredibly successful behaviours. Age, gender, and annual income are other factors that are necessary to examine as they can have a good impact on purchase intention. It is reasonable to assume that web interface features influence consumer purchase intentions, with the demographic profiles of Indian consumers acting as moderating variables. Web interface features reflect the attributes of an online shopping portal of service or product and are related to consumers' intentions to purchase.

CONCLUSION

In order to optimise sales and create favourable intentions to purchase online, the paper offers online businesses extremely valuable evidence. Through the identification of the significance of demographic parameters that function in tandem to mediate the relationship between web interface features and customer purchase intentions, the study advances our understanding of online shopping behaviour. When it comes to online shopping, consumers' perceptions of web interface features are important factors to take into account. It offers valuable insight into the key problems that clients have while utilising an online purchasing website, which is important for online shopping systems. This research provides valuable insights into the ways in which the demographic characteristics of Indian consumers influence their purchasing intentions with regard to web interface elements.

REFERENCES

Aggarwal, A., & Rahul, M. (2017). Impact of perceived usability and perceived information quality on Indian consumer purchase intentions in online shopping: Implication of TAM and SOR theory. *International Journal of Technology Transfer and Commercialisation, 15*(2), 160–183. DOI: 10.1504/IJTTC.2017.087683

Aggarwal, A., & Rahul, M. (2018). The effect of perceived security on consumer purchase intensions in electronic commerce. *International Journal of Public Sector Performance Management, 4*(1), 1–20. DOI: 10.1504/IJPSPM.2018.088691

Al Qeisi, K. I., & Al-Abdallah, G. M. (2014). Website design and usage behaviour: An application of the UTAUT model for Internet banking in UK. *International Journal of Marketing Studies, 6*(1), 75. DOI: 10.5539/ijms.v6n1p75

Al-Somali, S., Gholami, R., & Clegg, B. (2009). An investigation into the acceptance of onlinebanking in Saudi Arabia. *Technovation, 29*(2), 130–141. DOI: 10.1016/j.technovation.2008.07.004

Alreck, P., & Settle, R. B. (2002). Gender effects on Internet, catalogue and store shopping. *Journal of Database Marketing & Customer Strategy Management, 9*(2), 150–162. DOI: 10.1057/palgrave.jdm.3240071

Anand, A. (2007, May). E-satisfaction--a comprehensive framework. In *Internet and Web Applications and Services, 2007. ICIW'07. Second International Conference on* (pp. 55-55). IEEE.

Banerjee, N. (2017, January 2017), Online retail consumers to cross 100 million by 2017: ASSOCHAM-Resurgent India Retrieved from https://www.google. co .in/search?q=apa+citation+website&ie=utf-8&oe=utf-8&client=firefox-b& gfe_rd=cr&ei=J9VCWby9GI3y8AeW4JaQDw

Bauer, H. H., Falk, T., & Hammerschmidt, M. (2006). eTransQual: A transaction process-based approach for capturing service quality in online shopping. *Journal of Business Research, 59*(7), 866–875. DOI: 10.1016/j.jbusres.2006.01.021

Bellman, S., Lohse, G. L., & Johnson, E. J. (1999). Predictors of online buying behavior. *Communications of the ACM, 42*(12), 32–38. DOI: 10.1145/322796.322805

Boyer, K. K., & Hult, G. T. M. (2006). Customer behavioral intentions for online purchases: An examination of fulfillment method and customer experience level. *Journal of Operations Management, 24*(2), 124–147. DOI: 10.1016/j.jom.2005.04.002

Brucks, M., Zeithaml, V. A., & Naylor, G. (2000). Price and brand name as indicators of quality dimensions for consumer durables. *Journal of the Academy of Marketing Science*, *28*(3), 359–374. DOI: 10.1177/0092070300283005

Chau, P. Y., & Hu, P. J. (2002). Examining a model of information technology acceptance by individual professionals: An exploratory study. *Journal of Management Information Systems*, *18*(4), 191–229. DOI: 10.1080/07421222.2002.11045699

Chen, Q., Clifford, S. J., & Wells, W. D. (2002). Attitude toward the site II: New information. *Journal of Advertising Research*, *42*(2), 33–45. DOI: 10.2501/jar-42-2-33-45

Chiu, H. C., Hsieh, Y. C., & Kao, C. Y. (2005). Website personality and customer's behavioural intention: An exploratory study of the role of information asymmetry. *Total Quality Management & Business Excellence*, *16*(2), 185–197. DOI: 10.1080/14783360500054277

Cristobal, E., Flavián, C., & Guinaliu, M. (2007). Perceived e-service quality (PeSQ) Measurement validation and effects on consumer satisfaction and web site loyalty. *Managing Service Quality*, *17*(3), 317–340. DOI: 10.1108/09604520710744326

2016. Delhiites are the biggest shoppers on Flipkart, 2016 (2016, December) Retrieved from https://www.gadgetsnow.com/tech-news/2016-delhiites-are-the-biggest-shoppers-on-flipkart/articleshow/56178738.cms

Fink, D., & Nyaga, C. (2009). Evaluating web site quality: The value of a multi paradigm approach. *Benchmarking*, *16*(2), 259–273. DOI: 10.1108/14635770910948259

Grewal, D., Iyer, G. R., Krishnan, R., & Sharma, A. (2003). The Internet and the price–value–loyalty chain. *Journal of Business Research*, *56*(5), 391–398. DOI: 10.1016/S0148-2963(01)00227-2

Hausman, A. V., & Siekpe, J. S. (2009). The effect of web interface features on consumer online purchase intentions. *Journal of Business Research*, *62*(1), 5–13. DOI: 10.1016/j.jbusres.2008.01.018

Hiranrithikorn, P., & Banjongprasert, J. (2022). The effect of the website attributes on online impulse buying: An empirical investigation of utilitarian and hedonic motivations. *International Journal of Data and Network Science*, *6*(4), 1419–1426. DOI: 10.5267/j.ijdns.2022.5.009

Honeycutt, E. D.Jr, Flaherty, T. B., & Benassi, K. (1998). Marketing industrial products on the Internet. *Industrial Marketing Management*, *27*(1), 63–72. DOI: 10.1016/S0019-8501(97)00038-2

Hubona, G. S., & Kennick, E. (1996, January). The influence of external variables on information technology usage behavior. In *System Sciences, 1996.,Proceedings of the Twenty-Ninth Hawaii International Conference on,* (Vol. 4, pp. 166-175). IEEE. DOI: 10.1109/HICSS.1996.495323

Jarvenpaa, S. L., Tractinsky, N., & Saarinen, L. (1999). Consumer trust in an internet store: a cross-cultural validation. Journal of Computer-Mediated Communication, 5(2), 0-0.

Katta, R. M. R., & Patro, C. S. (2021). Influence of web attributes on consumer purchase intentions. In *Research Anthology on Strategies for Using Social Media as a Service and Tool in Business* (pp. 337–356). IGI Global. DOI: 10.4018/978-1-7998-9020-1.ch017

Kominski, R., & Newburger, E. (1999). Access denied: Changes in computer ownership and use: 1984-1997. In *Annual Meeting of American Sociological Association.*

Lian, T. P., & Lai, H. J. (2002). Effect of store design on consumer purchases: An empirical study of on-line bookstores. *Information & Management*, *39*(6), 431–444. DOI: 10.1016/S0378-7206(01)00129-X

Liu, X., He, M., Gao, F., & Xie, P. (2008). An empirical study of online shopping customer satisfaction in China: A holistic perspective. *International Journal of Retail & Distribution Management*, *36*(11), 919–940. DOI: 10.1108/09590550810911683

Longstreet, P., Brooks, S., Featherman, M., & Loiacono, E. (2022). Evaluating website quality: Which decision criteria do consumers use to evaluate website quality? *Information Technology & People*, *35*(4), 1271–1297. DOI: 10.1108/ITP-05-2020-0328

Lu, J., Yu, C. S., Liu, C., & Yao, J. (2003). Technology acceptance model for wireless internet. *Internet Research*, *13*(3), 206–222. DOI: 10.1108/10662240310478222

Miyazaki, A. D., & Fernandez, A. (2001). Consumer perceptions of privacy and security risks for online shopping. *The Journal of Consumer Affairs*, *35*(1), 27–44. DOI: 10.1111/j.1745-6606.2001.tb00101.x

Özkan, S., Bindusara, G., & Hackney, R. (2010). Facilitating the adoption of e-payment systems: Theoretical constructs and empirical analysis. *Journal of Enterprise Information Management*, *23*(3), 305–325. DOI: 10.1108/17410391011036085

Park, C. H., & Kim, Y. G. (2003). Identifying key factors affecting consumer purchase behavior in an online shopping context. *International Journal of Retail & Distribution Management*, *31*(1), 16–29. DOI: 10.1108/09590550310457818

Poddar, A., Donthu, N., & Wei, Y. (2009). Web site customer orientations, Web site quality, and purchase intentions: The role of Web site personality. *Journal of Business Research*, *62*(4), 441–450. DOI: 10.1016/j.jbusres.2008.01.036

Raijas, A., & Tuunainen, V. K. (2001). Critical factors in electronic grocery shopping. *International Review of Retail, Distribution and Consumer Research, 11*(3), 255–265. DOI: 10.1080/713770596

Ranganathan, C., & Ganapathy, S. (2002). Key dimensions of business-to-consumer web sites. *Information & Management, 39*(6), 457–465. DOI: 10.1016/S0378-7206(01)00112-4

Schaupp, L. C., & Belanger, F. (2005). A conjoint analysis of online consumer satisfaction. *Journal of Electronic Commerce Research*, *6*(2), 95–111.

Serenko, A., Turel, O., & Yol, S. (2006). Moderating roles of user demographics in the American customer satisfaction model within the context of mobile services. *Journal of Information Technology Management, 17*(4), 20–32.

Shin, J. I., Chung, K. H., Oh, J. S., & Lee, C. W. (2013). The effect of site quality on repurchase intention in Internet shopping through mediating variables: The case of university students in South Korea. *International Journal of Information Management, 33*(3), 453–463. DOI: 10.1016/j.ijinfomgt.2013.02.003

Srinivasan, S. S., Anderson, R., & Ponnavolu, K. (2002). Customer loyalty in e-commerce: An exploration of its antecedents and consequences. *Journal of Retailing*, *78*(1), 41–50. DOI: 10.1016/S0022-4359(01)00065-3

Swaminathan, V., Lepkowska-White, E., & Rao, B. P. (1999). Browsers or buyers in cyberspace? An investigation of factors influencing electronic exchange. *Journal of Computer-Mediated Communication, 5*(2), 0-0.

Szymanski, D., & Hise, R. T. (2000). Hise R. E-satisfaction: An initial examination. *Journal of Retailing*, *76*(3), 309–322. DOI: 10.1016/S0022-4359(00)00035-X

Trocchia, P. J., & Janda, S. (2000). A phenomenological investigation of Internet usage among older individuals. *Journal of Consumer Marketing*, *17*(7), 605–616. DOI: 10.1108/07363760010357804

Turban, E., King, D., Lee, J., & Viehland, D. (2002). Electronic commerce: A managerial perspective. *Prentice Hall: ISBN 0, 13*(975285), 4.

Turban, E., King, D., Lee, J. K., & Viehland, D. (2006). *Electronic commerce: A managerial perspective*. Prentice Hall.

Yoo, B., & Donthu, N. (2001). Developing a scale to measure the perceived quality of an Internet shopping site (SITEQUAL). *Quarterly journal of electronic commerce, 2*(1), 31-45.

Yoon, S. J. (2002). The antecedents and consequences of trust in online-purchase decisions. *Journal of Interactive Marketing, 16*(2), 47–63. DOI: 10.1002/dir.10008

APPENDIX

Table 8.

	Shopping Convenience (Shin et al., 2013)	Strongly Disagree 1 2 3 4 5 6 7 8 9 Strongly Agree
1	This website is incredibly easy to use.	1 2 3 4 5 6 7 8 9
2	Shopping on this website doesn't take much time.	1 2 3 4 5 6 7 8 9
3	This website provides simple ordering methods.	1 2 3 4 5 6 7 8 9
4	A novice customer doesn't need much assistance to make a purchase from this website.	1 2 3 4 5 6 7 8 9
5	I have no trouble navigating this website.	1 2 3 4 5 6 7 8 9

Table 9.

	Site design (Shin et al., 2013)	Strongly Disagree 1 2 3 4 5 6 7 8 9 Strongly Agree
6	The website has a pleasing aesthetic.	1 2 3 4 5 6 7 8 9
7	There is a good selection on this website.	1 2 3 4 5 6 7 8 9
8	The website has an expert appearance.	1 2 3 4 5 6 7 8 9
9	Using this website, completing a transaction is quick and simple.	1 2 3 4 5 6 7 8 9
10	It's simple to navigate this website.	1 2 3 4 5 6 7 8 9
11	This website offers a quick and precise search feature for many products and their subcategories.	1 2 3 4 5 6 7 8 9

Table 10.

	Transaction security (Shin.et al., 2013)	Strongly Disagree 1 2 3 4 5 6 7 8 9 Strongly Agree
17	This website protects client credit card information.	1 2 3 4 5 6 7 8 9
18	This website protects private purchasing data.	1 2 3 4 5 6 7 8 9
19	This website never gives out a customer's email address to any parties.	1 2 3 4 5 6 7 8 9

continued on following page

Table 10. Continued

	Transaction security (Shin.et al., 2013)	Strongly Disagree 1 2 3 4 5 6 7 8 9 Strongly Agree
20	This website does not misuse user data in any way.	1 2 3 4 5 6 7 8 9
21	The retailer's website is reliable overall.	1 2 3 4 5 6 7 8 9
22	My interactions with the retailer's website feel secure.	1 2 3 4 5 6 7 8 9

Table 11.

	Payment system (Shin et al., 2013)	Strongly Disagree 1 2 3 4 5 6 7 8 9 Strongly Agree
23	The site's payment process is straightforward.	1 2 3 4 5 6 7 8 9
24	Order identification is easy to understand and practical.	1 2 3 4 5 6 7 8 9
25	I have faith in this website's payment mechanism.	1 2 3 4 5 6 7 8 9
26	This website frequently makes excessive payment claims.	1 2 3 4 5 6 7 8 9
27	The payment procedure's instructions are quite clear.	1 2 3 4 5 6 7 8 9

Table 12.

	Customer Communication (Kim et al., 2009; Shin et al., 2013)	Strongly Disagree 1 2 3 4 5 6 7 8 9 Strongly Agree
28	Customers are able to comment on ideas or complaints on this website.	1 2 3 4 5 6 7 8 9
29	This website has a helpful FAQ section.	1 2 3 4 5 6 7 8 9
30	Users on this website can actively review products.	1 2 3 4 5 6 7 8 9
31	Customers can freely share their comments on this website.	1 2 3 4 5 6 7 8 9
32	I'll keep using (Internet provider) for all of my online needs.	1 2 3 4 5 6 7 8 9
33	When I'm ready to buy something, I like to use the internet store.	1 2 3 4 5 6 7 8 9

Table 13.

	Delivery (Chen et al., 2010)	Strongly Disagree 1 2 3 4 5 6 7 8 9 Strongly Agree
34	Delivery within the specified time frame is guaranteed by the website.	1 2 3 4 5 6 7 8 9
35	Users are informed about likely delays by the website.	1 2 3 4 5 6 7 8 9
36	Users are informed of shipping delays by the website.	1 2 3 4 5 6 7 8 9
37	To allay clients' fears, the website provides tools for tracking shipments.	1 2 3 4 5 6 7 8 9
38	Product pickup at the petrol station in the neighbourhood	1 2 3 4 5 6 7 8 9

Table 14.

	Product Value (Chen et al., 2010)	Strongly Disagree 1 2 3 4 5 6 7 8 9 Strongly Agree
39	Products on the website have features that live up to client expectations.	1 2 3 4 5 6 7 8 9
40	The website provides a thorough description of each product.	1 2 3 4 5 6 7 8 9
41	The prices of the things on the website are fair.	1 2 3 4 5 6 7 8 9
42	There are many different things available on the website.	1 2 3 4 5 6 7 8 9
43	This website's products are easily comparable to one another.	1 2 3 4 5 6 7 8 9

Table 15.

	Special Content Information (Al-Qeisi et al., 2014; Shin et al., 2013)	Strongly Disagree 1 2 3 4 5 6 7 8 9 Strongly Agree
44	Contact details (such as email addresses and customer support lines) are available on the website.	1 2 3 4 5 6 7 8 9
45	The website offers information about their goods and services (clearly stated terms and conditions).	1 2 3 4 5 6 7 8 9
46	The website offers specifics about customer policies, such as privacy and dispute information.	1 2 3 4 5 6 7 8 9

	Special Content Information (Al-Qeisi et al., 2014; Shin et al., 2013)	Strongly Disagree 1 2 3 4 5 6 7 8 9 Strongly Agree
47	The website offers customer service-related information.	1 2 3 4 5 6 7 8 9
48	The website offers details about exchange and refund policies.	1 2 3 4 5 6 7 8 9

Table 16.

	Purchase Intentions (Hausman, 2011; Shin et al., 2013)	Strongly Disagree 1 2 3 4 5 6 7 8 9 Strongly Agree
62	I plan to keep making purchases from this online store in the future.	1 2 3 4 5 6 7 8 9
63	I'll tell my friends and family about this online store.	1 2 3 4 5 6 7 8 9
64	For my online services, I'll keep using (Internet provider).	1 2 3 4 5 6 7 8 9
65	I would like to use the online store if there is a product I wish to buy.	1 2 3 4 5 6 7 8 9
66	I'm encouraged to come back to this location soon.	1 2 3 4 5 6 7 8 9
67	I'm going to buy something from this website quite soon.	1 2 3 4 5 6 7 8 9
68	I plan to make a purchase soon using this website.	1 2 3 4 5 6 7 8 9
69	I will most certainly purchase goods from this website in the near future.	1 2 3 4 5 6 7 8 9

Compilation of References

Abou-Shouk, M., & Soliman, M. (2021). The impact of gamification adoption intention on brand awareness and loyalty in tourism: The mediating effect of customer engagement. *Journal of Destination Marketing & Management*, *20*, 100559. DOI: 10.1016/j.jdmm.2021.100559

Abou-Shouk, M., & Soliman, M. (2021). The impact of gamification adoption intention on brand awareness and loyalty in tourism: The mediating effect of customer engagement. *Tourism and Hospitality Research*, *21*(3), 261–276. DOI: 10.1177/1467358420988048

Abrar, K. (2018). Impact of augmented reality on consumer purchase intention with the mediating role of customer brand engagement: Moderating role of interactivity in online shopping. Bahria University. *Journal of Management & Technology*, *1*(2), 64–80.

Acquisti, A., Brandimarte, L., & Loewenstein, G. (2015). Privacy and Human Behavior in the Age of Information. *Science*, *347*(6221), 509–514. DOI: 10.1126/science.aaa1465 PMID: 25635091

Adams, M. (2017). Big Data and Individual Privacy in the Age of the Internet of Things. *Technology Innovation Management Review*, *7*(4), 12–24. DOI: 10.22215/timreview/1067

Afacan, N. M. (2023). Gamification in metaverse. In *Metaverse: technologies, opportunities and threats* (pp. 187–202). Springer Nature Singapore. DOI: 10.1007/978-981-99-4641-9_13

Agarwal, R., Badghish, S., Yaqub, M. Z., & Pandey, R. (2025). Customer engagement through metaverse-empowered retail channels: Role of personalization. *International Journal of Retail & Distribution Management*, *53*(6), 467–484. DOI: 10.1108/IJRDM-07-2024-0344

Agenda, I. (2015). *"Industrial internet of things: unleashing the potential of connected products and services," 34*. Collaboration with Accenture.

Aggarwal, A., & Rahul, M. (2017). Impact of perceived usability and perceived information quality on Indian consumer purchase intentions in online shopping: Implication of TAM and SOR theory. *International Journal of Technology Transfer and Commercialisation*, *15*(2), 160–183. DOI: 10.1504/IJTTC.2017.087683

Aggarwal, A., & Rahul, M. (2018). The effect of perceived security on consumer purchase intensions in electronic commerce. *International Journal of Public Sector Performance Management*, *4*(1), 1–20. DOI: 10.1504/IJPSPM.2018.088691

Aghdaie, S. F. A., Ansari, A., & Telgerdi, J. (2022). Analysing the impact of gamification dynamics and e-WOM on impulsive buying. *International Journal of Procurement Management*, *15*(1), 40–61. DOI: 10.1504/IJPM.2022.119840

Aguirre Velasco, A., Cruz, I. S. S., Billings, J., Jimenez, M., & Rowe, S. (2020). What are the barriers, facilitators and interventions targeting help-seeking behaviours for common mental health problems in adolescents? A systematic review. *BMC Psychiatry*, *20*(1), 293. DOI: 10.1186/s12888-020-02659-0 PMID: 32527236

Aiolfi, S., & Luceri, B. (2024). See you on the Metaverse: A bibliometric expedition through the Metaverse landscape. *Technological Forecasting and Social Change*, *207*, 123605. DOI: 10.1016/j.techfore.2024.123605

Aksoy, L., Keiningham, T. L., Buoye, A., Lariviere, B., Williams, L., & Wilson, I. (2015). Does loyalty span domains? Examining the relationship between consumer loyalty, other loyalties and happiness. *Journal of Business Research*, *68*(12), 2464–2476. DOI: 10.1016/j.jbusres.2015.06.033

Al Omari, O., Al Sabei, S., Al Rawajfah, O., Abu Sharour, L., Aljohani, K., Alomari, K., Shkman, L., Al Dameery, K., Saifan, A., Al Zubidi, B., Anwar, S., & Alhalaiqa, F. (2020). Prevalence and Predictors of Depression, Anxiety, and Stress among Youth at the Time of COVID-19: An Online Cross-Sectional Multicountry Study. *Depression Research and Treatment*, *8887727*, 1–9. Advance online publication. DOI: 10.1155/2020/8887727 PMID: 33062331

Al Qeisi, K. I., & Al-Abdallah, G. M. (2014). Website design and usage behaviour: An application of the UTAUT model for Internet banking in UK. *International Journal of Marketing Studies*, *6*(1), 75. DOI: 10.5539/ijms.v6n1p75

Al-Adwan, A. S., Yaseen, H., Alkhwaldi, A. F., Jafar, R. M. S., Fauzi, M. A., & Abdullah, A. (2025). Treasure hunting for brands: Metaverse marketing gamification effects on purchase intention, WOM, and loyalty. *Journal of Global Marketing*, •••, 1–25. DOI: 10.1080/08911762.2025.2463897

Algashami, A. (2019). Gamification risks in collaborative information systems: identification and management method (Doctoral dissertation, Bournemouth University).

Algashami, A., Vuillier, L., Alrobai, A., Phalp, K., & Ali, R. (2019). Gamification risks to enterprise teamwork: Taxonomy, management strategies and modalities of application. *Systems*, *7*(1), 9. DOI: 10.3390/systems7010009

Algharabat, R., Rana, N. P., Alalwan, A. A., Baabdullah, A., & Gupta, A. (2020). Investigating the antecedents of customer brand engagement and consumer-based brand equity in social media. *Journal of Retailing and Consumer Services*, *53*, 101767. DOI: 10.1016/j.jretconser.2019.01.016

Aljuhmani, H. Y., Elrehail, H., Bayram, P., & Samarah, T. (2022). Linking social media marketing efforts with customer brand engagement in driving brand loyalty. *Asia Pacific Journal of Marketing and Logistics*, *35*(7), 1719–1738. DOI: 10.1108/APJML-08-2021-0627

Al-Msallam, S., Xi, N., & Hamari, J. (2023). Ethical considerations in gamified interactive marketing praxis. In *The Palgrave Handbook of Interactive Marketing* (pp. 963–985). Springer International Publishing. DOI: 10.1007/978-3-031-14961-0_41

Alqahtani, F., Al Khalifah, G., Oyebode, O., & Orji, R. (2019). Apps for Mental Health: An Evaluation of Behavior Change Strategies and Recommendations for Future Development. *Frontiers in Artificial Intelligence*, *2*, 30. Advance online publication. DOI: 10.3389/frai.2019.00030 PMID: 33733119

Alreck, P., & Settle, R. B. (2002). Gender effects on Internet, catalogue and store shopping. *Journal of Database Marketing & Customer Strategy Management*, *9*(2), 150–162. DOI: 10.1057/palgrave.jdm.3240071

Al-Somali, S., Gholami, R., & Clegg, B. (2009). An investigation into the acceptance of onlinebanking in Saudi Arabia. *Technovation*, *29*(2), 130–141. DOI: 10.1016/j.technovation.2008.07.004

Al-Zyoud, M. F. (2021). The impact of gamification on consumer loyalty, electronic word-of mouth sharing and purchase behavior. *Journal of Public Affairs*, *21*(3), e2263. DOI: 10.1002/pa.2263

Anand, A. (2007, May). E-satisfaction--a comprehensive framework. In *Internet and Web Applications and Services, 2007. ICIW'07. Second International Conference on* (pp. 55-55). IEEE.

Anixter, K., & Kohn, D. (2022). Incentive-based waste management and recycling systems: A review. *Waste Management (New York, N.Y.), 147*, 293–317. DOI: 10.1016/j.wasman.2022.04.027

Antonaci, A., Klemke, R., & Specht, M. (2019, August). The effects of gamification in online learning environments: A systematic literature review. In Informatics (Vol. 6, No. 3, p. 32). MDPI. DOI: 10.3390/informatics6030032

Arensman, E., Scott, V., De Leo, D., & Pirkis, J. (2020). Suicide and Suicide Prevention From a Global Perspective. *Crisis, 41*(Suppl 1), S3–S7. DOI: 10.1027/0227-5910/a000664 PMID: 32208759

Arora, C., & Razavian, M. (2021). Ethics of gamification in health and fitness-tracking. *International Journal of Environmental Research and Public Health, 18*(21), 11052. DOI: 10.3390/ijerph182111052 PMID: 34769570

Arora, S., & Agarwal, R. (2022). Plastic pollution: A review of challenges, policies, and strategies for managing plastic waste in India. *Journal of Environmental Management, 319*, 115740. DOI: 10.1016/j.jenvman.2022.115740

Arumugam, S. K., & Tyagi, A. K. (2023). Gamification for Industry 5.0 at the Core of Society 5.0. In *Concepts, Technologies, Challenges, and the Future of Web 3* (pp. 307–336). IGI Global. DOI: 10.4018/978-1-6684-9919-1.ch016

Arya, V., Sambyal, R., Sharma, A., & Dwivedi, Y. K. (2024). Brands are calling your AVATAR in Metaverse–A study to explore XR-based gamification marketing activities & consumer-based brand equity in virtual world. *Journal of Consumer Behaviour, 23*(2), 556–585. DOI: 10.1002/cb.2214

Aydin, O., Karaarslan, E., & Narin, N. G. (2024). Artificial intelligence, vr, ar and metaverse technologies for human resources management. *arXiv preprint arXiv:2406.15383*.

Baek, T. H., Yoon, S., & Kim, S. (2015). When environmental messages should be assertive: Examining the moderating role of effort investment. *International Journal of Advertising, 34*(1), 135–157. DOI: 10.1080/02650487.2014.993513

Baikins, P. (2025, March 27). *The State of Marketing Gamification: Challenges and opportunities*. GAMIFICATION+. https://gamificationplus.uk/the-state-of-marketing-gamification-challenges-and-opportunities/

Baldwin, C., & Baldwin, C. (2024, December 27). *Gamification in marketing*. Insider. https://useinsider.com/gamification-in-marketing/

Banerjee, N. (2017, January 2017), Online retail consumers to cross 100 million by 2017: ASSOCHAM-Resurgent India Retrieved from https://www.google. co .in/search?q=apa+citation+website&ie=utf-8&oe=utf-8&client=firefox-b& gfe_rd=cr&ei=J9VCWby9GI3y8AeW4JaQDw

Bartle, R. A. (2004). Designing virtual worlds. New riders, bell, M. W. (2008). Toward a definition of. *Journal of Virtual Worlds Research, 1*(1).

Bathla, D., & Ahuja, R. (2024). Leveraging Big Data Analytics for Customer Experience Excellence in Metaverse. In *Entrepreneurship and Creativity in the Metaverse* (pp. 128–142). IGI Global. DOI: 10.4018/979-8-3693-1734-1.ch010

Bauer, H. H., Falk, T., & Hammerschmidt, M. (2006). eTransQual: A transaction process-based approach for capturing service quality in online shopping. *Journal of Business Research, 59*(7), 866–875. DOI: 10.1016/j.jbusres.2006.01.021

Bell, I. H., Nicholas, J., Alvarez-Jimenez, M., Thompson, A., & Valmaggia, L. (2020). Virtual reality as a clinical tool in mental health research and practice. *Dialogues in Clinical Neuroscience, 22*(2), 169–177. DOI: 10.31887/DCNS.2020.22.2/lvalmaggia PMID: 32699517

Bellman, S., Lohse, G. L., & Johnson, E. J. (1999). Predictors of online buying behavior. *Communications of the ACM, 42*(12), 32–38. DOI: 10.1145/322796.322805

Benjamin, G. (2019). Playing at control: Writing surveillance in/for gamified society. *Surveillance & Society, 17*(5), 699–713. DOI: 10.24908/ss.v17i5.13204

Berger, A., Schlager, T., Sprott, D. E., & Herrmann, A. (2017). Gamified interactions: Whether, when, and how games facilitate self–brand connections. *Journal of the Academy of Marketing Science, 46*(4), 652–673. DOI: 10.1007/s11747-017-0530-0

Berggren, N., and Iselid, F. (2023). Unlocking the fashion Metaverse: exploring the impact of external factors on innovation diffusion in the Metaverse fashion industry.

Bharadwaj, A., Yadav, D., & Varshney, S. (2017). Non-hazardous solid waste management in Indian cities – A review. *Management of Environmental Quality, 28*(2), 163–178. DOI: 10.1108/MEQ-06-2015-0119

Bilgihan, A., Leong, A. M. W., Okumus, F., & Bai, J. (2024). Proposing a metaverse engagement model for brand development. *Journal of Retailing and Consumer Services, 78*, 103781. DOI: 10.1016/j.jretconser.2024.103781

Bitrián, P., Buil, I., & Catalán, S. (2020). Gamification in sport apps: The determinants of users' motivation. *European Journal of Management and Business Economics, 29*(3), 365–381. DOI: 10.1108/EJMBE-09-2019-0163

Bitrián, P., Buil, I., & Catalán, S. (2021). Enhancing user engagement: The role of gamification in mobile apps. *Journal of Business Research, 132*, 170–185. DOI: 10.1016/j.jbusres.2021.04.028

Bogoslov, I. A., Stoica, E. A., Georgescu, M. R., & Lungu, A. E. (2023). Gamification In E-Commerce: Advantages, Challenges, And Future Trends. *Revista Economica (Sibiu), 75*(2), 17–33. DOI: 10.56043/reveco-2023-0012

Bousba, Y., & Arya, V. (2022). Let's connect in metaverse. Brand's new destination to increase consumers' affective brand engagement & their satisfaction and advocacy. Journal of Content. *Community & Communication, 15*(8), 276–293.

Boyer, K. K., & Hult, G. T. M. (2006). Customer behavioral intentions for online purchases: An examination of fulfillment method and customer experience level. *Journal of Operations Management, 24*(2), 124–147. DOI: 10.1016/j.jom.2005.04.002

Braun, V., & Clarke, V. (2006). Using thematic analysis in psychology. *Qualitative Research in Psychology, 3*(2), 77–101. DOI: 10.1191/1478088706qp063oa

Brodie, R. J., Hollebeek, L., Juric, B., & Ilic, A. (2011). Customer engagement: Conceptual domain, fundamental propositions, and implications for research. *Journal of Service Research, 17*(3), 1–20. DOI: 10.1177/1094670511411703

Brucks, M., Zeithaml, V. A., & Naylor, G. (2000). Price and brand name as indicators of quality dimensions for consumer durables. *Journal of the Academy of Marketing Science, 28*(3), 359–374. DOI: 10.1177/0092070300283005

Buhalis, D., Leung, D., & Lin, M. (2023). Metaverse as a disruptive technology revolutionising tourism management and marketing. *Tourism Management, 97*, 104724. DOI: 10.1016/j.tourman.2023.104724

Bullock, M. (2024, November 21). *Why Gamification is Important & Its Benefits*. Spinify. https://spinify.com/blog/why-gamification-is-important/

Bunchball, I. (2010). Gamification 101: An introduction to the use of game dynamics to influence behavior. *White paper, 9*, 1-18.

Burke, Brian. "Gamify: How Gamification motivates people to do extraordinary things. Bibliomotion." *Inc., Apr* (2014).

Burnett, S. (2019),"Is it time to add gamification to your loyalty strategy? Forbes", available at: https://www.forbes.com/councils/forbesagencycouncil/2019/01/22/is-it-time-to-add-gamification-to-your-loyalty-strategy/ (accessed 28 March 2025).

Burns, J. M., Davenport, T. A., Durkin, L. A., Luscombe, G. M., & Hickie, I. B. (2010). The internet as a setting for mental health service utilisation by young people. *The Medical Journal of Australia*, *192*(11). Advance online publication. https://www.mja.com.au/journal/2010/192/11/internet-setting-mental-health-service-utilisation-young-people. DOI: 10.5694/j.1326-5377.2010.tb03688.x PMID: 20528703

Business Today. (2023). *IPL franchise investments create 1.8M viewership milestone for BGMI Masters Series*. https://www.businesstoday.in/

Cali, U., Ferdous, M. S., Karaarslan, E., Gourisetti, S. N. G., & Mylrea, M. (2022a). "SSI meets Metaverse for industry 4.0 and beyond," in Paper presented at the 2022 IEEE 1st global emerging technology blockchain Forum: blockchain and beyond (iGETblockchain). 1–6. DOI: 10.1109/iGETblockchain56591.2022.10087134

Cali, U., Kuzlu, M., Karaarslan, E., & Jovanovic, V. (2022b). "Opportunities and challenges in Metaverse for industry 4.0 and beyond applications," in Paper presented at the 2022 IEEE 1st global emerging technology blockchain Forum: blockchain and beyond (iGETblockchain), 1–6. DOI: 10.1109/iGETblockchain56591.2022.10087104

Castronova, E. (2008). *Synthetic worlds: the business and culture of online games*. University of Chicago press.

Central Pollution Control Board (CPCB). (2019). Annual report for the year 2018-19 on implementation of Plastic Waste Management Rules. https://cpcb.nic.in/uploads/plasticwaste/Annual_Report_2018-19_PWM.pdf

Chakraborty, U., & Biswal, S. K. (2024). Diffusion of Innovation in Direct-to-Avatar (D2A): A Study of Immersive Communication and Branding in the Metaverse. *Computers in Human Behavior*, *158*, 108318. DOI: 10.1016/j.chb.2024.108318

Chan, A., Kow, R., & Cheng, J. (2017). Adolescents' Perceptions on Smartphone Applications (Apps) for Health Management. *Journal of Mobile Technology in Medicine*, *6*(2), 47–55. DOI: 10.7309/jmtm.6.2.6

Cha, S. S., Kim, C. Y., & Tang, Y. (2024). Gamification in the Metaverse: Affordance, perceived value, flow state, and engagement. *International Journal of Tourism Research*, *26*(2), e2635. DOI: 10.1002/jtr.2635

Chaturvedi, A., Arora, R., & Ahmed, S. (2021). Challenges in municipal solid waste management: A case study of Delhi. *Waste Disposal & Sustainable Energy*, *3*(2), 123–136. DOI: 10.1007/s42768-021-00063-6

Chaudhuri, A., & Holbrook, M. B. (2001). The Role of Brand Loyalty / 81 The Chain of Effects from Brand Trust and Brand Affect to Brand Performance: The Role of Brand Loyalty. In *Journal of Marketing* (Vol. 65).

Chau, P. Y., & Hu, P. J. (2002). Examining a model of information technology acceptance by individual professionals: An exploratory study. *Journal of Management Information Systems, 18*(4), 191–229. DOI: 10.1080/07421222.2002.11045699

Chen, Q., Clifford, S. J., & Wells, W. D. (2002). Attitude toward the site II: New information. *Journal of Advertising Research, 42*(2), 33–45. DOI: 10.2501/jar-42-2-33-45

Chen, S. S., & Zhang, J. J. (2024). Market demand for metaverse-based sporting events: A mixed-methods approach. *Sport Management Review*, •••, 1–27. DOI: 10.1080/14413523.2024.2401640

Cheung, M. L., Pires, G. D., Rosenberger, P. J., Leung, W. K., & Sharipudin, M. N. S. (2021). The role of consumer-consumer interaction and consumer-brand interaction in driving consumer-brand engagement and behavioral intentions. *Journal of Retailing and Consumer Services, 61*, 102574. DOI: 10.1016/j.jretconser.2021.102574

Chien, W. J., & Wu, Y. L. (2015). The Effect of Mobile Gamification on Brand Loyalty.

Chin, W. W., Marcolin, B. L., & Newsted, P. R. (2003). A Partial Least Squares Latent Variable Modeling Approach for Measuring Interaction Effects: Results from a Monte Carlo Simulation Study and an Electronic-Mail Emotion/Adoption Study. *Information Systems Research, 14*(2), 189–217. Advance online publication. DOI: 10.1287/isre.14.2.189.16018

Chiu, H. C., Hsieh, Y. C., & Kao, C. Y. (2005). Website personality and customer's behavioural intention: An exploratory study of the role of information asymmetry. *Total Quality Management & Business Excellence, 16*(2), 185–197. DOI: 10.1080/14783360500054277

Chu, S. C., & Seock, Y. K. (2020). The power of social media in fashion advertising. *Journal of Interactive Advertising, 20*(2), 93–94. DOI: 10.1080/15252019.2020.1802955

Cristobal, E., Flavián, C., & Guinaliu, M. (2007). Perceived e-service quality (PeSQ) Measurement validation and effects on consumer satisfaction and web site loyalty. *Managing Service Quality, 17*(3), 317–340. DOI: 10.1108/09604520710744326

Cugelman, B. (2013). Gamification: What It Is and Why It Matters to Digital Health Behavior Change Developers. *JMIR Serious Games*, *1*(1), e3139. DOI: 10.2196/games.3139 PMID: 25658754

Damaševičius, R., Maskeliūnas, R., & Blažauskas, T. (2023). Serious Games and Gamification in Healthcare: A Meta-Review. *Information (Basel)*, *14*(2), 2. Advance online publication. DOI: 10.3390/info14020105

Damaševičius, R., & Sidekersniene, T. 2023, September. Designing immersive gamified experiences in the metaverse for enhanced student learning. In *2023 International Conference on Intelligent Metaverse Technologies & Applications (iMETA)* (pp. 1-6). IEEE.

Das, L., Poornachandrika, T. S., & Bhargava, D. (2024). Ethical Dilemmas in Gamified Marketing Approaches. In Marketing and Gamification (pp. 222-245). Routledge. DOI: 10.4324/9781032694238-16

Daşdemir, Y. (2022). A brain-computer interface with gamification in the Metaverse. *Dicle Üniversitesi Mühendislik Fakültesi Mühendislik Dergisi*, *13*(4), 645–652.

Das, T., Ganesh Kondamudi, S., Dawood Babakerkhell, M., Pal, D., Roy, R., & Funilkul, S. (2024). Intention for enhancing metaverse-based learning using gamification among university students: A study using Delphi and structural equation modelling approaches. *Cogent Business & Management*, *11*(1), 2380016. DOI: 10.1080/23311975.2024.2380016

Dastane, O., Rafiq, M., & Turner, J. J. (2024). Implications of metaverse, virtual reality, and extended reality for development and learning in organizations. *Development and Learning in Organizations*, *38*(5), 27–32. DOI: 10.1108/DLO-09-2023-0196

De Canio, F., Fuentes-Blasco, M., & Martinelli, E. (2021). Engaging shoppers through mobile apps: The role of gamification. *International Journal of Retail & Distribution Management*, *49*(7), 919–940. DOI: 10.1108/IJRDM-09-2020-0360

De Giovanni, P. (2023). Sustainability of the Metaverse: A transition to industry 5.0. *Sustainability (Basel)*, *15*(7), 6079. DOI: 10.3390/su15076079

Deci, E. L., & Ryan, R. M. (2000). The" what" and" why" of goal pursuits: Human needs and the self-determination of behavior. *Psychological Inquiry*, *11*(4), 227–268. DOI: 10.1207/S15327965PLI1104_01

Delgado, C. B. (2022). User experience (UX) in Metaverse: Realities and challenges. *Metaverse Basic Appl. Res.*, *1*, 9. DOI: 10.56294/mr20229

Delmerico, J., Poranne, R., Bogo, F., Oleynikova, H., Vollenweider, E., Coros, S., Nieto, J., & Pollefeys, M. (2022). Spatial computing and intuitive interaction: Bringing mixed reality and robotics together. *IEEE Robotics & Automation Magazine, 29*(1), 45–57. DOI: 10.1109/MRA.2021.3138384

Deloitte. (2023). *Gaming: The next level.* Deloitte Insights. https://www2.deloitte.com/

Deterding, S., Sicart, M., Nacke, L., O'hara, K., & Dixon, D. (2011). Gamification. using game-design elements in non-gaming contexts. In *CHI'11 extended abstracts on human factors in computing systems* (pp. 2425-2428).

Deterding, S., Dixon, D., Khaled, R., & Nacke, L. (2011, September). From game design elements to gamefulness: defining" gamification". In *Proceedings of the 15th international academic MindTrek conference: Envisioning future media environments* (pp. 9-15). DOI: 10.1145/2181037.2181040

Digra Conference. (2024). *Digital playgrounds and cognitive development: Implications for India's edutainment strategies* [Conference preprint]. *Digital Games Research Association.* https://www.digra.org/

Dinev, T., & Hart, P. (2004). Internet privacy concerns and their antecedents - measurement validity and a regression model. *Behaviour & Information Technology, 23*(6), 413–422. Advance online publication. DOI: 10.1080/01449290410001715723

Doğan-Südaş, H., Kara, A., & Karaca, E. (2023). Effects of gamified mobile apps on purchase intentions and word-of-mouth engagement: Implications for sustainability behavior. *Sustainability (Basel), 15*(13), 10506. DOI: 10.3390/su151310506

Dos Remedios, L., 2023. The influence of the Metaverse on Brand Management: A study. *communities, 2*(2), p.5.

Dutta, D., Srivastava, Y., & Singh, E. (2023). Metaverse in the tourism sector for talent management: A technology in practice lens. *Information Technology & Tourism, 25*(3), 331–365. DOI: 10.1007/s40558-023-00258-9

Dwivedi, Y., Hughes, L., Wang, Y., Alalwan, A. A., Ahn, S., Balakrishnan, J., ... & Wirtz, J. (2023). How metaverse will change the future of marketing: Implications for Research and Practice Psychology and Marketing.

Dwivedi, A. (2015). A higher-order model of consumer brand engagement and its impact on loyalty intentions. *Journal of Retailing and Consumer Services, 24*, 100–109. DOI: 10.1016/j.jretconser.2015.02.007

Dwivedi, Y. K., Hughes, L., Ismagilova, E., Aarts, G., Coombs, C., Crick, T., Duan, Y., Dwivedi, R., Edwards, J., Eirug, A., Galanos, V., Ilavarasan, P. V., Janssen, M., Jones, P., Kar, A. K., Kizgin, H., Kronemann, B., Lal, B., Lucini, B., & Williams, M. D. (2021). Artificial Intelligence (AI): Multidisciplinary perspectives on emerging challenges, opportunities, and agenda for research, practice and policy. *International Journal of Information Management*, *57*, 101994. DOI: 10.1016/j.ijinfomgt.2019.08.002

Ebrahimi, O. V., Pallesen, S., Kenter, R. M. F., & Nordgreen, T. (2019). Psychological Interventions for the Fear of Public Speaking: A Meta-Analysis. *Frontiers in Psychology*, *10*, 488. Advance online publication. DOI: 10.3389/fpsyg.2019.00488 PMID: 30930813

Edwards, E. A., Lumsden, J., Rivas, C., Steed, L., Edwards, L. A., Thiyagarajan, A., Sohanpal, R., Caton, H., Griffiths, C. J., Munafò, M. R., Taylor, S., & Walton, R. T. (2016). Gamification for health promotion: Systematic review of behaviour change techniques in smartphone apps. *BMJ Open*, *6*(10), e012447. DOI: 10.1136/bmjopen-2016-012447 PMID: 27707829

Eigenraam, A. W., Eelen, J., Van Lin, A., & Verlegh, P. W. (2018). A consumer-based taxonomy of digital customer engagement practices. *Journal of Interactive Marketing*, *44*(1), 102–121. DOI: 10.1016/j.intmar.2018.07.002

Eisingerich, A. B., Marchand, A., Fritze, M. P., & Dong, L. (2019). Hook vs. hope: How to enhance customer engagement through gamification. *International Journal of Research in Marketing*, *36*(2), 200–215. DOI: 10.1016/j.ijresmar.2019.02.003

EY–FICCI. (2024). *Tuning into consumer: Indian media & entertainment report 2024*. Ernst & Young. https://www.ey.com/

Fajar, M., David, D., Sihombing, P., Kekal, H., Aditya, I., Ilham, R., & Keswara, Y. S. (2022). The Metaverse to enhance safety campaign toward shipping industry (case study: The development and implementation of Metaverse in government-owned corporation). *International Journal of Emerging Technology and Advanced Engineering*, *12*(08), 1–11. DOI: 10.46338/ijetae0822_01

Falco, G. (2020). *Customer engagement through gamification marketing in China: A focus on the luxury market* [Unpublished manuscript or thesis if not published].

Fatmawati, I., & Amanati, A. K. (2023). How does consumer experience with cosmetics products create EWOM, satisfaction, and loyalty? *Jurnal Manajemen Bisnis*, *14*(1), 53–71. DOI: 10.18196/mb.v14i1.14525

Financial Express. (2023). *India's 442M gamers embracing play-to-earn models via Web3 integration*. https://www.financialexpress.com/

Fink, D., & Nyaga, C. (2009). Evaluating web site quality: The value of a multi paradigm approach. *Benchmarking*, *16*(2), 259–273. DOI: 10.1108/14635770910948259

Fitria, T. N. (2022, December). Using game design techniques (gamification) in teaching and learning process: A review. *Prosiding Seminar Nasional & Call for Paper STIE AAS*, *5*(1), 1–18.

Flavián, C., Ibáñez-Sánchez, S., Orús, C., & Barta, S. (2024). The dark side of the metaverse: The role of gamification in event virtualization. *International Journal of Information Management*, *75*, 102726. DOI: 10.1016/j.ijinfomgt.2023.102726

Flores, B., & Flores, B. (2025, March 7). How gamification engages your audience—benefits, challenges, case studies and future trends - Agility PR Solutions. *Agility PR Solutions - Media Relations. . .Streamlined*. https://www.agilitypr.com/pr-news/public-relations/how-gamification-engages-your-audience-benefits-challenges-case-studies-and-future-trends/

Fornell, C., & Larcker, D. F. (1981). Evaluating Structural Equation Models with Unobservable Variables and Measurement Error. *JMR, Journal of Marketing Research*, *18*(1), 39–50. Advance online publication. DOI: 10.1177/002224378101800104

Gamayanto, I., Wibowo, S., & Prayitno, A. (2024). The Concept of gamification, metaverse & AI to develop hybrid learning systems inside education. [International Journal of Information System and Technology]. *IJISTECH*, *7*(6), 370–378.

Games India, E. P. I. C. (2024). *Case study: Virtual concert engagement and experiential marketing in India*. EPIC Games.

Ganesan, S. (2020). Recycle Mate: A gamified recycling app to promote waste segregation. https://www.recyclemate.co/ 10.

Gao, Z., Chen, S., Sun, H., & Wen, X. (2021). Impact of gamification on college students' learning engagement. *Frontiers in Psychology*, *12*, 1185353.

Garrido, S., Oliver, E., Chmiel, A., Doran, B., & Boydell, K. (2022). Encouraging help-seeking and engagement in a mental health app: What young people want. *Frontiers in Digital Health*, *4*, 1045765. Advance online publication. DOI: 10.3389/fdgth.2022.1045765 PMID: 36620186

Getman, A. P., Yaroshenko, O. M., Demenko, O. I., Lutsenko, O. Y., & Prokopiev, R. Y. (2024). Gamification for staff motivation: Impact on work efficiency and corporate culture at the international level. *Journal of Economics and Management, 46*, 274–299. DOI: 10.22367/jem.2024.46.11

Girvan, C. (2018). What is a virtual world? Definition and classification. *Educational Technology Research and Development, 66*(5), 1087–1100. DOI: 10.1007/s11423-018-9577-y

Glover, I. (2013). Play as you learn: Gamification as a technique for motivating learners. In *Proceedings of world conference on educational multimedia, hypermedia and telecommunications 2013* (pp. 1999e2008). Chesapeake, VA: Association for the Advancement of Computing in Education.

Gough, C. (2024). Health & fitness clubs. Statista. https://www.statista.com/topics/1141/health-and-fitness-clubs/

Goyette, I., Ricard, L., Bergeron, J., & Marticotte, F. (2010). E-WOM scale: Word-of-mouth measurement scale for e-services context. *Canadian Journal of Administrative Sciences, 27*(1), 5–23. DOI: 10.1002/cjas.129

Grewal, D., Iyer, G. R., Krishnan, R., & Sharma, A. (2003). The Internet and the price–value–loyalty chain. *Journal of Business Research, 56*(5), 391–398. DOI: 10.1016/S0148-2963(01)00227-2

Gupta, D. R. (2025). The Dark Side of Gamification: Ethics, Privacy, Surveillance, and Monitoring in the Use of Gamified Elements. In Gamification and Global Business Management: Mapping the Future (pp. 167-198).

Gursoy, D., Malodia, S., & Dhir, A. (2022). The Metaverse in the hospitality and tourism industry: An overview of current trends and future research directions. *Journal of Hospitality Marketing & Management, 31*(5), 527–534. DOI: 10.1080/19368623.2022.2072504

Hadavi, A., & Alizadehsalehi, S. (2024). From BIM to Metaverse for AEC industry. *Automation in Construction, 160*, 105248. DOI: 10.1016/j.autcon.2023.105248

Hair, J. F., Hult, G. T. M., Ringle, C. M., Sarstedt, M., & Thiele, K. O. (2017). Mirror, mirror on the wall: A comparative evaluation of composite-based structural equation modeling methods. *Journal of the Academy of Marketing Science, 45*(5), 616–632. Advance online publication. DOI: 10.1007/s11747-017-0517-x

Hajarian, M., & Hemmati, S. (2020, September). A gamified word of mouth recommendation system for increasing customer purchase. In *2020 4th International Conference on Smart City, Internet of Things and Applications (SCIOT)* (pp. 7-11). IEEE. DOI: 10.1109/SCIOT50840.2020.9250209

Hamari, J., & Koivisto, J. (2013, June). Social Motivations To Use Gamification: An Empirical Study Of Gamifying Exercise. In *ECIS* (Vol. 105, No. 5, pp. 18-19).

Hamari, J., Koivisto, J., & Sarsa, H. (2014, January). Does gamification work?--a literature review of empirical studies on gamification. In *2014 47th Hawaii international conference on system sciences* (pp. 3025-3034). Ieee.

Hamari, J. (2013). Transforming homo economicus into homo ludens: A field experiment on gamification in a utilitarian peer-to-peer trading service. *Electronic Commerce Research and Applications*, *12*(4), 236–245. DOI: 10.1016/j.elerap.2013.01.004

Hamari, J., & Koivisto, J. (2015b). Working out for likes: An empirical study on social influence in exercise gamification. *Computers in Human Behavior*, *50*, 333–347. DOI: 10.1016/j.chb.2015.04.018

Hamari, J., Koivisto, J., & Sarsa, H. (2014). Does gamification work?—A literature review of empirical studies on gamification. *Proceedings of the 47th Hawaii International Conference on System Sciences*, 3025-3034. DOI: 10.1109/HICSS.2014.377

Hamari, J., Xi, N., Legaki, Z., & Morschheuser, B. (2023). *Gamification. In Hawaii International Conference on System Sciences* (p. 1105).

Hammedi, W., Leclercq, T., & Poncin, I. (2019). Customer engagement: The role of gamification. In *Handbook of research on customer engagement* (pp. 164–185). Edward Elgar Publishing. DOI: 10.4337/9781788114899.00014

Hammedi, W., Leclercq, T., & van Riel, A. (2017). The use of gamification mechanics to increase employee and user engagement in participative healthcare services: A study of two cases. *Journal of Service Management*, *28*(4), 640–661. DOI: 10.1108/JOSM-04-2016-0116

Harapan, H., Itoh, N., Yufika, A., Winardi, W., Keam, S., Te, H., Megawati, D., Hayati, Z., Wagner, A. L., & Mudatsir, M. (2020). Coronavirus disease 2019 (COVID-19): A literature review. *Journal of Infection and Public Health*, *13*(5), 667–673. DOI: 10.1016/j.jiph.2020.03.019 PMID: 32340833

Harwood, T., & Garry, T. (2015). An investigation into gamification as a customer engagement experience environment. *Journal of Services Marketing*, *29*(6/7), 533–546. DOI: 10.1108/JSM-01-2015-0045

Hassan Butt, A., Ahmad, H., Muzaffar, A., Irshad, W., Usman Mumtaz, M., & Zubair Ahmad Khan, T. (2024). WeChat Gamification: Mobile Payment Impact on word of mouth and customer loyalty. *Spanish Journal of Marketing - ESIC.*

Hassan, L. (2017). Governments should play games: Towards a framework for the gamification of civic engagement platforms. *Simulation & Gaming*, *48*(2), 249–267. DOI: 10.1177/1046878116683581

Hassan, L., & Hamari, J. (2020). Gameful civic engagement: A review of the literature on gamification of e-participation. *Government Information Quarterly*, *37*(3), 101461. DOI: 10.1016/j.giq.2020.101461

Hassen, D. E., & El-Amine, S. (2021). Incentive model designs for crowdsourcing: Review and research directions. *Computer Science Review*, *39*, 100350. https://doi.org/doi:10.1016/j.cosrev.2020.100350

Hausman, A. V., & Siekpe, J. S. (2009). The effect of web interface features on consumer online purchase intentions. *Journal of Business Research*, *62*(1), 5–13. DOI: 10.1016/j.jbusres.2008.01.018

Health, C. for D. and R. (2022, September 29). Device Software Functions Including Mobile Medical Applications. FDA; FDA. https://www.fda.gov/medical-devices/digital-health-center-excellence/device-software-functions-including-mobile-medical-applications

Henseler, J., Ringle, C. M., & Sarstedt, M. (2015). A new criterion for assessing discriminant validity in variance-based structural equation modeling. *Journal of the Academy of Marketing Science*, *43*(1), 115–135. Advance online publication. DOI: 10.1007/s11747-014-0403-8

Hermawan, J. H., & Tjhin, V. U. (2023). The effect of gamification on customer engagement in e-commerce. *Journal of Theoretical and Applied Information Technology*, *101*(19), 5952–5954.

He, T. (2022). From single-player games to Metaverse: A futuristic analysis of challenging legal issues in the video game industry in China. *GRUR Int.*, *71*(10), 952–966. DOI: 10.1093/grurint/ikac039

Hiranrithikorn, P., & Banjongprasert, J. (2022). The effect of the website attributes on online impulse buying: An empirical investigation of utilitarian and hedonic motivations. *International Journal of Data and Network Science*, *6*(4), 1419–1426. DOI: 10.5267/j.ijdns.2022.5.009

Ho, X. N. L. (2024). *Exploring Factors That Influence Gen Z Consumers' Adoption of Metaverse and Brand Experience through Metaverse* (Master's thesis, Illinois State University).

Hoeppner, B. B., Hoeppner, S. S., Seaboyer, L., Schick, M. R., Wu, G. W. Y., Bergman, B. G., & Kelly, J. F. (2016). How Smart are Smartphone Apps for Smoking Cessation? A Content Analysis. *Nicotine & Tobacco Research: Official Journal of the Society for Research on Nicotine and Tobacco, 18*(5), 1025–1031. DOI: 10.1093/ntr/ntv117 PMID: 26045249

Hofacker, C. F., De Ruyter, K., Lurie, N. H., Manchanda, P., & Donaldson, J. (2016). Gamification and mobile marketing effectiveness. *Journal of Interactive Marketing, 34*(1), 25–36. DOI: 10.1016/j.intmar.2016.03.001

Högberg, J., Ramberg, M. O., Gustafsson, A., & Wästlund, E. (2019). Creating brand engagement through in-store gamified customer experiences. *Journal of Retailing and Consumer Services, 50*, 122–130. DOI: 10.1016/j.jretconser.2019.05.006

Hollebeek, L. (2011). Demystifying Customer Brand Engagement: Exploring the Loyalty Nexus. *Journal of Marketing Management, 27*(7-8), 785–807. DOI: 10.1080/0267257X.2010.500132

Hollebeek, L. D., Das, K., & Shukla, Y. (2021). Game on! How gamified loyalty programs boost customer engagement value. *International Journal of Information Management, 61*, 102308. DOI: 10.1016/j.ijinfomgt.2021.102308

Honeycutt, E. D.Jr, Flaherty, T. B., & Benassi, K. (1998). Marketing industrial products on the Internet. *Industrial Marketing Management, 27*(1), 63–72. DOI: 10.1016/S0019-8501(97)00038-2

Hsu, C. L. (2023). Enhancing brand love, customer engagement, brand experience, and repurchase intention: Focusing on the role of gamification in mobile apps. *Decision Support Systems, 174*, 114020. DOI: 10.1016/j.dss.2023.114020

Hsu, C. L., & Chen, M. C. (2018). How gamification marketing activities motivate desirable consumer behaviors: Focusing on the role of brand love. *Computers in Human Behavior, 88*, 121–133. DOI: 10.1016/j.chb.2018.06.037

Huang, R., Ritzhaupt, A. D., Sommer, M., Zhu, J., Stephen, A., Valle, N., Hampton, J., & Li, J. (2020). The impact of gamification in educational settings on student learning outcomes: A meta-analysis. *Educational Technology Research and Development, 68*(4), 1875–1901. DOI: 10.1007/s11423-020-09807-z

Hubona, G. S., & Kennick, E. (1996, January). The influence of external variables on information technology usage behavior. In *System Sciences, 1996.,Proceedings of the Twenty-Ninth Hawaii International Conference on,* (Vol. 4, pp. 166-175). IEEE. DOI: 10.1109/HICSS.1996.495323

Huotari, K., & Hamari, J. (2017). A definition for gamification: Anchoring gamification in the service marketing literature. *Electronic Markets*, *27*(1), 21–31. DOI: 10.1007/s12525-015-0212-z

Hutter, K., Hautz, J., Dennhardt, S., & Füller, J. (2013). The impact of user interactions in social media on brand awareness and purchase intention: The case of MINI on Facebook. *Journal of Product and Brand Management*, *22*(5/6), 342–351. DOI: 10.1108/JPBM-05-2013-0299

Hwang, J., & Choi, L. (2020). Having fun while receiving rewards?: Exploration of gamification in loyalty programs for consumer loyalty. *Journal of Business Research*, *106*, 365–376. DOI: 10.1016/j.jbusres.2019.01.031

Hyrynsalmi, S., Kimppa, K., Koskinen, J., Smed, J., & Hyrynsalmi, S. (2017). The Shades of Grey: Datenherrschaft in Data-Driven Gamification. DDGD@ MindTrek, 4-11.

Hyundai. (n.d.). *Hyundai vitalizes future mobility in Roblox Metaverse space* [Press release]. https://www.hyundai.news/eu/articles/press-releases/hyundai-vitalizes-future-mobility-in-roblox-metaverse-space.html (Retrieved March 8, 2025)

Ibrahim, E. N. M., Jamali, N., & Suhaimi, A. I. H. (2021). Exploring gamification design elements for mental health support. *International Journal of Advanced Technology and Engineering Exploration*, *8*(74), 114–125. DOI: 10.19101/IJATEE.2020.S1762123

IDGS-MIB WAVES Initiative. (2025). *GameForge: Bridging academia and industry in gaming through Chitkara and NorthCap universities*. Ministry of Information and Broadcasting.

Ilhamalimy, R. R., & Ali, H. (2021). Model perceived risk and trust: e-WOM and purchase intention (the role OF trust mediating IN online shopping IN shopee Indonesia). *Dinasti International Journal of Digital Business Management*, *2*(2), 204–221. DOI: 10.31933/dijdbm.v2i2.651

Inchamnan, W. (2023). Gamification Pedagogy Trigger Design for Creative Experiences in Metaverse Class Room. [JASET]. *Journal of Applied Science and Emerging Technology*, *22*(2), 251539. DOI: 10.14416/JASET.KMUTNB.2023.02.003

Induji, R. T., & Somasundari, K. M. VinothKumar, K.R., Swapna, S., Brindha, S. and Kumar, S.K. (2024). Entry of the Metaverse in Human Resource Management: A Paradigm Shift in Workplace Dynamics. In *Anticipating Future Business Trends: Navigating Artificial Intelligence Innovations: Volume 1* (pp. 73-80). Cham: Springer Nature Switzerland.

Intelligence, M. (2020), Gamification market– growth, trends, COVID-19 impact, and Forecasts (2021-2026), Report, available at https://www.mordorintelligence.com/industry-reports/gamification-market (accessed 29 March 2025).

Invest India. (2023). *Gaming industry in India: Market overview & investment opportunities*. https://www.investindia.gov.in/

Jagatheesaperumal, S. K., & Rahouti, M. (2022). Building digital twins of cyber physical systems with Metaverse for industry 5.0 and beyond. *IT Professional, 24*(6), 34–40. DOI: 10.1109/MITP.2022.3225064

Jami Pour, M., & Binaei, H. (2024). The Ethical Challenges of Gamification in Iran: Uncovering the Dark Side. *Journal of Business and Management, 16*(2), 415–446.

Jami Pour, M., Rafiei, K., Khani, M., & Sabrirazm, A. (2021). Gamification and customer experience: The mediating role of brand engagement in online grocery retailing. *Nankai Business Review International, 12*(3), 340–357. DOI: 10.1108/NBRI-07-2020-0041

Jang, S., Kitchen, P. J., & Kim, J. (2018). The effects of gamified customer benefits and characteristics on behavioral engagement and purchase: Evidence from mobile exercise application uses. *Journal of Business Research, 92*, 250–259. DOI: 10.1016/j.jbusres.2018.07.056

Jarvenpaa, S. L., Tractinsky, N., & Saarinen, L. (1999). Consumer trust in an internet store: a cross-cultural validation. Journal of Computer-Mediated Communication, 5(2), 0-0.

Jayasiri, H. B., Purushothaman, C. S., & Vennila, A. (2013). Plastic litter accumulation on high-water strandline of urban beaches in Mumbai, India. *Environmental Monitoring and Assessment, 185*(9), 7709–7719. DOI: 10.1007/s10661-013-3129-z PMID: 23430068

Jeon, H.-J., Youn, H.-C., Ko, S.-M., & Kim, T.-H. (2021). Blockchain and AI meet in the metaverse. In Fernández-Caramés, T. M., & Fraga-Lamas, P. (Eds.), *Advances in the convergence of blockchain and artificial intelligence* (pp. 73–82). Intech Open., DOI: 10.5772/intechopen.99114

Jetir. (2023). *Esports and its 100B impact on India's digital economy: A study from Hyderabad's competitive scene. Journal of Emerging Technologies and Innovative Research (JETIR), 10*(6), 1002–1015. https://www.jetir.org/

Jiang, W., Han, B., Habibi, M. A., & Schotten, H. D. (2021). The road towards 6G: A comprehensive survey. *IEEE Open Journal of the Communications Society, 2*, 334–366. DOI: 10.1109/OJCOMS.2021.3057679

Johnson, D., Deterding, S., Kuhn, K.-A., Staneva, A., Stoyanov, S., & Hides, L. (2016). Gamification for health and wellbeing: A systematic review of the literature. *Internet Interventions : the Application of Information Technology in Mental and Behavioural Health, 6*, 89–106. DOI: 10.1016/j.invent.2016.10.002 PMID: 30135818

Jovanović, A., & Milosavljević, A. (2022). VoRtex Metaverse platform for gamified collaborative learning. *Electronics (Basel), 11*(3), 317. DOI: 10.3390/electronics11030317

Kadry, A. (2022). The Metaverse revolution and its impact on the future of advertising industry. *J. Des. Sci. Appl. Arts, 3*(2), 347–358. DOI: 10.21608/jdsaa.2022.129876.1171

Kaede, S., Hiroki, S., & Shuichi, N. (2023). The Metaverse in the tourism industry: A new horizon after the COVID-19 pandemic. *Wakayama Tour. Rev., 4*, 32–35. DOI: 10.19002/24363839.4.32

Kafilaleh, Y., & Asadi, H. (2022). Identifying and prioritizing key branding factors in the pharmaceutical industry in Metaverse: An integrated DEMATEL-ANP approach. [TRS]. *Tobacco Regulatory Science*, •••, 3026–3034.

Kalyani, P. (2017). Study on smartphone gaming adoption patterns among India's youth demographic, highlighting correlations between affordable device penetration and gaming market expansion. *International Journal of Research in Finance and Marketing, 7*(11), 112–126.

Kamboj, S., Rana, S., & Drave, V. A. (2020). Factors driving consumer engagement and intentions with gamification of mobile apps. [JECO]. *Journal of Electronic Commerce in Organizations, 18*(2), 17–35. DOI: 10.4018/JECO.2020040102

Kanat, M. (2019). The relationship between online game addiction and communication skills among college students. *Journal of Behavioral Addictions, 8*(2), 213–221. PMID: 31120318

Karta. (n.d.). *Sunsilk City*. https://www.karta.game/project/sunsilkcity (Retrieved March 8, 2025)

Katta, R. M. R., & Patro, C. S. (2021). Influence of web attributes on consumer purchase intentions. In *Research Anthology on Strategies for Using Social Media as a Service and Tool in Business* (pp. 337–356). IGI Global. DOI: 10.4018/978-1-7998-9020-1.ch017

Kennedy, E., & Guzmán, F. (2016). Co-creation of brand identities: Consumer and industry influence and motivations. *Journal of Consumer Marketing*, *33*(5), 313–323. DOI: 10.1108/JCM-07-2015-1500

Khaddage, F., Lattemann, C., & Acosta-Díaz, R. (2014). Mobile Gamification in Education Engage, Educate and Entertain via Gamified Mobile Apps.

Kim, H., Munson, M. R., & McKay, M. M. (2012). Engagement in Mental Health Treatment Among Adolescents and Young Adults: A Systematic Review. *Child & Adolescent Social Work Journal*, *29*(3), 241–266. DOI: 10.1007/s10560-012-0256-2

Kim, J., & Castelli, D. M. (2021). Effects of gamification on behavioral change in education: A meta-analysis. *International Journal of Environmental Research and Public Health*, *18*(7), 3550. DOI: 10.3390/ijerph18073550 PMID: 33805530

Kim, J., & Ha, J. (2021). User experience in VR fashion product shopping: Focusing on tangible interactions. *Applied Sciences (Basel, Switzerland)*, *11*(13), 6170. DOI: 10.3390/app11136170

Kim, S. J., Kim, K. H., & Mattila, P. (2012). The role of fashion in the characters of online games. *Journal of Global Fashion Marketing*, *3*(2), 81–88. DOI: 10.1080/20932685.2012.10593110

Kim, T. W., & Werbach, K. (2016). More than just a game: Ethical issues in gamification. *Ethics and Information Technology*, *18*(2), 157–173. DOI: 10.1007/s10676-016-9401-5

Kim, T. W., & Werbach, K. (2022). Excerpt from ethics of gamification. In *Ethics of Data and Analytics* (pp. 375–385). Auerbach Publications. DOI: 10.1201/9781003278290-55

Klock, A. C. T., Santana, B. S., & Hamari, J. (2023). Ethical Challenges in Gamified Education Research and Development: An Umbrella Review and Potential Directions. In Toda, A., Cristea, A. I., & Isotani, S. (Eds.), *Gamification Design for Educational Contexts* (pp. 37–48). Springer. DOI: 10.1007/978-3-031-31949-5_3

Koivisto, J., & Hamari, J. (2019). The rise of motivational information systems: A review of gamification research. *International Journal of Information Management*, *45*, 191–210. DOI: 10.1016/j.ijinfomgt.2018.10.013

Kominski, R., & Newburger, E. (1999). Access denied: Changes in computer ownership and use: 1984-1997. In *Annual Meeting of American Sociological Association*.

Koohang, A., Nord, J. H., Ooi, K. B., Tan, G. W. H., Al-Emran, M., Aw, E. C. X., Baabdullah, A. M., Buhalis, D., Cham, T.-H., Dennis, C., Dutot, V., Dwivedi, Y. K., Hughes, L., Mogaji, E., Pandey, N., Phau, I., Raman, R., Sharma, A., Sigala, M., & Wong, L. W. (2023). Shaping the metaverse into reality: A holistic multidisciplinary understanding of opportunities, challenges, and avenues for future investigation. *Journal of Computer Information Systems*, *63*(3), 735–765. DOI: 10.1080/08874417.2023.2165197

Koster, R. (2021). *Online world or metaverse?* Raph's Website. https://www.raphkoster.com/2021/09/02/online-world-or-metaverse/

Kothgassner, O. D., Goreis, A., Bauda, I., Ziegenaus, A., Glenk, L. M., & Felnhofer, A. (2022). Virtual reality biofeedback interventions for treating anxiety: A systematic review, meta-analysis and future perspective. *Wiener Klinische Wochenschrift*, *134*(S1, Suppl 1), 49–59. DOI: 10.1007/s00508-021-01991-z PMID: 34989862

KPMG. (2023). *India's media and entertainment sector: The digital reset*. https://home.kpmg/in • Lumikai & Google. (2024). *State of India interactive media report*. https://www.lumikai.com/

Kulkarni, K., Adithya, V. V., Hitesh, K., & Kumari, N. (2023). Brand Management in the Metaverse. In *The Business of the Metaverse* (pp. 95–112). Productivity Press. DOI: 10.4324/b23404-6

Kumar, G., Singh, R. K., Arya, V., & Mishra, S. K. (2024). Analyzing barriers in adoption of artificial intelligence for resilient health care services to society. *Global Journal of Flexible Systems Managment*, *25*(1), 179–197. DOI: 10.1007/s40171-024-00373-4

Kumari, H., & Gujral, H. K. (2023). A STUDY ON GAMIFICATION & ITS EFFECTS ON CONSUMER BEHAVIOUR. *International Journal of Advanced Research in Computer Science*, *14*(4).

Kumar, J., Arora, M., & Erkol Bayram, G. (Eds.). (2024). *Exploring the Use of Metaverse in Business and Education*. IGI Global. DOI: 10.4018/979-8-3693-5868-9

Kumar, V., Aksoy, L., Donkers, B., Venkatesan, R., Wiesel, T., & Tillmanns, S. (2010). Undervalued or overvalued customers: Capturing total customer engagement value. *Journal of Service Research*, *13*(3), 297–310. DOI: 10.1177/1094670510375602

Kumar, V., & Pansari, A. (2016). Competitive advantage through engagement. *JMR, Journal of Marketing Research*, *53*(4), 497–514. DOI: 10.1509/jmr.15.0044

Kuo, M. S., & Chuang, T. Y. (2016). How gamification motivates visits and engagement for online academic dissemination—An empirical study. *Computers in Human Behavior*, 55(A), 16–27.

Lamba, S. S., & Malik, R. (2024). Retention in the Metaverse: Customer Engagement Using Big Data. In *Augmenting Customer Retention Through Big Data Analytics* (pp. 291-309). Apple Academic Press.

Landers, R. N., Bauer, K. N., & Callan, R. C. (2017). Gamification of task performance with leaderboards: A goal setting experiment. *Computers in Human Behavior*, *71*, 508–515. DOI: 10.1016/j.chb.2015.08.008

Leclercq, T., Hammedi, W., & Poncin, I. (2018). The boundaries of gamification for engaging customers: Effects of losing a contest in online co-creation communities. *Journal of Interactive Marketing*, *44*(1), 82–101. DOI: 10.1016/j.intmar.2018.04.004

Leclercq, T., Poncin, I., & Hammedi, W. (2017). The engagement process during value co-creation: Gamification in new product-development platforms. *International Journal of Electronic Commerce*, *21*(4), 454–488. DOI: 10.1080/10864415.2016.1355638

Lee, H., Yoo, S., & Kim, Y. (2015). "Design and implementation of an energy trading model for smart factories," in Paper presented at the 2015 IEEE 20th conference on emerging technologies and factory automation (ETFA), 1–4. DOI: 10.1109/ETFA.2015.7301568

Lee, C. T., Ho, T. Y., & Xie, H. H. (2023). Building brand engagement in metaverse commerce: The role of branded non-fungible tokens (BNFTs). *Electronic Commerce Research and Applications*, *58*, 101248. DOI: 10.1016/j.elerap.2023.101248

Lee, C. W. (2022). Application of Metaverse service to healthcare industry: A strategic perspective. *International Journal of Environmental Research and Public Health*, *19*(20), 13038. DOI: 10.3390/ijerph192013038 PMID: 36293609

Lee, E., Hammer, B., Kim, J. K., Page, Z., Emrick, T., & Hayward, R. C. (2011). Hierarchical Helical Assembly of Conjugated Poly (3-hexylthiophene)-block-poly (3-triethylene glycol thiophene) Diblock Copolymers. *Journal of the American Chemical Society*, *133*(27), 10390–10393. DOI: 10.1021/ja2038547 PMID: 21627317

Lee, J. J., & Hammer, J. (2011). Gamification in education: What, how, why bother? *Academic Exchange Quarterly*, *15*(2), 146.

Lem, A. J., Liddicoat, C., Bissett, A., Cando-Dumancela, C., Gardner, M. G., Peddle, S. D., Watson, C. D., & Breed, M. F. (2022). Does revegetation cause soil microbiota recovery? Evidence from revisiting a revegetation chronosequence 6 years after initial sampling. *Restoration Ecology*, *30*(8), e13635. DOI: 10.1111/rec.13635

Lian, T. P., & Lai, H. J. (2002). Effect of store design on consumer purchases: An empirical study of on-line bookstores. *Information & Management, 39*(6), 431–444. DOI: 10.1016/S0378-7206(01)00129-X

Liboriussen, B. (2011). Collective building projects in second life: User motives and strategies explained from an architectural and ethnographic perspective. In Zagalo, N., Morgado, L., & Boa-Ventura, A. (Eds.), *Virtual worlds and metaverse platforms: New communication and identity paradigms* (pp. 33–46). IGI Global., DOI: 10.4018/978-1-60960-854-5.ch003

Lim, D. H., Lee, J. Y., & Park, S. (2024). The metaverse in the workplace: Possibilities and implications for human resource development. *Human Resource Development Review, 23*(2), 164–198. DOI: 10.1177/15344843231217174

Litterati. (2023). Litterati: A global community cleaning the planet one piece at a time. https://www.litterati.org/

Litvin, S., Saunders, R., Maier, M. A., & Lüttke, S. (2020). Gamification as an approach to improve resilience and reduce attrition in mobile mental health interventions: A randomized controlled trial. *PLoS One, 15*(9), e0237220. DOI: 10.1371/journal.pone.0237220 PMID: 32877425

Liu, C. C., Lin, Y. Y., Lo, F. Y., Chang, C. H., & Lin, H. M. (2024). From readers to players: Exploring student engagement in a gamified metaverse and its effect on reading interest. *Education and Information Technologies*, •••, 1–27.

Liu, R., Liu, L., Lee, M., & Chen, J. (2019). When will consumers be ready? A psychological perspective on consumer engagement in social media brand communities. *Internet Research, 29*(4), 704–724. DOI: 10.1108/IntR-05-2017-0177

Liu, X., He, M., Gao, F., & Xie, P. (2008). An empirical study of online shopping customer satisfaction in China: A holistic perspective. *International Journal of Retail & Distribution Management, 36*(11), 919–940. DOI: 10.1108/09590550810911683

Lo, C. K., & To, W. M. (2023). Exploring the Impact of Gamification and AI on Personalized Learning: A Review. *International Journal of Research Publication and Reviews, 6*(4), 5543–5548.

Locke, E. A., & Latham, G. P. (2002). Building a practically useful theory of goal setting and task motivation: A 35-year odyssey. *The American Psychologist, 57*(9), 705–717. DOI: 10.1037/0003-066X.57.9.705 PMID: 12237980

Loia, F., Capolupo, N., & Adinolfi, P. (2025). Training me softly. Metaverse-based immersive and gamified learning through a knowledge management perspective. *Journal of Knowledge Management*, *29*(5), 1465–1489. DOI: 10.1108/JKM-08-2024-0929

Loijas, J. (2024). How Gamification Shapes Learning And Interaction In Virtual Educational Events.

Longstreet, P., Brooks, S., Featherman, M., & Loiacono, E. (2022). Evaluating website quality: Which decision criteria do consumers use to evaluate website quality? *Information Technology & People*, *35*(4), 1271–1297. DOI: 10.1108/ITP-05-2020-0328

Luarn, P., Chen, C.-C., & Chiu, Y.-P. (2023). Enhancing intrinsic learning motivation through gamification: A self-determination theory perspective. *The International Journal of Information and Learning Technology*, *40*(5), 413–424. DOI: 10.1108/IJILT-07-2022-0145

Lu, J., Yu, C. S., Liu, C., & Yao, J. (2003). Technology acceptance model for wireless internet. *Internet Research*, *13*(3), 206–222. DOI: 10.1108/10662240310478222

Madakam, S., Lake, V., Lake, V., & Lake, V. (2015). Internet of things (IoT): A literature review. *J. Comput. Commun.*, *3*(05), 164–173. DOI: 10.4236/jcc.2015.35021

Mahadev Madgule, N. (2023). Vinayaka, Yeshwant M. Sonkhaskar, Dhiren Ramanbhai Patel, R. Karthikeyan, P. Selvakumar,(2023). Mechanical properties and microstructure of activated TIG welded similar joints of Inconel alloys by desirability approaches. *Materials Today: Proceedings*, *77*, 528–533. DOI: 10.1016/j.matpr.2022.12.250

Mahajan, S., Pandey, P. K., Behera, J., Pandey, P. K., & Beg, R. A. (2018). *Hybrid Work Models, Metaverse Integration, and Talent Management Strategies: Navigating Post-Pandemic Realities*. Green Metaverse for Greener Economies.

Markets and Markets. (2022). *Metaverse Market for Automotive worth $16.5 billion by 2030*. https://www.marketsandmarkets.com/PressReleases/automotive-metaverse.asp

Marques, G., Drissi, N., Díez, I. de la T., de Abajo, B. S., & Ouhbi, S. (2021). Impact of COVID-19 on the psychological health of university students in Spain and their attitudes toward Mobile mental health solutions. *International Journal of Medical Informatics*, *147*, 104369. DOI: 10.1016/j.ijmedinf.2020.104369 PMID: 33388481

Martínez-López, F. J., Anaya-Sánchez, R., & Gázquez-Abad, J. C. (2020). Consumer engagement and loyalty in social media environments: The role of content and interaction. *Journal of Retailing and Consumer Services, 54*, 102027.

Mattke, J., & Maier, C. (2021). Gamification: Explaining brand loyalty in mobile applications. *AIS Transactions on Human-Computer Interaction, 13*(1), 62–81. DOI: 10.17705/1thci.00142

Mazzù, M. F., Pozharliev, R. I., & Della Sala, I. (2024). How Metaverse Creates Value for Luxury Brands. In *Sinergie-SIMA Conference 2024 «Management of sustainability and well-being for individuals and society.*

McCall, R., & Baillie, L. (2017). Ethics, Privacy, and Trust in Serious Games. In Handbook of Digital Games and Entertainment Technologies (p. 611).

McClure, C., & Seock, Y. K. (2020). The role of involvement: Investigating the effect of brand's social media pages on consumer purchase intention. *Journal of Retailing and Consumer Services, 53*, 101975. DOI: 10.1016/j.jretconser.2019.101975

Meenakshy, M., Saxena, R., & Srivastava, M. (2020). Gamification: Increasing electronic word of mouth in tourism. *SCMS Journal of Indian Management, 17*(4), 51–62.

Mehrabian, A., & Russell, J. A. (1974). An approach to environmental psychology. 'e MIT Press

Meral, M. (2019). The effect of online game addiction on academic performance and learning attitudes. *The Turkish Online Journal of Educational Technology, 18*(3), 45–52.

Michie, S., Richardson, M., Johnston, M., Abraham, C., Francis, J., Hardeman, W., Eccles, M. P., Cane, J., & Wood, C. E. (2013). The behavior change technique taxonomy (v1) of 93 hierarchically clustered techniques: Building an international consensus for the reporting of behavior change interventions. Annals of Behavioral Medicine: A Publication of the Society of Behavioral Medicine, 46(1), 81–95. DOI: 10.1007/s12160-013-9486-6

Ministry of Environment. Forest and Climate Change. (2016). Plastic Waste Management Rules, 2016. https://cpcb.nic.in/uploads/plasticwaste/PWM_Rules_2016.pdf

Mink, J., Yuile, A. R., Pal, U., Aviv, A. J., & Bates, A. (2022, April). Users Can Deduce Sensitive Locations Protected by Privacy Zones on Fitness Tracking Apps. *Proceedings Of The 2022 CHI Conference On Human Factors In Computing Systems*, 1-21. DOI: 10.1145/3491102.3502136

Mittal, G., & Bansal, R. (2023). Driving force behind consumer brand engagement: the metaverse. In *Cultural marketing and metaverse for consumer engagement* (pp. 164–181). IGI Global. DOI: 10.4018/978-1-6684-8312-1.ch012

Miyazaki, A. D., & Fernandez, A. (2001). Consumer perceptions of privacy and security risks for online shopping. *The Journal of Consumer Affairs*, *35*(1), 27–44. DOI: 10.1111/j.1745-6606.2001.tb00101.x

Mordor Intelligence. (2024). *India gaming market - Growth, trends, and forecasts (2024–2034)*. https://www.mordorintelligence.com/

Mukherjee, S., & Gupta, G. (2024). Re-Imaging Human Resource Strategic Approaches: Adoption of Metaverse. In *The Role of HR in the Transforming Workplace* (pp. 95-103). Productivity Press.

Müller-Stewens, J., Schlager, T., Häubl, G., & Herrmann, A. (2017). Gamified Information Presentation and Consumer Adoption of Product Innovations. *Journal of Marketing*, *81*(2), 8–24. DOI: 10.1509/jm.15.0396

Nagarajah, A. (2022, December 20). *How gamification in marketing affects consumer behavior?* eVULX. https://evulx.com/how-gamification-in-marketing-affects-consumer-behavior/

Nandy, B., Sharma, G., Garg, S., Kumari, S., George, T., Sunanda, Y., & Sinha, B. (2015). Recovery of hydrocarbons from waste plastics by thermal pyrolysis and catalytic pyrolysis. *Energy & Fuels*, *29*(6), 3544–3557. DOI: 10.1021/acs.energyfuels.5b00472

NASSCOM. (2023). *Gaming: The emerging frontier in India's digital economy*. https://nasscom.in/

Nayak, A., Patnaik, A., Satpathy, I., Patnaik, B. C. M., & Baral, S. K. Metaverse: The Transformation of Customer Engagement with Brands in the Digital Age. In Green Metaverse for Greener Economies(2024) (pp. 270-284). CRC Press.

Newzoo. (2021). Global games market report 2021. https://newzoo.com/ insights/trend-reports/newzoo-global-games-market-report-2021-freeversion

Ng, P. H., Chen, P. Q., Sin, Z. P., Jia, Y., Li, R. C., Baciu, G., Cao, J., & Li, Q. 2023, November. From classroom to metaverse: a study on gamified constructivist teaching in higher education. In *International conference on web-based learning* (pp. 92-106). Singapore: Springer Nature Singapore. DOI: 10.1007/978-981-99-8385-8_8

Nicholson, S. (2012). A user-centered theoretical framework for meaningful gamification. *Gamesþ Learningþ Society*, *8*, 1.

Nicola, M. (2022). Gamification marketing in metaverse contexts: can the employment of immersive gamification experiences that leverage customer's creativity and sociality be a useful tool to influence customer engagement in metaverse applications?.

Nicola, M., (2022). gamification marketing in metaverse contexts: can the employment of immersive gamification experiences that leverage customer's creativity and sociality be a useful tool to influence customer engagement in metaverse applications?.

Nieto-Escamez, F. A., & Roldán-Tapia, M. D. (2021). Gamification as online teaching strategy during COVID-19: A mini-review. *Frontiers in Psychology*, *12*, 648552. DOI: 10.3389/fpsyg.2021.648552 PMID: 34093334

Nurtanto, M., Kholifah, N., Ahdhianto, E., Samsudin, A., & Isnantyo, F. D. (2021). A review of gamification impact on student behavioral and learning outcomes. iJIM, 15(21), 23.

Nwakanma, C., Njoku, J., Okafor, C., & Kim, D. (2022). "Prospect and industry issues of Metaverse and digital twin adoption in nigerian maritime," in Paper presented at the Proceedings of the 1sth international Conference on maritime IT convergence. South Korea: Jeju Island, 1–4.

Nyström, T. (2021). Exploring the Darkness of Gamification: You Want It Darker? In Arai, K. (Ed.), *Intelligent Computing* (pp. 479–495). Springer. DOI: 10.1007/978-3-030-80129-8_35

O'Brien, H. (2018). *A Holistic Approach to Measuring User Engagement.*, DOI: 10.1007/978-3-319-73374-6_6

Observer Research Foundation. (2024). *Harnessing gaming potential: Policy proposals for India's gaming economy.* https://www.orfonline.org/

Oliver, R. L. (1999). Whence consumer loyalty? *Journal of Marketing*, *63*(4, suppl1), 33–44. DOI: 10.1177/00222429990634s105

Oluwaseyi, J. and Stilinski, D., (2024). The Strategic Implications of the Metaverse for Brand Building and Customer Experience.

OMIgroup. (2022). Open Metaverse interoperability group. Omigroup. Available at: https://omigroup.org/

Orji, R., Vassileva, J., & Mandryk, R. (2012). LunchTime: A slow-casual game for long-term dietary behavior change. *Personal and Ubiquitous Computing*, *17*(6), 1211–1221. Advance online publication. DOI: 10.1007/s00779-012-0590-6

Ouariachi, T., Elving, W. J., & Pierie, F. (2017). Playing for a sustainable future: Games to model and appraise paths towards sustainable behavior change. *Proceedings of the 11th European Conference on Games Based Learning*, 492-499.

Özdemir Uçgun, G., & Şahin, S. Z. (2023). How does Metaverse affect the tourism industry? Current practices and future forecasts. *Current Issues in Tourism*, *27*(17), 2742–2756. DOI: 10.1080/13683500.2023.2238111

Özkan, S., Bindusara, G., & Hackney, R. (2010). Facilitating the adoption of e-payment systems: Theoretical constructs and empirical analysis. *Journal of Enterprise Information Management*, *23*(3), 305–325. DOI: 10.1108/17410391011036085

Öztürk, B. and Hersono, R., (2023). Playing to Win: How Gamification Can Boost Customer Engagement and Turn Non-Fans into Brand Advocates.

Packin, N. G., & Chagal-Feferkorn, K. (2025). This Is Not a Game: The Addictive Allure of Digital Companions. *Seattle University Law Review*, *48*(3), 693. DOI: 10.2139/ssrn.5133614

Palma Ruiz, J. M. (2022). Gaming revenue dynamics: A cross-continental analysis with Asia-specific implications. *International Journal of Interactive Media and Gaming*, *5*(2), 89–104.

Palmer, D., Lunceford, S., & Patton, A. J. (2012). The engagement economy: How gamification is reshaping businesses. *Deloitte Review*, *11*, 52–69.

Pandey, S., Kumar, A., & Sharma, A. (2024). Sustainable solar drying: Recent advances in materials, innovative designs, mathematical modeling, and energy storage solutions. *Energy*, *308*, 132725. DOI: 10.1016/j.energy.2024.132725

Pansari, A., & Kumar, V. (2017). Customer engagement: The construct, antecedents, and consequences. *Journal of the Academy of Marketing Science*, *45*(3), 294–311. DOI: 10.1007/s11747-016-0485-6

Park, C. H., & Kim, Y. G. (2003). Identifying key factors affecting consumer purchase behavior in an online shopping context. *International Journal of Retail & Distribution Management*, *31*(1), 16–29. DOI: 10.1108/09590550310457818

Park, J. H. (2021). The direction and implications of the content industry in the Metaverse era. *SSRN*, (21), 6–5. DOI: 10.2139/ssrn.4194255

Park, S., & Kim, S. (2022). Identifying world types to deliver gameful experiences for sustainable learning in the metaverse. *Sustainability (Basel)*, *14*(3), 1361. DOI: 10.3390/su14031361

Pavlus, J. (2010). The game of life.(Cover story). *Scientific American, 303*(6), 43–44. DOI: 10.1038/scientificamerican1210-43

Payal, R., Sharma, N., & Dwivedi, Y. K. (2024). Unlocking the impact of brand engagement in the metaverse on Real-World purchase intentions: Analyzing Pre-Adoption behavior in a futuristic technology platform. *Electronic Commerce Research and Applications, 65*, 101381. DOI: 10.1016/j.elerap.2024.101381

Peng, W., Lin, J. H., Pfeiffer, K. A., & Winn, B. (2012). Need satisfaction supportive game features as motivational determinants: An experimental study of a self-determination theory guided exergame. *Media Psychology, 15*(2), 175–196. DOI: 10.1080/15213269.2012.673850

Pero, J. (2022). *Sorry, Metaverse is the word of the year whether you like it or not.* Inverse.

Plastic Bank. (2023). Plastic Bank: A global network of ethical Plastic Collectors and recyclers. https://plasticbank.com/

Poddar, A., Donthu, N., & Wei, Y. (2009). Web site customer orientations, Web site quality, and purchase intentions: The role of Web site personality. *Journal of Business Research, 62*(4), 441–450. DOI: 10.1016/j.jbusres.2008.01.036

Pooyandeh, M., Han, K., & Sohn, I. (2022). Cybersecurity in the AI-based Metaverse: A survey. *Applied Sciences (Basel, Switzerland), 12*(24), 12993. DOI: 10.3390/app122412993

Prabadevi, B., Deepa, N., Victor, N., Gadekallu, T. R., Maddikunta, P. K. R., & Yenduri, G.. (2023). Metaverse and the fashion industry: A systematic literature review. *J. Glob. Fash. Mark., 15*(1), 131–154. DOI: 10.1080/20932685.2023.2270587

Prabowo, S. H. W., Murdiono, A., Martha, J. A., Zutiasari, I., & Murad, S. M. A. (2023). May. Gamification of Ubiquitous-Based Learning Media as an Initiative of Open-World Metaverse Conversion for Problem Based Learning (PBL) in Business and Management Courses. In *BISTIC Business Innovation Sustainability and Technology International Conference (BISTIC 2022)* (pp. 86-97). Atlantis Press. DOI: 10.2991/978-94-6463-178-4_10

Punwatkar, S., & Verghese, M. (2025). Investigating the impact of gamification on customer engagement, brand loyalty and purchase intent in marketing. *Journal of Applied Research and Technology, 23*(1), 94–102. DOI: 10.22201/icat.24486736e.2025.23.1.2592

PwC & Ministry of Information and Broadcasting. (2024). *From sunrise to sunshine: The growth trajectory of India's gaming sector*. https://www.pwc.in/

Qian, T. Y., Matz, R., Luo, L., & Xu, C. (2022). Gamification for value creation and viewer engagement in gamified livestreaming services: The moderating role of gender in esports. *Journal of Business Research, 145*, 482–494. DOI: 10.1016/j.jbusres.2022.02.082

Qin, Y. (2022). Investment potential analysis on Chinese stock market in Metaverse-take VR industry as a sample. Paper presented at the 2022 7th international conference on financial innovation and economic development (ICFIED 2022), 1001–1007. DOI: 10.2991/aebmr.k.220307.165

Raftopoulos, M. (2014). Towards gamification transparency: A conceptual framework for the development of responsible gamified enterprise systems. *Journal of Gaming & Virtual Worlds*, *6*(2), 159–178. DOI: 10.1386/jgvw.6.2.159_1

Raijas, A., & Tuunainen, V. K. (2001). Critical factors in electronic grocery shopping. *International Review of Retail, Distribution and Consumer Research, 11*(3), 255–265. DOI: 10.1080/713770596

Ramakrishnan, T., Mohan Gift, M. D., Chitradevi, S., Jegan, R., Hency Jose, P. S., Nagaraja, H. N., & Hailegiorgis, S. M. (2022). Study of numerous resins used in polymer matrix composite materials. *Advances in Materials Science and Engineering*, *2022*(1), 1088926.

Rane, N., Choudhary, S. and Rane, J., (2023). Metaverse for Enhancing Customer Loyalty: Effective Strategies to Improve Customer Relationship, Service, Engagement, Satisfaction, and Experience. *Service, Engagement, Satisfaction, and Experience (November 1, 2023).*

Rane, N., Choudhary, S., & Rane, J. (2023). Metaverse marketing strategies: enhancing customer experience and analysing consumer behaviour through leading-edge Metaverse technologies, platforms, and models. Platforms, and Models (November 3, 2023).

Rane, N. (2023). Metaverse marketing strategies: enhancing customer experience and analysing consumer behaviour through leading-edge Metaverse technologies, platforms, and models. *Available atSSRN*. DOI: 10.2139/ssrn.4624199

Rane, N., Choudhary, S., & Rane, J. (2023, November 1). *Metaverse for enhancing customer loyalty: Effective strategies to improve customer relationship, service, engagement, satisfaction, and experience. SSRN*. https://ssrn.com/abstract=4624197 or DOI: 10.2139/ssrn.4624197

Ranganathan, C., & Ganapathy, S. (2002). Key dimensions of business-to-consumer web sites. *Information & Management, 39*(6), 457–465. DOI: 10.1016/S0378-7206(01)00112-4

Rasool, A., Shah, F. A., & Islam, J. U. (2020). Customer engagement in the digital age: A review and research agenda. *Current Opinion in Psychology, 36*, 96–100. DOI: 10.1016/j.copsyc.2020.05.003 PMID: 32599394

Rather, R. A. (2023). Metaverse marketing and consumer research: Theoretical framework and future research agenda in tourism and hospitality industry. *Tourism Recreation Research*, •••, 1–9. DOI: 10.1080/02508281.2023.2216525

Rauschnabel, P. A., Felix, R., & Hinsch, C. (2019). Augmented reality marketing: How mobile AR-apps can improve brands through inspiration. *Journal of Retailing and Consumer Services, 49*, 43–53. DOI: 10.1016/j.jretconser.2019.03.004

Raza, A., Rehmat, S., Ishaq, M. I., Haj-Salem, N., & Talpur, Q. U. A. (2024). Gamification in financial service apps to enhance customer experience and engagement. *Journal of Consumer Behaviour, 23*(4), 1653–1670. DOI: 10.1002/cb.2294

RedSeer. (2022). *Online gaming in India: The next wave*. https://redseer.com/

Rivadeneira, J. E., Silva, J. S., Colomo-Palacios, R., Rodrigues, A., & Boavida, F. (2023). User-centric privacy preserving models for a new era of the Internet of Things. *Journal of Network and Computer Applications, 217*, 103695. DOI: 10.1016/j.jnca.2023.103695

Robertson, A., & Peters, J. (2021). *What is the metaverse, and do I have to care?* The Verge. https://www.theverge.com/22701104/metaverse-explained-fortnite-roblox-facebook-horizon

Rosário, A. T., Lopes, P. R., & Rosário, F. S. (2023). Metaverse in Marketing: Challenges and Opportunities. *Handbook of Research on AI-Based Technologies and Applications in the Era of the Metaverse*, 204-227.

Rowicka, M., & Postek, S. (2023). Who likes to learn new things? How Gamification User Types and Satisfaction but not the frustration of basic psychological needs explain the preference for learning new things. *Acta Psychologica, 236*, 103925. DOI: 10.1016/j.actpsy.2023.103925 PMID: 37116268

Rozak, H. A., & Fachrunnisa, O., Sugiharti, Taswan, & Fitriati, I. R. (2023, August). Metaverse and Modification Needs of Human Resources Management Practices and Policies: An Overview. In *International Conference on Intelligent Networking and Collaborative Systems* (pp. 285-294). Cham: Springer Nature Switzerland. DOI: 10.1007/978-3-031-40971-4_27

Rozalén, S. M. (2024). Gamification as a Persuasive Technology: Characteristics and Ethical Implications. *Journal of Ethics and Emerging Technologies*, *34*(1), 1–19.

Ruggiu, D., Blok, V., Coenen, C., Kalloniatis, C., Kitsiou, A., Mavroeidi, A. G., Milani, S., & Sitzia, A. (2022). Responsible innovation at work: Gamification, public engagement, and privacy by design. *Journal of Responsible Innovation*, *9*(3), 315–343. DOI: 10.1080/23299460.2022.2076985

Ryan, R. M., & Deci, E. L. (2000). Self-determination theory and the facilitation of intrinsic motivation, social development, and well-being. *The American Psychologist*, *55*(1), 68–78. DOI: 10.1037/0003-066X.55.1.68 PMID: 11392867

Ryan, R. M., Rigby, C. S., & Przybylski, A. (2006). The motivational pull of video games: A self-determination theory approach. *Motivation and Emotion*, *30*(4), 344–360. DOI: 10.1007/s11031-006-9051-8

Saeed, A., Ali, A., & Ashfaq, S. (2024). Employees' training experience in a metaverse environment? Feedback analysis using structural topic modeling. *Technological Forecasting and Social Change*, *208*, 123636. DOI: 10.1016/j.techfore.2024.123636

Safitri, A., Husin, N., Arifah, I. D. C., Dewi, R. S., Kharisma, F., & Kautsar, A. (2024, January). Metaverse User Experience, Customer Engagement, and Brand Awareness Relation as SMEs Marketing Strategies in Virtual Worlds. In *2024 ASU International Conference in Emerging Technologies for Sustainability and Intelligent Systems (ICETSIS)* (pp. 1092-1096). IEEE. DOI: 10.1109/ICETSIS61505.2024.10459506

Sardi, L., Idri, A., & Fernández-Alemán, J. L. (2017). A systematic review of gamification in e-Health. *Journal of Biomedical Informatics*, *71*, 31–48. DOI: 10.1016/j.jbi.2017.05.011 PMID: 28536062

Schaupp, L. C., & Belanger, F. (2005). A conjoint analysis of online consumer satisfaction. *Journal of Electronic Commerce Research*, *6*(2), 95–111.

Seaborn, K., & Fels, D. I. (2015). Gamification in theory and action: A survey. *International Journal of Human-Computer Studies*, *74*, 14–31. DOI: 10.1016/j.ijhcs.2014.09.006

Segmentify. (2024, July 4). *The Ultimate guide to gamification in Marketing*. Segmentify. https://segmentify.com/blog/gamification-marketing-guide/

Selinger, E., Sadowski, J., & Seager, T. (2015). Gamification and morality.

Serenko, A., Turel, O., & Yol, S. (2006). Moderating roles of user demographics in the American customer satisfaction model within the context of mobile services. *Journal of Information Technology Management*, *17*(4), 20–32.

Shah, R., Shah, S., & Pathak, P. (2025). Metaverse work culture: The emergence of virtual-first companies and HR's role. *Strategic HR Review*. Advance online publication. DOI: 10.1108/SHR-03-2025-0029

Sharholy, M., Ahmad, K., Mahmood, G., & Trivedi, R. C. (2008). Municipal solid waste management in Indian cities – A review. *Waste Management (New York, N.Y.)*, *28*(2), 459–467. DOI: 10.1016/j.wasman.2007.02.008 PMID: 17433664

Sharma, V., Payal, R., Dutta, K., Poulose, J., & Kapse, M. (2024). A comprehensive examination of factors influencing intention to continue usage of health and fitness apps: A two-stage hybrid SEM-ML analysis. *Cogent Business & Management*, *11*(1), 2391124. Advance online publication. DOI: 10.1080/23311975.2024.2391124

Sharma, W., Lim, W. M., Kumar, S., Verma, A., & Kumra, R. (2024). Game on! A state-of-the-art overview of doing business with gamification. *Technological Forecasting and Social Change*, *198*, 122988. DOI: 10.1016/j.techfore.2023.122988

Sheetal, T., Tyagi, R., & Singh, G. (2023). Gamification and customer experience in online retail: A qualitative study focusing on ethical perspective. *Asian Journal of Business Ethics*, *12*(1), 49–69. DOI: 10.1007/s13520-022-00162-1

Shen, Y. S., Choi, H. C., Joppe, M., & Yi, S. (2020). What motivates visitors to participate in a gamified trip? A player typology using Q methodology. *Tourism Management*, *78*, 104074. DOI: 10.1016/j.tourman.2019.104074

Shin, J. I., Chung, K. H., Oh, J. S., & Lee, C. W. (2013). The effect of site quality on repurchase intention in Internet shopping through mediating variables: The case of university students in South Korea. *International Journal of Information Management*, *33*(3), 453–463. DOI: 10.1016/j.ijinfomgt.2013.02.003

Shi, Y., Qian, Y., & Cao, L. (2019). Gamification recycling: Study into the factors influencing the continuation intention of the use of a gamified recycling system. *Sustainability*, *11*(6), 1532. DOI: 10.3390/su11061532

Sidorenko-Bautista, P., Castillo-Abdul, B., Herranz-de-la-Casa, J. M., & Abellán-Hernández, M. (2025). Marketing, advertising, and branding in Fortnite: How do brands and companies connect today to audiences through the metaverse? *Cogent Social Sciences*, *11*(1), 2458058. DOI: 10.1080/23311886.2025.2458058

Sigala, M. (2015). Gamification for crowdsourcing marketing practices: Applications and benefits in tourism. *Advances in crowdsourcing*, 129-145.

Sigala, M. (2015). The application and impact of gamification funware on trip planning and experiences: The case of TripAdvisor's funware. *Electronic Markets*, *25*(3), 189–209. DOI: 10.1007/s12525-014-0179-1

Simms, B. (2019, May 13). *5 Benefits of Using Gamification in your Digital Marketing Strategy*. #DMWF World Series. https://www.digitalmarketing-conference.com/5-benefits-of-using-gamification-in-your-digital-marketing-strategy/

Singh, A., Lakhera, G., Ojha, M., Mishra, A. K., & Kumari, J. (2022). Exploring the Use of Gamification in HR Processes for Staff Engagement in Hotels and Restaurants. In *AI, Blockchain, and Metaverse in Hospitality and Tourism Industry 4.0* (pp. 253-262). Chapman and Hall/CRC.

Singh, K. (2023). Evaluation planning for artificial intelligence-based industry 6.0 Metaverse integration. Intelligent Hum. Syst. Integration (IHSI 2023). *Integrating People Intelligent Syst.*, *69*(69). Advance online publication. DOI: 10.54941/ahfe1002892

Sinha, N. (2021). *Introducing Gamification for Advancing Current Mental Healthcare and Treatment Practices.*, DOI: 10.1007/978-981-15-9897-5_11

Smiderle, R., Rigo, S. J., Marques, L. B., Peçanha de Miranda Coelho, J. A., & Jaques, P. A. (2020). The impact of gamification on students' learning, engagement and behavior based on their personality traits. *Smart Learning Environments*, *7*(1), 3. DOI: 10.1186/s40561-019-0098-x

Smith, B. (2025, March 17). *Gamification in Marketing: Trends for 2025*. https://www.rhapsodymedia.com/blog/gamification-in-marketing-trends-for-2025

Smith, E., Herbert, J., Kavanagh, L., & Reidsema, C. (2013). The effects of gamification on student learning through the use of reputation and rewards within community moderated discussion boards.

Sousa-Vieira, M. E., López-Ardao, J. C., Fernández-Veiga, M., & Rodríguez-Rubio, R. F. (2023). Study of the impact of social learning and gamification methodologies on learning results in higher education. *Computer Applications in Engineering Education*, *31*(1), 131–153. DOI: 10.1002/cae.22575

Spajić, J., Mitrović, K., Lalić, D., Milić, B., & Bošković, D. (2022, September). Personalized brand experience in metaverse. In *10th International Conference on Mass Customization and Personalization–Community of Europe (MCP-CE 2022)* (pp. 21-23).

Spanellis, A. (2023). Gamification for sustainable consumption: Ethical issues and future promises. In *Research Handbook on Ethical Consumption* (pp. 366–381). Edward Elgar Publishing. DOI: 10.4337/9781802202021.00031

Sreenivasulu, A., & Manimozhi, T. Satheesh kumar P., Selvakumar P. and Singh P.,(2022). “The Model of Smart Sensing Device For Sensitive Nanoclusters Modification in Sensing Properties,” 2022 2nd International Conference on Advance Computing and Innovative Technologies in Engineering (ICACITE), Greater Noida, India, 2022, pp. 1043-1047, DOI: 10.1109/ICACITE53722.2022.9823846

Srinivasan, S. S., Anderson, R., & Ponnavolu, K. (2002). Customer loyalty in e-commerce: An exploration of its antecedents and consequences. *Journal of Retailing*, *78*(1), 41–50. DOI: 10.1016/S0022-4359(01)00065-3

Srisawat, S., & Piriyasurawong, P. (2022). Metaverse Virtual Learning Management Based on Gamification Techniques Model to Enhance Total Experience. *International Education Studies*, *15*(5), 153–163. DOI: 10.5539/ies.v15n5p153

Srivastava, G., Bag, S., Rahman, M. S., Pretorius, J. H. C., & Gani, M. O. (2023). Examining the dark side of using gamification elements in online community engagement: An application of PLS-SEM and ANN modeling. *Benchmarking*, *30*(9), 2921–2947. DOI: 10.1108/BIJ-03-2022-0160

Statista. (2024). Biggest social media platforms. Statista. https://www.statista.com/statistics/272014/global-social-networks-ranked-by-number-of-users/

Sugumaran, K. M. D., Pandiyarajan V., Y. B S, Selvakumar P. and M. S, (2024). “Analysis of Electromyography Signals for Control of Mechanical Prosthesis using Machine Learning Techniques,” 2024 2nd International Conference on Intelligent Data Communication Technologies and Internet of Things (IDCIoT), Bengaluru, India, 2024, pp. 1059-1067, DOI: 10.1109/IDCIoT59759.2024.10467707

Su, N., Mariadoss, B. J., & Reynolds, D. (2019). Emotional and cognitive involvement of consumers with hotel brands on social networking sites. *Journal of Hospitality and Tourism Insights*, *2*(4), 377–390. DOI: 10.1108/JHTI-10-2018-0064

Swaminathan, V., Lepkowska-White, E., & Rao, B. P. (1999). Browsers or buyers in cyberspace? An investigation of factors influencing electronic exchange. *Journal of Computer-Mediated Communication, 5*(2), 0-0.

Sweileh, W. (2023). Analysis and mapping of scientific literature on virtual and augmented reality technologies used in the context of mental health disorders (1980 – 2021). *The Journal of Mental Health Training, Education and Practice*, *18*(4), 288–305. Advance online publication. DOI: 10.1108/JMHTEP-04-2022-0019

Szymanski, D., & Hise, R. T. (2000). Hise R. E-satisfaction: An initial examination. *Journal of Retailing*, *76*(3), 309–322. DOI: 10.1016/S0022-4359(00)00035-X

Tayal, S., Rajagopal, K., & Mahajan, V. 2022, March. Virtual reality based metaverse of gamification. In *2022 6th International Conference on Computing Methodologies and Communication (ICCMC)* (pp. 1597-1604). IEEE. DOI: 10.1109/ICCMC53470.2022.9753727

Tena Ochoa, K. A. (2023). *An explorative Impact Analysis of Digitalization in Automotive Customer Journey and Retail Experience* (Doctoral dissertation, Wien).

Thaler, R. H., & Sunstein, C. R. (2008). *Nudge: Improving decisions about health,wealth, and happiness*. Yale University Press.

Thomas, N. J., Baral, R., Crocco, O. S., & Mohanan, S. (2023). A framework for gamification in the metaverse era: How designers envision gameful experience. *Technological Forecasting and Social Change*, *193*, 122544. DOI: 10.1016/j.techfore.2023.122544

Thomason, J. (2022). Metaverse, token economies, and non-communicable diseases. *Global Health Journal (Amsterdam, Netherlands)*, *6*(3), 164–167.

Tlili, A., Huang, R., & Kinshuk, X. (2023). Metaverse for climbing the ladder toward 'industry 5.0'and 'society 5.0. *Service Industries Journal*, *43*(3-4), 260–287. DOI: 10.1080/02642069.2023.2178644

Tomé Klock, A. C., Santana, B. S., & Hamari, J. (2023). Ethical Challenges in Gamified Education Research and Development: An Umbrella Review and Potential Directions. In Gamification Design for Educational Contexts (pp. 37-48). Springer.

Topuzova, I. (2025, March 13). *What is gamification in marketing?* Dot.vu Blog. https://blog.dot.vu/gamification-in-marketing/

Torres, P., Augusto, M., & Neves, C. (2022). Value dimensions of gamification and their influence on brand loyalty and word-of-mouth: Relationships and combinations with satisfaction and brand love. *Psychology and Marketing*, *39*(1), 59–75.

Trocchia, P. J., & Janda, S. (2000). A phenomenological investigation of Internet usage among older individuals. *Journal of Consumer Marketing*, *17*(7), 605–616. DOI: 10.1108/07363760010357804

Truong, V. T., Le, L. B., & Niyato, D. (2023). Blockchain meets Metaverse and digital asset management: A comprehensive survey. *IEEE Access : Practical Innovations, Open Solutions*, *11*, 26258–26288. DOI: 10.1109/ACCESS.2023.3257029

Tsai, C. C., & Lin, S. S. (2020). The relationship between online game addiction and peer relationships among adolescents. *Computers & Education*, *148*, 103809.

Tsiliakos, M., & Bassing, S. 2024, April. Eduverse: Exploring Gamification and the Metaverse in Architectural Pedagogy. In *ACCELERATED DESIGN, Proceedings of the 29th International Conference of the Association for ComputerAided Architectural Design Research in Asia (CAADRIA) 2024, Volume 3, 59-68* (pp. 59-68). Association for Computer-Aided Architectural Design Research in Asia (CAADRIA).

Turban, E., King, D., Lee, J., & Viehland, D. (2002). Electronic commerce: A managerial perspective. *Prentice Hall: ISBN 0, 13*(975285), 4.

Turban, E., King, D., Lee, J. K., & Viehland, D. (2006). *Electronic commerce: A managerial perspective*. Prentice Hall.

Vaismoradi, M., Turunen, H., & Bondas, T. (2013). Content analysis and thematic analysis: Implications for conducting a qualitative descriptive study. *Nursing & Health Sciences, 15*(3), 398–405. DOI: 10.1111/nhs.12048 PMID: 23480423

Valmohammadi, C., Asayesh, F., Mehdikhani, R., & Taraz, R. (2025). Influencer marketing, ewom, e-brand experience, and retail e-brand loyalty: Moderating influence of e-brand love. *Journal of Relationship Marketing, 24*(1), 66–92. DOI: 10.1080/15332667.2024.2405292

Venly. (2025). *Web3 gaming white paper: Blockchain and NFT innovation in India's AVGC-XR sector*. https://www.venly.io/

Verma, R., Vinoda, K. S., Papireddy, M., & Gowda, A. N. S. (2016). Toxic pollutants from plastic waste- A review. *Procedia Environmental Sciences, 35*, 701–708. DOI: 10.1016/j.proenv.2016.07.069

Vijayakumar, G., Rajkumar, M., Rajiv Chandar, N., Selvakumar, P., & Duraisamy, R. (2024). Muniyandi Rajkumar, Rajiv Chandar N, Selvakumar P and Ramesh Duraisamy, (2024). Environmentally friendly TDS removal from waste water by electrochemical ion exchange batch-type recirculation (EIR) technique. *Environmental Science. Water Research & Technology, 10*(4), 826–835. DOI: 10.1039/D3EW00793F

Vincent, B., Daniele, R., & Christopher, C. (2022). Responsible innovation at work: gamification, public engagement, and privacy by design.

Wang, X., Shi, T., Bai, W., Peng, K., Li, J., & Shi, Y. (2022). "The research of Metaverse application in intelligent railway passenger station," in Paper presented at the international conference on Metaverse, 111–117. DOI: 10.1007/978-3-031-23518-4_10

Wang, L., Gunasti, K., Shankar, R., Pancras, J., & Gopal, R. (2018). (Forthcoming). Impact of gamification on perceptions of word-of-mouth contributors and actions of word-of-mouth consumers. *Wang, L., Gunasti K., Shankar, R., Pancras, J. Gopal, R., Impact of Gamification on Perceptions of Word-of-Mouth Contributors and Actions of Word-of-Mouth Consumers, MISQ. Management Information Systems Quarterly.*

Wang, T., Fan, L., Zheng, X., Wang, W., Liang, J., An, K., Ju, M., & Lei, J. (2021). The impact of gamification-induced users' feelings on the continued use of mHealth apps: A structural equation model with the self-determination theory approach. *Journal of Medical Internet Research*, *23*(8), e24546. DOI: 10.2196/24546 PMID: 34387550

Wang, Y., & Kosinski, M. (2018). Deep neural networks are more accurate than humans at detecting sexual orientation from facial images. *Journal of Personality and Social Psychology*, *114*(2), 246–257. DOI: 10.1037/pspa0000098 PMID: 29389215

Wang, Y., Su, Z., Zhang, N., Xing, R., Liu, D., Luan, T. H., & Shen, X. (2022). A survey on metaverse: Fundamentals, security, and privacy. *IEEE Communications Surveys and Tutorials.*

Wang, Z., & Yang, X. (2024). Building brand loyalty through value co-creation practices in brand communities: The role of affective commitment and psychological brand ownership. *Journal of Research in Interactive Marketing*.

Wanick, V., & Stallwood, J. (2023). Brand storytelling, gamification and social media marketing in the "metaverse": A case study of the Ralph Lauren winter escape. In *Reinventing fashion retailing: Digitalising, gamifying, entrepreneuring* (pp. 35–54). Springer International Publishing. DOI: 10.1007/978-3-031-11185-3_3

Waste-Free World. (2023). Waste-Free World: Incentivizing communities to recycle. https://wastefreeworld.org/

Weiss, J. (2019, January). Gamification and Scholarly Ethical Perspectives on Industries, A Bibliometric Analysis. *Proceedings of the 52nd Hawaii International Conference on System Sciences*. DOI: 10.24251/HICSS.2019.827

Werbach, K., & Hunter, D. (2012). *For the win: How game thinking can revolutionize your business*. Wharton Digital Press.

White, M., & Shellenbarger, T. (2018). Gamification of nursing education with digital badges. *Nurse Educator*, *43*(2), 78–82. DOI: 10.1097/NNE.0000000000000434 PMID: 28817476

Widiyanti, D. E., Kim, E. B., & Shin, S. Y. (2022). "Enhancing the use of Metaverse in industry: advertisement management system," in *Proceedings of the korea communications society conference*, 753–754.

Wolf, T., Weiger, W. H., & Hammerschmidt, M. (2020). Experiences that matter? The motivational experiences and business outcomes of gamified services. *Journal of Business Research, 106*, 353–364. DOI: 10.1016/j.jbusres.2018.12.058

Woo, A., & Forbes Agency Council. (2021). *Mapping the metaverse: How can brands make the most of this new world?* https://www.forbes.com/sites/forbesagencycouncil/2021/11/30/mapping-the-metaverse-how-can-brands-make-the-most-of-this-new-world/?sh=3edd3fdb6534

Wu, C., Zhou, Y., Wang, R., Huang, S., & Yuan, Q. (2022). Understanding the Mechanism Between IT Identity, IT Mindfulness and Mobile Health Technology Continuance Intention: An Extended Expectation Confirmation Model. *Technological Forecasting and Social Change, 176*(C), 121449. https://ideas.repec.org//a/eee/tefoso/v176y2022ics0040162521008805.html. DOI: 10.1016/j.techfore.2021.121449

Xi, N., & Hamari, J. (2019). Does gamification satisfy needs? A study on the relationship between gamification features and intrinsic need satisfaction. *International Journal of Information Management, 46*, 210–221. DOI: 10.1016/j.ijinfomgt.2018.12.002

Xi, N., & Hamari, J. (2020). Does gamification affect brand engagement and equity? A study in online brand communities. *Journal of Business Research, 109*, 449–460. DOI: 10.1016/j.jbusres.2019.11.058

Xu, Y. (2011). Literature review on web application gamification and analytics. CSDL Technical Report 11-05. Retrieved from https://csdl.ics.hawaii.edu/techreports/11-05/11-05.pdf

Xu, F., Buhalis, D., & Weber, J. (2017). Serious games and the gamification of tourism. *Tourism Management, 60*, 244–256. DOI: 10.1016/j.tourman.2016.11.020

Xu, F., Weber, J., & Buhalis, D. (2013). Gamification in tourism. In *Information and Communication Technologies in Tourism 2014* (pp. 525–537). Springer. DOI: 10.1007/978-3-319-03973-2_38

Xu, M., Ng, W. C., Lim, W. Y. B., Kang, J., Xiong, Z., Niyato, D., Yang, Q., Shen, X., & Miao, C. (2022). A full dive into realizing the edge-enabled Metaverse: Visions, enabling technologies, and challenges. *IEEE Communications Surveys and Tutorials, 25*(1), 656–700. DOI: 10.1109/COMST.2022.3221119

Yadav, M., & Dangi, A. (2023). The Impact of Gamification on Cognitive Brand Engagement in E?Commerce Context, *Pacific Business Review International*, 15(8).

Yadav, K., Arora, A., Yadav, R., & Saini, C. P. (2022). Gamified apps and customer engagement: Modeling in online shopping environment. *Transnational Marketing Journal, 10*(3), 593–605. DOI: 10.33182/tmj.v10i3.2062

Yadav, S., Pandey, S. K., & Sharma, D. (2024). Marketing beyond reality: A systematic literature review on metaverse. *Management Research Review, 47*(7), 1029–1051. DOI: 10.1108/MRR-06-2023-0456

Yamba-Yugsi, M., Contreras-Espinosa, R. S., & Eguia-Gomez, J. L. 2024. Exploring the Emerging Potential of the Metaverse in Education: Gamification, Advantages, and Limitations. In *Navigating Virtual Worlds and the Metaverse for Enhanced E-Learning* (pp. 111-133). IGI Global.

Yamba-Yugsi, M., Contreras-Espinosa, R. S., Maldonado-Mahauad, J., & Gomez, J. L. E. (2023). EXAMINING THE OPPORTUNITIES OF THE METAVERSE AND GAMIFICATION IN EDUCATION: Benefits, and constraints. *Video Journal of Social and Human Research, 2*(2), 47–64. DOI: 10.18817/vjshr.v2i2.32

Yan, R. (2022). "A sustainable fashion industry business model revolution based on the Metaverse: practices and reciprocal processes,", 4. Econ. Manag., 363–369. DOI: 10.54097/hbem.v4i.3526

Yang, C., Yang, P., & Feng, Y. (2022). Effect of achievement-related gamification on brand attachment. *Industrial Management & Data Systems, 122*(1), 251–271. DOI: 10.1108/IMDS-02-2021-0088

Yang, L. (2023). Recommendations for Metaverse governance based on technical standards. *Humanities & Social Sciences Communications, 10*(1), 1–10. DOI: 10.1057/s41599-023-01750-7

Yang, W., Fang, M., Xu, J., Zhang, X., & Pan, Y. (2024). Exploring the Mediating Role of Different Aspects of Learning Motivation between Metaverse Learning Experiences and Gamification. *Electronics (Basel), 13*(7), 1297. DOI: 10.3390/electronics13071297

Yang, Y., Asaad, Y., & Dwivedi, Y. (2017). Examining the impact of gamification on consumer engagement. *Computers in Human Behavior, 69*, 98–106.

Yang, Y., Asaad, Y., & Dwivedi, Y. (2017). Examining the impact of gamification on intention of engagement and brand attitude in the marketing context. *Computers in Human Behavior, 73*, 459–469. DOI: 10.1016/j.chb.2017.03.066

Yang, Y., & Koenigstorfer, J. (2020). Determinants of physical activity maintenance during the Covid-19 pandemic: A focus on fitness apps. *Translational Behavioral Medicine*, *10*(4), 835–842. DOI: 10.1093/tbm/ibaa086 PMID: 32926160

Yan, M., Filieri, R., Raguseo, E., & Gorton, M. (2021). Mobile apps for healthy living: Factors influencing continuance intention for health apps. *Technological Forecasting and Social Change*, *166*, 120644. DOI: 10.1016/j.techfore.2021.120644

Yee, N. (2005). Motivations for play in online games. *Cyberpsychology & Behavior*, *9*(6), 772–775. DOI: 10.1089/cpb.2006.9.772 PMID: 17201605

Yee, N. (2014). *The Proteus paradox: How online games and virtual worlds change us—And how they don't.* Yale Univeristy Press.

Yee, N., Ducheneaut, N., & Nelson, L. (2012). Online gaming motivations scale: Development and validation. In *Proceedings of the SIGCHI Conference on Human Factors in Computing Systems*, Austin, Texas, USA. DOI: 10.1145/2207676.2208681

Ye, S., & Lin, Y. (2023). The impact of short video addiction on students' behavioral engagement. *Computers in Human Behavior*, *137*, 107420.

Yolanda, F. (2020). Pengaruh Electronic Word Of Mouth Di Media Sosial Instagram Terhadap Brand Loyalty OVO (Survei Terhadap Pengguna OVO Pada Generasi Z) (Doctoral dissertation, Universitas Mercu Buana Jakarta).

Yonemura, K., Yajima, K., Komura, R., Sato, J., & Takeichi, Y. (2017). Practical Security Education on Operational Technology Using Gamification Method. 2017 7th IEEE International Conference on Control System, Computing and Engineering (ICCSCE), 284–88.

Yoo, B., & Donthu, N. (2001). Developing a scale to measure the perceived quality of an Internet shopping site (SITEQUAL). *Quarterly journal of electronic commerce*, *2*(1), 31-45.

Yoon, S. J. (2002). The antecedents and consequences of trust in online-purchase decisions. *Journal of Interactive Marketing*, *16*(2), 47–63. DOI: 10.1002/dir.10008

Zaib Abbasi, A., Hussain, K., Kaleem, T., Rasoolimanesh, S. M., Rasul, T., Ting, D. H., & Rather, R. A. (2023). Tourism promotion through vlog advertising and customer engagement behaviours of generation Z. *Current Issues in Tourism*, *26*(22), 3651–3670. DOI: 10.1080/13683500.2022.2144156

Zaki, Y., Wu, M. S., Hamdan, A., & Alsharabi, H. (2024). A Conceptual Framework for Metaverse Marketing Strategies in the Fashion Industry: Exploring the Role of Brand Experience and Brand Equity. In *Opportunities and Risks in AI for Business Development* (Vol. 1, pp. 311–321). Springer Nature Switzerland. DOI: 10.1007/978-3-031-65203-5_28

Zeiser, A. (2015). Transmedia marketing: From film and TV to games and digital media. In *Transmedia marketing*. https://www.proquest.com/books/transmedia-marketing/docview/2148110801/se-2?accountid=11526%0Ahttps://hud.alma.exlibrisgroup.com/discovery/openurl?institution=44HUD_INST&vid=44HUD_INST:Services&sid=ProQ%3Aebookcentral1&genre=book&issn=&volume=&issue=&spag

Zhang, S. (2023). "Metaverse technology enabled figure skating industry upgrade," in Paper presented at the 3rd international conference on internet, education and information technology (IEIT 2023), 383–394. DOI: 10.2991/978-94-6463-230-9_45

Zhang, J., Quoquab, F., & Mohammad, J. (2025). "Do video game players dream of metaverse traveling?" The role of gamification technology and game immersion experience. *Tourism Review*. Advance online publication. DOI: 10.1108/TR-09-2024-0821

Zhang, L., Shao, Z., Benitez, J., & Zhang, R. (2023). How to improve user engagement and retention in mobile payment: A gamification affordance perspective. *Decision Support Systems*, *168*, 113941. DOI: 10.1016/j.dss.2023.113941

Zhang, R., Wen, K., Cai, R., & Liu, H. (2023). The application of Metaverse in the construction industry: Exploring the future architectural trends of virtual and real integration. *J. Civ. Eng. Urban Plan.*, *5*(3), 65–72. DOI: 10.23977/jceup.2023.050309

Zichermann, G., & Cunningham, C. (2011). *Gamifcation by Design: Implementing Game Mechanics in Web and Mobile Apps*. O'Reilly Media, Inc.

Zichermann, G., & Cunningham, C. (2011). *Gamification by design: Implementing game mechanics in web and mobile apps*. O'Reilly Media, Inc.

Zizo, S. (2023, December 3). *A gamified language learning experience: a case of duolingo*. https://www.linkedin.com/pulse/gamified-language-learning-experience-case-duolingo-studio-zizo-feb4f

Zolfaghari, M., Shirmohammadi, M., Shahhosseini, H., Mokhtaran, M., & Mohebbi, S. Z. (2021). Development and evaluation of a gamified smart phone mobile health application for oral health promotion in early childhood: A randomized controlled trial. *BMC Oral Health*, *21*(1), 18. DOI: 10.1186/s12903-020-01374-2 PMID: 33413304

Сизикова, А. (2024). Tools of Brand Promotion Metaverse. *Коммуникации. Медиа. Дизайн*, *9*(3), 135–158.

About the Contributors

Garima Malik is an Associate Professor in the Marketing area at Birla Institute of Technology Management (BIMTECH), Greater Noida. She is a Fellow of Xavier School of Management, XLRI Jamshedpur, India, and a recipient of the K.V. Raju (Narajuan Award) Gold Medal awarded to an outstanding Ph.D. student. She has more than twenty years of academic experience. She guided the ten Ph.D students . Summer Faculty Research Fellow (2021) From IIT Delhi. Her research interests span various areas, including gamification, customer brand engagement, co-creation and gaming marketing experience. She authored more than 55+ research papers. In addition to her research contributions, Dr. Malik has written Seven books, two of which are textbooks, and five are case study and edited books. Her research papers are published in various leading journals such as Journal of Destination & Marketing Management, Economic Survey, Marketing Intelligence Planning, Service Marketing Quarterly, R&D Management Employee Relations International Journal of Bank Marketing, Tourism Analysis, Journal of Event Management, Information Technology & Tourism, International Journal of Healthcare Management, Journal of Global Marketing, Innovative Marketing, Pacific Asia Journal of the Association for Information Systems, Journal of Science and Technology Policy Management, among others.

Dharmendra Singh is an Associate Professor and program head (Finance) at Modern College of Business and Science, Muscat (Oman). He possesses over 23 years of rich professional experience in the field of finance. He holds a Ph.D. in Finance, professional certifications including Certified Financial Planner (CFP), an Associate Diploma in Life Insurance from the Insurance Institute of India, and a CFA from ICFAI. He has published several articles & research papers in ABDC, CABS, and Scopus Q1-ranked international and refereed journals. He has published five edited books with renowned publishers. His research areas include banking, corporate finance, entrepreneurial finance, and financial markets. He has delivered training programs in association with CMA, Oman. He also serves as a reviewer for high-ranking journals. He is a member of the Financial Planning Standard Board (FPSB), the Indian Econometric Society, and the Insurance Institute of India.

Rohit Bansal is an associate professor at the Department of Management Studies. He holds a PhD Degree in Finance from IIT Roorkee. He has more than ten years of research and teaching experience. His research areas include Behavior Finance, Corporate Finance, Sustainable Finance, and Financial Services. He regularly contributes articles to refereed journals and books. He has contributed chapters to several books published by reputed national and international publishers. To his credit, he has several case studies, research papers, book chapters, conference papers and presentations. He has also published research papers in ABDC-ranking journals. Dr. Bansal has published research papers in the International Journal of Consumer Studies, International Journal of Emerging Markets, Journal of Emerging Markets Case Studies, Asian Case Research Journal, Qualitative Research in Financial Markets, and Oil & Gas Journal.

***

Kamini S. Bhardwaj is an accomplished academician with over 17 years of rich teaching experience in Business Administration, Human Resource Management, Economics, and Business Communication across reputed institutions in India. Her journey has spanned classroom lectures, personality development training, online tutoring for international curricula (IB, IGCSE, A Levels), and conducting impactful student development programs.

Swati Bhatnagar is an Asst. Professor in the Marketing Department at New Delhi Institute of Management. She has graduated from Hindu College, Delhi University and did MBA from ICFAI Business School, Gurgaon. She did her Ph. D from Delhi Technological University .She is also UGC NET qualified.She has a cumulative experience of more than 21 years. She has a corporate experience of 5 years with Birla Sunlife and ICICI Prudential AMC Ltd. And academic experience with Amity Business School and New Delhi Institute of Management for over 15 years. Her area of expertise is sales, behavioral and structural dimensions of Distribution Channel Management and emerging area of Marketing Analytics. She has presented papers in various national and international conferences and has authored many research papers and chapters in Scopus indexed journals.

Ritesh Dwivedi has more than 17 years of working experience with various Development Agencies, Research projects with reputed agencies and Academic

Institutions. He has served at University of Lucknow and University of Garhwal before joining Amity University Uttar Pradesh, Noida campus. He has rich working experience in the area of social entrepreneurship and rural management and continuously engaged in teaching MBA level students and guiding research scholars in the same academic area. He has more than 65 research papers / book chapters in his credit of publications in refereed Social Science / Management Journals. He has delivered lectures in different MDPs, training programs and webinars on relevant socio-economic aspects.

Nirupama is a distinguished academician with over 22 years of experience in Commerce and Management Education. She is currently serving as a Professor in the MBA Program at Saveetha School of Management, bringing extensive expertise in Finance and Accounting. A multi-award-winning educator and researcher, she has published widely in reputed national and international journals. Dr. Nirupama has actively contributed to Academic Leadership, Curriculum Development, and Faculty Development initiatives.

Nazia Hasan is currently working as an Assistant Professor at TMIMT,Teerthanker Mahaveer University, Moradabad. She has more than 15 years of work experience in the field of commerce. Her area of teaching includes accounting and finance. Her field of research are microfinance, fintech, social entrepreneurship.

Deepa Kapoor, is a Professor of Marketing at Amity University Uttar Pradesh. Dr. Deepa holds a Ph.D. from the University Business School, Panjab University, Chandigarh, and has been working in academia for more than 15 years, teaching Digital Marketing, Advertising, and Public Relations.

Her research interests are in the areas of Advertising, Services Marketing, Digital Marketing and Consumer Behaviour. She has co-edited two books, and her research papers have been published in reputed international journals.

She has been instrumental in conducting Training Program on Digital Marketing for national and international participants. She has co-edited two books, and her research papers have been published in reputed 'A' and 'B' category international journals. She is actively involved in various institutional building activities, including the Program Review and Outcome Assessment Committee and the IQAC.

K. Naresh Babu is the Dean cum Principal at Sree Abirami College of Occupational Therapy in Coimbatore, Tamil Nadu. With a distinguished career in the field of occupational therapy, he plays a key role in academic leadership and clinical education. His institution is affiliated with The Tamil Nadu Dr. M.G.R.

Medical University, Chennai. Dr. Naresh Babu is known for his dedication to advancing occupational therapy education and for mentoring the next generation of healthcare professionals.

Anam Khanam is a research scholar at Department of Commerce and Business Studies, Jamia Millia Islamia. She has done her M. Com in Business Management from Jamia Millia Islamia. Her work is on green marketing, green purchase intention and greenwash. She has qualified UGC NET (Assistant Professor) examination.

Ruchi Khandelwal, an academician in the field of Marketing and Strategy has a proven teaching career of over 20 years. She is an alumnus of the Delhi University and Aligarh Muslim University with her postgraduate from the prestigious Delhi school of Economics and her doctorate from Faculty of Management Studies and Research. She is a passionate teacher, and her lucid teaching style infuses very well amongst the target audience. Currently working as Deputy Director with Amity School of Business, AUUP, she balances her passion for teaching and her interest in research with her knack for administration very amicably. Dr. Ruchi's research interest lies in the Consumer Decision Making, Psychology of Marketing, Technology and Consumer Behavior, Entrepreneurship and Strategy. She has presented her research at several national and international conferences.

T.C. Manjunath was born on 6th February 1967. He did his BE from RV College of Engg. in 1989, ME in Robotics & Automation from LD College of Engg. in 1992 with First Rank and PhD in Systems & Control Engg. from IIT Bombay in the year 2007. He is currently working as the Dean Research R D and as Professor in the Dept. of Computer Science & Engineering with specialization in IoT, Cyber Security & Blockchain Technology in Rajarajeswari College of Engineering, Bengaluru, Karnataka. He has completed B.E. Degree from R.V. College of Engg., M.E. Govt.'s LD College of Engg., Gujarat Univ., Ahmedabad in First Rank and Ph.D. in Systems and Control Engineering from the Indian Institute of Technology Bombay IIT Bombay He has got a teaching academic, research and administrative experience of more than 35+ years 10 years as Principal, 8 years as HoD rest as faculty and has published more than 1200+ research papers in various national & international journals and conferences, with 175+ patents, 25 book-chapters, 25 awards and also published 25 text books in various field of science, engineering and technology, completed projects worth Rs. 9 Crores till date apart from guiding 10 PhD scholars. He is a member of 30 Professional Society Chapters and is a fellow of IE, IETE, AMIEE and a chartered engineer. He got the best research scholar award in 2006 in IIT Bombay amongst all the research scholars of the institute. He has got 10 awards in academics and research activities.

Angad Munshi has been working at New Delhi Institute of Management (NDIM) since June, 2024. He is an accomplished entrepreneur with over 14 years of experience in B2B sales, business development, vendor management, business strategy, and growth management. He has worked with several leading Indian startups, including Zomato, Ola, Paytm, Swiggy, and the Modi Group, where he played a pivotal role in setting up new teams and divisions. Currently, Mr. Munshi is pursuing doctorate from the Indian Institute of Foreign Trade (IIFT), New Delhi, with a focus on F&B service marketing. His extensive experience across various industries, coupled with his academic pursuits, positions him as a valuable leader and expert in the fields of business strategy and marketing.

Sarita Nagvanshi has been working at New Delhi Institute of Management (NDIM) since June, 2024. She has a Ph.D in Commerce from Amity University. Ms. Nagvanshi has published several research articles, conference papers, and book chapters in peer-reviewed, Scopus-indexed journals. Her research interests are in the areas of consumer behavior, digital marketing, social media marketing, and sustainability. She has experience in teaching various marketing courses as a scholar and teaching assistant at Amity University, Noida, Uttar Pradesh. Driven by a passion for fostering research-driven education and practical learning, Ms. Nagvanshi is committed to contributing to academic excellence and innovation in the field of marketing.

P. Selvakumar is currently an Associate Professor in the Department of Science and Humanities at Nehru Institute of Technology, Coimbatore, Tamil Nadu, India. Prior to joining Nehru Institute of Technology, he held positions as an Assistant Professor in the Department of Science and Humanities various engineering colleges in Coimbatore, Tamil Nadu, India, spanning from 2011 to 2023. Dr.P. Selvakumar's academic and research interests lie primarily in the field of phytochemistry. He has made significant contributions to his field, with an impressive record that includes 30 journal publications, 12 patents, and 20 conference papers. Additionally, he has organized 5 seminars and conferences, further demonstrating his commitment to academic and scientific exchange. Throughout his career, Dr. P.Selvakumar has been recognized for his dedication and excellence in teaching, having been honored with several awards, including the Best Teacher Awards. He holds a prominent position in the academic community, contributing actively to research.

Rukshar is Research Scholar at Department of Commerce and Business Studies, Jamia Millia Islamia, New Delhi, India. She holds a master's degree in commerce and bachelors in education from the University of MJPR, Bareilly. Her research interests include marketing, consumer satisfaction and promotional strategies regarding online education. She has also qualified UGC NET (Assistant Professor) examination. She has proficiency in software like SmartPLS and SPSS. Rukshar is the corresponding author and can be contacted at rukhsarsaifi365@gmail.com .

Guru Basava Aradhya S is a seasoned academician with 17 years of experience in management education. He currently serves as the Director & Professor at Chandigarh School of Business, Mohali. He holds a Ph.D. in Management and has mentored five Ph.D. scholars. His expertise includes HR, marketing, and business analytics. A prolific researcher, he has published in SCOPUS, ABDC, and UGC CARE journals. He has organized numerous international conferences and contributed to NAAC and NBA accreditations. His industry collaborations include faculty exchange programs and consultancy projects. Passionate about academia, he actively fosters innovation, research, and student development.

S. Seenivasan is currently working as a Associate Professor Department of Mechanical Engineering at Rathinam Technical Campus, Coimbatore,TamilNadu, India. He completed BE (Mechanical Engineering) in the year of May 2009 at Kumaraguru College of Technology, Coimbatore and ME (Engineering Design) in the year May 2012 at Anna University Regional campus,Coimbatore. Ph.D (Mechanical Engineering) in the Year 2021 at Anna University, Chennai, in the area of Composite Materials,machine learning,deep learning . He has 12 years of teaching & 5 Years of Research Experience.

Md Sajjad is a research scholar at Department of Commerce and Business Studies, Jamia Millia Islamia. He has done his M. Com (Business Management) from Jamia Millia Islamia. His work is on work life balance, leadership, organizational behavior and human resource management. He has been awarded a fully funded Ph.D. scholarship (JRF) for his research, provided by UGC in India.

Index

I

L

M

O

P

R

S

T

U

V

W

www.ingramcontent.com/pod-product-compliance
Lightning Source LLC
LaVergne TN
LVHW080606300926
849162LV00005B/1059